John Chidubem Nwaogaidu

Globalization and Social Inequality

D1663872

Beste Grüße

Dr. Nwaogaidu Chidubem

John Chidubem Nwaogaidu

Globalization and Social Inequality

An Empirical Study of Nigerian Society

LIT

Dank gilt Prof. Dr. Hanns Wienold und Prof. Dr. Christoph Weischer

Gedruckt auf alterungsbeständigem Werkdruckpapier entsprechend
ANSI Z3948   DIN ISO 9706

Disssertation zur Erlangung der Doktorwürde

D 6

Bibliographic information published by the Deutsche Nationalbibliothek
The Deutsche Nationalbibliothek lists this publication in the Deutsche
Nationalbibliografie; detailed bibliographic data are available in the Internet at
http://dnb.d-nb.de.

ISBN 978-3-643-90323-5
Zugl.: Münster (Westf.), Univ., Diss., 2012

A catalogue record for this book is available from the British Library

©LIT VERLAG GmbH & Co. KG Wien,
Zweigniederlassung Zürich 2013
Klosbachstr. 107
CH-8032 Zürich
Tel. +41 (0) 44-251 75 05
Fax +41 (0) 44-251 75 06
E-Mail: zuerich@lit-verlag.ch
http://www.lit-verlag.ch

LIT VERLAG Dr. W. Hopf
Berlin 2013
Fresnostr. 2
D-48159 Münster
Tel. +49 (0) 2 51-620 320
Fax +49 (0) 2 51-23 19 72
E-Mail: lit@lit-verlag.de
http://www.lit-verlag.de

Distribution:
In Germany: LIT Verlag Fresnostr. 2, D-48159 Münster
Tel. +49 (0) 2 51-620 32 22, Fax +49 (0) 2 51-922 60 99, E-mail: vertrieb@lit-verlag.de

In Austria: Medienlogistik Pichler-ÖBZ, e-mail: mlo@medien-logistik.at
In Switzerland: B + M Buch- und Medienvertrieb, e-mail: order@buch-medien.ch
In the UK: Global Book Marketing, e-mail: mo@centralbooks.com
In North America: International Specialized Book Services, e-mail: orders@isbs.com

DEDICATION

To

My Parents

Late Syvester Ogbonnaya Nwaogaidu

And

Ezinneora Elizabeth Ifeyinwa Nwaogaidu

ACKNOWLEDGEMENTS

Some years ago as I was parking my luggage for a journey across the sea, it never occurred to me that it would be a sojourn of discovery. I came and I saw another world that is fascinating, full of possibilities. I came also to realize how the world society is rapidly changing, with many network-linkages that connect the seas, lands and space together. But in these linkages, some societies are pushing forward whereas some others are drawing backward, and finding it difficult to detect where they belong. I began to think, whether the so-much talked-about globalization is real or mirage. I also thought about the socio-economic and political partitions between societies and among individuals. Then I came again to understand that the very things that connect are also those things that divide. Hence these thoughts and insights motivated my research on globalization and social inequality in the Nigerian society.

But the success of this work would not have been possible without the collaborative supports of individuals and groups from whose stock of knowledge and moral supports I benefited. My gratitude first of all goes to God, without whom my sojourn to Europe would have been a 'mission impossible'. I thank immensely my Bishop Most Rev. Dr. Francis Okobo, who gave me the opportunity to further my studies. For my two Professors: Prof. Dr. Hanns Wienold and Prof. Dr. Christoph Weischer through whom my doctoral mission in Sociology was successfully accomplished, I remain ever grateful for your intensive supervisions and scholarly suggestions that helped to shape and reshape this work to its perfection.

I owe a lot of thanks to the Diocese of Muenster who invited, accommodated and assisted me financially here in Germany. I am also indebted to the entire parish members of St. Maria Himmelfahrt Ahaus for your priceless love and solidarity during my stay with you. I thank immensely Dr. Uche Obodoechina whose effort the cordial relationship with the parish was established.

I lack words to express my sincere gratitude to many good friends in Germany whose companionship and encouragement have helped me in this journey of life. I take the risk to mention only but few: Mrs. Ingrid Altenhövel, Mr. Hermann Vollmer & Mrs. Barbara Brockmann, Family viii

of Josef Gesenhues, Prof. Dr. & Mrs. Manfred & Doris Gerwing, Mrs. Gertrude Löns, Mrs. Margild Kaiser, Mrs Marianne Strickling, Mr. Bernhard & Mrs. Mechthild Gersmeier, Mr. & Mrs. August & Gisela Bierhaus, Mrs. Hilde Süß, Family of Karl-Josef Lürwer, Dr. & Mrs. Silas & Sigrid Okwor, Mrs. Petra Fuchs, Mr. & Mrs. Heinrich & Maria Aertker, Mr. & Mrs. Hermann Nöfer, Mr. Norbert Rehring & Family, Mr. Alöis Helling & Family, Mrs. Maria Enning, Mr. Robert Huber & Family, and priests Propst Jürgen Quante, Pfr. Heinrich Plassmann and Kanonikus Uwe Börner. I thank also my colleagues in the Graduate School of Sociology Muenster for your challenges through seminars, conferences and colloquium that offered me the strength to write. And special thanks go to many well-wishers and friend in Nigeria for your love and support. Without you and without your help this thesis would not have seen the light of the day.

I cannot forget to thank my fellow priest's friends: Frs. Moses Ugwu, Matthew Ezea, Cajetan Iyidobi, Eugene Odo, Johnson Ozioko, Donatus Eze, Charles Onuh, Victor Anoka, Donatus Ogudo, Augustine Asogwa, Sylvester Ozioko, George Abah, Hyginus Eke, Justus Idike, Victor Ezema, Samuel Uzondu, Timothy Asogwa, Anthony Adani, Francis Okigbo, Edwin Ozioko, Ambrose Aba, Thaddeus Eze, Chris Mama, for your inspirations and comradeship.

The dedicated page acknowledged the deep heart I have for my parents. And also my success story would not have been without my siblings: Caroline, Christiana, Theresa, Simeon, Samuel and Anthonia and many close relatives whose prayers, support and encouragement have been my bulwark of strength.

Chidubem Nwaogaidu
Muenster, December 01, 2012

CONTENTS

LISTS OF TABLES AND FIGURES xii
ACRONYMS AND ABBREVIATIONS xv

1 INTRODUCTION.. ... 1

   1.1 The Research Process 8
     1.1.1 The Problem and Study Objective 8
     1.1.2 Rationale and Method of Study 11

PART I
THEORETICAL FRAMEWORK

2 UNDERSTANDING SOCIAL STRUCTURE 15

   2.1 The Concept of Inequality 18
     2.1.1 Social Dimension of Inequality 21
     2.1.2 Political Dimension of Inequality 22
     2.1.3 Economic Dimension of Inequality 24
   2.2 Complexities of Inequality Variations 26
     2.2.1 Social Positioning 27
     2.2.2 Changing Patterns of Relational Attribute 30
   2.3 Essential Components of Inequality Categories 32
     2.3.1 Identity and Difference 33
     2.3.2 Difference Perspectives 35
        2.3.2.1 Natural Difference 36
        2.3.2.2 Cultural Difference 37
        2.3.2.3 Constructive Difference 41
   2.4 Conclusion 43

3 THEORETICAL ANALYSIS ON GLOBALIZATION 45

   3.1 Dualistic Conception of Modernization Theory 46
   3.2 Dependency Theory as a Historical Model 48
   3.3 Significance of World-Systems Theory 52
   3.4 Theoretical Propositions on Globalization 57
     3.4.1 Factors of Globalization 62

3.4.1.1 Economic Factor 62
3.4.1.2 Social Factor 63
3.4.1.3 Political Factor 64
3.4.2 Recasting the Globalization Antinomies 65
3.4.2.1 Unequal Power and Economic Relations 66
3.4.2.2 Globalization and Inequality Nexus 71
3.4.3 Globalization Implications for Social Formation 75
3.5 Complexity of State Formation in Africa 78
3.5.1 Internal Formation Blockade as Consequence of
       Political Instrumentalization of Disorder 86
3.5.2 Critical Analysis of Chabal and Daloz Position 93
3.6 Conclusion 97

PART II
NIGERIA IN THE PAST AND PRESENT

4   FORMATION OF STATE AND POLITICAL LEGACY 101

4.1 Nature of State in Nigeria 101
4.1.1 Regional/Ethnic Formation 103
4.1.2 Subtle Demarcation between State and Civil Society 108
4.2 Political Evolution and Democratization 113
4.2.1 The Heritage of Colonial Indirect Rule 116
4.2.2 Military Interventions and Dictatorship 120
4.2.3 Democratic Transition vis-à-vis Political
       Liberalization 123
4.2.3.1 The Antecedents of Civilian Administration 126
4.2.3.2 The Endemic Culture of Neo-patrimonialism 129
4.3 Institutional Paradox of State Formation 133
4.3.1 The Role of Traditional Rulers 133
4.3.2 The Role of Religion 137
4.3.3 The Role of Interest Groups 141
4.4 Conclusion 143

5   ECONOMIC DEVELOPMENT AND GLOBAL INFLUENCE ... 145

5.1 Incorporation into Global Economy 146
5.1.1 Free Market Economy 149

5.1.2 Structural Adjustment Programme 150
5.2 Economic Performance since Independence 154
5.2.1 Oil and Gas Economy 160
5.2.1.1 The Scale of Dependency on Oil Economy 163
5.2.1.2 The Strength of Multinational Oil Company 166
5.2.2 Agricultural Sector 169
5.2.3 Manufacturing Sector 172
5.2.4 Services 175
5.2.4.1 Electricity and Communication 175
5.2.4.2 Import and Export 178
5.2.5 Informal Sector of the Economy 185
5.3 Current Economic Reform Agenda 186
5.4 Consequence of Global Economic Integration 190
5.4.1 Comparative Market Decline 191
5.4.2 Deceleration of Economic Growth by Global
Financial Crisis 193
5.4.3 Environmental Degradation 194
5.4.4 Emergence of Conflicts/Grass-Root Movements 197
5.5 Conclusion 199

PART III
SOCIAL STRUCTURAL ANALYSIS AND INEQUALITY

6 TOWARDS CONTEXTUAL STUDY OF THE SOCIAL
STRUCTURE 203

6.1 Configuration of Social Networks 203
6.2 Indicators of Structural Differences 210
6.2.1 Income Distribution 220
6.2.2 Minimum Wage and Maximum Difference 227
6.2.3 Education as Structural Determinant 236
6.2.4 Urban and Rural Dichotomy 243
6.2.5 Regional Differentiation 250
6.3 Inequality in an Intersectional Perspective 258
6.3.1 Class Distinction 260
6.3.2 Ethnic Identity Struggle 264
6.3.3 Gender Disparity 267
6.4 Inequality and Globalization: Social Consequences 274
6.4.1 Insecurity and Fear 275

6.4.2 Emerging Individualism 278
6.4.3 Clash of Interests and Violence 280
6.5 Conclusion 283

PART IV
NIGERIA: THE FUTURE OF THE PRESENT

7 CHALLENGES 289

7.1 The Approach for Immediate Action 289
7.1.1 Change of Mind-Set 290
7.1.1.1 The Imperative of Patriotism 291
7.1.1.2 Aiding Priority through Collective/
Collaborative Initiatives 293
7.1.2 The Need for Subsidized Education System 296
7.1.3 Safety-Net for the Poor 299
7.1.4 Matching Economic Growth with Sustainable
Development 302
7.1.5 Enhancement of Social Cohesion 304
7.2 The Axes of Future Plan 305
7.2.1 The Necessity of Good Governance 306
7.2.1.1 Entrenching Political and Economic
Decentralization 309
7.2.1.2 Increased Local Participation in National
Matters 314
7.2.1.3 Renewed Civil Society Engagement 315
7.2.2 Balancing the Asymmetries of Globalization 318
7.2.2.1 Fostering Globalization from Below 321
7.2.2.2 Organized Information Networks 324

GENERAL CONCLUSION.. 329

BIBLIOGRAPHY.. 343

LISTS OF TABLES AND FIGURES

TABLES:

Table 2.1: Comparing Average Annual Growth Rate of GDP
per Capita (PPP), 1980-2006 154
Table 2.2: Percentage Distribution of Sectoral Contribution to GDP
in Real Terms (at 1990 basic prices), 2001-2006 157
Table 2.3: Major Nigerian Oil Production Ventures 167
Table 2.4: The Physical Infrastructural Shortage in Nigeria (2009) 176
Table 2.5: Nigeria's Top Import Partners (2008) 181
Table 2.6: Nigeria's Top Export Partners (2008) 181
Table 3.1: Social Indicators in Nigeria and some Comparator
Countries (2007) 212
Table 3.2: Nigeria Core Welfare Indicator by Zones, 2006 (%) 213
Table 3.3: Measures of Economy and Inequality of
Selected Countries 2007 215
Table 3.4: Federal and State Shares of Petroleum Proceeds,
1960-1999 224
Table 3.5: Some Federal Government Policies on Minimum
Wage from 1974 to 2011 229
Table 3.6: Federal Minimum Wage (1980-2007) 230
Table 3.7: Approximate Comparison of Monthly Salaries of
Selected Public Sectors (2007) 231
Table 3.8: Secondary School Output in Northern and
Southern Nigeria, 1912–2005 239
Table 3.9: Primary and Secondary Schools Statistics 2004-2008 240
Table 3.10: Economic Grouping by Class 1996 & 2004 262
Table 3.11: Gender Disparity in Core Development Indicators,
2006 (%) 269
Table 3.12: Distribution in National Assembly by Type, Year &
Gender from 1999-2011 (%) 273

FIGURES:

Figure 2.1: Comparing Average Annual Growth Rate of GDP
per Capita (PPP), 1975-2005 155
Figure 2.2: Nigeria GDP - real growth rate (2000-2010) 156
Figure 2.3: Average Rate of Inflation (1980-2011) 158

Figure 2.4: Nigerian Crude Oil Production, 1980-2004
(includes Lease Condensate) 161
Figure 2.5: Nigerian Natural Gas Production, 1980-2002 162
Figure 2.6: Export and Import Levels 1988-2008 (US$ mill.) 183
Figure 3.1: Nigeria's Human Development Index by Zones 2008 214
Figure 3.2: National Poverty Incidence from 1980-2010 216
Figure 3.3: Lorenz Curve Showing Inequalities in Nigeria (2004) 218
Figure 3.4: National Inequality Trends 1985-2010 (Gini Coefficient) . 219
Figure 3.5: Average Sectoral Monthly Wage 2009
and 2010 (Naira) 232
Figure 3.6: National Unemployment Rate (2000-2011) 234
Figure 3.7: Total Number of Teachers in Federal
Universities, 2001/2002-2005/2006 242
Figure 3.8: Trends in Poverty Levels between Urban and Rural
Areas 1980-2010 (%) 245
Figure 3.9: Inequality Trends by Urban and Rural Sectors,
1985-2010 (Gini Coefficient) 247
Figure 3.10: Nigerians in US Diaspora 1961-2008 249
Figure 3.11: Spreads and Trends in Poverty Levels by Zones,
1980-2010 (%) 252
Figure 3.12: Inequality Trends by Geo-Political Zones,
1985-2010 (Gini Coefficient) 254
Figure 3.13: Percentage Rate of Labour Force Participation
by Gender 2009 270
Figure 3.14: Enrolment Distribution in Nigerian University
by Gender 2003-2010 (%) 272

DIAGRAM/MAPS:

Diagram 3.1: Social Network Formation 208
Map 3.2: Presidential Election Results by Geopolitical
Zones, 2011 257
Map 3.1: Major Ethnic Groups in Nigeria 264

ACRONYMS AND ABBREVIATIONS

ACN:	Action Congress of Nigeria
APC:	Arewa People Congress
ASUU:	Academic Staff Union for Universities
BP:	British Petroleum
CAN:	Christian Association of Nigeria
CBN:	Central Bank of Nigeria
CEO:	Chief Executive Officer
CLO:	Civil Liberties Organization
CPC:	Congress for Progressive Change
EFCC:	Economic and Financial Crimes Commission
EIA:	Environmental Impact Assessment
FEPA:	Federal Environmental Protection Agency
FOS:	Federal office of Statistics
GDP:	Gross Domestic Product
GII:	Global Information Infrastructure
GNP:	Gross National Product
GSM:	Global System for Mobile communication
HDI:	Human Development Index
HDR:	Human Development Report
ILO:	International Labor Organization
IMF:	International Monetary Fund
JAMB:	Joint Admission and Matriculation Board
JNI:	Jama'at Nasr al-Islam
JSS:	Junior Secondary School
LEEDS:	Local Economic Empowerment Development Strategy
LNG:	Liquefied Natural Gas
MASSOB:	Movement for the Actualization of the Sovereign State of Biafra
MD:	Managing Director
MDGs:	Millennium Development Goals
MEND:	Movement for the Emancipation of the Niger Delta
MOCs:	Multinational Oil Companies
MTN:	Mobile Telephone Networks
MWH:	Million Megawatt-Hours
NANS:	National Association of Nigerian Students
NBA:	Nigerian Bar Association
NBS:	National Bureau of Statistics

NCC:	Nigerian Communications Commission
NEEDS:	National Economic Empowerment Development Strategy
NEITI:	Nigeria Extractive Industry Transparency Initiative
NEPAD:	New Partnership for Africa's Development
NGOs:	Non-Governmental Organizations
NITEL:	Nigerian Telecommunication Company
NLC:	Nigerian Labor Congress
NLNG:	Nigeria Liquefied Natural Gas Corporation
NLSS:	Nigeria Living Standard Survey
NMA:	Nigerian Medical Association
NNOC:	Nigerian National Oil Corporation
NNPC:	Nigerian National Petroleum Corporation
NPC:	Northern People's Congress
NSE:	Nigerian Stock Exchange
NSEs:	Nigerian Society of Engineers
NUC:	National Universities Commission
NUPENG:	Nigeria Union of Petroleum and Natural Gas Workers
NUT:	Nigerian Union of Teachers
NYSC:	Nigerian Youth Service Corp
OIC:	Organization of the Islamic Conference
OPC:	Odua People Congress
OPEC:	Organization of Petroleum Exporting Countries
PDP:	People Democratic Party
PIB:	Petroleum Industry Bill
SAP:	Structural Adjustment Programme
SEEDS:	State Economic Empowerment Development Strategy
SPDC:	Shell Petroleum Development Company of Nigeria Ltd.
SSS:	Senior Secondary School
TNCs:	Transnational Corporations
UAC:	United Africa Company
UBE:	Universal Basic Education
UNDP:	United Nations Development Programme
UPE:	Universal Primary Education
WDI:	World Development Indicator
WTO:	World Trade Organization

1.   INTRODUCTION

Across time and space, regions and nations, socio-political and economic disparities among individuals and groups continue to manifest themselves by means of different institutional and organizational arrangements that govern social relations. These arrangements could vary from place to place, but have one common denominator which is societal change. Thus the structure of state in Nigerian with its historical antecedents has been punctuated with different societal changes. The changes are associated with transformations from local to modern society, from colonial to independent state and then to post-colonial state. These stages of formation have also some consequential undertones such as political instability, ethnic rivalry, inequality components, and other social malaise. It follows that in this era of globalization, various transformation mechanisms are beginning also to generate other new forms of structurization and inequality differences both within and among individuals, groups, regions and countries. In that sense, social inequality remains a daunting challenge to any nation. In Nigeria as a case study, even after fifty years of her independence from the British hegemony and imperialism, a significant number of her citizens still exist on the peripheries and as such are subjected to conditions that are appalling despite huge reserve of oil and gas, and other solid minerals. In other words, marginalized and vulnerable, different groups and individuals continue to face the difficult task of sustaining their livelihoods in a country that is endowed with human and rich natural resources. It is on this standpoint that I am compelled to investigate the structural formation in the Nigerian society and how that manifests itself in inequality differentials in this globalization period.

It then follows that the issue of understanding, defining, and evaluating the inequality configurations in social relationships and their links to globalization have been a very serious concern to social theorists, who have been consistently attempting to analyze and tackle this main subject point. Again, given the tensions and conflicts associated with establishing social, political, economic and cultural interactions in a pluralistic world and some difficult experiences in the past, the subject matter of this research acquires a pressing urgency in the field of social sciences. The study will open up the fact that no society pattern is constant but continues to transform in different phases. If not, there would not have been inventions and progressive society changes. As the society transforms, so also are the social categories that govern the structural differences. But in this current age of global interactions and integrations, it seems that the structural formation has become more challenging for the developing worlds.

Suffice it to say that inequality as a way of structural formation and social differentiation exists in all parts of the world, yet it varies from country to country with its attending consequences. It seems to be more rampant especially in the developing nations than in the developed ones because of the associative factors of unequal balance of globalization asymmetries occasioned by the global capitalism and their institutional arrangements. The global imbalance acquires more concern within the organizational structure of the global institutions such as International Monetary Fund (IMF), World Bank, World Trade Organization (WTO), etc. that condition the global interactions. These institutions tend to promote the global homogenization of economic, socio-cultural and political formation, but on the contrary, their integration processes are usually hampered by unequal participation and policy impositions especially on the developing economies. The impositions, of course are governed by the ethos of capitalism. This idea however demonstrates the magnitude of globalization ideology as a force towards global process of integration of local, regional and national into social, economic and political activities as well as the worldwide systems of interaction. Indeed globalization has not only constituted a formation process but also a system formation that has been the major cause of spatial disparities and interdependencies in socio-political and economic development across regions and countries.

Putting it in another way, globalization has different dimensions with various consequences, which could either be negative-generating or positive-generating. Thus in so far as globalization has generated a positive results in some instances, its negative features will however be collectively addressed in this research work, taking appropriate cognizance of the fact that the issues identified can have deleterious consequences on social inequality and overall developmental strategies. On the other hand, by identifying and qualifying the effects of globalization on socio-political and economic developments and the social life-pattern of the population especially the dialectical changes associated with its processes and systems, this work will have values in formulating a positive sociological synthesis in addressing the problem of inequality and globalization in Nigeria.

The study however takes into account variety of factors that have contributed significantly to social inequality in Nigeria. It proposes a comparative framework of inequality approach, focusing not only on income and class differences but also on underlying manifestations of inequality categories in terms of choices and opportunities that people have, and how that delimit inter-relational patterns of social formation. In that instance, the present research work will however take into account difference standpoints in order to tackle the problem of inequality. It will question the rationale behind the changes in inequality differences over time, that is to say, changes experienced during social transformation and changes from the economies based on agrarianism and communal redistribution to the present day capitalist economy. From this major transformation, the work will provide suitable insight into the causes and nature of inequality with its attending consequences of modernization. The emerging conclusions will affirm the very fact that the magnitude of inequality-inducing nature of neoliberal restructuring has been especially severe on developing countries.

Moreover, the work investigates the procedural manifestation of cross-ethnic and cross-regional variations in the political and economic status of household levels; based partly on the social policy or political regime, and partly on access to the economy and social infrastructure. These procedural overviews are regarded as inequality-inducing mechanism. And as such, the work presents here empirical analysis using various statistical data to estimate the relationship between globalization and social inequality at the national, local and household levels. This estimation will of course capture overall impacts of socio-political and economic distributions on the variables of individual and group interests, and also measuring the effects of the changes in gross domestic product (GDP) on outcome variables across sectors within the country's economy. The empirical survey will not be restricted to purely economic considerations but will also take into account the human dimensions of economic phenomena of change as they affect the inequality differences both locally and nationally.

Thus, the research project is structured into four parts. Part one explores the theoretical framework which for a study of this nature is of critical importance. The framework commences with analytical clarifications of some of the basic tenets and key notions, namely: inequality and globalization. It argues how inequality could be a complex and multidimensional problem-inducing mechanism, in the sense that it is socially, politically and economically structured and historically encompassing. Through the categories of inequality, different identities are formed. Also this point is expanded through the analysis on how the exclusion of certain groups or individuals in the mainstream of the society could endanger the pattern of social relationships. Hence by examining the changing patterns of inequality differentials and their bifurcation of the social system, as well as how different categories of inequality manifest among and within groups and individuals, the work will then proceed to investigate some of the developmental and globalization theoretical formulations. The investigation is with the intention of laying a suitable theoretical foundation that can help in buttressing the present topic. Thus, the main critical focus has its basis on how the theoretical debates on development and globalization could justify the present crisis of modernization being experienced in Africa and Nigeria as a case in point. Presenting globalization not only as an economic factor, but also as political and social factors, the work unveils the antinomies of globalization and how unequal power asymmetries have generated a steady decline in developmental opportunities and the increase of inequality.

Alongside the implications of global formation processes, the discourse on the state formation will be critically analyzed in part one especially how the post-colonial states in Africa and Nigerian in particular are being challenged by the current wave of globalization. It suffices to say that although the formation of the state in Nigeria has undergone considerable changes, yet it has also been subjected to further transformation within and without, and initiating new class formation and struggle between the rulers and the ruled, creating two major classes, namely: dominant and oppressed groups with their associated consequences. This division is majorly underlined by the new formation of capital accumulation that manifests itself in putting the market-based reformulation of capital relations into more and more difficult condition for the underprivileged majority. In this perspective, the state and its apparatuses are being personalized by a system action of 'internal blockade' described as 'political in-strumentalization of disorder'. This body of knowledge is based on the analytical framework, which is championed by Chabal, Patrick and Daloz, Jean-Pascal. Their propositions attempt to examine the emerging crisis of socio-political and economic developments and underdevelop-ments in Africa, drawing from the body of knowledge of post-Weberian social and political theory, but not without some limitations to their theo-retical postulations.

Part two of the work takes on an historical as well as a critical survey of the past and present conditions of the Nigerian state. This survey is basi-cally from the point of view of political and economic developments of the modern state. By analysing the nature of state formation in Nigeria, the work examines the interplay between the state and civil society, and other constituent elements of state formation and their role dichotomies. Given the roles played by colonial administration in democratization processes and the aftermath of military interventions, the post-colonial state of Nigeria still encounters major political quagmire. The state is entrenched with the endemic culture of 'neo-patrimonialism' and other paradoxical institutional frameworks such as religion, traditional institu-tions and various interest groups. In these instances, the work describes what may be regarded as the major question facing the country, namely the struggle for access to and control of resources, fierce competition for the control of state apparatuses and ethnic identity manipulations, which seem to have installed corruption into the political system.

Moreover, the work also evaluates various empirical data that illustrate majorly on the 'why' the post-colonial state of Nigeria has not made much economic developmental progress in comparison with other coun-tries of relative developmental history. This evaluation goes a long way to excavate the influence of colonialism on the state formation in Africa through a link to the contemporary situational crisis, as well as major issues arising from contemporary globalization such as changing proc-esses of incorporation into global capitalism encapsulated in its mode of development. On the other hand, the work identifies the endemic nature of mono-cultural oil economy that has constituted a 'paradox of poverty' in the midst of plenty as a consequence of undiversified economic devel-opment, and then its impact on the other sectors of the economy. The study further addresses the recent issue of global financial and economic crises, which have presented significant economic, political and social developmental challenges for all countries around the world. The far-reaching consequences of the crises have been identified both on the resource distribution as well as national budgets, creating serious challenges to economic growth and social development in Nigeria. As a globalization instance, the work looks at certain implications of global integration especially the crisis of oil economy as it pertains to the relationship between Multinational Oil Companies (MOC) and the Nigeria government on the one hand, and on the other hand the predicament of Niger-Delta region whose soil harbors the oil economy. This investigation aims to interrogate the concept of globalization especially as it patterns to the resource conflicts and social deprivations in Niger Delta region. Besides, the attempts to reform and diversify the economy seem to have not yielded much result. Instead the country has further been subjected into comparative market declines, consequence of the global integration.

Part three however offers a topology of social structure and inequality. It investigates the changing structure of the endogenous social networks, and how poor household incomes and human development indices have enhanced the possibility of inequality incidence both within and among individuals and groups. From the indicators of social and human developments, I will argue in this thesis that the worsening unequal distribution of life chances such as employment opportunities, educational attainment, health-care services, incomes etc., which are sustained by selfish accumulation of wealth and subsequently amassing of power by political elites, endanger socio-economic stability through crime increase and violence. In other words, the nation's wealth has continued to remain in the hands of few Nigerians, with the resultant implications of minimum wage and maximum differences in the distribution of incomes both within and among groups and individuals. Specifically, the work will further examine the basic trends of inequality based on urban and rural dichotomy and disparities among the geopolitical zones, and how the differences induce inequality rate. In those instances, I will also emphasize how the underlying categories of inequality such as ethnic origin, gender and class manifest in diverse ways to produce new forms of differentiations. These differentiations are highlighted by the intersectional nature of inequality categories in the day-to-day experiences. Here some statistical data will be analyzed and variables used in the analysis will be defined as guidelines for possible evaluations and for future research applications. On the other hand, the study analysis will further underline the consequential effects of globalization and inequality on social development especially as regards the emerging individualism and the increasing threats of security in the development of the country.

Nevertheless, the tensions and challenges facing the Nigerian state will be ipso facto heuristically discussed before the general conclusion in part four. The burden of this part of the work is not only to offer most distinctive and helpful insights into problem solutions and future options with regard to the development of equitable, productive, and sustainable nation-state in a globalized world, but also an avenue to analyze various social actions against the impediments imposed by an unequal global integration and society interaction. In that sense, the study provides suggestive socio-political- and economic-intervention alternatives with the capacity of reducing social inequality. The suggestions will attest to the fact that socially integrated societies with collective initiatives, governed by interventionist public institutions with regulative mechanisms and good governance, have more potentialities for equitable development and economic growth. This last part of work also evaluates various determinant challenges that can best be tackled in alleviating the problem discourse and most importantly the renewed efforts in balancing the globalization asymmetries that has been the niche of global inequality.

Finally, the conclusion summarises the lines of thought of the research study, and also pinpoints the possible contributions of the study to the socio-political and economic development of a stable society. It will first of all reveal how the developmental trajectory of the Nigerian state has not positively impacted on the well-being of the population. Instead, there exist conflicting interests and poor policy implementation strategies, which have both internal and external influences. Thus the conclusion attests to the fact that development of the nation-state involves among others an in-depth understanding of the procedural changes in the society and how that changes could be explored to maximize positive transformation that is culturally-based and contextually applicable to the situational problems. Therefore, this research work is conceived from broader theoretical, historical as well as structural perspectives in order to raise important questions that may hopefully continue to be discussed in the field of sociology.

1.1.   The Research Process

1.1.2.   The Problem and Study Objective

What Problems does the Work seek to address?

The work explores several of the latest endeavours that tend to theorize globalization and inequality, as well as reflecting on the wide range of debates on globalization and social inequality, which are quite relevant to Nigerian case. Thus the question on how the impacts of globalization have produced and are still producing not only increasing poverty but also inequalities within and among different groups and individuals will be well analysed. The analysis is also consistent with empirical evidence that the spatial increase of income difference and wage inequality observed following globalization takes place mainly on 'within' the non-poor groups than poor group and then 'among' individuals and groups. Hence the wave of globalization being associated in this work with the phenomenon of increasing inequality has also the attribute of changing forms of socio-economic and political relations, which results to instability, conflicts and violence. Moreover, this work also concentrates on the pervasiveness of inequality, which has been worsened through the integration of the Nigerian state into global capitalism without sustaining growth of the local economy. By applying both classical and contemporary explanations of social inequality and how the categories of inequality manifest themselves, this research work examines the effect of inequality both on individuals and groups respectively.

Objective of the Study:

By uniting various methodological approaches, this research work tends to investigate on a suitable theoretical framework in order to achieve a common base that justifies the inherent problems associated with globalization and inequality. Based on that, I tend to argue in this study that notwithstanding the inevitability of globalization, the severe consequences it has on social inequality may be overwhelming. Moreover, as a distinguishing trait of many contradictions associated with the political and economic trajectories, globalization impacts on the state of Nigeria brings about a number of specific issues. On the one hand, the formation of state by the colonial powers was not strongly consolidated to withstand the external impositions; rather the state became independence in 'principle', with constant awakening influence of western factors. On the other hand, by analysing the structural crystallization of the Nigerian society that is being affected by modernization, the study gives insights into how inequality is manifesting both in the national and global interaction. It follows that the issues at stake continue to raise the question on the state formation and the integration into global capitalism that features the political fragility being governed by the politics of neo-patrimonialism, and the powerful external influences through the neo-liberalism. Through historical antecedents, the issue of state formation brings out the basic tenets of state disintegration and deformation made possible by its improper institutionalization or non-emancipation by colonial powers.

In the context of the analysis, there will also be need for a suitable response to the burning issues in order to devise some pragmatic measures that can help in reducing the far-reaching consequences of globalization on social life of the people. In this effect, the work aims at examining the ways in which state institutions and civil society organizations can contribute to a more inclusive globalization process that is practicable and as such acceptable. This contribution will represent an unprecedented effort to ensuring sustainable development that fosters growth as well as reduces inequality. In this line of thought, more relevant and reliable solutions to meet up with the challenges and exigencies of the moment shall here be attempted, which as it were will aim at discovering, to what extent a more equitable access to life chances could help to combat inequality differences. Therefore, the objective of the research is not to produce scientifically measurable quantitative materials but to identify salient issues, raise series of questions, trigger debates and rekindle interests for further research processes. And then to get a general grid of the scope through which the reports to be evaluated will have a value for a qualitative result.

Research Priority:

In keeping with its purpose of enabling empirical analysis, the connections between globalization and social inequality in developing nations are best described through an understanding of the social structural changes build upon by the waves of globalization. The empirical research pinpoints to the very fact that the more interaction between inequality and globalization, the more problematic is development. In this instance, the implications of globalization and inequality enhancing mechanisms and how globalization influences the global inequality are found to be important. In following this discourse, this work will focus on the following questions:

> Has the globalization drive through its uneven processes any influence on the society and if so, how could the influence be attributed to the nature of state formation in Nigeria?

> In the current instance of neoliberal influence through democratization, how has Nigeria been affected and what are the responses to the many challenges of modern democracy?

> Have cosmopolitan ideas and discourse about global capitalism with particular reference to free trade enhanced equality, economic growth and social cohesion?

> Have the social changes emanating from the global integration any influence on the endogamous pattern of social network, so also on the pattern of income distribution and ethnic associations? In particular, how do those changes affect the individuals and groups both within and without?

> Finally, what are the possible challenges that could be drawn out from the above questions?

These and more are what this research work will critically tend to examine, notwithstanding the difficulties that may be associated with finding the original and documented data-base, and also the scarce availability of reliable research sources on the subject-topic from the indigenous authors. However, addressing the above questions would help towards identifying the critical issues at hand, as well as constructing and developing alternative solutions to the problems imposed by globalization and social inequality relevant not only to Nigeria but also to other developing countries of Africa.

1.1.2. Rationale and Method of the Study

The rationale of the research study is to establish clarity on the subject-topic based on literature reviews, supplemented by empirical research methodology through data analysis as well as discussions with resource persons. The basis of this approach points mainly on the subjective experiences and perceptions of the research objects needed for a qualitative result. However, the literature review covers academic publications both published and unpublished. The literature majorly centers on the study topic: globalization and inequality, relying basically on the works that has stood the test of time. Further disaggregated report sources include: National Bureau of Statistics (NBS), Government and United Nations reports, Country reports, policy documents and Press releases. Though there might be some contradictions following the statistical data reports, yet by way of proper analysis and harmonization of the reports the study could achieve definitive results. Furthermore, other official documents and papers published on the Websites are also of importance in gathering secondary information relevant to the research process. Nevertheless, the empirical part of the research is carried out in a qualitative and purposive way, adapted to the regional and socio-cultural specificities of the national context. This method therefore provides the research work with detailed analysis and relevant comparative cases, which highlight the impact of globalization on social inequality.

In addition, informal conversations were carried out in some of the current issues that bother on development, in order to have a glimpse of the day-to-day experiences of the people. Hence listening to voices within the society are of immense help in analyzing and understanding the people's problems and aspirations behind the observed situations.The purpose is to gain an understanding of the 'why' of issues and articulate the problems observed, and not merely a description of the events or situations on ground. On the other hand, the work is designed based on existing data reports; and on the other way round, estimations are required to be made in some aspects due to scarce availability of the required data. Following this perspective of investigation, the research study aims to interpret events and to reflect on sample results that might gain acceptance as well as assume an objective procedure in the study project. In essence, this method will help in validating some of the findings to be made towards procedural interventions. Hence, this procedure assumes the background through which this research work finds its basic methodological drive.

Finally, with the nature of the study, various assumptions could be made as a vehicle of instigation of more debates and new ideas in this area of research. Although this may be termed as a limitation to the research project, yet the conclusions that are to be made would be a step towards more dynamic and reliable contribution to the nexus between globalization and social inequality study.

PART I

THEORETICAL FRAMEWORK

2   UNDERSTANDING SOCIAL STRUCTURE

The changing structure of the global society as well as the new dimensions of social relationships in the 21st century have propelled a more critical research into the foundation and forms of social inequality. To understand the real import of social structure is an essential constituent of inequality studies and a fundamental concept in sociological enquiry. But the concept is often quite undefined because of its subtle and complex nature in explaining the character and the spatial realities of social conditions common to most sociological concepts. In the context of this study, social structure is generally viewed as a concept that provides a descriptive pattern of social relationship, differentiation and stratification, independent of individuals or groups in a given society. It defines social relations in terms of the mode of interactions, as well as the tensions that exist both within a given society and an environment and among individuals and groups that are characterized by different positions they occupy in the society. It is not just about the components of the society, but social structure preoccupies itself with the social groupings in the society formation.

However, to have a consensus definition of social structure that could be acceptable by all sociologists has been a quite difficult project. It is on that note that Lopez rightly argues that, "although there is no consensus regarding the term itself, there is an implicit contemporary consensus regarding how sociologists, and other social theorists, should agree over it: the debate over, and about, social structure is seemingly always a 'structure and agency' debate. Structure and agency are seen as mutually implicated with one another, both logically and substantively, and the tension between the two is seen as providing one of the crucial nodal point around which sociological theory develops, and has developed in the past."[1] It follows that agency-structure problem thus questions the nature of objects and their relationship in social settings. Though methodologically substantiating or transcending this dualistic conception has been a subject of sociological debate over the years. But some sociolo-

---

[1] Lopez, Jose (2003): Society and its Metaphors: Language, Social Theory and Social Structure. London & New York: Continuum, p. 4.

16

gists like Jeffrey Alexander in his four-volume work 'Theoretical Logic in Sociology' suggest a multidimensional approach that unites the two concepts of agency and structure, in order "to overcome the debilitating dualism of one-dimensional thought."[2] In fact, he alleges the superiority of his approach over the dualistic conception, either through structure or human agency in achieving a balance between 'determinism'[3] and 'voluntarism'[4], but his failure to justify the empirical adequacy of his position limited his methodic approach in constructing the required framework that is needed for structural analysis. Nevertheless, his multidimensional approach gave room for a new form of functionalism that seeks to assess society situations from different standpoints and then appreciates the importance of normative dimension of human actions.

In a related study, Lopez and Scott propose that social structure could be discussed under three dimensions that would capture various realities of social relations. They include: 'institutional structure', 'relational structure' and 'embodied structure'. Thus, the institutional structure entails "those cultural or normative patterns that define the expectations of agents hold about each other's behaviour and that organize their enduring relations with each other." The relational structure on the other hand is seen "as comprising the relationships themselves, understood as patterns of causal interconnection and interdependence among agents and their actions, as well as the positions that they occupy." Finally, embodied structure is "found in the habits and skills that are inscribed in human

---

[2] Alexander, Jeffrey (1982): Theoretical Logic in Sociology, Vol. 1. London and Heney: Routledge and Kegan Paul, p. 125.

[3] This idea points to the Marxist's historical determinism that views human action as consequent of material relation. Wood comments that "the central claim of historical materialism [or often referred to as economic determinism] is that people's economic behavior, their 'mode of production in material life', is the 'basis' of their social life generally, that this 'economic basis' generally 'conditions' or 'determines' both the society's remaining institutions and the prevalent ideas or forms of social consciousness" (Wood, Allen W. (2004): Karl Marx 2nd Edition. New York and London: Routledge, p. 63).

[4] This is connected to Emile Durkheim's conception of 'normative order as voluntaristic' and Talcott Parsons' idea of 'normative solution to social order' in reference to system of norms and values that is compatible with voluntaristic mode of action. It implies that the nature of 'social reality' is conceived in relation to the human action as object of means-end rationality (Cf.: Parsons, Talcott (2003): Das System moderner Gesellschaften (6. Auflage). Weinheim/München: Juventa Verlag).

bodies and minds and that allow them to produce, reproduce and trans-form institutional structures and relational structures."[5] By implication, these three-dimensional structures constitute the conceptual frameworks through which different realities of social formation or organization could be captured. Although for Lopez and Scott, institutional and embodied structures seem to be similar to each other, yet they differ in terms of their singular manifestations in particular actions or circumstances. As structural patterns of interaction, the institutional, relational and embod-ied structures combine to form the fundamental basis through which indi-viduals or groups are structurally constructed in themselves and at the same time project their common interests as an institutional framework in contrast to the general goods.

Similarly, Alexander in his analysis explains that the institutional concept of structure is linked to the functionalist macro-level notion of social structure that has its root in Durkheim's thesis on 'the existence of social facts'[6] as well as the 'structural functionalism'[7] formulated by Talcott Parsons in his system theory. Alexander however asserts that "the con-cept of institutional structure is so familiar with embodied structure that its diversity and variety is easily overlooked."[8] However, in contrast to the agency-structure debate, relational structure is characterized within the social milieu of interactionism, which appears to connect individuals and groups to a basic network of relationship. This idea in a way differs from the other social structural dimensions on the account that it formal-izes itself through the reference to social network as the connecting line

---

[5] Lopez, Jose/Scott, John (2000): Social Structure. Glasgow: Harper Collins, pp. 3-4.

[6] Durkheim is of the view that the existence of social facts transcends the individual con-sciousness to embrace the collective consciousness, which exists inside the individuals that make them to socialize (See: Durkheim, Emile (1992): Über soziale Arbeitsteilung: Studie über die Organisation höherer Gesellschaften. Frankfurt am Main: Suhrkamp).

[7] In this thesis, the essence of function is to safeguard the social system, which contains in its particular structure, the units and boundaries that make up the system. He arrives to the function of system through the existence of structure (See: Parsons, Talcott (2003): p. 111ff).

[8] Alexander, Malcolm L. (2007): Visualizing Social Structure: Bridging the Gap between Contemporary Social Theory and Social Network Analysis. In: Curtis, B./Matthewman, S./McIntosh T. (eds.): Public Sociologies: Lessons and Trans-Tasman Comparisons, TASA & SAANZ Joint Conference 2007. http://www.tasa.org.au/conferences/conference papers07/papers/199.pdf [accessed: 22.03.2010]

that governs the pattern of relationships. This pattern of relationship, which is incorporated in relational structure, will be broadly examined in part three of this work. In other words, the social structure is revealed by the commonality of interpersonal relationships, which tie individuals and groups together, and derive its formation from the character of social networks.

Still on the pattern of social relationship, here Giddens points to "the fact that the social contexts of our lives do not consist just of random assortments of events or actions; they are structured, or patterned, in distinct ways."[9] This 'structuration' according to Giddens, has influence over important social groupings and social networks, and also explains the dynamics of the wider range of human relationships in a distinctive form. This relationship is arranged in a mutually dependent mode of interaction, which seeks to protect and maintain a definitive institutional order. In this conception, the institutional arrangement always reflects on the interests and positions inherent in human interactions, whereby some occupy higher status and others a subordinate one within the social groupings that form the bases for social relationship. Thus following this theoretical discourse thus far, the analysis will intend to examine the social structural arrangements based on inequality relations and interactional differences.

2.1 The Concept of Inequality

The study of inequality occupies an important place in sociological research. Inequality is a regular feature in social interactions and conditions based on differences in class, locality, race, ethnicity and gender. It has diverse forms, which divide people into social groups of 'unequal rewards'[10] and different living standards. Simply put, Scott & Marshall note

---

[9] Giddens, Anthony (2006): Sociology, 5th Edition. Cambridge: Polity Press, p. 8.

[10] Grusky argues that "the degree of inequality in a given reward or asset depends, of course, on its dispersion or concentration across the individuals in the population. Although many scholars seek to characterize the overall level of societal inequality with a single parameter, such attempts will obviously be compromised insofar as some types of rewards are distributed more equally than others" (Grusky, David B. (2001): 'The Past, Present, and Future of Social Inequality'. In: Grusky, David B. (ed.): Social Stratification: Class, Race, and Gender in Sociological Perspective 2nd Edition. Westview Press, pp. 5-6. http://www.scribd.com/doc/37719956/Gruskyinequality [accessed: 18.11.2010]).

that "it entails an unequal rewards or opportunities within a group or groups within a society."[11] In the real sense, inequality seems to be inevitable considering the fact that the manifestation of equality is almost impossible in the community of relationships. But it is even when inequality becomes intolerable that it has difficult implications for social integration and cohesion. Intolerable inequality however means a significant departure from distributional justice such that groups affected view it as a social aberration or a serious deviation from the socio-cultural norms. The various discrepancies involved in intolerable inequality could feed directly into civil strife given the proper catalyst. In other words, when particular groups are suppressed and denied what are their rights, the society is usually endangered through social conflicts and disorder.

However, inequality discourse is chiefly associated with 'social changes' in the society, which manifest themselves in various aspects of social life within a long period of time. Social change (Sozialer Wandel) on the other hand is characterized by 'modifications or variations'[12] that entails "significant alteration of social structures (that is, of patterns of social action and interaction), including consequences and manifestations of such structures embodied in norms (rules of conduct), values, and cultural products and symbols."[13] In fact, social change could be attributed to as either a transformation or alteration (i.e. transformation as a form of progressive new order, and alteration as a way of external influence and imposition). These two aspects of social change have effect both on people's social life and behavior in a particular society, characterized by inclusion and exclusion (i.e. inclusion as an integrating factor of production and exclusion from participation seen as disintegrating factor). For instance, exclusion could be lack of access to basic needs such as education, health care, housing, employment opportunities, participation in

---

[11] Scott, John/Marshall, Gordon (eds.) (2005): 'Inequality': Oxford Dictionary of Sociology, 3rd Edition. New York: Oxford University Press, pp. 306-307.
[12] Social change is "a term used to describe variations or modifications of any aspect of social processes, social patterns, social interactions, or social organisations" (Jones, Marshall: Basic Sociological Principles, p. 1. Cited in: Sharma, Rajendra K. (2007): Fundamentals of Sociology. New Delhi: Atlantic Publ., p. 305).
[13] Moore, Wilbert E. (1968): 'Social Change'. In: Sills, David (ed.): International Encyclopedia of the Social Sciences, Vol. 14. New York: The Free Press, p. 366.

politics, status symbol etc, and inclusion as a formation of class difference and interest groups.

From the above perspective, inequality could be fashioned by a range of structural factors that indicate people's status, identity and where they live. This idea goes to highlight socio-cultural formation that is associated with identity discourse and its contribution to inequality differences. It must however be pointed out that the discourse on inequality differs from poverty discourse, although the two have comparative consequences on individuals and groups. Hence inequality can be high where poverty is low depending on its mode of appearance and socio-cultural phenomenon involved. That means that the poor can jump from poverty to richness but at the same time the inequality gaps between the newly rich and the already rich may not be affected and still have the tendency to widen all the more due to the already structural mechanisms of formation. Hence, the fundamental assumption of inequality study is on how to bridge the gap among individuals or groups in their various social formations.

Therefore, the various views on inequality in sociology are frequently posited on the basis of analytic constructions. In this way, some of the protagonists agree more or less on the social reality of classification of inequality. For instance, Osberg identifies certain dimensions of classifying inequality: "For some, the important issue is the differences among all individuals in potential command over goods and services – if society as a whole produces a certain amount of output, how is the total pie sliced up? For some, the situation of the poor is a particular important dimension of inequality, since there is a long tradition of ethical concern with inequality which stresses the relative well-being of the most disadvantaged members of the society. For others, the crucial questions are those which surround the concentration of ownership, wealth and power in capitalist societies. And for still others the social policies which affect inequality command the most interest."[14] These classifications by Osberg give room for examination of various dimensions of inequality. Thus the points of consideration are not only on the vertical axis but also on the horizontal axis of social relationship. This analysis will then focus on

---

[14] Osberg, Lars (1991): 'Introduction'. In: Osberg, Lars (ed.): Economic Inequality and Poverty: International Perspectives. New York: M.E. Sharpe, Inc., p. xi.

social, political, and economic dimensions that take into considerations the different life chances that characterize inequality. These various dimensions also relate to each other in terms of their consequences within and among groups, but have their distinguishing characteristics in social relationships.

2.1.1 Social Dimension of Inequality

In discussing social dimension of inequality, various areas of interests are considered; such as social welfares or security (employment and health opportunities) and social positions (pertaining to discriminations experienced in life situations). According to Barlösius, social dimension of inequality results from two causes: "firstly, from differences of the provision with material things, but also with supply levels like medical and education facilities, and secondly, the social positions are not for all equally attainable, because as such they presuppose the affiliation to exquisite cliques. Thus, not all differences and access limitations are relevant for inequality but only such which certainly show some resistance and as well have positive or negative effect on the possible actions of the concerned."[15] In that instance, social inequality exists where an unequal distribution of wealth or power could hinder some people from obtaining the same standard of living or positions in society. In this conception, two basic elements are at stake: the socially-defined categories such as class, gender, ethnicity etc. that position people differently, and the unequal access to social goods. Hence, when these two elements are neglected in social relationships, they form the bases through which groups or individuals are subjugated and subjected to minority social grouping.

Moreover, the socially-defined categories of inequality as well as the accessibility to the social goods are majorly characterized by the unequal distribution of life chances. In other words, such an unequal access to life chances is regarded as social stratification. Giddens is of the opinion that sociologists speak of social stratification to describe inequalities that exist among individuals and groups within human societies. Nevertheless, stratification is not only in terms of assets or property, but it can also

---

[15] Barlösius, Eva (2004): Kämpfe um soziale Ungleichheit: Machtheoretische Perspektiven. Wiesbaden: VS Verlag für Sozialwissenschaften, S. 11-12 (Translation is mine).

occur because of other attributes, such as gender, age, religious affiliation, educational level etc.[16] These attributes constitute the integral factors that define social inequality and as such describe how relevant opportunities are distributed across the various groups in the society.

In fact, social inequality is everywhere, but manifest strongly in places
where there are limited availability of opportunities and accessibilities to
broadly and desirable social goods and/or to social positions, or in places
that are equipped with unequal power and/or interaction possibilities.
And in that way lasting restrictions are experienced, which however impair or favor the life chances of the certain individuals, groups and parties
involved.[17] However, the impairment of life chances could be directed to
absence of rights people ought to have such as freedom of speech and
assembly, voting rights, property rights as well as social privileges such
as incomes, access to basic health care, education and other social welfares and infrastructural amenities. On the other hand, one could as well
identify other socio-cultural transformations that could widen the margin
of difference, such as access to new technological networks that create
boundaries in social system. With the rapid socio-cultural changes, the
phenomena of inequality seem to have increased. Many parts of the world
are now becoming more reliant on the new technology such as internet
and mobile telephone so that peoples' access to such technologies affects
their life chances. These new changes may be experienced differently by
different social groups and individuals who regularly interact with each
other, and as such contributing to complexities in social structures.

2.1.2   Political Dimension of Inequality

Political dimension of inequality mainly centers on the areas of participation and representation: participation in the affairs of the state especially
on political matters, and how various groups are politically represented.
Here Bartels notes that "studies of participatory inequality seem to be
inspired in significant part by the presumption that participation has im-

---

[16] Giddens, Anthony (2006): Sociology, p. 295.
[17] Kreckel, Reinhard (1992): Politische Soziologie der sozialen Ungleichheit. Frankfurt
am Main: Campus, S. 17.

portant consequences for representation."[18] Thus, participation is at the heart of political inequality. Political participation creates an avenue through which groups or individuals could be informed about their interests, preferences, and needs in policy formulation, and as well actively get involved in decision making regarding the affairs of the community or the society. The implications of participation on equal representation refer mostly to the rights of political parties concerning the electoral processes, and the extent by which the individuals or groups in the state have rights over decisions concerning the state.

Moreover, the measure by which the citizens have equal participation over government decisions is an important aspect of democracy. Thus, one of the essential principles in a democratic setting is the consideration of the basic preferences of the citizens and their general interests in political issues. Participation can be made manifest in the manner in which people express their rights through voting in the electoral processes. Apart from voting rights, other political activities in the state such as belonging to political parties and the right to engage the citizens through campaign also matter in effective participation. The citizens should in this sense feel that they are part of the state and therefore have the right to vie for any elective position. But unfortunately, many obstacles limit especially the opportunities of women, the poor and the minorities in political processes. This limitation may be as a result of exclusion, intimidation or domination by the ruling class and also because of the fact that the political processes are often governed by economic availability and economic power to which the minorities have little or no access.

On the other hand, political inequality transmits to political stratification when it is associated with the lack of opportunities in political competition. It directly overlaps with other forms of inequality in producing variations in relationships. As such, various individuals and groups tend to device different means to cope with the ranging situations. For instance, the diverse interest groups can use the available resources in their possession such as power and wealth to preserve their positions and respective interests. Through this means, they suppress other groups and influence

---

[18] Bartels, Larry M. (2005): Economic Inequality and Political Representation. Princeton University, p. 3. http://www.princeton.edu/~bartels/economic.pdf [accessed: 24.05.2010]

the making of political processes and government decisions through their wealth and power. On the horizontal level of relationship, they compete within themselves in the bid to have control over the state apparatuses.

Hence Johnston believes that "the interrelations of individuals, as well as those of groups, are thought of either as situated on the same horizontal level or as hierarchically superimposed upon each other. Shifting from group to group sometimes does not involve any social rise or descent; at other times it is thought of as inseparable from the vertical dimensions [...]. The discrimination between the vertical and the horizontal dimensions expresses something which really exists in the social universe: the phenomena of hierarchy, ranks, dominion and subordination, authority and obedience, promotion and degradation. All these phenomena and corresponding interrelations are thought of in the form of stratification and superposition."[19] That is to say that the political space by way of domination and superimposition is dominated by the powerful few, who really use their subordinates to achieve their political interests. But the powerful groups also utilize their power and high social ranks to stratify others who prove to be obstacles in their political decisions as well as blocking any advancement that could lead to opposition. Finally, it is always very difficult to surmount such powerful groups because they have the economic and political powers to determine the mode of political operations and how the introduction of certain new political formations could be executed. In the end, the political system continues to be hampered by domination, which deepens the political gap among and within different political groups.

2.1.3   Economic Dimension of Inequality

Economic dimension of inequality is fundamentally based on disparity in the distribution of wealth as well as income differences that affect life chances and shape other spheres of society such as culture and politics. This dimension does not delimit itself only on income disparities but also correlated with other inequality determinants in affecting the social structures of the society. Economic inequality thus reflects on power positions

---

[19] Johnston, Barry V. ed. (1998): Pitirim A Sorokin 1889-1968: On the Practice of Sociology – The Heritage of Sociology. Chicago: University of Chicago Press, pp. 211-212.

among various categories of privileged and unprivileged groups or individuals. By means of definition, economic inequality could be referred to as disparities in income distribution, but broadly to an unequal access to the general wealth, which constitutes the major factor in social system. In other words, it entails unequal distribution of goods and services among groups and individuals within a society or between countries. This inequality distribution could be generally referred to as unequal outcomes in relation to unequal opportunity to the basic resources. Again, economic inequality is usually characterized by conflict arising as a result of struggle for economic interests or the pursuit of more accumulation.

An investigation on the economic dimensions of inequality is not a step away from sociological discourse, but rather central in making sense of the sociological concern of inequality. The issue of measuring economic inequality has been a crucial problem in research fields. Thus, in analyzing various approaches in inequality measurement, Sen and Foster contend that "the measures of inequality that have been proposed in the economic literature fall broadly into two categories. On the one hand, there are measures that try to catch the extent of inequality in some objective sense, usually employing some statistical measure of relative variation of income, and on the other there are indices that try to measure inequality in terms of some normative notion of social welfare so that a higher degree of inequality corresponds to a lower level of social welfare for a given total of income."[20] They further argue that "the two approaches in terms of their practical use would not be all that different from each other. Even if we take inequality as an objective notion, our interest in its measurement must relate to our normative concern with it, and in judging the relative merits of different objective measures of inequality, it would indeed be relevant to introduce normative consideration."[21] Following both approaches, the extent of inequality of income and wealth is often traditionally measured by the 'Gini Coefficient' which was first applied by 'Gini'[22]. One way of viewing

---

[20] Sen, Amartya/Foster, James (1997): On Economic Inequality, Expanded Edition with a Substantial Annexe. New York: Oxford University Press, p. 2.
[21] Sen, Amartya/Foster, James (1997): p. 3.
[22] The Gini Coefficient measurement was formulated by Gini, Corrado (1912) in his analysis of "Variability and Mutability".

measure as Sen and Foster noted, is in terms of the Lorenz Curve, whereby the percentages of the population arranged from the poorest to the richest are represented on the horizontal axis and the percentages of income enjoyed by the bottom X% of the population is shown on the vertical axis.[23] In finding a yearly index result as applied to a given country, Gini Coefficient entails 'multiple observations for a given country in a given year'. But this measurement may hardly be able to account for other areas of inequality such as social status or health opportunity. Nevertheless, the use of Gini Coefficient in measuring of economic inequality is quite determinant in analyzing the income differences and wealth disparities within a given population. The measurement therefore enables for more meaningful assessment of economic distribution in the society.

2.2   Complexities of Inequality Variations

The questions of where does one belong, who does what and how individuals and groups ought to protect their common interests often preoccupy one on the idea of formulating and, at the same time, determining the yardstick in variations involved in an unequal social relationship. Reconciling these phenomena of relationship allows the interplay of different categories that constitute the complex nature of inequality especially taking into account the issue of diversity and existence of multiple identities as the delimiting factors. Thus, describing, predicting and explaining such complexities provide some basic facts about structural changes and the consequential positioning in the society. However, various positionings in the society tend to bring in the conventional specificities that are associated both with cultural and historical pattern of relational processes. In the first instance, the specificities relate with each other, forming a bond of commonality and networks, and in some other instances, they project the terms and conditions of differentiations that put 'one' in contrast with the 'other' in social relationship.

Consequently, these two instances of specificities exist mostly within a group, but have the tendency to manifest themselves differently among groups and individuals. In this manifestation, Mahalingam is of the opin-

---

[23] Sen, Amartya/Foster, James (1997): p. 29-30.

ion that it is "the triangulation of a subject vis-à-vis her or his location and social positioning along class, gender, race, and or caste. This process is dynamic, multidimensional, and historically contingent."[24] As a multidimensional inequality condition that is historically construed, which was also proposed by Theodor Geiger, the variations are analyzed through the integral formation of the cultures, historical phenomena and social categories that relate with other structural variables to produce multiple inequality. This idea brings out the new inequality consciousness by appreciating the ideological formulations over the categorical assumptions. Using this framework, this analysis recognizes the complex nature of inequality and seeks to address the challenges superimposed by using qualitative research methodology. For a more detailed elaboration of this complex formation, how individuals and groups are positioned in a given social environment as well as the changing processes involved in the attributes that form the pattern of relationships would be addressed as follows.

2.2.1 Social Positioning

In examining further the complex nature of inequality variations, social positioning as a delimiting factor of inequality looks into relational patterns in the social environment. The usage of the term 'social positioning' stems from the functionality of individual mode of location in a given environment or social grouping and not quite as a form of social status. The relevant standpoint of social positioning is on how the categories such as gender, ethnicity, race, age, sexuality and class are perceived in different social locations and at the same time contouring the basic attributes that constitute their differences in social relations. This perception is basically located in the people's normative experiences of everyday life or what Smith calls 'relations of ruling' in her 'institutional ethnographic approach'[25] to daily relationship as a standpoint. Social positioning how-

---

[24] Mahalingam, Ramaswami (2007): 'Essentialism and Cultural Narratives: A Social-Marginality Perspective'. In: Fuligni, Andrew J. (ed.): Contesting Stereotypes and Creating Identities: Social Categories, Social Identities and Educational Participation. New York: Russell Sage Foundation, p. 45.

[25] This approach was introduced by Smith to account for most unrecognized variable in social relationships. According to Smith, "institutional ethnography is distinctive among sociologies in its commitment to discovering 'how things are actually put together,' 'how

28

ever captures multiple dimensions of relationships that characterize people's daily life, which seems more often than not as conflict-enhancing. It creates the conditions of contradiction and resistance, thereby producing complexities in the relations of ruling, which govern human interactions.

Naples further comments that, "Smith's institutional ethnographic approach to standpoint offers more of a methodological guidepost for investigation than other dimensions of standpoint. While attending to the relations of ruling in everyday life, Smith's approach includes sensitivity to the power of 'discourse' and textual bases of ruling as they organize daily life in ways that are not necessarily visible to the social actor."[26] In elaborating this point of view, social positioning brings out the dominant features that characterize the subjugation of one group against the other as a consequence of vulnerability. In other words, social positioning offers the necessary conditions in understanding and investigating how the daily lived experiences of different categories of inequality interact to produce complexity in inequality variations.

By analyzing "what role does inequality play?" according to Cole, "draws attention to the ways that multiple category memberships position individuals and groups in asymmetrical relation to one another, affecting their perceptions, experiences and outcomes. This question helps [...] to view the categories such as race and gender as structural categories and social processes rather than primarily as characteristics of individuals [...]."[27] In such instance, social categories structure groups' access to social, economic, and political resources and at the same time determine how privi-

---

it works'." (Smith, Dorothy E. (2006): 'Introduction'. In: Smith, Dorothy E. (ed.): Institutional Ethnography as Practice. Oxford: Rowman and Littlefield Publishers, Inc., p. 1).

[26] Naples, Nancy A. (2003): Feminism and Method: Ethnography, Discourse Analysis, and Activist Research. New York/London: Routledge, p. 198. For Jäger, 'discourse' implies a practice of articulation that does not passively represent social conditions, but rather constructs and organizes them as a flow of social knowledge supplied through time (Jäger, Siegfried (1999): Kritische Diskursanalyse: Eine Einführung. Duisburg: DISS-Studien, S. 23). Für Foucault „Diskurse sind das, worum und womit man kämpft; [...]." (Foucault, Michel (1991): Die Ordnung des Diskurses. Frankfurt am Main: Fischer-Taschenbuch-Verlag, S. 11)

[27] Cole, Elizabeth R. (2009): Intersectionality and Research in Psychology. In: American Psychologist: 2009 American Psychological Association. Vol. 64, No. 3, p. 173. http://aurora.wells.edu/~vim/Intersectionality_Psy.pdf [accessed: 11.09.2009]

leges are grounded in historical and social contexts.[28] Thus the historical and social contexts form the structural factors, which perceive such phenomena like cultural barriers, poverty as vestiges of domination and disempowerment. On the other hand, the socially structural factors in reference to income, accessibility and recognition of one's status have methods which are structurally registered into social associations. These methods however manifest in different spheres and operational capacities that further present themselves in network of relationships as a way of producing greater inequalities and identity complexity.

Furthermore, discussions on identity formation often raise challenging and difficult issues such as class differences and gender disparities that need not be overlooked but articulated with proper deliberation and concentration. Identity construction however repositions individuals and groups in their various interactive experiences that define social positioning. The reposition may either consciously or unconsciously influence one's position in relation to the ways in which one's own idea of belonging and not belonging in society or group are exercised or manifested. For instance, the dominant groups exercise more influence through subordination of the minorities or the less privileged. However, such categories as sex, race, nation, religion, occupation etc. constitute identity construction and understood as such in relation to each other. In that case, individuals and groups struggle for protection of interests through projection of their basic identities that function as differentiating categories.

Specifically, it is proposed that with identity constructions along difference categories of inequality, one must first of all ensure the reduction of insecurities in one's own social positioning through disassociation and exclusion from others, and secondly by increasing security through unions and a strengthened protection of oneself. By implication, individuals could strive not only to safeguard themselves through formation of network of sustainability, but also uphold an extensive and diverse differentiation system of situation approach. In this condition, individuals would attempt to reduce other insecurities with reinforced recourses to traditional backgrounds such as lineages, and/or new differentiation lines through isolation and then increase own security through strengthening of one's

---

[28] Cf. Cole, Elizabeth R. (2009): p. 176.

identity positioning. This reduction could be referred to as social struggle, but implies more to the manifestation of various categories of inequality which cannot wholly justify the inherent differences and changes that exist within each identity construction. But rather reflects on the dynamic and multidimensional nature of structural changes that are more diffused in interpreting specific locations of different relationships initiated through social positioning.

2.2.2   Changing Patterns of Relational Attributes

With the growing complex nature of social relationships, especially the ever changing relational structure as articulated by Lopez and Scott in terms 'patterns of causal interconnection and interdependence' or medium for socio-political and economic integration and interaction, investigation on the different variables of inequality assume here the centre stage. It is even more pertinent in the contemporary democratic society whereby the question frequently arises on 'who belongs' and 'who does not belong' or rather put; the issue of 'inclusion and exclusion'[29] in the social network. The questions are constructed in the interrelationships of different social categories like gender, class, race, ethnicity, sex and other social divisions. From these categories, the individuals construct different attributes and identities, and reproduce them quite in various symbolic representative mechanisms being influenced through material accumulations. Thus, understanding this construction according to Josephson is necessary in determining: "how experiences of domination can change and can vary for different groups and for different individuals within groups, even while they are reproducing long-standing inequalities and

---

[29] Connected to the concept of exclusion and inclusion is the question of power, inspired by Michel Foucault. Knudson notes that "the Foucauldian use of the concept of power and power relations involves both exclusion and inclusion. With the concepts of exclusion and inclusion power may be analysed as continually moving. Rather than viewing exclusion barely as a matter of suppression, exclusion involves discourses of opposition and productive power with negotiations about the meaning of gender, race, ethnicity etc." (Knudsen, Susanne V. (2004): Intersectionality - A Theoretical Inspiration in the Analysis of Minority Cultures and Identities in Textbooks. In: Caught in the Web or Lost in the Textbook, Paris, p. 67. http://www.caen.iufm.fr/colloque_iartem/pdf/knudsen.pdf [accessed: 12.08.2009]. See also: Foucault, Michel (1980): Colin Gordon (ed.) Power/Knowledge. Selected Interviews and other Writings 1972-1977. New York: Pantheon Books).

hierarchies."[30] The key standpoint is that the categories are terrains of social network as well as constitution in inequality differences. This idea relates to the three analytical frameworks of social embodiment which include macro (imagined community), meso (collective organizations) and micro levels (local community) that refer to how different power hierarchies mutually constitute each other and reproduce in different forms of relational attributes. The frameworks however illustrate the dynamic nature of inequality categories and how they relate in a reciprocal manner to affect each other in the social network.

The relational attributes however manifest mainly as a hegemonial discourse towards the mode of representation. This point brings out the individuals' daily performances, which contribute to their own subjectivity and at same time support the exercise of power in implementation of decisions and method of representation. Thus the decisive position is that, between 'we' and 'the other'[31], and here lies as well other assessment of differences such as: modern/old, central/periphery, civilized/uncivilized, white/black, rational/emotional etc. These differences are reproduced in various ways, which however capture the specific notations of inequalities such as gender, class, ethnicity etc that wedge out proper or accurate representation. They also boil down in questioning how the examined phenomena of attributes and processes of interactions with norms and ideologies function in different perspectives of representation. Such mode of representation in the society is sensibly integrated through common values, cultural order and convictions in the social structure. Hence relational attributes of representations as the "bearers of such valuable structures"[32] of inequality, stand at the set performance of interactionism. Such interactionism pushes the individual to socialize and therefore brings out the significant elements of the social categories in the social praxis.

---

[30] Josephson, Jyl (2005): 'The Intersectionality of Domestic Violence'. In: Sokoloff, Natalie J./Pratt, Christina (eds.): Domestic Violence at the Margins: Readings on Race, Class, Gender and Culture. USA: Rutger University Press, p. 86.
[31] Eichelpasch, Rolf/Rademacher, Claudia (2004): Identität. Bielefeld: Transcript Verlag, S. 84ff.
[32] Schützeichel, Rainer (2007): ‚Soziale Repräsentationen'. In Schützeichel, Rainer (Hrsg.): Handbuch Wissenssoziologie und Wissensforschung. Konstanz: UVK, S. 451.

2.3   Essential Components of Inequality Categories

The categories of inequality are defined using the social structural changes that are considered to have particular consequences on social relationships. The categories however influence the manner in which the structural factors are constituted and reproduced in the variety of ways, creating contradictions and conflicts under the conditions of social, political
and economic networks. Thus social categories such as gender, class, sex,
ethnicity etc. manifest themselves both as structural positioning and as
intersectional notions of relational attributes. Though the category of
class mostly assumes the dominant positioning, yet each has its own specific notation or separate base upon which identity and differences are
constructed. Bringing out the essential components of inequality categories assume here part of the critical response to the conception that social
positioning and the identities people possess are articulated within the
social categories.

The above response remains clear perhaps in analyzing the social categories of inequality in relation to their contingency and dimensionality. In
that sense, the categories of inequality are based on their mode of contingency especially in terms of their changeable patterns in individual circumstances, and their dimensionality in relation to their manifestations
and consequences in different life situations. According to Mahalingam,
"a person's race, class, and gendered experience are embedded in a particular social and cultural matrix that influences the person's beliefs about
various social categories and about the origins of social differences."[33] It
is obvious here that the social categories intrinsically impact and condition individuals' locations especially their functions and performative
instances. These formations also depend on certain historical and social
factors such as religion, ethnic origins or race that predominantly reveal
differences in various distinctive structures. One stands here to reason
that the categories often contribute something to the manner in which the
structural, participatory or identity phenomena have some advantages and
disadvantage on one's experiences. These phenomena are simply essential especially when one analyzes such relationship or interdependence
between different asymmetries of inequality and the social categories that

---

[33] Mahalingam, Ramaswami (2007): p. 45.

produce them. In this way, social categories are viewed as normative framework in understanding the reciprocity of inequality differences as well as the complexity of individual identities.

2.3.1 Identity and Difference

Identity and difference are the key elements that determine the institutional and relational framework in social formation. To understanding these notions of difference and identity, and the ways in which they manifest to exacerbate marginalization and oppression, the changing patterns of social categories assume a defining role. As the changes relate to identity differences, Woodward posits that "identity is often most clearly defined by difference, that is, by what it is not. Identities may be marked by polarization, for example in the most extreme forms of national or ethnic conflicts, and by the marking of inclusion or exclusion – insiders and outsiders, 'us' and 'them'."[34] However, the polarization marked by identity and difference is not exclusively an issue of ethnicity or gender or class inequalities, but also a location where there are often simultaneous and compounding relationships of different identities. These identities are repositioned in relation to various phenomena of locations that manifest in the categories of inequality and other social formations.

Hund then observes that "differences that had been considered insignificant before now develop so as to become the foundation of categorical differentiation. The emphasis of mutuality was however replaced by the stress of dissimilarity."[35] In other words, what assumes the object of similarity, by and large constitutes also the object of difference. It points to the diversity of human and social locations in a given environment. In this instance, Sen notes that "the demands of equality in different spaces do not coincide with each other precisely because human beings are so diverse. It is because we are so deeply diverse, that equality in one space frequently leads to inequality in other spaces. The force of the question 'equality of what?', thus, rests to a great extent on the empirical fact of

---

[34] Woodward, Kathryn ed. (1997): Identity and Difference. London: SAGE Publ., p. 2.
[35] Hund, Wulf D. (2003): Inclusion and Exclusion: Dimensions of Racism. In: Wiener Zeitschrift zur Geschichte der Neuzeit, 3. Jg. Heft 1/6 – 19, p. 14. http://www.wiso.uni-hamburg.de/fileadmin.pdf [accessed: 25.09.2009]

our dissimilarity – in physical and mental abilities and disabilities, in epidemiological vulnerability, in age, in gender, and of course, in the social and economic bases of our well-being and freedom."[36] This diversity makes possible the discovery of who may or may not be considered as belonging to a given community. But it becomes more complex in determining the modality, in the sense that as society and people continue to change so also new forms of differences and identities continue to emerge.

Moreover, the emergence of identity is a complex process that demands proper examination of the existing elements of differences within a particular identity, less influenced by external impositions such as modernity, but contextually constructed attributes and characteristics. The construction reflects the system of descriptions understood in relation to the core dimensions of identity. The essence of these descriptions is argued by Foucault thus; "from the elements that the system juxtaposes in great detail by means of description, it selects a particular few. These define the privileged and, in fact, exclusive structure in relation to which identities or differences as a whole are to be examined. Any difference not related to one of these elements will be considered irrelevant."[37] This idea suggests that the awareness of differences by an individual within the social or cultural context often determines the way identity development process of the individual is been shaped and redefined.

Hall on the other hand recognizes that the destabilization of the status of identity in the Western ideological context is being governed by a particular kind of force. This force is the object of change and continuity in identity formation and experiences. He however argues that, "the logic of identity is the logic of something like a 'true self'. And the language of identity has often been related to the search for a kind of authenticity to one's experience, something that tells me where I come from. The logic and language of identity is the logic of depth – in here, deep inside me, is my Self which I can reflect upon. It is an element of continuity. I think most of us do recognize that our identities have changed over time, but

---

[36] Sen, Amartya (1995): Inequality Reexamined. New York: Harvard Univ. Press, p. 117.
[37] Foucault, Michel (2004): The Order of Things: An Archaeology of the Human Sciences (First Published in 1966 in French). New York: Routledge, p. 152.

we have the hope or nostalgia that they change at the rate of a glacier. So, while we're not the fledglings that we were when we were one year old, we are the same sort of person."[38] In this conception, the logic of identity implies that identity changes over time, as a result of the social order in which the logic of 'true self' reflects on the changing conditions, but at the same time retains the unchangeable essential components such as the inner traits that make possible for continuity.

Contextualizing identity in this form brings out the differences that characterize the notion of individual traits and associations. As a result of various experiences, whereby the social categories manifest in a unique structural pattern, individuals tend to exhibit different identity formation in relational context. Addressing the position of identity and difference in social relationship is beneficially in detecting the structural barriers that constitute inequality dimensions. Therefore, in dealing with a particular group that sees itself as possessing different identities, I strongly argue that belongingness does not guarantee equality in the sense that one could belong to a privileged group and at the same time discovers oneself in a disadvantaged few. I will still come back to this point in part three of this work.

2.3.2 Difference Perspectives

Perceiving difference as a mechanism through which the social categories of inequality is formulated and sustained, provides basis for assessing identity formation. This mechanism according to Weedon, "is produced by economic, political, social and cultural factors that influence groups and individuals. In the global context these include the division of the world into radically different economic zones characterized by extremes of wealth and poverty. Factors which produce difference as oppression further include class, caste, colonial and racist practices and heterosexism."[39] To speak of difference in this sense is thus to speak of divisions

---

[38] Hall, Stuart (2007): 'Ethnicity: Identity and Difference'. In: Ching, Erik Kristofer/Buckley, Christina/Lozano-Alonso Angélica (eds.): Reframing Latin America: a Cultural Theory Reading of the Nineteenth and Twentieth Centuries. USA: University of Texas Press, p. 77.
[39] Weedon, Chris (2000): Feminism, Theory, and the Politics of Difference. Oxford: Blackwell Publishers, p. 180-181.

associated with conflict. This conception implies that it is always easy to detect how the existing difference can become a potential source of inequality especially if there is some perception of oppression or marginalization. Hence the social categories such as gender, ethnicity, sex and class produce hierarchically structured forms of differences in naturally, culturally and constructively specific modes.

2.3.2.1 Natural Difference

Certain structural compositions that militate against equality are considered to be a natural phenomenon. This phenomenon creates differences among individuals and groups that could result to oppression and discrimination. The manifestations of these differences are more eminent in gender studies. In defining the boundary of natural formation, one of the starting points of feminist theory has been the distinction between 'sex' and 'gender', which seem to have enabled feminist critique to confront the ideology of natural differences between women and men. In this conception, two opposing arguments have emerged. Liberals on the one hand have spent a lot of time arguing that differences between men and women are created by socialization alone; which may be through upbringing, education, media influence and so on. They have preferred to believe that because they do not want an unchosen quality like the manhood or womanhood to significantly influence who someone is. In this perspective, liberal's first principle is that one should be self-created by one's own individual will and reason that characterize what defines one as human. In this sense, the liberal attempts to overthrow the influence of inherited sex role, which is still a contesting issue today. On the other hand, Modern science has continued to undermine and disprove the liberal position on account of unsubstantial categorization of certain traits such as genes and hormones of individuals. It is difficult to deny the role of body composition in guaranteeing the natural differences that aid oppressive relationships. Thus, the conservative attitude which strongly suggests that there are natural differences between men and women, which may be reflected in the nature of social life, and particularly family life, is increasingly being vindicated on the daily experiences.

Nevertheless, the question whether race or ethnicity reflects natural difference is still well contested by many scholars. Against this backdrop, Bulmer and Solomos opine that "race and ethnicity are not 'natural' cate-

37

gories, even though both concepts are often represented as if they were. Their boundaries are not fixed, nor is their membership uncontested. Racial and ethnic groups, like nations, are 'imagined communities'. They are ideological entities, made and changed in struggle. They are discursive formations, signaling a language through which differences may be named and explained."[40] In that case, there is always something that is real about race or ethnicity. Okere thus argues that "even if it is a mere invention created ad hoc by ethnocentric Europeans and foisted upon a world they were just poised to colonize and exploit; even if it has no ontological status and is no part of nature; it may yet be something with a merely functional status, but even so, something. Though race may be no more than a social construct or an externally imposed attribute, it is not mere mental fiction. Their scientific basis may be doubtful but their social consequences can be substantial because of the heavy weight of meaning history has conferred on them."[41] As a historical factor in essence, the manner in which the impact of race or ethnicity is shaping the formation of social and political identities cannot be ignored. Therefore, history plays a major role in constructing this complex identity relationship that has been achieved for a long period of time through shared belief and mutual commitment.

2.3.2.2 Cultural Difference

Culture provides a major context for identity formation and social distinction. The influence of culture on people's relationship characterizes the embodied structures that make possible the manifestation of particular traits inherited or as a result of historical consequence. In this context,

---

[40] Solomos, John/Schuster, Lisa (2000): 'Citizenship, Multiculturalism and the politics of Identity Politics: Contemporary Dilemmas and Policy Agendas'. Koopmans, Ruud/Statham, Paul (eds.): Challenging Immigration and Ethnic Relations Politics: Comparative European Perspectives. Oxford: Oxford University Press, p. 79. 'Imaginary community' as a concept was first formulated by Benedict Anderson whose construction process like nation is imagined, because the members of even the smallest nation will never know most of their fellow-members, meet them, or even hear of them, yet in the minds of each lives the image of their communion (Anderson, Benedict (1983): Imagined Communities: Reflection on the Origin and Spread of Nationalism. London: Verso Editions, p. 15).
[41] Okere, Theophilus (2005): Philosophy, Culture and Society in Africa: Essays. Nsukka-Nigeria: Afro-Orbis Publications, p. 53.

Okere defines culture as "the way of life of a people, their traditional behavior in a broad sense, including their ideas, arts and artifacts. It is the social heritage which an individual acquires from his group. It denotes an historical transmitted pattern of meanings embodied in symbols, by a system of inherited conceptions expressed in symbolic forms by means of which men communicate, perpetuate and develop their knowledge about an attitude towards life."[42] For Shorter, "culture is made up of 'invention' and 'convention'. 'Convention' refers to what is held in common, 'agreed upon', in society. 'Invention' refers to the appropriation of the culture by individuals, who thereby contribute to its ongoing development."[43] These two notions from Shorter however explain the changing nature of culture as a 'dynamic phenomenon'. That means that even though culture may be changeable to suit a particular historical moment, its essential components still remain stable as a source of its continuity.

Subsequently, culture is also a potential source of conflict and division in the sense that it forms a distinguishing as well as a unifying factor. Hall recognizes that, notwithstanding that "there are many points of similarity, there are also critical points of deep and significant difference which constitute 'what or who we really are'; or rather - since history has intervened − 'what we have become'. We cannot speak for very long, with any exactness, about 'one experience, one identity', without acknowledging its other side - the ruptures and discontinuities which constitute, precisely, the uniqueness."[44] As 'critical points of deep and significant differences', culture distinguishes one from the other either as a group or nation, drawing its own definition from particular customs, norms and concepts. For instance, the 'Osu' (caste system[45]) in the southern part of

---

[42] Okere, Theophilus (2005): p. 28.
[43] Shorter, Aylward (1998): African Culture: An Overview. Nairobi: Paulines Publications, p. 23.
[44] Hall, Stuart (1997): 'Cultural Identity and Diaspora'. In: Woodward, Kathryn (ed.) Identity and Difference. London: Sage Publication, p. 52.
[45] As a form of class society, Giddens explains that "a caste system is a social system in which one's social status is given for life. In caste societies, therefore, different social levels are closed, so that all individuals must remain at the social level of their birth throughout life. Everyone's social status is based on personal characteristics – such as perceived race or ethnicity […], parental religion or parental caste – that are accidents of

Nigeria offers here a case in point. Specifically, it is a disgusting practice mostly among the Igbos in Nigeria that is derived from their native religious beliefs and customs. The Osu is considered to be owned by the local deities and separated from the 'Nwadiala' who possess the full citizen right in the cultural community. However, the differences that exist between an Osu and Nwadiala are well pronounced in the area of marriage. An Osu cannot marry Nwadiala. According to this belief, if Nwadiala marries an Osu, he defiles the family and becomes a curse to the entire kinship lineage. That is why the Nwadiala families are always up in arms against any of their associates who attempt to marry an Osu.

On the other hand, culture plays an important role in the perception of one's identity as 'distinct from the other'. It means that understanding one's culture is a way of breaking the borders that secret the differences, which tend to separate one from the other. This understanding involves identifying those elements of the culture that could be share by the other. Actually, one argues that without perceiving strong elements of cultural identity, it is virtually hard to articulate and understand the points of similarity. In this perspective, culture attempts to describe the dimension of identities rooted in certain customs, values, traditions, and heritages. It describes the collective identity that manifests itself in individual positioning in a particular social situation. Thus the collective identity in a culture can transform over time through new discoveries, but still can also retain its essential component as a historical reality.

In other words, culture is marked by persistence and continuity depending on their mode of appearances. According to Barth, "this makes it possible to understand one final form of boundary maintenance whereby cultural units and boundaries persist. Entailed in ethnic boundary maintenance are also situations of social contact among persons of different cultures: ethnic groups only persist as significant units if they imply marked difference in behaviour, i.e. persisting cultural differences. Yet where persons of different culture interact, one would expect these differences to be reduced, since interaction both requires and generates a congruence of codes and values - in other words, a similarity or community of culture.

---

birth and are therefore believed to be unchangeable" (Giddens, Anthony (2006): Sociology, p. 297).

40

Thus the persistence of ethnic groups in contact implies not only criteria and signals for identification, but also a structuring of interaction which allows the persistence of cultural differences."[46] For example: if one was born and grew up into one particular culture say Igbo ethnic culture in Nigeria and later decided to earn a living in another ethnic culture say Yoruba, that does not diminish the relevant of the original or native culture but forms a sequence of cultural contact. For one to make a return after a long absence in the former, one is to experience what Hall refers to as the "shock of the 'doubleness' of similarity and difference."[47] This idea implies that it is a 'profound difference of culture and history' which is determinant in distinguishing cultural identity. In that case, the underlying elements of both cultures position the Igbos and Yorubas as both alike and different, as a result of cultural contact as well as the perception of interconnectedness of both cultures in certain norms.

Moreover, Barth argues that the interconnection can best be analyzed "by looking at the agents of change: what strategies are open and attractive to them, and what are the organizational implications of different choices on their part? The agents in this case are the persons normally referred to somewhat ethno-centrically as the new elites: the persons in the less industrialized groups with greater contact and more dependence on the goods and organizations of industrialized societies. In their pursuit of participation in wider social systems to obtain new forms of value they can choose among the following basic strategies: i) they may attempt to pass and become incorporated in the pre-established industrial society and cultural group; ii) they may accept a 'minority' status, accommodate to and seek to reduce their minority disabilities by encapsulating all cultural differentiae in sectors of non-articulation, while participating in the larger system of the industrialized group in the other sectors of activity; iii) they may choose to emphasize ethnic identity, using it to develop new positions and patterns to organize activities in those sectors formerly not found in their society, or inadequately developed for the new purposes."[48] All these strategies are important in defining the boundary of intercon-

---

[46] Barth, Fredrik (1969): Ethnic Groups and Boundaries: The Social Organization of Cultural Difference. Boston: Little, Brown and Company, pp. 15-16.
[47] Hall, Stuart (1997): p. 53.
[48] Barth, Fredrik (1969): p. 33.

nectedness. Although Barth did not expatiate on the cultural traits that enclosed those boundaries, yet these strategies are potential source of cultural dynamism and unifying factors in which certain cultural dichotomy could eventually be averted.

Finally, living in a diversity of cultures, one must understand one another not necessarily from the boundaries of separation but also as bearers of a common humanity with different cultural identities. In this sense, one realizes not only the ways in which the cultural differences manifest themselves in various circumstances, but also the ways in which cultures are interconnected. Therefore, one also comes to recognize that the very thing that differentiates is also the very thing that could unite.

2.3.2.3 Constructive Difference

A focus on the reality of differentials must take into account the existing dichotomies that manifest in individuals' or groups' social relationships as a result of constructed differences. Thus the existence of inequality is not merely endangered by natural or cultural realities, but majorly by what others think of another to represent by way of socially constructed attributes based on prejudices and stereotyped traits. Sometimes the constructed differences are accompanied by several beliefs. It is imperative that such beliefs may not be real or in existence but may have been originated out of popular conceptions. These beliefs are the basis through which categorizations are usually formed. They manifest differently depending on the social and cultural settings in which they find their meanings and consequences.

Most significant in the process of constructive difference is the conception of ethnic relationship. Ethnicity has remained a paradigm and much cited example of the constructivist view of difference. This idea was pictured by Croucher, who states that "ethnicity should not be viewed as ancient, unchanging, or inherent in a group's blood, soul, or misty past; nor be reduced to a rational means ends calculation of those intent on manipulating it for political or economic ends: 'Rather ethnicity itself is to be understood as a cultural construction accomplished over historical time. Ethnic groups in modern settings are constantly recreating themselves, and ethnicity is continuously being reinvented in response to changing realities' both within the group and the host society."[49] In this view, ethnicity is said to be a social construct rather than a constant, which corresponds to Anderson's idea on invented community.[50] According to Conzen, "the concept of invention allows for the appearance, metamorphosis, disappearance, and reappearance of ethnicities."[51] This conception implies that ethnicity changes in a historical circumstance with different attributes or traits that expand the cultural relationships when they are still relevant to the group.

However, Croucher further notes that "what is useful about constructivist approach is not merely that it turns needed attention to the emergence and maintenance of the ethnic group itself, but also that it combines valuable insights from the primordialist and instrumentalist views without replicating the analytical weaknesses of either. Because the emphasis is on construction, this approach borrows a great deal from the instrumentalists' focus on specific contexts and circumstances – whether they are economic or political, immediate, or structural. In other words, the construction of ethnic identities and ethnic group relations takes place under specific circumstances and can only be understood through a careful examination of those circumstances – for example, who has access to political, economic, and cultural resources, who does not, who lives where, who works where and with whom? […] Finally what must be clearly understood about the constructivist approach is that an emphasis on social definition, invention, or imagination does not signify superficiality or inconsequentiality of the constructed identities."[52] In other words, the existence of those social phenomena remain quite relevance in determining the meaning and construction of identities, especially where the character of social realities remain insecure. In fact, the constructed categories of identity are the major source of differentiation by which individuals and groups expe-

---

[49] Croucher, Sheila L. (1997): Imagining Miami: Ethnic Politics in a Postmodern World. USA, Virginia: University Press, p. 15.
[50] See: Anderson, Benedict (1983): Imagined Communities, pp. 5-7.
[51] Conzen, Kathleen et al (1992): 'The Invention of Ethnicity: A Perspective from the USA'. In: Journal of American Ethnic History Vol. 12, No. 1. USA, Illinois: University Press, p. 2.
[52] Croucher, Sheila L. (2004): Globalization and Belonging: The Politics of Identity in a Changing World. Oxford: Rowman & Littlefield Publishers, pp. 128-129.

rience inequality. They capture different social processes by the existence of valued norms and traits that promote complex relational hierarchies. Therefore, constructive approach is very essential especially in identifying the various characteristics or traits that have influences on people's interaction within the social and cultural milieus.

2.4   Conclusion

In this section, we have aimed towards establishing and affirming the characteristics of social structural formation and the various approaches to inequality study. From the study thus far, inequality and how it influences structural formations are viewed from different facets of social relations. These facets, which mostly aid domination and subordination of the disadvantaged by the privileged groups, are most often than not neglected, thereby causing wide range of disparities in social relationships. Hence the conditions of disparities determine the pattern of changes in the social structure.

In order to understand the underlying causalities of inequality, particularly as they affect different social groupings, considerations were given to different aspects of inequality. Thus the emphasis on multidimensional social structural approach in this work was to relate the existing pattern of differences that manifest in individuals and groups in terms of their positioning, distribution of attributes and mode of integration into socio-cultural, economic and political relations.[53] In that way, ranking individuals and groups in term of positioning and relational attributes create the complex variations in inequality make-ups, which constitute the differences and causal interaction among the social compo-

---

[53] Goldthorpe clearly identifies that "one can think of inequality as it exists within a society in terms of the distributions of attributes of its individual members that are in some sense ranked: individuals differ – i.e. are unequal – in their incomes, wealth, standards of consumption, the desirability of their occupations, their educational attainments, the extent of their social and cultural participation, etc. Treating social inequality in this way is often valuable, at least for descriptive purposes. However, inequality can also be thought of, at a deeper level, in terms of social relations in the context of which individuals are in some sense advantaged or disadvantaged" (Goldthorpe, John H. (2009): 'Analysing Social Inequality: A Critique of Two Recent Contributions from Economics and Epidemiology'. In: European Sociological Review. Oxford: Oxford University Press, pp. 2-3).

nents that exist in the social system. In this perspective, this study took on a broader analytical tool in investigating and determining inequality within different stratums of social relationships as well as specific categories that constitute inequality differences.

Finally, analyzing the structural inequality differences require both the vertical and horizontal derivatives in the context of natural, cultural and constructive perspectives in the distribution of social attributes and identity differences. On the vertical dimension, it directs to the hierarchical composition of the social structure, which assumes the major source of differences. On the other hand, the horizontal phenomenon is mainly based on relational attributes consequence of cultural dynamics. In this sense, the changes in the cultural aspects of social relations that reflect in interaction processes are major determining factors in constructing the physical criteria of inequality. The manifestation of these changes and their relational attributes contribute significantly to the pattern of social interactions as well as in widening the complexities of the contextual influences on inequality differences that impair social relations. The nature of interaction could however be gradual or rapid depending on the mode of responses to the social changes. The rapid changes consequent of the globalization influence evolve both the bifurcation of the social system as well as developmental transition. And this evolving is what I will investigate in the next chapter. Therefore, the usefulness of this study approach will enhance a broader knowledge of inequality differentials that manifest in a given environment, and also it forms a useful tool in policy formations and implementations that can gear towards sustainable development.

3 THEORETICAL ANALYSIS ON GLOBALIZATION

Theoretical investigations on inequality and globalization have continued to be a vital focal point and important repertoire of sociology in the recent time. Their studies have been characterized by boundary of differences between empirical realities and scientific analysis on society relations, resulting to various shifts on theoretical approaches. Due to new changes in the social system especially in international production and technological innovations, globalization is seen both as a developmental strategy and also as a means of socio-political and economic consolidation through an organizational framework. Thus Cheru notes that, "a striking feature of globalization is the very fact of social change expressed in a 'multiplicity of transitions' occurring simultaneously at numerous and in some cases mutually contradictory levels. These multiplicity of changes occur in different ways for different economies, different cities and different agents within them. The effects, which can either be positive or negative, are manifest in a wide array of contexts – from the social and cultural to the economic, environmental and political."[54] As a long term society process, the context in which globalization manifests in society integration becomes relevant in determining the real consequences it has in defining the boarders of differences. It however contributes to various transformations in the society. In this examination, we shall view globalization as a developmental process as well as a system theory that marks the boundary in the social system.

Various theories have so far been employed by sociologists and political scientists to investigate the developmental crisis as it affects the developing countries especially in Africa. Some of these theories, though being contested, seem to rely on the fundamental notion that Africa is towing a different developmental trajectory as against the Western developmental strategies. On that account, I will first of all examine briefly some of those views on development processes such as modernization theory, dependency theory and world-systems theory, and why Africa is not

---

[54] Cheru, Fantu (2005): Globalization and Uneven Urbanization in Africa: The Limits to Effective Urban Governance in the Provision of Basic Services. Los Angeles: African Studies Center, p. 1. http://www.international.ucla.edu/media/files/57.pdf [accessed: 12. 03.2010]

catching up with the rest of the world in developmental exercises. Moreover, the current wave of globalization seems to have intensified the African predicaments. It follows that the weakness of the state structures in Africa is seen as a consequence of global integration. Hence, this work explores how the current theories on globalization have advanced over the years and as such, how globalization impacts on inequality differences both locally and internationally have not only resulted to risk factors and increase of conflicts, but have also contributes to the distortion of the social order. Having that in mind, the work will therefore proceed to construct its framework based on the recent prevailing views on sociopolitical development, as well as African crisis of modernization associated with the issue of state formation.

3.1   Dualistic Conception of Modernization Theory

Modernization theory was developed to harmonize the prevailing theoretical trends brought in by evolutionism and functionalism. The theory was championed by the North American scholars in the early fifties. The main assumption of the theory is that modernization is the result of rationalization and differentiation in developmental process. As a dualistic conception, it is based on the contrasting dichotomy between traditional (agrarian, hierarchical-autocratic status-) society and modern (industrial, rational, bureaucratic, class-based, democratic performing-) society. This dichotomy is mirrored down to the following expressions; "developed – underdeveloped", "north – south" and "first – third world", with the assumption that the "second world" stands at the threshold of industrialization. According to Kößler, "the parochial nature of modernization theory, which reflected on the theory of developmental model of dualistic structure placed 'modern' against 'traditional' sectors in economy and society."[55] The theory of course describes the pattern of changes on the mode of production as well as the processes of integration into modern economy. In contrast to the evolutionism on the one hand, social change is seen not as immanent, but necessarily established, in that endogenous factors hinder development as well as prevent it, such that it needs the exogenous stimuli sides of the developed societies to eliminate the 'development

---

[55] Kößler, Reinhart (1994): Postkoloniale Staaten: Elemente eines Bezugsrahmens. Hamburg: Deutsches Übersee-Institut, S. 76 (The translation is mine).

impediments' which is explained from socio-economic and cultural conditions. On the other hand, in contrast to the interdependence of various institution of the society as proposed by the functionalist, modernization theory agree to the need to have a harmonized component parts that make up the society.

The theory however argues that "low-income societies can develop economically only if they give up their traditional ways and adopt modern economic institutions, technologies and cultural values that emphasize savings and productive investment."[56] It implies that the impediment of development in the traditional societies is seen as a result of certain cultural phenomena such as values, beliefs and norms, which have prevented the application of the required modernization ideals. This impediment is what Rostow called 'ceiling' against development. He notes that "the central fact about the traditional society was that a ceiling existed on the level of attainable output per head. This ceiling resulted from the fact that the potentialities which flow from modern science and technology were either not available or not regularly and systematically applied."[57] With this assumption, African traditional institutions are regarded as an impediment to modernization process in the sense that they are not complied with the industrialization processes and modern technologies followed by the Western conception of development.

Modernization theory is criticized on many grounds following its assumptions on single path to development that constitutes a binary opposite between the local and national. The criticism could be analyzed as follows: developmental process is seen as ethnocentric (Euro-centric), determinate and universal; the explanation of developmental impediments on endogenous conditions is then deficit, circular (for example: pointing to the idea of 'vicious circle poverty'[58]), and not historical, since it neglects power structures like colonialism, imperialism and world market conditions; the establishing of the beginning of development (traditional

---

[56] Giddens, Anthony (2006): Sociology, p. 405.
[57] Rostow, Walt Whitman (1990): The Stages of Economic Growth: A Non-Communist Manifesto, Third Edition. Cambridge: Cambridge University Press, p. 4.
[58] The 'vicious circle of poverty' is explained as constituting variations in circular designs that impedes developmental outcomes both on individuals and groups.

society) and the goal of development (modern society as endpoint) ignores the perspective for dependent path and possibly the various directions of development (bifurcations); and the assumption of autonomous development (after what could be termed the 'Take-Off'[59] process) makes push for development politics redundant.[60] Finally, the major flaw of the theory is that it specifically treats African societies as if they have no historical origin, neglecting the influence and contributions of external factors to her woes. It also fails to justify the mechanisms and their applicability through which the continent could break the jinx of underdevelopment. In the final analysis, the theory is unable to capture Africa's cultural realities especially the indigenous institutions, which could also aid in facilitating development.

3.2   Dependency Theory as a Historical Model

Dependency theory was initiated by some scholars mainly from the developing world in contrast to modernization approach to development. It was first applied in the study of underdevelopment in Latin America and later used as an analytical tool in the contextual African developmental crisis. The theory later shifted from the idea of impeding indigenous character of development to the sporadic predicaments associated with world capitalist economy as a historical process of exploitation and underdevelopment. In this context, Mamdani argues that "[...] dependency theorists juxtaposed development with underdevelopment. Of the bipolar-

---

[59] According to Rostow, "the take-off is the interval when the old blocks and resistances to steady growth are finally overcome. The forces making for economic progress, which yielded limited bursts and enclaves of modern activity, expand and come to dominate the society. Growth becomes its normal condition [...] During the take-off new industries expand rapidly, yielding profits a large proportion of which are reinvested in new plant; and these new industries, in turn, stimulate, through their rapidly expanding requirement for factory workers, the services to support them, and for other manufactured goods, a further expansion in urban areas and in other modern industrial plants. The whole process of expansion in the modern sector yields an increase of income in the hands of those who not only save at high rates but place their savings at the disposal of those engaged in modern sector activities. The new class of entrepreneurs expands; and it directs the enlarging flows of investment in the private sector. The economy exploits hitherto unused natural resources and methods of production." (Rostow, Walt Whitman (1990): pp. 6-8)
[60] See: Goetze, Dieter (2002): Entwicklungssoziologie: Eine Einführung. Weinheim/ München: Juventa, S. 21.

ity, the lead term – 'modern', 'industrial', 'capitalist', or 'development' – was accorded both analytical value and universal status."[61] In fact, this approach according to Petithomme "introduced a historical explanation of developed countries' asymmetrical domination over developing countries. Africa's economical decline was explained by the prevalence of 'neo-colonial' practices, leading the postcolonial African state to be a direct descendant of its colonial ancestor."[62] It then follows that through the process of imperialism, colonialism and neo-colonialism, the 'core'[63] capitalist regions have constituted a developmental blockade to the development of the 'peripheral'[64] low-income regions. Hence, dependency school argues that the 'core' regions represent the marginal line of economic deprivations that exploit the 'peripheral' regions such as Africa. This developmental asymmetry based on the preferential role of the core regions has even persisted through the mercantile system of neo-liberal policies.

However, the capitalist economic policies have rather intensified and deepened the poverty level of peripheral regions, which have constituted the major market outlet in terms of raw material sources for the wealthy and powerful countries. In this development, capitalism involves exploration of the natural resources by the transnational corporations and exploitation of human resources through cheap labor in order to maximize profits. This formation process implies that most of the transnational corporations represent the interests of their core indigenous countries, who employ various means to ensure the growth of their own economy to the

---

[61] Mamdani, Mahmood (1996): Citizen and Subject: Contemporary Africa and the Legacy of Late Colonialism. Princeton, New Jersey: Princeton University Press, p. 9.
[62] Petithomme, Mathieu (2007): Political Power and the Development of Underdevelopment in Sub-Saharan Africa. 4th ECPR General Conference, p. 3. http://www.essex.ac.uk/pisa.pdf [accessed: 14.02.2010]. See also: Amin, Samir (1973): Neo-Colonialism in West Africa. Hardmondsworth: Penguin Books, p. 275.
[63] According to Friedmann, "core regions are defined as territorially organized subsystems of society which have a high capacity for generating and absorbing innovative change" (Friedmann, John (1973): Urbanization, Planning and National Development. Newbury Park California: SAGE Publications, p. 51).
[64] On the other hand, "peripheral regions are subsystems whose development path is determined chiefly by core region institutions with respect to which they stand in a relation of substantial dependency" (Friedmann, John (1973): p. 51).

underdevelopment of the peripheral countries mainly the Sub-Saharan Africa.

Similarly, Scott and Marshall aptly point out that the relationship between core and periphery regions is said to be a spatial and substantial dependency, which involves "the export of capital from the former to the latter; a reliance on Western manufactured goods and services which thwarts indigenous development efforts; further deterioration in the terms of trade for the newly independent countries; and a continuation of the processes of cultural Westernization which guarantee the West's market outlets elsewhere in the world. Apparently, the operations of transnational corporations in the Third World are seen as the principal agents of contemporary neo-colonialism, since [...] these are seen as exploiting local resources and influencing international trade and national governments to their own advantage."[65] It follows that the economic relationship between the people at the core and peripheral regions only contribute to the affluence of the core and the exploitation of the peripheral. Or what may be described as a developmental parasite that pitches the 'super-world' against the 'lesser-world' in the bid to control both their economic and political power/sovereignty.

Furthermore, Giddens notes that, "while political and military power is usually ignored by market-oriented theorists, dependency theorists regard the exercise of power as central to enforcing unequal economic relationships. According to this theory, whenever local leaders question such unequal arrangements, their voices are quickly suppressed."[66] The suppression of local authorities could either be by economic sanctions or aiding the overthrowing of the ruling government that does not succumb to the western policies. This issue of influence however boils down to the fact that those who hold the power would always have the advantage and control of the economy, and they determine the rate at which the distributional activities should be enhanced. Also the economic conditionality by the neo-liberal policies has influence on the participation of most African states in the capitalist economy. Dependency theory however proposes that should African state remain in the world capitalist economy, the de-

---

[65] Scott, John/Marshall, Gordon (2005): 'Neo-Colonialism', p. 442.
[66] Giddens, Anthony (2006): Sociology, p. 410.

velopmental possibility would be difficult considering the fact that unequal economic relationship makes progress impossible to achieve.

One of the limitations of the dependency theory is that, it overlooks the
many domestic/internal socio-political variables such as interest groups,
cultural constraints etc. which are very important in explaining developmental processes.[67] On the other hand, Kößler contends that "the dependency theory in its different forms could neither overcome the modernistic
impulse nor a secret dualism completely: Where it seemed to deny 'internal' factors of the underdevelopment or covered this fact through the
priority attack on the hierarchical world market connections, it however
got again and again in danger to call such inner social structures either
all-embracing or 'capitalistic' and then to constrict the concept of capitalism to a circulation sphere, or, actually overlooking the inner social dynamics, and with it also the problem of state structures."[68] Thus the implication of the theory is that the African indigenous structures are redundant, neither a stumbling-block to development nor incapable of uplifting
the continent from underdevelopment, rather the trajectories of development should be seen from the Western model.

Finally, in this consideration, there is the need for an important body of
work that could properly explain the developmental crisis in Africa and
particularly in Nigeria. In this way, the irresponsible political actors will
be at the centre of political analysis in examining the persistence of underdevelopment. This idea stands to highlight that "while dependency
theories help to account for much of the economic backwardness in Africa, they are unable to explain the occasional success story among such

---

[67] Vaughan argues that while "the dependency theory was preoccupied with the advance
of global capitalism, the marginality of third world economies, and the role of 'compra-
dor' classes in the economies of new states, dependency theorists underestimated the
critical role that indigenous structures [...] might play in the transformation of African
states. In short, while modernization analyses dismissed indigenous structures as dysfunctional to a Western-style developmental process, the dependency paradigm reduced these
institutions to mere reflections of social class. Thus, the dependency paradigm's instrumentalist Marxist preoccupations ignored the continuing relevance of indigenous structures as modern expressions of communal and class interests" (Vaughan, Olufemi (2000):
Nigerian Chiefs: Traditional Power in Modern Politics, 1890s-1990s. Rochester, New
York: University of Rochester Press, pp. 4-5).
[68] Kößler, Reinhart (1994): S. 76 (The translation is mine).

low-income countries as Brazil, Argentina and Mexico or the rapidly expanding economies of East Asia."[69] Therefore, considering the former 'Third World' nations that have relatively expanded their economic horizons through proper utilization of developmental opportunities, one will then question the credibility of generalizations of the dependency theory as it fails to establish the intricacies and implications of the internal political factors in African crisis of development.

3.3   Significance of World-Systems Theory

In developmental and capitalist economy, World-System theory as first associated with Immanuel Wallerstein is significantly important in explaining the dynamics of social system. In his two major works first published in 1974, namely: 'The Rise and Future Demise of the World Capitalist System: Concepts for Comparative Analysis' and 'The Modern World System: Capitalist Agriculture and the Origins of the European World-Economy in the Sixteenth Century', Wallerstein sees modern world-system (or the capitalist world-economy) as a historical social system that explains world economy and politics as interrelated in analyzing social structural changes and developmental crisis. He draws most of his ideas from dependency theory. In relation to dependency theory, world system theory follows the discussion on the household production and the changing structure of market economy. But on its theoretical standpoint, it describes the forcible process of expansion of the Western Europe, the incorporation and different peripheral 'zones' of the capitalistic world system in the course of colonialism, imperialism and new International division of labor.

However, the discussions on the renewed social transformations and intersociety relations point to the spread of the capitalist world-systems comprising of borders and units; borders in terms of diversities and units in terms of interactions and integrations. Here Wallerstein describes the world system as "a social system that has 'boundaries, structures, member groups, rules of legitimation, and coherence'. Its life is made up of the conflicting forces which hold it together by tension and tear it apart as each group seeks eternally to remold it to its advantage. It has the

---

[69] Giddens, Anthony (2006): Sociology, p. 413.

characteristics of an organism, in that it has a life-span over which its characteristics change in some respects and remain stable in others. Life within it is largely self-contained, and the dynamics of its development are largely internal."[70] He further points out two basic notations that characterize his theory. He argues that "it is a 'world system' not because it encompasses the whole world, but because it is larger than any juridically-defined political unit. And it is a 'world economy' because the basic linkage between the parts of the system is economic, although this was reinforced to some extent by cultural links and eventually [...] by political arrangement and even confederal structures."[71] Such structures and political arrangement in the capitalist world system are characterized by an unequal flow and endless accumulation of capital resources, and as such what may be referred to as 'one system among many' dynamic parts. This idea suggests that the structure of the capitalist world-economy, and the ability of some groups to play within the system, is central in understanding how the groups tend to exploit the means of production and the labor of others in a wide array of political and economic interests.

Wallerstein structurally divides his capitalist world-economy into core, semi-periphery and periphery. This 'division' of world economy according to him involves "a hierarchy of occupational tasks, in which tasks requiring higher levels of skill and greater capitalization are reserved for higher-ranking areas. Since a capitalist world-economy essentially rewards accumulated capital, including human capital, at a higher rate than 'raw' labor power, the geographical maldistribution of these occupational skills involves a strong trend toward self-maintenance [...]. Hence, the ongoing process of a world-economy tends to expand the economic and social gaps among its varying areas in the very process of its development."[72] In this way, the social system is definitively characterized by "the existence within it of a division of labor, such that the various sectors or areas within are dependent upon economic exchange with others

---

[70] Wallerstein, Immanuel (1974): The Modern World-System: Capitalist Agriculture and the Origins of the European World Economy in the Sixteenth Century. New York: Academic Press, p. 347.
[71] Wallerstein, Immanuel (1974): The Modern World-System, p. 15.
[72] Wallerstein, Immanuel (1974): The Modern World-System, p. 350.

54

for the smooth and continuous provisioning of the needs of the areas. Such economic exchange can clearly exist without a common political structure and even more obviously without sharing the same culture."[73] The economic exchange accounts to the permanent character of different class structures between the core and periphery in the world-system. In other words, the modern world-system is characterized by an unequal geographically and occupationally exchange distribution not only over wage labor/value-added tax within society but also over unequal distribution between core and periphery, and the structurally innovative semi-peripheral areas of the modern world-system.

In the structural division of the world system, Chase-Dunn notes that the "core areas are those where core production is concentrated, while peripheral areas contain mostly peripheral production. Core production is capital-intensive and uses skilled, high-wage labor. Peripheral production is labor-intensive and utilizes low-wage labor which often subject to extra-economic coercion."[74] In fact, core areas exploit the opportunity of cheap labor in extracting the raw materials from the periphery. Here Rodney recognizes this relationship of exploitation based on unequal economic exchange through trade contacts between the periphery and the core as "symptoms of underdevelopment and the secondary factor that make for poverty."[75] In other words, peripheral areas are highly influenced by core nations that employ various means in assuming control over the economic resources. More often than not, the periphery nations on that basis are forced to follow the economic policies that favor mostly the core nations, and with long-term negative impact on their own economic relations.

However, Wallerstein further states that "the structural differences of core and peripheral are not comprehensible unless we realize that there is a third structural position: that of the semi-periphery [...]. Our logic is not

---

[73] Wallerstein, Immanuel (2004): 'The Rise and Future Demise of the World-Capitalist System'. In: Lechner, Frank J./Boli, John (eds.): The Globalization Reader 2nd Edition. Oxford: Blackwell Publishing Ltd., p. 63.
[74] Chase-Dunn, Christopher (1981): 'Interstate System and Capitalist World-Economy: One Logic or Two?' In: International Studies Quarterly, Vol. 25, No. 1. JSTOR, p. 19.
[75] Rodney, Walter (2012): How Europe Underdeveloped Africa. Cape Town/Dakar /Nairobi & Oxford: Pambazuka Press, p. 22.

merely inductive, sensing the presence of a third category from a comparison of indicator curves. It is also deductive. The semi-peripheral is needed to make a capitalist world-economy run smoothly."[76] As a 'necessary structural elements in a world economy'[77] towards organizational balance, semi-peripheral forms the basis for innovation and social transformation. According to Chase-Dunn, "this is because semi-peripheral societies have access to both core and peripheral cultural elements and techniques, and they have invested less in existing organizational forms than core societies have. So they are freer to recombine the organizational elements into new configurations and to invest in new technologies, and they are usually more motivated to take risks than are older core societies."[78] In this perspective, Anthony then observes that "the semi-periphery acts as both a political and economic buffer between the core and the peripheral areas as well as an alternative arena to engage in unfair economic practices."[79] This development aids the semi-peripheral states to maintain the hierarchical structure that consolidates the modern world-system through capital accumulation. Hence, they are more diversified in their economic production and as such less dependent on the core than peripheral regions.

More significantly, Wallerstein in his work 'The Three Stages of African Involvement in the World Economy' differentiates three-world stages of incorporation of Africa into capitalist world economy. The first stage he called the 'Informal Empire', which extends from around 1750 to 1900 and was mainly propelled by the Atlantic slave trade and cash crop production, the second is the formal colonial era from 1900 to sometime between 1960 and 1980 sustained by imperialism, and the third stage, which is the time of formal independence of African states within the

---

[76] Wallerstein, Immanuel (2004): 'The Rise and Future Demise of the World-Capitalist System', p. 67.
[77] Wallerstein, Immanuel (1974): The Modern World-System, p. 350.
[78] Chase-Dunn, Christopher (2005): 'Social Evolution and the Future of World Society'. In: Herkenrath, Mark/König, Claudia/Scholtz, Hanno/Volken, Thomas (eds.): Globalizations from 'Above' and 'Below' – The Future of World Society. Journal of World-Systems Research Vol. XI, No. 2, p. 173. http://jwsr.ucr.edu [accessed: 23.07.2009]
[79] Anthony, Robert Michael (2009): Primacy and Polity: The Role of Urban Population in Political Change. Dissertation: The Ohio State University, p. 49.

present World-System.[80] He made this distinction not necessarily for historical development of Africa or European rise to 'hegemony'[81], but in view of his discussion on capitalist world system governed by unending accumulation of capitals. This distinction is also critical to the determination of regulatory institutions that have shaped the tremendous capital accumulations. In effect, the regulatory force in the capitalist world-economy has been the object of endless accumulation of capital or what Arrighi characterized as 'systemic cycles of accumulation'[82]. The regulatory institutions are usually accompanied by organizational changes that create a long-term influence on relational differences on the global market economy and the intensification of hegemonic power struggle.

However, world-systems theory has been criticized on many grounds, including the putative Euro-centrism and overemphasis on the significance of economic factors in history. Looking at it in another way, world-system theory takes a global perspective as the unit of analysis of social systems. But how this thought has relationship with each other, or how they can structurally change into another becomes problematic. The theory however relies on the capitalist dialectical production and accumulation, which have been the major crisis of capitalism. Thus, the trimodal structure of the capitalist world-economy cannot account for the crisis of profitability in the world system rather it has intensified the unprecedented revolution of time and space as differentiating as well as unifying procedures. In that instance, the global economy has been majorly characterized by asymmetrical relationship, creating diversities in both economic and political relations.

---

[80] See: Wallerstein, Immanuel (1976): 'The Three Stages of African Involvement in the World Economy'. In: Gutkind, Peter/Wallerstein, Immanuel (eds.): The Political Economy of Africa. Los Angeles: Univ. of California Press, pp. 31-55.

[81] The three hegemonies of the modern world-system include the Dutch hegemony of the seventeenth century, the British hegemony of the nineteenth century, and the U.S. hegemony of the twentieth century. However, world-systems analysts see a strong analogy between the decline of British hegemony after 1870 and the trajectory of the United States after the 1970s (Chase-Dunn, Christopher (2005): p. 176).

[82] According to Arrighi, systemic cycles of accumulation are "characterized by a fundamental unity of the primary agency and structure of the world-scale processes of capital accumulation" (Arrighi, Giovanni (1994): The Long Twentieth Century: Money, Power, and the Origins of Our Times. London/New York: Verso, p. 6).

Therefore, using only the categories of modern world-systems theory to account for the diverse cultural and economic formations in the world systems seems both empirically and theoretically simplistic. Lewellen affirms this position by arguing that "although Wallerstein was a major influence on contemporary globalization theory, much of what he describes has already changed or is in the process of transformation. The division-of-labor structure is based on an industrialized core and a pre- or nonindustrial periphery. Today, the core has moved into a postindustrial phase and to a great extent the periphery, even some of the poorest countries, has taken over the function of manufacture and the refinement of raw materials. The neat functional integration of world system theory seems increasingly simplistic given the rapid transfer of industrialism and mass consumerism to the Third World, the unfettered fluidity of financial flows, and worldwide media saturation."[83] Finally, Wallerstein's World System Theory which initially attracted many supporters was also criticized especially by historians on the ground that it seems historically unattainable and therefore ahistorical, since the theory selectively chose some historic facts to support its theoretical world-system without accounting for other various spatial and temporary events in world history. This criticism will therefore lead us to examine further some theoretical propositions on globalization processes.

3.4 Theoretical Propositions on Globalization

Globalization as a concept has different meanings for different political and social theorists. For some theorists, it is a changing process, but for others, it is a revolutionary system of development. In this analysis, globalization is viewed not so to speak a revolutionary new development in the history of social relationship, but rather a 'process'[84] and a 'system'[85]

---

[83] Lewellen, Ted C. (2002): The Anthropology of Globalization: Cultural Anthropology enters the 21st Century. USA: Greenwood Publishing Group, p. 14.

[84] Prakash and Hart explains globalization in terms of "a set of processes leading to the integration of economic activity in factor, intermediate and final goods and services markets across geographical boundaries, and the increased salience of cross-border value chains in international economic flows" (Prakash, A. /Hart, Jeffrey A. (1999): Globalization and Governance. London/New York: Routledge, p. 3). Likewise, Steger maintains that "globalization is a multidimensional set of social processes that create, multiply, stretch, and intensify worldwide social interdependencies and exchanges while at the

58

of development, which has continued to introduce various debates in both academic and general discourse. The discourse on globalization emerged mainly in the last few decades following the changing structures of the society that presupposes uniformity as well as diversity in political, cultural and social relations. This form of relation points to the dynamic nature of globalization both as a unifying as well as a diffusing element of political, economic and social conditions. Understanding the real import of the concept today leads one to many theoretical presuppositions. Generally, it involves 'changes toward transformations'[86] over time and space resulting to unified global economic, political, socio-cultural and technological developments, in which the nation-states are constantly being integrated and reintegrated, as well as national authorities losing their sovereignties. These changes affect all countries of the world, but rather unevenly distributed with respect to their influences. Of course, to understand the concept of globalization means that its potentials and risk factors involved in those changes must be taken into consideration.

Just like modernization theory, globalization theory however deals with various directional flow of development associated with Western influence, but differs in terms of transformative social forces derived from the influence of modern technology and communication networks. Again, globalization theory like world-systems theory dwells on the recent changes as they affect the social, political and economic structures in a global perspective but differs from world-systems theory in terms of its rate of transformation. For globalization theorists, transformation in this

---

same time fostering in people a growing awareness of deepening connection between the local and the distance" (Steger, Manfred B. (2003): Globalization: A Very Short Introduction. Oxford: Oxford University Press, p. 13).

[85] Luhmann identifies globalization with system theory. He points that communication technology as a characteristic of today's world society forms the boundary of social system, which has broken and transformed the accessibility to worldwide interaction. (See: Luhmann, Niklas (1999): Funktionen und Folgen formaler Organisation (5. Auflage). Berlin: Duncker &. Humblot). In that way, social system has also the function of integration that gears towards a particular formation (See: Parsons, Talcott (2003): p. 12).

[86] Steger explains thus: "Changes in the way in which people undertake economic production and organize the exchange of commodities represent one obvious aspect of the great transformation of our age" (Steger, Manfred B. (2003): p. 37). This is further facilitated by the mobility of people and capital, and the subsequent transformation through information technological networks.

sense is a gradual process that ought to be adapted to through social relations, interactions and integrations. In this perspective, globalization emphasizes sociological movement especially underpinned by movement of people, goods and capitals. It regenerates the cultural variables, particularly communications and new technologies that tend to influence social systems through intensification of economic, political, social and cultural relations across boundaries.

However, the debates on globalization bring out its important features without an emphatic assertion on its definition. It means that globalization is more or less described rather than defined. Steger notes that "since its earliest appearance in 1960s, the term 'globalization' has been used in both popular and academic literature to describe a process, a condition, a system, a force, and an age."[87] These descriptions form the fundamental elements of globalization. Nevertheless, this study basically views globalization as a 'process' of integration evident in cultural and technological innovations, and a 'system' of interaction that links different regions and countries into worldwide social relations. In this instance, McGrew asserts that "globalization has two distinct dimensions: scope (stretching) and intensity (or deepening). On the one hand, it defines a set of processes which embrace most of the globe or which operate worldwide; the concept therefore has a spatial connotation. Politics and other social activities are becoming stretched across the globe. On the other hand, it also implies an intensification in the levels of interaction, interconnectedness or interdependence between the states and societies which constitute the world community."[88] In fact, the intensification has gone beyond the traditional alliances by breaking down the barriers by way of interaction and integration. Thus these two conditions point to the unfolding organizational changes such as in production, financial market, global institutions, and social transformations being affected by neoliberal policies, neo-imperialism, cultural homogenization, increased mobility of people, communications and new technologies etc. These organizational changes

---

[87] Steger, Manfred B. (2003): p. 7.
[88] McGrew, Anthony G. (1992): 'Conceptualizing Global Politics'. In: McGrew, Anthony G. /Lewis, Paul G. (eds.): Global Politics: Globalization and the Nation-states. Cambridge: Polity Press, p. 23.

60

alter the structural balances of both social, political and economic processes and systems as a result of adoption of new methods and practices.

Oman on the other hand tries to explain globalization in terms of economic growth that transcends the activities of other social systems. He asserts that it is "the growth, or more precisely the accelerated growth, of economic activity that spans politically defined national and regional boundaries. It finds expression in greater cross-border movement (for a given level of domestic activity) of tangible and intangible goods and services, including ownership rights, via trade and investment, and often of people, via migration. It can be, and normally is, facilitated and stimulated by a lowering of impediments to cross-border activity both via technological progress (notably in transportation and communications) and via a lowering of policy of political impediments (e.g. tariffs, investment restrictions, conflicting national standards or regulations on the environment, labour, etc.)."[89] In this perspective, the global market takes the arena of political and economic competitions, which accelerates growth as well as constitutes impediments for the developing nation-states due to unequal participation in the global competition.

From another perspective, a number of theorists, most of them with roots in regulation theory are beginning to readdress the relationship between globalization theory and state theory by arguing that "nation-states are the principal agents of globalization as well as the guarantors of the political and material conditions necessary for global capital accumulation."[90] In effect, globalization process is aided by the intervention of the state as a form of mediation in directing the state capital to the global market and transnational corporations, as well as limiting capital accumulation to particular interest groups and organizations. In this instance, exclusion becomes inevitable and a major threat of globalization, considering that

---

[89] Oman, Charles (1999): 'Globalization, Regionalization, and Inequality'. In: Hurrell, Andrew/Woods, Ngaire (eds.): Inequality, Globalization, and World Politics. New York: Oxford University Press, p. 37.
[90] Barrow, Clyde W. (2005): 'The Return of the State: Globalization, State Theory, and the New Imperialism'. In: New Political Science: A Journal of Politics and Culture Vol. 27, No. 2. London: Routledge, p. 124. See also: Mentan, Tatah (2010): The State in Africa: An Analysis of Impacts of Historical Trajectories of Global Capitalist Expansion and Domination in the Continent. Cameroon: Langaa RPCIG, p. 67.

the power of the nation-states in the developing countries as ownership of the means of production are suppressed in having control of the 'push and pull' factors of the global processes as well as the capacity to enhance policy development and implementation. Consequently, the nation-state stands in compromising the institutional framework and then empowers some interest groups or individuals in the accumulation of capital.

Wood moreover observes that "to say all this is certainly not to deny that the relations between capital and nation-state take many different forms. The relations among advanced capitalist economies and among their national states are obviously very different from the relations between them and weaker national entities. And the room for national maneuver varies accordingly."[91] In this same way, Barrow asserts that "it is important to recognize that while globalization is a multilateral process, it is one that unfolds in a context where states are not only unequal in their political and military power, but are representing 'nations' already deeply penetrated by [global] capital."[92] This process of integration creates not only uneven power blocs but also forms boundary of differences, which continues to exist in the capitalist economy, countering the development of nation-state especially in Africa.

As a result, globalization process according to Wood has initiated "an imperial hegemony that need not rely on military conquest or political rule but dominates by means of economic imperatives and the 'laws' of market. It is in this respect more than any other that globalization has moved beyond earlier forms of imperialism."[93] Hence globalization in its current form is in fact a new dimension of imperialism without formal empire, but sustained by common interests of the imperial collaborators, using the political elites as their instrument of operation and governance. In this instance, the so-called 'First World countries' can penetrate the national boundaries of the 'Third World countries'; manipulate their political and economic systems and expand their economic dependency, in order to ensure dominance and control. Unfortunately, the developing

---

[91] Wood, Ellen M. (2002): 'Global Capital, National States'. In: Rupert, Mark/Smith, Hazel (eds.): Historical Materialism and Globalization. New York: Routledge, p. 28.
[92] Barrow, Clyde W. (2005): p. 137.
[93] Wood, Ellen M. (2002): p. 28.

countries have not demonstrated a remarkable strength to withstand the pressure of this global influence. Therefore, the basic assumption of globalization is that the political and economic processes and socio-cultural systems are the major determinate of global relations. In order to have a better eye-view of the above propositions, various factors of globalization will then be investigated.

3.4.1 Factors of Globalization

There are many factors that promote globalization, but this work concentrates on three basic factors of globalization. These factors are necessary tools in clarifying several misunderstandings and misinterpretations on globalization systems and processes. They are viewed in the following dimensions of economic, social and political.

3.4.1.1 Economic Factor

Globalization as an economic factor deals with intensification of market integrations as well as changes involved in the flow of capital in the regional and global networks. These changes potentially transform the means of production and accumulation of capital from traditional to modern and from local to advanced technological means. But the transformation also manifest in different economic conditions other than equal fiscal relationships. According to Chase-Dunn "economic globalization means nothing less than globe-spanning economic relationships. The interrelationships of world markets – namely, finance, goods and services – and the networks created by transnational corporations are the most important manifestations of economic globalization [...]. Economic globalization has also been accelerated by what telematics has done to the movement of money. It is commonly claimed that the market's ability to shift money from one part of the globe to another at the push of a button has changed the rules of policy-making, putting economic decisions much more at the mercy of market forces than before."[94] Thus the new dynamics of market tradition involves an increase of economic interde-

---

[94] Chase-Dunn, Christopher (2000): 'Globalization: A World-Systems Perspective'. In: Ciprut, Jose V. (ed.): Of Fears and Foes: Security and Insecurity in an Evolving Global Political Economy. USA: Greenwood Publishing Group Inc., p. 122.

pendence and competition, which tends to integrate regional economies into global economy within the framework of global capitalism. Such powerful international organizations like International Monetary Fund (IMF), World Bank and World Trade Organization (WTO) etc. are the agents of integration by introducing institutional changes and new economic policies. They therefore subject the nation-states to market forces, which oppose their sovereignty and delimit the national economic regulations.

3.4.1.2 Social Factor

As ongoing changes brought about by social and cultural transformation over time and space, globalization is envisaged "as sociological factor but part of it could be considered also under the cultural category, since most of it has to do with the transfer or values, either under the impact of markets (convergence) or under the power of capitalism."[95] This aspect of globalization as Chase-Dunn noted "relates to the diffusion of two sets of cultural phenomena: a) the proliferation of individualized values, originally of Western origin, to ever larger parts of the world population. These values are expressed in social constitutions that recognize individual rights and identities and transnational and international efforts to protect 'human rights', b) the adoption of originally Western institutional practices. Bureaucratic organization and rationality, belief in a law-like natural universe, the values of economic efficiency and political democracy have been spreading throughout the world since they were propagated in the European Enlightenment."[96] Thus, through these two phenomena of cultural proliferation propelled by new communication technologies according to Chase-Dunn, the native culture may be seen as subsuming in the global culture, consequent of the changes in the value systems. Hence the interactive space of the social system is widely opened-up by globalization, influencing the traditional way of thinking and acting. This open-

---

[95] Dutceac, Anamaria (2004): Globalization and Ethnic Conflict: Beyond the Liberal – Nationalist Distinction. In: The Global Review of Ethnopolitics Vol. 3, no. 2, p. 22.
[96] Meyer, John W. (1996): 'The Changing Cultural Content of the Nation-State: A World Society Perspective'. In: Steinmetz, George (ed.) New Approaches to the State in the Social Sciences. Ithaca: Cornell University Press; Markoff, John (1996): Waves of Democracy: Social Movements and Political Change. Thousand Oaks CA: Pine Forge Press. Cited in: Chase-Dunn, Christopher (2000): p. 121.

ing-up as an inevitable process, has permeated the ethos and civilizations of the nation-states, cutting loose their traditional social formation with the view of embracing the new order of global formation.

3.4.1.3 Political Factor

Globalization as a political factor entails the 'deepening' and 'stretching' of political interrelations within and beyond the national boundaries. It questions the sovereignty of nation-state and emergence of global interdependence under the veil of democratic development. In his analysis, Steger discusses political globalization based on the origins of the modern nation-state system, which could be traced back to the seventeenth-century in Europe. This formation broke out new consensual normative order that ushered in the 'evolution of political arrangements'. The evolution of political arrangements however goes beyond the frame-work of nation-state. It involves also the principle of state sovereignty without its engagement, growing intergovernmental organizations, and the future prospects for global governance.[97]

Although the sovereign powers of individual states are still effective to some extent, yet the much concentration of sovereignty as consequence of global governance has geared towards the regulation of the political structures of states by intergovernmental and global institutions. Such institutions include the European Union, the League of Nations and United Nations etc. This formation has advantage with regard to the increase and enhancement of political participation, devolution of power and border interactions evident in the wide-spread of democracy around the world and a gradual disappearance of the old territorial borders. But on the other hand, the procedural practices and representational outcomes have shifted the struggle for power competition in the international scene, which obviously is to the detriments of the developing nations. This conclusion will then lead us to examine the consequential features of globalization especially on the developing countries of Africa.

---

[97] Steger, Manfred B. (2003): pp. 56-57. See also: Steger, Manfred B. (2010): Globalization: A Brief Insight. New York: Sterling Publishing Co. Inc., p. 73.

3.4.2   Recasting the Globalization Antinomies

Globalization is associated with antinomies as a result of logical contradictions between a particular mode of activities and a universal system of imposition. It 'pulls upwards and pushes downwards'[98] as well as categorizes and demarcates the manner in which the nature of global participation is understood. In this sense, globalization presents different faces, some of which may be positive while some others may be negative but could also complement to each other in instituting gainers and losers. According to Rajaee, "globalization operates as a two-edged sword. It emancipates but also represses, and it brings together and unites but also divides and forms new hierarchies."[99] The new hierarchies crystallize the construction of localities apparently responsible for the tensions emanating from global interrelationships. What were initially particular in one locality are now seen to transcend the boundary of differences and form a universal concept. On the other hand, certain phenomena that once appeared to be autochthonous or sacred in a particular society or culture are allowed to diminish in the universal space, thereby losing their specific relevance in the contemporary global era.

Therefore, Robertson views "contemporary globalization in its most general sense as a form of institutionalization of the two-fold process involving the universalization of particularism and the particularization of universalism. [...] it is around the universalism-particularism axis of globalization that the discontents of globality manifest themselves in reference to new, globalized variations on the oldish theme of Gesellschaft and Gemeinschaft."[100] In other words, globalization introduces new for-

---

[98] Giddens states that "globalization not only pulls upwards, but also pushes downwards, creating new pressures for local economic autonomy" (Giddens, Anthony (2002): Runaway World: How Globalisation is Reshaping our Lives. London: Profile Books, p. 13). Under this dialectical nature of globalization, one would argue that the developing countries and economies have always the greater share of the downward movement. For instance, with the recent global economic crunch or indeed the global crisis of capitalism provoked by the neo-liberal recklessness of the multinational and financial corporations, the developing economies largely suffered the consequences.
[99] Rajaee, Farhang (2000): Globalization on Trail: The Human Condition and the Information Civilization. West Hartford, USA: Kumarian Press Inc., p. 96.
[100] Robertson, Roland (1992): Globalization: Social Theory and Global Culture. London: SAGE Publications, p. 102. See also: Rajaee, Farhang (2000): p. 96.

mations, which according to Walby "leads variously to new forms of universalism or the maintenance or invention of new particularisms. There is neither simple homogenization nor simple maintenance of differences, but rather the forming and re-forming of social differences and inequalities."[101] In that perspective, globalization regenerates structural formations in the society, which emanate as the consequence of tensions between the universal and the particular. Hence, the tensions have been the most interesting challenge of contemporary globalization especially as they affect the developing societies with regard to the openness to global participation and integration.

3.4.2.1 Unequal Power and Economic Relations

Understanding the power play in the global arena vindicates the nature of economic relationship that exists between regions and nations. Globalization has systematically contributed to regional and global competitions in an unequal power and economic relations, thus widening the power blocs of the northern and western countries to the limitation of the southern and the eastern influences. It was the same process, which was operative in the 19th century during the scrambling of the newly discovered African states by the European powers both for economic benefits and political influences. This scramblation was rather covered under the veil of colonialism, economic empowerment, social mobility and expansion of global relationships. Shaka aptly gives an instance that such "discursive practices underlying the Euro-African contact, as both products and producers of the uneven power relations between both continents, […] is best understood within the context of the emergent experiences of the trans-Atlantic slave trade, colonialism, post-colonialism and the continuing experience of neo-colonialism and globalization."[102] The present-day experiences of the most African states suggest a power play by more consolidated and powerful nations towards the weakness of African institutional development. It is then not surprising that the current wave of globalization,

---

[101] Walby, Sylvia (2009): Globalization & Inequalities: Complexities and Contested Modernities. London: SAGE Publication, p. 47.
[102] Shaka, Femi O. (2004): Modernity and African Cinema: A Study in Colonialist Discourse, Postcoloniality, and Modern African Identities. Trenton, New Jersey: Africa World Press Inc., p. 9.

which initiates other forms of unequal power and economic relations such as liberalization processes in following the antecedents of history, introduces also drastic changes in social, political and economic formations. The changes are said to be part of the by-products of new global capitalist policies and integration.

In several instances, globalization leads to the adoption of many neoliberal economic and political policies to the disadvantages of some nation-states especially in Africa. The contours of this neoliberal consensus were famously identified by Tony Blair in 2001 in his speech. 'The Power of Community can Change the World'. Here he comments on the partnership with Africa, between the developed and developing world based around the 'New African Initiative' thus: "On our side: provide more aid, untied to trade; write off debt; help with good governance and infrastructure; training to the soldiers, with UN blessing, in conflict resolution; encouraging investment; and access to our markets so that we practice the free trade we are so fond of preaching. But it's a deal: on the African side: true democracy, no more excuses for dictatorship, abuses of human rights; no tolerance of bad governance, from the endemic corruption of some states [...]."[103] Of course, these ideas are important, but one basic fact about Blair's new initiatives is that they might not be properly implemented but rather sustaining and pointing backwards to the external interference in Africa development. In other words, his initiatives basically sort to promote the revisited ideas of the modernization school, saying that the development of the region is possible, only if the governments in Africa will manage to co-opt the principles of western model of development into their administrative governance.

Nevertheless, with spatial interconnectedness of states and societies that both imposes constraints as well as empowers some sections of the society, Held et al perceives globalization, as "akin to a process of 'structuration' in so far as it is a product of both the individual actions of, and the cumulative interactions between, countless agencies and institutions across the globe. Globalization is associated with evolving dynamic

---

[103] Blair, Tony (2001): The Power of Community can Change the World. Address at the Labour Party Conference. http://www.americanrhetoric.com/speeches/tblair10-02-01.htm [accessed: 30.08.2009]

68

global structure of enablement and constraint. But it is also a highly stratified structure since globalization is profoundly uneven: it both reflects existing patterns of inequality and hierarchy while also generating new patterns of inclusion and exclusion, new winners and losers."[104] Obviously, in this global political, social and economic structuralization, the main propelling factor is the world capitalist economy. In his modern world systems theory as we have already seen, Wallerstein classified the world economy into core, semi-periphery, and periphery, which provide a framework for analyzing the socio-economic history of the various regions and their functions in the World System. Through capitalism, the world system ushers in new order that goes beyond national boundaries, penetrating vast regions which have never been before and forming regional and national differences. As such, Giddens states that "In the late twentieth century, where colonialism in its original form has all but disappeared, the world capitalist economy continues to involve massive imbalances between core, semi-periphery, and periphery."[105] In these imbalances, the major centers of power are capitalist states in which the capitalist economic enterprise assumes the main mode of formation and production.

Capitalism according to Mossmann, "gives priority to the endless accumulation of capital. A product will only be produced if it brings more capital on the market as its production costs have been. The capitalist always wants to get the highest profit out of its product, what is called surplus value."[106] The 'surplus value' however tends to govern the mode

---

[104] Held, David/McGrew, Anthony/Goldblatt, David/Perraton, Jonathan (1999): Global Transformations: Politics, Economics and Culture. California: Stanford University Press, p. 27.
[105] Giddens, Anthony (1990): The Consequences of Modernity. Cambridge: Polity Press, p. 69.
[106] Mossmann, Jannis (2007): Modern World System Theory: Essay. Norderstedt: GRIN Verlag, p. 3. Surplus value was also used by Karl Marx as a measure of worker exploitation by capitalism. He considered his theory of surplus-value as his most important contribution to the progress of economic analysis. It is through this theory that the wide scope of his sociological and historical thought enables him simultaneously to place the capitalist mode of production in its historical context, and to find the root of its inner economic contradictions and its laws of motion in the specific relations of production on which it is based. (cf. Mandel, Ernest: Marx's Theory of Surplus Value, in: http://www.international viewpoint.org/ [accessed: 02.06.2010]).

of production through continuous accumulation. Here Chase-Dunn argues that "capitalist mode of production exhibits a single logic in which both political-military power and the appropriation of surplus value through production and sale on the world market play an integrated role."[107] In this sense, both political power and economic production operate in related and interchangeable system of interactions, exacerbating adverse effect on the market integration, and as a consequence on the participating limitations on the part of the developing economies. This unequal formation is thus a basic attribute of globalization ideology, which expands spatial networks of economic activities and power relations that is unevenly experienced.

Moreover, this unequal formation dominates the current interconnected global system with long distance trade ties and routes, embodied with regulated economic system, production and exchange. Of course, the 'regulated' system of interaction according to Giddens, "allows wide scope for the global activities of business corporations, which always have a home base within a particular state but may develop many other regional involvements elsewhere. Then, business firms, especially the transnational corporations, may wield immense economic power, and have the capacity to influence political policies in their home base and elsewhere."[108] The character of this development is the extension of influence beyond borders, through policies that control and determine the methods of interactions and integrations. It implies then that the fate of developing economies and states majorly lies on the Western influence. And this influence according to Okere is "neo-colonialism at work. It is

---

[107] Chase-Dunn, Christopher (1981): pp. 20-21. According to Chase-Dunn, "the theorists of global capitalism contend that the most recent wave of integration has created a single tightly wound global bourgeoisie that has overthrown the dynamics of the hegemonic sequence (hegemonic rise and fall and interstate rivalry). While most world-systems theorists hold that the U.S. hegemony continues the decline that began in the 1970s, many other observers interpret the demise of the Soviet Union and the relatively greater U.S. economic growth in the 1990s as ushering in a renewal of U.S. hegemony [...]. The theorists of global capitalism contend that the U.S. government and other core states have become the instruments of an integrated global capitalist class rather than of separate and competing groups of national capitalists" (Chase-Dunn, Christopher (2005): p. 180).

[108] Giddens, Anthony (1990): p. 70.

really the continuation of slavery/imperialism by other means [...]."[109] In this set-up, the independence of the states notwithstanding, some various forms of imperialistic rules occasioned through neo-colonialism, advance with socio-cultural penetration and manipulation of political powers, in order to reinforce control over the economic processes of the peripheral state.[110] Thus the reinforcement and advancement are to be actualized without military presence, but the force of its penetration could never be overcome by the peripheral states.

In fact, the imperialistic tendencies have continued to manifest in the Nigerian context, especially in the current economic relations and global integration, giving an undue advantage to the advanced capitalist states through massive extractions and surplus transfers. For instance, Ihonvbere rightly observes in the Nigerian context that "the political economy was not just underdeveloped, but it was also structurally incorporated into a hostile, exploitative, and unequal international system. Its weaknesses made it extremely vulnerable to the vagaries of the world capitalist system. This system, into which the economy is integrated, has not been restructured in any way in favor of poor, dependent, and vulnerable economies like Nigeria. This means that at best what the postcolonial dominant classes have done is to attempt to integrate themselves and the Nigerian economy within this unequal exchange relations, which, given the structure of internal and external power balances, has continued to operate against the development of the Nigerian economy."[111] Thus this intensive structure of integration through external domination has also influence on the sovereignty of the state. For example, with the influence of globalization, the direct investment under the joint venture conditions that was operative in 1960s and 1970s, changed measurably Nigerian economic formation, such that the government was obliged to the decisions of the international policies, resulting to structural uncer-

---

[109] Okere, Theophilus (2005): p. 191.
[110] This idea was also described by Davidson as 'clientele sovereignty' which is "the practice of granting a sort of independence [...] with the concealed intention of making the liberated country a client state, and controlling it effectively by means other than political ones" (Davidson, Basil (1971): Which Way Africa? The Search for a New Society 3rd Edition. Middlesex, England: Penguin Books, p. 122).
[111] Ihonvbere, Julius O. (1994): Nigeria: the Politics of Adjustment & Democracy. New Brunswick, New Jersey: Transaction Publishers, p. 15.

tainty on both the social politics and economic development. Therefore, under the conditions of dominant power and the capitalist economic policy, the realities of regional and national differences present various empirical facts in different business and social environments as well as in the political mechanisms.

3.4.2.2 Globalization and Inequality Nexus

In this period of globalization, the changing structure of inequality is assuming new dimensions of differentiation in the manner which has never been before in the past. The growing character of inequality both on regional and national dimensions has conferred on the society different orientation and cyclical relationship between the economy and social politics. This character of inequality manifests in varied capabilities as part of long-term changes caused by globalization. In other words, like inequality, globalization is associated with change, both upward and downward changing mechanisms. Today, these changes have made possible the segmentation of the society into different modes of interactions and integrations, displacement of the institutional arrangements and formation of other mechanisms of adaptation, thereby initiating new forms of social inequality. Hence, this section enquires on the interconnections between globalization and inequality both as interdependent elements and also phenomena of structural changes that influence institutional framework either by declination or regeneration.

The focus on change particularly explains the inevitable reconfiguration of the social order as consequence of technological innovations. Change is indeed one peculiar feature about the current wave of globalization. It is the emerging forces and nature of the social structural changes that globalization carries which consequently corrode traditional culture and political autonomy, and increase inequality both within and among groups. These changes involved in globalization could be: i) in the form of decline in social safety networks that may result in increasing degrees of relative deprivation; ii) increasing competition for resources that greatly affects the inequality differences; and iii) exploitations that involves unequal balance of transaction that infringes on 'international trade rights'[112]. These phenomena of structural changes bring along with them some particular 'risks'[113] as a result of: i) the opening up of dangerous probabilities; ii) the cultural alienations and identity displacements as a result of new technological developments; iii) the increasing restructuring of the 'international division of labour'[114]; and iv) the increasing desire for profit and capital accumulation.

Subsequently, the desire for profit and capital accumulation as the distinctive factor of globalization has also emanated from the recent economic changes being driven by neoliberal policies. In that case, the integration of the nation-state into global economy is mostly governed by neoliberal principles that have led to resource accumulation and unequal distribution, which have also increased inequality differences. In this perspective, some may see globalization as similar to neoliberalism in terms of market formations, but in the real sense they differ. Although neoliberalism promotes free market, Walby however argues that, "neoliberalism is not the same as globalization [...]. While neoliberalism is often rhetorically associated with globalization, it is but one of the projects that competes for hegemonic position. Although neoliberalism can be treated as a contemporary wave, it is continuous with an earlier project and practice of liberalism."[115] Nevertheless, neoliberalism could then be seen as a driving force of the hegemonial influence that is occasioned by the current wave of globalization. It is on this note that globalization is both an

---

[112] Miller notes that it has been argued that "international trade is exploitative because the prices at which the traded commodities exchange reflect large differences in wage levels between rich and poor countries" (Miller, David (1999): ‚Justice and Global Inequality'. In: Hurrell, Andrew/Woods, Ngaire (eds.): Inequality, Globalization, and World Politics. New York: Oxford University Press, p. 205).

[113] Risks in this sense can be viewed as the probability of harm arising from technological and economic change (Globalization: http://www.infed.org/biblio/globalization.htm [accessed: 12.08.2009]

[114] 'Globalization' might be considered to mean another way of saying an 'international division of labor'. Instead of the extent of the market being increased within one community, globalization is the means by which the division of labor, the extent of the market, is increased amongst people world-wide (Weber, Cameron M. (2008): "Adam Smith and Globalization". Brooklyn, NY. http://cameroneconomics.com/smith.pdf [accessed: 12.04.2010]).

[115] Walby, Sylvia (2009): p. 45.

economic factor as well as a political factor, which has ushered in new dimensions of structural changes.

In the recent times, the neoliberal economic regime has been the force of relative deprivation on the developing countries' economic and political systems. Through hegemonial manipulations and enforcement of democratic imbuement in underdeveloped state structures, globalization has initiated new systems of formation and practices. Perhaps, viewing the political development and economic liberalization in the lens of the current wave of democratization provides in this study a comparative instrument of enquire. According to Bratton and Van de Walle, "the process of democratization is the analogue in the realm of political authorities of the breakdown of feudal systems of economic production and aristocratic social status, representing a general trend toward the inclusion of previously excluded groups in large-scale institutions. The driving forces of these systemic changes are impersonal forces such as technological innovation and its application to production, the spread of market-based social relations, and the emergence of new social identities."[116] However, Bratton and Van de Walle may be right in their position but on the other hand, there is the need to point out that in so far as the democratic exercise engendered by liberalization processes has included the previously excluded groups, it has also on the other side sidetracked some and widened the gap in political participation, as the dominant groups continue to weld more influence in the political scenario. This unequal formation is as a result of interplay between neoliberal economic regime and political liberalization that pitch democratic participation at risk especially among the so-called newly democratic societies.

Bollen and Jackman are right when they observe that the level of economic development of a particular country is a constituent element in explaining the dominant variable as a determinate factor of democratization process. But it is equally clear that this cannot be the only way because of other additional impeding factors that influence democracy and

---

[116] Bratton, Michael/Van de Walle, Nicolas (1997): Democratic Experiments in Africa: Regime Transitions in Comparative Perspective. Cambridge: Cambridge University Press, p. 20.

74

that are associated with the timing of development.[117] In other words, the practice of democracy depends on the level of economic development. However, if the neoliberal dominant variable which eludes the sovereignty of the state is not in check, it gives rise to political instability which according to Bollen and Jackman is "a drop in political democracy and it is a matter of degree; some declines are much more severe than other."[118] In fact, Held maintains that by eroding national sovereignty, globalization then undermines a central tenet of liberal democracy, for liberal democracy is premised on the sovereignty of nation-states and assumed that the state has control over its own fate, subject only to compromises it must make and to the limits imposed upon it by other actors.[119] It is here that one can say that globalization is the subject of social difference and inequality. And the sovereign limitation is of course one of the greatest problems of the developing democracies under the hegemonial Western impositions through the institutional systems of neo-liberalism.

Finally, with the interplay of neoliberal economic regime and political liberalization, the dominant groups made up of political elites and businessmen are giving undue advantage over the marginalized and vulnerable groups (i.e. lower classes with little or no voices) in consolidating their positions of power and support. This undue advantage is possible because the dominate groups have the political influence which aid them in solidifying their resource accumulation base. In that sense, the distribution of resources and power serve mostly their interests. Therefore, in holding their positions tenacious, the dominant groups through their hegemonial influence may on the one hand control the accumulation base but on the other hand turn out to create distributional crises that are detrimental to social formation and economic growth.

---

[117] Bollen, Kenneth/Jackman, Robert (1985): 'Economic and Noneconomic Determinants of Political Democracy in the 1960's'. In: Research in Political Sociology, Vol. 1. JAI Press Inc, p. 28.

[118] Bollen, Kenneth/Jackman, Robert (1989): 'Democracy, Stability, and Dichotomies'. In: American Sociological Review, Vol. 54, p. 619.

[119] Held, David (1995): Democracy and the Global Order: From the Modern State to Cosmopolitan Governance. London: Polity Press, p. 141.

3.4.3 Globalization Implications for Social Formation

The implications of globalization as a system of global interaction as well as a process of production that tends towards socio-economic integration have brought about radical opposite effects in creating new opportunities of capital inflow as well as posing new challenges to social mobility. As already noted, it follows that while globalization has increased opportunities for economic development and growth in some areas, there have also been major structural changes in social formation evident in the increase of social disparities and inequality differences in other areas. This new structural changing pattern governs not only the structures of the economy but also has unprecedented influence on social and political arrangements that have been the bane of underdevelopment and the risk resources especially in the Sub-Saharan Africa. In other words, globalization has offered not only new opportunities in the field of modern technologies and social mobilization but has also initiated other sources of social risks that have embraced both the developing world and the developed world.

It is pertinent to note that the opportunities associated with globalization are accompanied with some risk factors brought about by the dictates of the 'market mechanisms'[120] and industrial development. In this sense, Beck argues that "the gain in power from techno-economic 'progress' is being increasingly overshadowed by the production of risks."[121] As such, Beck and others discuss the risks production from the point of view of 'reflexive modernization'[122], which is defined as a theoretical attempt to

---

[120] One of the acclaimed economic historian of the 20th century, Polanyi warned in his classic work 'The Great Transformation' that "to allow the market mechanism to be the sole director of the fate of human beings and their natural environment, indeed even of the amount and use of purchasing power, would result in demolition of society" (Polanyi, Karl (1944): The Great Transformation. Boston, MA, USA: Beacon Press, p. 73).

[121] Beck, Ulrich (1992): Risk Society: Towards a New Modernity (First Published in 1986 in German). London: SAGE Publication, p. 13.

[122] The idea of reflexive modernization as a component part of the three-stage periodization of social change describes the idea that there is a movement from the simple modernity to the third stage of modernity. Scott Lash and Brian Wynne in their introduction to 'Risk Society' point out that, there was "first pre-modernity, then simple modernity and finally reflexive modernity [...] modernity is very much coextensive with industrial society and the new reflexive modernity with the risk society" (Beck, Ulrich (1992): Risk

76

make sense of some of the broad currents of social changes affecting the structures of the society. The changes involve emanation of new problems, which according to Beck et al implies that 'modernity has begun to modernize its own foundations'.[123] As an irresistible threat to social formation, the process of modernization has assumed the character of a risk society (Risikogesellschaft),[124] whereby progress can only be achieved through reorganization and reformation of the social and political institutions. In his theoretical analysis, Beck inclines sometimes to Marxism and sometimes to postmodernism, which contain strong items of epochal changes that have no defined boundaries. Although Beck applied this analysis to the classical industrial society, yet it has also strong intent on the developing societies which is the main focus here. Thus the developing countries are less likely to benefit from the globalization process and as well more on the receiving ends of the globalization risks production through the changes emanating from social structural formation.

Furthermore, the changes also affect the traditional class culture as well as compel the social agents of formation towards individualization that gives today's modernization process its peculiar character. In other words, the inevitability of globalization shaping the social formation as consequence of changes inherent in the process constitutes the major risks that could cut across borders and affects also those that benefit from them. Though some are more affected than others, yet these risks contain what Beck called a 'boomerang effect'[125] that breaks up the pattern of

---

Society, p. 3). Scott and Marshall however note that: "Whereas industrial society was concerned primarily with the production of goods, the risk society is organized around the management and distribution of 'bads' or dangers, not only those associated with physical risk deriving from the application of technological processes but also with the consequences of risky organizational activity and social relations" (Scott, John/Marshall, Gordon (2005): 'Reflexive Modernization', p. 555).

[123] See: Beck, Ulrich/Bonss, Wolfgang/Lau, Christoph (2003): The Theory of Reflexive Modernization: Problematic, Hypotheses and Research Programme. In: Theory, Culture & Society Vol. 20, No. 2. London: SAGE Publications, p. 19.

[124] Risk society is a (latent) revolutionary society in which a state of normalcy and a state of exception overlap. (Beck, Ulrich (2009): World at Risk (First Published in German in 2007). Cambridge: Polity Press, p. 76.)

[125] Risks according to Beck "display a social *boomerang effect* in their diffusion: even the rich and powerful are not safe from them. The formerly 'latent side effects' strike back even at the centers of the production. The agents of modernization themselves are emphat-

class and national society.[126] In this perspective, Beck argues that "ine-qualities in class and risk society can therefore overlap and condition one another; the latter can produce the former. The unequal distribution of social wealth offers almost impregnable defensive walls and justifications for the production of risks."[127] Under this condition, "attachments to so-cial classes become weaker, people are separated from the traditional support networks provided by family or neighbourhood, and work loses its importance as a focus of conflict and identity formation. Ascribed differences of ethnicity, gender, age, and nationality – provide the basis for new life-styles and self-conceptions that replace class solidarities."[128] Thus the new class formation associated with risk production then com-promises the role of state, and deforms the traditional structure of the society and force to embrace the new order regime of capital develop-ment and differentiations. Actually, the deformation comes with emotive force that could thwart the social progress and social formation.

Looking at the preponderant nature of globalization on social formation, the validity of class culture dangles between the political determinants and economic determinants that issue the choice of reference governed by status protection. For instance, Bratton and Van de Walle argue that, "state elites in Africa have sought political power primarily to obtain and defend economic benefits, to the point that they have blocked private accumulation by independent groups in society, thus undermining the entire project of economic development."[129] This attitude of the elites seems to be a dominant practice in most African states. In Africa, most political elites seek for political power not actually for the patriotic love of their countries, but in order to enlarge and protect their economic base and then reenergize their economic control towards extension of political influence. This elitist's domination becomes evident through the usurpa-tion of power and state resources; and as a consequence of capitalist ac-

---

ically caught in the maelstrom of hazards that they unleash and profit from" (Beck, Ulrich (1992): Risk Society, p. 37).
[126] See: Beck, Ulrich (1992): Risk Society, p. 23.
[127] Beck, Ulrich (1992): Risk Society, p. 44.
[128] Scott, John & Marshall, Gordon (2005): 'Reflexive Modernization', p. 556.
[129] Bratton, Michael/Van de Walle, Nicolas (1997): p. 47.

cumulation trend, it retards by and large the social progress of non-industrial state.

Practically, the state, which is controlled by a dominant/ruling class and a major source of wealth accumulation, becomes subjected to profit orientation. For instance, frequent yearnings for the creation of new governing states in Nigeria political arena are another avenue to encourage and extend the accumulation production of the dominant class. Here Ekekwe notes that, "state creation promotes class interest; the proliferation of state capital and bureaucracies provide seats of political power for the petty bourgeoisie. Such power is mostly turned to purposes of accumulation through corruption and booty capitalism."[130] This system of accumulation becomes the existing pattern of class definition that ignores the traditional social groupings, which as such reflects the expression of Connell's 'categorical theory of class'[131]. In this perspective, the existing social formation is implicated by the changing nature of the social relation being rooted in the acceleration of the dominant force of globalization exercises and with its intending implications on state formation.

3.5   Complexity of State Formation in Africa

Considering the arbitrariness in which the external forces in the veil of globalization have influenced the internal politics and economic development of the continent, the state formation in African is said to be in a complex formative process. The nature of this complexity is against the presumption of the state theorists that emphasize the uniqueness of each country's developmental pattern. Thus the first turning point of state formation in Africa was the outcome of colonial order, and recently, it has reached to a complex relationship between two worlds of developed and underdeveloped sustained by neocolonial hegemony. In this under-

---

[130] Eme, Ekekwe (1986): Class and State in Nigeria. London: Longman, p. 167.
[131] The idea of categorical theory is defined as "the mere ordering of people, as against the generative, which starts with fundamental processes and ends with structures or social groupings" (Ifidon, Ehimika A. (1999): 'Social Rationality and Class Analysis of National Conflict in Nigeria: A Historiographical Critique'. In: Journal of Africa Development Vol. 24, Nos. 1 & 2, p. 154. See also: Connell, R. W. (1977): Ruling Class, Ruling Culture: Studies of Conflict, Power and Hegemony in Australian Life. Cambridge: Cambridge University Press, p. 4).

standing, Huntington affirms that "the world is in some sense two, but the central distinction is between the West as the hitherto dominant civilization and all others, which, however have little if anything in common among them. The world, in short, is divided between a Western one and a non-Western many."[132] This formation was defined by Huntington in terms of material interest variations, which has compromised the power of the state and its fundamental unites to the vested interests of the few. This arrangement cannot be neglected in the sense that the state constitutes the common ideological background in building up of socio-cultural, economic and political structures in defense of national interest. Hence, this analysis dwells more on the crises of reproduction of the capital relations as well as socio-cultural and political class domination as they affect the state formation in the post-colonial countries of Africa. It also postulates how the growing capitalist development has been a constituting factor in the weakening of state formation, consequent of individual's and group's interests.

However, Marxists theorists try to relate the forms and functions of state to the nature of capital, which 'acts at the behest of the capitalist class' as the instrumentalists would rather suggest. In that case, the state functions as the institutional means for the reproduction of class interests and capital accumulation. Poulantzas however opines that "capitalist states rule in the long-term political interest of capital, which raises the question of how the putative interests of capital are translated into state actions." He further argues that "the question of who controls the state is irrelevant in this instance. The capitalist states act on behalf of the capitalist class, not because state officers consciously contrive to do so, but because the various parts of the state apparatus are structured in such a way that the long-term interests of capital are always to the fore and dominant." On the other hand, the pluralists see the state as an arena of competition by various interest groups. Hence "both the Marxist and pluralist approaches to the state may be said to be society-centred: that is, they view the state as reacting to the activities of groups within society, be they classes or pressure groups."[133] Thus various mechanisms are here at stake on the

---

[132] Huntington, Samuel P. (1996): The Clash of Civilizations and the Remaking of World Order. New York: Simon & Schuster, p. 36.
[133] Scott, John/Marshall, Gordon (2005): 'State', p. 632.

activities of various groups' reactions: such as competing for sovereignty, political power, economic domination and social influence that are both internally and externally induced. These mechanisms then suggest that state increasingly provides the opportunity for class domination[134], and as such encourages preferences and the variations in interests.

Following Marx position, Kößler and Wienold argue that "if the state would represent the common interest as against the particularity of the individuals or families as Hegel viewed it, then the common interest is anchored in the structure of class dominion. That means that the individual capitalists are not capable to control the state."[135] However, the distinctions between state and society that informs these debates are said to be quite misleading because both state and society are networks of institutional order. Meanwhile, Mitchell argues that understanding the state as a phenomenon of decision making distinct from society becomes inadequate, in the sense that, "the state should not be taken as a free-standing entity, whether an agent, instrument, organization or structure, located apart from and opposed to another entity called society."[136] Thus, the consideration on state and society is viewed in this analysis as such. Even though this understanding is mainly based on the dialectical nature of state and society, yet it brings out the power relation that governs them as factors for conflicting interests. Hence it is especially on the level of characteristic that one could speak of state-society convergence in the modern political formation, as source of capital accumulation and political domination. This is because the boundaries of relationship or

---

[134] Ake asserts that "the state is a specific modality of class domination, one in which the system of institutional mechanisms of class domination are differentiated from the ruling-class and appears as an objective force standing alongside society. The essential feature of the state form of domination is that the system of institutional mechanisms of domination is autonomized and becomes largely independent of social classes including the hegemonic social class. The state is really [...] a contradiction of interests, of powers and of social forces." (Ake, Claude (1989): 'How Politics Underdevelops Africa'. In: Ihonvbere, O. Julius (ed.): The Political Economy of Crisis and Underdevelopment in Africa: Selected Works of Claude Ake. Lagos: JAD Publishers, p. 44).
[135] Kößler, Reinhart/Wienold, Hanns (2001): Gesellschaft bei Marx. Münster: Westfälisches Dampfboot, p. 223 (The translation is mine).
[136] Mitchell, Timothy (1991): 'The Limits of the State: Beyond Statist Approaches and Their Critics'. In: American Political Science Review Vol. 85, No. 1, p. 95.

rather the nature of interactions between the state and society are ambiguous and still contestable.

Be that as it may, the state as a set of institutions cannot act on its own[137], but depends on the various actors within the state structures in making decisions and implementing policies. Thus, Lasswell and Kaplan following Laski's empiricist conception of the state have argued that the acts of the state are "the concrete acts of certain persons and groups."[138] In other words, Ifidon explains further that "the state is in fact a social institution, and reflects the tensions and conflicts among sociopolitical groups. Indeed, it is instrumental in determining and sustaining outcomes, it is also importantly an object of appropriation by competing groups; hence the state is a source of violence (against non-ruling social groups)."[139] It is therefore here that the competing groups or what Kößler regarded as 'strategic groups'[140] play out their dominant role against their subordinates by using the state as the means, which has been the main line of inequality curves in most of the developing countries. In this regard,

---

[137] Jessop maintains that "an adequate account of the state should treat it 'as a set of institutions that cannot, qua structural ensemble, exercise power'. In turn this postulate sustained the related arguments that, first, 'one can legitimately define the state in various ways since it has no essential unity which establishes unambiguous institutional boundaries'; and that, secondly, 'whatever one's chosen definition, it is essential to consider the complex forms of articulation among state institutions and between state and non-state institutions in the overall production of capital accumulation and political domination" (Jessop, Bob (1990): State Theory: Putting the Capitalist State in its Place. USA: Pennsylvania State University Press, p. 8).

[138] Ifidon, Ehimika A. (1998): 'The Appropriated State: Political Structure and Cycles of Conflict in Nigeria, 1900 — 1993'. In: African Journal of Political Science Vol. 3, No. 2, p. 3. See also: Lasswell, H. D. /Kaplan, A. (1950): Power and Society: A Framework for Political Inquiry. New Haven/London: Yale Univ. Press, p. 184.

[139] Ifidon, Ehimika A. (1998): p. 3.

[140] Hans-Dieter Evers und Tilman Schiel haben – zunächst vor allem im Hinblick auf die Verhältnisse in Südostasien – folgende Definition gegeben: "Strategische Gruppen besteht aus Personen, die durch ein gemeinsames Interesse an der Erhaltung oder Erweiterung ihrer gemeinsamen Aneignungschancen verbunden sind. Diese Appropriationschancen beziehen sich nicht ausschließlich auf materielle Güter, sondern können auch Macht, Prestige, Wissen oder religiöse Ziele beinhalten. Das gemeinsame Interesse ermöglicht strategisches Handeln, d.h. langfristig ein ‚Programm' zur Erhaltung oder Verbesserung der Appropriationschancen zu verfolgen" (Evers, Hans-Dieter/Schiel, Tilman (1988): Strategische Gruppen: Vergleichende Studien zu Staat, Bürokratie und Klassenbildung in der Dritten Welt. Berlin (W), S. 10. Cited in: Kößler, Reinhart (1994): S. 183).

Bayart notes that "in Africa as elsewhere, the state is a major manufacturer of inequality. The 'development' which it boastfully claims to promote, and in whose name it attempts to ban political competition and social protest, plays its part in this process."[141] Hence the ideological construction in this category is the control and exploitation of the state resources by political actors, which has its roots in the nature of state formation in Africa. The manifestation of this exploitation is visible in the structural differences among individuals, as well as the regional dichotomies.

Moreover, the phenomena of exploitation explain the contradictory nature of African state that accommodates the autonomization of the interest groups or strategic groups as the major force in the institutional domination of the state. The interest groups however constitute the driving force especially for those groups with limited resources, whereby the state becomes the only available avenue for power and economic accumulation. In fact, this arrangement centralizes the political and economic resources to those groups to the detriment of developmental strategies that will be beneficial for the common good. In that case, Kößler explains that developmental strategies aim not only at a more diverse economic structure but also require a more broadly diversified platform of appropriation chances. However, these chances remain narrow with the availability of positions in the state apparatus or at least connected with the easy access to their owners.[142] As a result, inefficient regimes will reproduce themselves through the control of the state apparatus by the strategic and privileged groups. This tendency is sustained through the selfish appropriation of the state resources and the use of those resources to build networks of sustainability.

With the peculiar nature of the socio-political and economic history of different states presently in Africa, their formation processes can be hardly separated from the colonial domination and post-colonial integrated economies. In fact, it has been argued that the complexity in the formation of states in Africa is the outcome of colonial legacies. Olayode

---

[141] Bayart, Jean-Francois (2009): The State in Africa: The Politics of the Belly, Second Edition. Cambridge: Polity Press, p. 60.
[142] Kößler, Reinhart (1994): p. 165.

aptly observes that, "the colonial state in Africa was therefore a state lacking in natural legitimacy since it was an external imposition. Given its primary objectives of subjugation and exploitation of the people, the 'state' relied on force and violence, especially due to its monopoly of the instruments of coercion for the realization of its imperialist objectives. The colonial state was governed by the principle of amorality since the people did not accept the state in terms of the society's morality. This created a duality in citizenship commitment and consciousness formation. The primordial identification became primary over 'national allegiance' [...]. For example, indirect rule facilitated the practice by indigenous agents of 'straddling' between administration and business, between 'official duties and lucrative activities'. The fusion of public and private spheres upon which these straddling practices were predicated has led to the privatization of many state functions in post-colonial Africa."[143] Thus these imperialist objectives and the privatization of state through the dominance of political elites have constrained the suitable consolidation of states in Africa. As a result, some see many states in Africa as weak with limited capacities to combat and promote development. Because the weak structures of the states are profitable to colonial powers and the political elites in misappropriating the state resources, in essence, that have continued to retard proper institutionalization of states in Africa.

Furthermore, Olayode emphasizes that "the attainment of independence however did not fundamentally transform the structure of the African states. The political class that supplanted the colonial officers was committed to the protection of the 'colonial legacy'. The emerging nationalists whose political tutelage was under colonialism continued to operate with a 'bureaucracy trained and tested in the authoritarian habits and practices of the departed colonialists'. The African state thus retained its forceful and authoritarian character."[144] In other words, the postcolonial states in Africa have retained most of the organizational structures of

---

[143] Olayode, Kehinde (2005): 'Reinventing the African State: Issues and Challenges for Building a Developmental State'. In: African Journal of International Affairs, Vol. 8, Nos. 1&2. Council for the Development of Social Science Research in Africa (CODESRIA), pp. 27-28. http://www.codesria.org/IMG/pdf/2-Olayode.pdf [accessed: 15.10.2010] See also: Ekeh, Peter, (1975): 'Colonialism and the Two Publics in Africa'. In: Comparative Studies in Society and History, Vol. 17, No. 1.
[144] Olayode, Kehinde (2005): p. 28.

84

colonial formation, which have continued to weaken their internal structures. In effect, the politically incapacitated nature of post-colonial African states such as Nigeria are characterized by a deficit in the institutional arrangements occasioned by the weak structures of the state and the emerging 'new local and international actors'[145] in the appropriation of state. Some of these deficits are identified by Kirwin and Cho as: i) "lack of a command over sufficient resources; ii) dependency on external funds; iii) no concrete plan of development; iv) lack of territorial control; and v) lack of support and legitimacy with its population and the international community."[146] However, these deficiencies will be later expatiated in part two of this work. In fact, some or if not all of these characteristics constitute the incapacitation of state and great obstacles to socioeconomic and political development in Nigeria.

As I have already noted, the running of the state in Africa has been attributed to the action of certain dominant groups that control its structures. The dominant groups hold to ransom the institutional structures through their dominant role. This arrangement alters the position of the 'underprivileged' or the subordinated as well as weakens the regulative function of the state. The implication of this according to Ifidon is that "the state in Africa is neither autonomous nor impersonal: it is not law that rules, but groups, their interests and members. True, it is centralised, but centralisation has been a condition for the emergence of the appropri-

---

[145] Duffield emphasizes that "since the 1970s however, nation-state capacity has been increasingly qualified by the emergence of new supranational, international, and local actors. These new actors have appropriated state authority from 'above' and 'below'. The power of the international financial institutions to override national economic planning, for example, is also well known. The same is true of international non-governmental organizations (NGOs), intergovernmental organizations, and multinational companies in terms of the social and development policies of the countries in which they operate. At the same time, within countries, local organizations together with newly privatized agencies and other commercial actors have taken on a wide range of roles formally associated with nation-states and the public domain" (Duffield, Mark (2000): Globalization, Transborder Trade, and War Economies. In: Berdal, Mats/Malone, David (eds.): Greed and Grievance: Economic Agendas in Civil Wars. Colorado: Lynne Rienner Publishers Inc., pp. 70-71).

[146] Kirwin, Matthew/Cho, Wonbin (2009): Weak States and Political Violence in Sub-Saharan Africa: A Comparative Series of National Public Attitude Surveys on Democracy, Market and Civil Society in Africa. In: AFROBAROMETER Working Paper No. 111, p. 5. http://www.afrobarometer.org/papers/AfropaperNo111_2.pdf [accessed: 11.05.2010]

ated state, while further centralisation has been effected by the appropriated state to reproduce itself."[147] In essence, one can argue that the operation of the state and its apparatuses are the subject of the appropriating groups or the privileged groups. The groups are privileged in so far as they still have the opportunity to control power and appropriate the state resources because of limited demarcation between politics and economy. On the other hand, another group could one day arise to their challenge and take control either through force or foul means. That is the reason why every interest group or privileged group always sees state appropriation as a political struggle. This struggle is in order to maintain and preserve their own positions in the polity either by way of recycling of political actors or dictatorship; for the fear that the new local actors could upturn the appropriation arrangement. As a result, it could then be said that improper institutionalization of state structures and apparatuses in Africa is traceable to the 'consequence of the appropriated state' by the political elites occasioned by the system of neo-patrimonialism.

In conclusion, in view of the intents and limitations that may be envisaged in the above theoretical debates, one is then required to enquire more on a theoretical formulation that could best explain the challenges that confront Africa especially Nigeria within the scope of inequality development. That will help us to have better knowledge of the trends of inequality both locally and globally and how they have influenced the formation of state in Nigeria. Consequently, evaluations of the propositions above may seem to have assumed the needed paradigm, but by further scrutinization of the theories on social inequality and globalization, a new perspective may be emerged. And this line of thought, even though not wholly, seemed to have been applied by Chabal, Patrick and Daloz, Jean-Pascal in their study of African society and modernity crisis that is linked to non-emancipated state's internal formations. This thought therefore, assumes an important theoretical construction in this study on globalization and inequality in Nigeria.

---

[147] Ifidon, Ehimika A. (1998): p. 4.

3.5.1 Internal Formation Blockade as Consequence of Political Instrumentalization of Disorder

The axiom: 'Instrumentalization of Disorder' is associated with Chabal, Patrick and Daloz, Jean-Pascal, who in 1999 published a book titled, 'Africa Works: Disorder as Political Instrument.'[148] Reviewing this book will constitute the main focus of the present discussion. Though the book was written by non-Africans, it has generated much controversies, debates and uneasiness among many African scholars. It dwells majorly on the problem of underdevelopment in Africa and strongly argues that the present economic, social and political situations are consequent of political instrumentalization of disorder. However, the authors applied five dimensional approaches in their theoretical construct, which include: i) the empirical observation of present-day realities; ii) the use of universal analytical tools; iii) the multi-disciplinary approach; iv) a comparative method; and v) a historical inquiry.[149] Of all these methodologies, historical approach is more emphasized and well illustrated in the work, and thus, that takes a preeminent position in this present analysis.

In their historical inquiry, Chabal and Daloz maintain on the one hand that processes are explained in their proper historical context and on the other hand, analysis is 'to be grounded in an understanding of the historical continuities – the deep history' – which is known to be of importance in the comprehension of the Western societies. In that pers-pective, they assert that "an historical approach is one which attempts to explain events in contemporary Africa within the long span which connects the present to the pre-colonial past. What is meant here can be expressed in two connected propositions: i) the present-day crisis, or more broadly disorder, in Africa is a crisis of modernity; and ii) this crisis of modernity is rooted in the deep history of the societies in which it is taking place."[150] Thus they try to relate crisis in Africa with disorder as a vibrant notation in describing the present integration of Africa to modernity. It is a crisis of modernity in the sense that Africa toes a multi-faceted path to modernization

---

[148] I am highly grateful to Prof. Dr. Reinhard Kößler who recommended this book.

[149] Chabal, Patrick/Daloz, Jean-Pascal (1999): Africa Works: Disorder as Political Instrument. US & Canada: Indiana University Press, pp. xvi-xvii.

[150] Chabal, Patrick/Daloz, Jean-Pascal (1999): Africa Works, p. xviii.

not compatible with Western model and subsequently requires a particular dynamics in search of viable political model.

According to Chabal and Daloz, "to understand the nature of this particular dynamics is to use a universal conceptual apparatus – that is, one constructed according to clear analytical categories congruent with post-Weberian social and political theory. We use such a paradigm to examine the logic of African politics from the local viewpoint [...]. Our aim is to go beyond the two most common approaches currently in vogue. The first turns on a variant of the image of Africa as a traditional, unchanging of timeless continent, incapable of adapting to modernity. The second rests on what amounts to paternalism in that it systematically exculpates Africans for their (mis)deeds on the grounds that the continent's present predicament is the result of uncontrollable external forces. We hope in this way to show how a scientifically grounded approach is compatible with what would be called analytical empathy – that is, the capacity to explain what makes sense to Africans in con-ceptually rational terms."[151] In that way, Chabal and Daloz tried to dissociate themselves from the 'two dominant schools of thought'[152] in vogue, which according to them makes their paradigm more exclusive in African studies. Consequently, this methodological approach or rather analytical framework for Chabal and Daloz forms the new paradigm in any theoretical construction on African crisis of development.

This new paradigm is called 'Political Instrumentalization of Disorder' and is defined as: "the process by which political actors in Africa seek to maximize their returns on the state of confusion, uncertainty, and sometimes even chaos, which characterizes most African polities. Although there are obviously vast differences between countries in this respect, we would argue that what all African states share is a generalized system of patrimonialism and an acute degree of apparent 'disorder', as evidenced

---

[151] Chabal, Patrick/Daloz, Jean-Pascal (1999): Africa Works, p. 144.
[152] The first of this school of thought "might be termed Eurocentric in that it takes for granted the validity of what are self-evidently historically determined Western concepts such as development, corruption, civil society or even the state. The other interprets Africa's politics on the basis of generalized, or catch-all, 'African' causalities by way of metaphorical notions such as, for instance, 'the politics of the belly'" (Chabal, Patrick/Daloz, Jean-Pascal (1999): Africa Works, p. 144).

88

by a high level of governmental and administrative inefficiency, a lack of institutionalization, a general disorder for the rules of the formal political and economic sectors, and a universal resort to personal(ized) and vertical solution to societal problems."[153] This paradigm that characterizes Africa is quite distinct in the sense that "[...] it attempts to show how the political, social and economic 'logics' of contemporary Africa come together in a process of modernization which does not fit with the Western experience of development."[154] Putting it in another way, the development which has occurred in Africa is not according to Western conception of development, but rather a complex developmental trajectory that has been prone to crisis. It is obviously rooted in the instrumentalization of disorder, which is both functional and of 'different order'[155] that involves the overlapping of modernity and traditional culture as a unique path to development.

However, the uniqueness of the African developmental trajectory has restrained innovations and as such, Africa's social, economic and political logic of development results in another concept of 'modernity', which explains various crises occurring in Africa today. Following the position of Chabal and Daloz, Van den Boom comments that "instead of modernising, Africa seems to return to 'tradition', which according to the authors

---

[153] Chabal, Patrick/Daloz, Jean-Pascal (1999): Africa Works, pp. xviii-xix. "To speak of disorder is not, of course, to speak of irrationality. It is merely to make explicit the observation that political action operates rationally, but largely in the realm of the informal, uncodified and unpoliced – that is, in a world that is not ordered in the sense in which we usually take our own politics in the West to be" (Chabal, Patrick/Daloz, Jean-Pascal (1999): Africa Works, p. xix.).
[154] Chabal, Patrick/Daloz, Jean-Pascal (1999): Africa Works, p. 143. They note that "the common assumption of existing paradigm is that modernization is the coherent outcome of the combined and self-reinforcing effects of social and economic development as experienced in the West. This is another way of saying that modernization is perceived as the form of development which makes it possible to evolve an economically dynamic, technologically sophisticated and politically open society" (Chabal, Patrick/Daloz, Jean-Pascal (1999): Africa Works, p. 145).
[155] Leftwich observes that "given the very slim prospects for the formal institutionalization of politics in Africa through the evolution of typically western form of constitutional, legal and bureaucratic order (Weber's modern state), their thesis is that the alleged 'disorder' of African politics is 'in fact a different 'order', a functional one which discloses its own political rationality" (Leftwich, Adrian (2000): States of Development: On the Primacy of Politics in Development. Cambridge: Polity Press, p. 95).

is demonstrated by the increasing importance of ethnicity, tribal politics, religion and witchcraft."[156] On the other hand, the internal components of the society are said to be built on ineffective institutions, which promote corruption and constraint the bureaucratic formation. This implies that the African state and bureaucracy do not correspond to the classical Weberian notions of state as an 'institution sui generis', and seem to resist the modernization drive by the West. As the root cause of Africa's woe, Reno comments that "[...] Africans' failure to build institutionally distinct and effective bureaucratic states makes the development of citizenship impossible, since there is no rule-based state as a neutral arbiter. Instead, rulers use state office for personal benefit, and exploit ethnic grievances to build personal patronage networks, and divide communities against one another, rule through personality-based clientelist networks."[157] In such an instance, the state is personalized through the system of patrimonialism shrouded in corruption and disorder, in such a way that the system limits the citizens from seeking accountability of the state operations from their rulers. Hence the system of patimonialism constitutes the overall causation, which weakens the political structures and practices, as well as the likely source in instrumentalizing disorder in different societal categories.

Two central features of the persistent disorder are illustrated by Chabal and Daloz, which include i) the communal belonging, and ii) reciprocal and vertical relations. These two features bring out other traits of the disorder such as corruption, crime, war etc. Hence, people instrumentalize all these traits of the disorder in politics, and so influence political participation and representation in the state. In the first instance, the communal belonging implies that people have a shared belief in the relation of power and identify themselves as being part of a local community, i.e. ethnic group, village, family, caste, among others.[158] They find their identities, rationalities, and actions on this communal belonging. In this sense, iden-

---

[156] Van den Boom, Rob (2001): 'Africa's Crisis: A Crisis of Modernity'. In: Newsletter: Association for Law and Administration in Developing and Transition Countries (ALADIN), Vol. 2, No. 3, p. 4. http://www.aladinweb.org [accessed: 13.04.2010]
[157] Reno, William (2003): Patrick Chabal and Jean-Pascal Daloz. 1999. Africa Works: the Political Instrumentalization of Disorder (Book Review). In: Journal of Asian and African Studies Vol. 38, No. 1, p. 91. http://jas.sagepub.com [accessed: 16.11.2009]
[158] Chabal, Patrick/Daloz, Jean-Pascal (1999): Africa Works, p. 156.

tity is of course seen as being more inclusive and extensive than in Western countries, because it embraces several belongings people have.[159] The identity's inclusiveness and extensiveness makes politics all-encompassing, which may include: public, private, cultural, religious, and family spheres. Thus the communal belonging is instrumentalized in politics such as in voting and participation in political activities. The imperative of this practice is that democratic development is hindered by communal belonging and as such, undermines also the prospects for social and economic development.

Secondly, the reciprocal and vertical relations situate the activities of local politics in Africa. Even though other societies in the West are not quite immuned from these political manipulations, yet they are more pronounced in African politics. The pronouncement however explains why politics in Africa is rarely constituted by full political participation and representation; rather it is occasioned by reciprocal and vertical neo-patrimonial relations between the electorate and the political actors. These formations are instrumentalized in politics, because the relationship between the politicians and the electorate is determined by the political actors and their distributional formats. Chabal and Daloz on that note assert that "what is significant in Africa is the extent to which vertical and/or personalized, relations actually drive the very logic of the political system. It is not just that politics are swayed by personal considerations or that the personal is manipulated for political reasons. It is also, and perhaps more importantly, that the overall aim of politics is to affect the nature of such personal relations."[160] Hence, the political processes are rather characterized with the dominant role by the political elites, who control and determine the rules and procedures of socio-political and economic relationships. Moreover, in the reciprocal relationship between the political elites and their clients, Chabal and Daloz say that "in the end, there is an interlocking neo-patrimonial logic between the deep ambitions

---

[159] According to Chabal and Daloz, African identity is "more inclusive in that it contains the multiple aspects of the relationship between individual and community [...]. It is more extensive in that it projects with varying degrees of intensity into the other realms of human existence: social, economic, religious, cultural, etc." (Chabal, Patrick/Daloz, Jean-Pascal (1999): Africa Works, p. 52).

[160] Chabal, Patrick/Daloz, Jean-Pascal (1999): Africa Works, p. 158.

of the political elites and the well-grounded expectations of the clients."[161] Building such relations means extending the communal belonging, because these relations create such a belonging where it does not actually exist. There is, though, an underlying premise of patron-client relations: If the patron fails to fulfill his part of the relationship, the client may change to another patron. Such relations may take several forms, but Chabal and Daloz concentrate majorly on clientelistic (personalized) and neo-patrimonial (non-personalized) forms that relate to each other in instrumentalizing disorder in politics.

In fact, the communal belonging, as well as reciprocal and vertical relations leads to another trait of the theory, i.e. the non-separation between public and private spheres. In this perspective, civil society according to Chabal and Daloz does not actually exist because of non-separation of public and private spheres. In other words, people instrumentalize their positions in both circles of dependency. That implies that no associations or interest groups are thus fully independent from the state and its apparatuses, which means that civil society as an independent entity does not exist in actual sense. Chabal and Daloz then argue that "the emergence of a properly institutionalized civil society, led by politically independent citizens, separate from governmental structures, is only possible where there is a strong and strongly differentiated state."[162] Consequently, due to the non-separation of public enterprise from private interest, political actors and public employees in Africa always seek to profit on their positions, exploiting state resources based on consumption rather than on production input. They also collaborate with the customary actors such as village chiefs when that could also aids in profiting from the public resources.

Moreover, another factor of the disorder, which is derived from the vital role of reciprocal and vertical relations in politics, is that political success, accountability, and legitimacy are measured by the number of clients one was able to buy through with the public resources, either in the form gifts or properties. As a result, political actors personalize community resources and also use the material goods in their possession to dis-

---

[161] Chabal, Patrick/Daloz, Jean-Pascal (1999): Africa Works, p. 162.
[162] Chabal, Patrick/Daloz, Jean-Pascal (1999): Africa Works, p. 21.

tribute to their various clients rather than for common good. In this way, they aim to obtain accountability and legitimacy as well as the fortification of their network of relations through the state wealth. Hence, short-term goals characterize political formation. Consequently, ideological arguments are not quite important in politics, and in that conception, political parties do not stay in opposition if they do not profit from it as a means of delivering resources to their constituents.[163] It is then not necessary to be in opposition in so far as one is not strong enough to sustain the clientele needs.

Finally, another trait of the theory is the recycling of political elites, which have become a regular practice in the political formation. In that perspective, even if new political actors appear on the scene, they will always try to mobilize their actions in building their own circle of trust in order to sustain their influences and positions. In this sense, Van den Boom notes that here Pareto's theory on the 'circulation of elites'[164] can be used to explain the elite's relative longevity in political positions in Africa. By the flexibility and adaptability of the system, by maintaining patron-client relations through distribution practices, the elites are able to consolidate their positions.[165] In that case, no political office holder or politician would ever like to voluntarily relinquish his or her position for the other outside the same circle of trust. By that, political struggle is accompanied with the motive of preserving and sustaining the neo-patrimonial interests through every available means. Thus the social ordering of the society becomes impossible in so far as disorder has been instrumentalized in politics, giving rise to crisis of modernity. Therefore, the crisis which affects the development of the African continent according to the authors cannot and would never be overcome without proper institutionalization of the state.

---

[163] Chabal, Patrick/Daloz, Jean-Pascal (1999): Africa Works, p. 55.

[164] "The pivot of Pareto's theory was a mechanistic view of society which stressed equilibrium as the key to social stability. He began with a concept of "residues" which accounted for individual differences in the members of society, went on to a division of society based not on classes, but on "elites" and "masses" and then proposed that it was in the circulation of "elites" that the clue to maintaining equilibrium in society was to be found" (Delaney, Joan (1971): Pareto's Theory of Elites and Education. Studium no. III. http://sunzi.lib.hku.hk/hkjo/view/32/3200052.pdf [accessed: 23.05.2010])

[165] Van den Boom, Rob (2001): p. 4.

3.5.2 Critical Analysis of Chabal and Daloz Position

While applying the state of art of social and political sciences especially the Weberian notions of modern state, the analytical framework by Chabal and Daloz gives an overview of African crisis of modernity in a provocative instance. In their views, there are internal blockages or interpenetration of the other traditional settings such as kinship, interest groups and community ties etc. in post-colonial Black African states that hinder the formation of bureaucratic order, and as such undermine the role of state in safeguarding the social system. In this instance, civil society in Africa is only but an illusion that does not constitute an independent category of organization separate from an autonomous state. But in this observation, the application of Eurocentric perspective or ideal-type of the Weberian bureaucratic state as the yardstick to justify the 'modernity' of African states seems to be questionable and insufficient in establishing the cause of underdevelopment in Africa. This is because of the fact that Africa has different history and is built on different ideological background which the authors failed to establish. It is then wrong to assume that there were absolutely no beginnings of African statehood before the advent of Europeans in the continent in the late nineteenth century. In fact, what seems to be a residual category in the state is actually the civil society, even though not well developed like the Western conception, but plays some mediation roles in the function of the state. Hence a better conceptual framework may be required to explain the modern state and its relationship with civil society in Sub-Saharan Africa.

On the other hand, Chabal and Daloz argue that the fundamental problem facing Africa is that of corruption and ineffective institutional arrangements that gave rise to instrumentalization of disorder. From this conception, it seems that corruption is uniquely African and constitutes her major disorder, which may not be obtainable elsewhere. In that sense, the 'unique' nature of corruption obtainable in Africa as against the Western type is seen as a disregard to the social diversity in relation to internal structure of the society as the sole cause of corruption. The idea however overlooks the very external influences that aid and sustain corruption in Africa such as market interests, foreign investments, political hegemony etc. These external factors propel the political elites or the dominant class in instituting corruption in the system.

Moreover, the nature of corruption in Africa does not of course show that the phenomenon is particularistic in Africa. Rather it indicates that the historical antecedents that influenced both the internal and external structures of the society must be taken into consideration. On this, Bayart et al argue that "it is not that the societies or the political systems of the subcontinent are more corrupt than others, as is often believed. There is no reason to suppose that Japan, China, India, Russia, Turkey, Italy (or France for that matter), are any less tainted by this phenomenon. But, in Africa, the interaction between the practice of power, war, economic accumulation and illicit activities of various types forms a particular political trajectory which can be fully appreciated only if it is addressed in historical depth. One of the characteristics of this trajectory is the exploitation by dominant social groups, or by dominant actors of the moment, or a whole series of rents generated by Africa's insertion in the international economy in a mode of dependence."[166] This mode of dependency brings out the historical antecedents of the state formation in Africa as the legacy of colonialism as well as the integral nature of the globalization systems and processes that constitute problem factors in African social formations. One would then believe that without the fundamental support of the dominant groups by the capitalist economic policies that favour them, and the external support to the political elites that geared towards neo-imperialism, the issue of corruption would have relatively assumed another dimension, such that it would have been made unattractive through proper institutional building.

On the issue of ineffective institutional arrangement, Chabal and Daloz propose that bureaucratic institutions in Africa operate as 'empty shell' without organized structures. However, most of the post independent African states inherited bureaucratic ideals and democratic institutions not properly institutionalized during the colonial periods. Besides, the Western model of autonomous state was never applied by the colonial actors in order to sustain the independence of the African states and their state structures. Even though Chabal and Daloz acknowledged the fact that "the bureaucratic and political structures of states in Africa put in place under colonial rule were run at the lowest possible costs and to

---

[166] Bayart, Jean-Francois/Ellis, Stephen/Hibou, Beatrice (1999): The Criminalization of the State in Africa. Indiana: Indiana University Press, p. xvi.

ensure the profitable exploitation of the colonies"[167], yet they failed to acknowledge the fact that the infiltration of the societies by the colonial powers weakened the efficiency of the state structures dominated by the interest groups and the political elites. Nevertheless, the structure of state institutions may seem to be bureaucratic in nature but the political elites have personalized the institutions and operate them as extension of their clientelism and neo-patrimonial formation.

However, Chabal and Daloz also accepted the fact that the colonial period induced some changes characterized by artificial demarcation of territories without serious concern to the existing homogeneous formation. Unfortunately, they reject the fact that colonialism was the foremost influence in shaping the societies in Africa in their present formation. They argue that "colonial rule was neither the fundamental rupture which many envisaged it to be nor a mere interlude in the placid history of the continent."[168] Hence "the time has long passed when we, Westerners, had to expiate the colonial crime of our forefathers."[169] For them, African crisis of modernity lies fundamentally on the 'strong instrumental and personalized characteristics' of traditional Africa practices, which the 'colonial bureaucratic institutionalization never managed to overcome'.[170] Unfortunately, this view does not portray the turn of events in the African history and development. Considering the fact that African traditional society was relatively institutionalized and functional, though in an indigenous context before the advent of colonial powers, we have to question all the more the authenticity of Chabal and Daloz's position on colonialism. Nevertheless, Mbembe rightly points out that "Postcolonial African regimes have not invented what they know of government from scratch. Their knowledge is the product of several cultures, heritages, and traditions of which the features have become entangled over time, to the point where something has emerged that has the look of 'custom' without being reducible to it, and partakes of 'modernity' without being wholly includ-

---

[167] Chabal, Patrick/Daloz, Jean-Pascal (1999): Africa Works, p. 12.
[168] Chabal, Patrick/Daloz, Jean-Pascal (1999): Africa Works, p. 11.
[169] Chabal, Patrick/Daloz, Jean-Pascal (1999): Africa Works, p. xviii.
[170] Chabal, Patrick/Daloz, Jean-Pascal (1999): Africa Works, pp. 12-13.

96

ed in it."[171] In other words, what is obtainable in Africa today is the by-product of traditional and colonial formations operating in different wave lengths. Hence it becomes very clear that the formation of state in Africa is linked to the historical antecedents that shaped the present-day Africa.

On the other hand, one is propelled to investigate the place of globalization in Chabal and Daloz thesis and its influence in developmental crisis. Their work suggests that unsuccessful implementation of neo-liberal policies such as structural adjustment policy was because it has been politically instrumentalized. They argue that "structural adjustment has been 'Africanized', in the sense that it has been adapted to the realities of the patrimonial system."[172] However, they failed to realize the consequences of the policy in generating growth, and therefore systematical exonerated the Bretton Woods institutions on the conditionalities they imposed through the economic reform policies that deepened African dependency on the West.

Finally, Hungwe and Hungwe observe that "the book would have been strengthened by paying attention to the role of conflictual social relations in African societies, and in particular the role of unequal power relations in African societies."[173] By that consideration, the book will also assist in bringing out the contributions of globalization to the power asymmetries in global arena. It is good to note that globalization has been detrimental to developing nations, who are yet unable to make head-ways in the global competition but rather on the receiving ends of unequal power relations that favour the foreign economic actors in exploiting the rich resources of the African states. It is also possible then to assume that contradictions associated with this development also questions the neutrality of bureaucratic formation, because of the changing nature of social relations that constitute the state dynamics. Therefore, the state as a neutral arbiter becomes unrealistic as a result of the external influences that distort the institutional arrangements and sovereignty of the state.

---

[171] Mbembe, Achille (1992): 'The Banality of Power and the Aesthetics of Vulgarity in the Postcolony', translated by Janet Roitman. In: Public Culture Journal Vol. 4, No. 2. Duke University Press, pp. 24-25.

[172] Chabal, Patrick/Daloz, Jean-Pascal (1999): Africa Works, p. 123.

[173] Hungwe, Kedmon/Hungwe, Chipo (2000): Essay Review on Africa Works: Disorder as Political Instrument. In: Zambezia Vol. 27, No. 2. Univ. College of Rhodesia, p. 281.

Notwithstanding the shortcomings of Chabal and Daloz's stance to address some burning issues on development, and their seemingly exaggerated positions on the crisis of modernity in Africa, yet their work leaves much to be desired. Its importance in facilitating a theoretical construction and debate on African development and modernity cannot be undermined. On the other hand, this critical analysis of Chabal and Daloz's position has also been an important tool for assessing its explanatory values and applicability in African studies. Hence the theory of political instrumentalization of disorder combined with its critique offers us a useful background to the study topic. The background analysis is to be properly applied to inequality and globalization, and to specifically illustrate its tendency in the Nigerian contextual state formation.

3.6   Conclusion

We have attempted in this chapter to establish a basic theoretical background relevant to socio-historical development of Africa in the world system. Based its investigations on problem discovery and important possibilities of definitive results, the work categorically examines the changing structure of the society whereby globalization was seen as a long-term process of integration and system of interaction in the society. The integration of Africa into capitalist economy or what Wallerstein regarded as expansion of Europe through capitalist world economy brought about inclusion of some and exclusion of many in the institutional arrangement. This was due to the introduction of new technologies and new mode of capital accumulation. Hence the world economy has been on a process of transformation, which has resulted to today's capital accumulation. The changes in the global order have created and are still creating asymmetrical relations between regions and nations, peoples and cultures. In that instance, the integration of Africa into the contemporary global economy has been a process of transformation and structural changes both in space and time, but whether the continent has been able to create a real unit in time in the global scale leaves many questions to be desired.

Nevertheless, the debate on globalization was viewed as a rhetorical social formation with decisive contra-positioning of consequences. The standpoint of the theoretical investigation was that globalization has positive as well as negative consequences, but its negative phenomena on the developing economies and states like Africa made it more unbearable. Hence, the task of this study is to empirically map out several and divergent phenomena of globalization that have constituted a niche to global integration and social formation. The significant of this point could successfully aid in identifying the complexities of Nigerian state in order to formulate new agendas that could enable her effective participation in the global networks.

On the other hand, the state in Africa has been in the crisis of legitimacy, with poor institutional development and weak economic growth for over half a decade since independence. Various attempts have been made so far by many scholars to establish a basic framework that will govern the explanation of African crisis of modernity. The main point of controversy has been the issue of class domination as consequent of hegemonic structures implanted by colonial imperialism and capitalist formation. This formation goes to show how various dominant classes or interest groups compromise the legitimation of state formation and as such control and appropriate the fundamental units of the state whenever there is opportunity in protecting their own interests.

Finally, the bone of contention remains the appropriation of state and unlimited capital accumulation influenced by both external and internal forces of the society. This process is being sustained partly by the imbalances created through the global asymmetries and partly as a consequence of non-defined separation between politics and economy. It means that if one has money, one has also power and could exercise both in the pursuit of what one has not. In that perspective, opposition in African politics is only possible if the opposing parties are able to withstand the financial weight of the ruling class and buy over supporters that can constitute the power blocs. But to achieve that is always impossible in the African context, because the ruling party will exploit the state resources at every nook and cranny in maintaining the status quo. Therefore, the saying 'if you cannot beat them, join them' forms the basic pattern of political formation in most African states. And this formation is what I will historically and empirically address in the next chapter.

PART II

NIGERIA IN THE PAST AND PRESENT

4 FORMATION OF STATE AND POLITICAL LEGACY

In this chapter, the thesis tries to scrutinize the political structure of Nigeria and the various components that played role in its evolution. The analysis takes on a historical survey into the past that connects to the present turn of events. It is a transition from colonial to post-colonial state, punctuated with events and transformations. The understanding of political transition in this manner explains events and their continuities and discontinuities in highlighting those significant historical aspects of state formation and the development of the modern state. Most of the backup knowledge in this investigation is drawn from the theoretical constructions already examined in chapter three. Thus three major issues are to be discussed namely; the nature of state in Nigeria, political evolution and democratization, and finally, the institutional paradox of state formation.

4.1 Nature of State in Nigeria

The state formation in Nigeria especially in terms of the general trends of political and social evolution has been a contesting issue among the indigenous social and political scientists. In an attempt to explain this issue, the formation of state in Nigeria has been categorized into three complex phases of structural transformation: pre-colonial, colonial and post-colonial eras. Unfortunately, this categorization has not wholly captured the trends of socio-political events that have shaped the historical processes as regards the continuity and discontinuity prominent in the institutional arrangement of the Nigerian state. However, under this complex formation, other subdivisions seen in the nature of contemporary state of Nigeria could as well emerge; such as neo-colonial state as dependent on external global factors, modern state, neo-patrimonial state etc. But whether these divisions account for the pre-existed structures, make one to believe that any understanding of state formation in Nigeria must be grounded on the historical antecedents in terms of events and outcomes over time. Thus this study attempts here to explain different political and economic struggles that are shaped by the quest for collective identities, and competitions among various interest groups and political elites.

Analyzing the nature of state in Nigeria, the thesis identifies such important elements like power relations and class structures. In fact, understanding the nature of state in Nigeria explains its distinctiveness, especially the various roles history and culture played out in the construction of varieties in interaction processes as well as the specific functions performed by various power structures. According to Eisenstadt et al, "the clue to an understanding of the origins of the state and of the variability of political systems in general, and of early and pristine states in particular, may be found in the types of interaction between them, that is, in the interrelationship between the social division of labor and the structural differentiation of society it entails, and the different coalitions of elites and the functions of regulation of power and construction of trust and meaning they perform."[1] These institutional interrelationships optimize the evolutional forces, which allow for variability of structures that fundamentally captures the pre-eminent roles of the different power structures in the state both internally and externally. Thus the state is embodied with powers bound by different interests, in which case, the institutional design of the state plays a critical role in determining the structures and modes of interaction that coercively bind the people to the state.

Fundamentally, this thesis is based on the fact that the state in Nigeria is highly centralized and mostly relies on clientelistic and neo-patrimonial relationships. Though the state is separate from traditional kinship bonds, yet it sustains the network of reciprocal relationship in its institutional arrangement.[2] In such instance, the crystallization of various interest groups only gears towards the accumulation and appropriation of state

---

[1] Eisenstadt, Shmuel N./Abitbol, Michel/Chazan, Naomi (1988): 'State Formation in Africa, Conclusions'. In: Eisenstadt, S. N. /Abitbol, M. /Chazan, N. (eds.): The Early State in African Perspective. The Netherlands: E. J. Brill, Leiden, p. 168.

[2] Paul here comments that; "on the one hand, the early states used and verticalized basic and probably universal familial forms of reciprocity and distribution, which in a way dressed themselves in family-like costumes to veil the fundamental break in the evolution of social organization which the advent of statehood indeed was. On the other hand, the violent and hostile character of the state did not reduce, but rather underlined the importance of extra- and anti-statal solidarity ties. Kinship, which as such is already a social as well as biological phenomenon, became ethnicity, or rather political tribalism, i.e., as regards the number of people, a more encompassing and culturally enlarged and standardized form of imaginary kinship, that served as the basis for political and economic competition within the arena of state" (Paul, Axel T. (2008): 'Reciprocity and Statehood in Africa: from Clientelism to Cleptocracy'. In: International Review of Economics Vol. 55, Nos. 1-2. Springer-Verlag, p. 223).

resources, as well as the increase in the competition for political control. This crystallization implies that notwithstanding that the state is different from kinship pattern of relationships, yet it fosters these relationships by transforming them to political instrument of sustainability. In other words, the traditional pattern of relationship is transformed into new object of competition, which the state embraces and sustains its structures.

One may be prompted then to ask: How does the formation of state in Nigeria interact with the contemporary situation as regards the social changes imminent in the institutional arrangements? In such consideration, the penetration of European merchants in search of wealth contributed in changing the pattern and means of domination that restructured the formation of state in Nigeria. It also led to intensive capital accumulation, which resulted to the development of capital market and centralization of state system that has been the main base of class formation, and consequently the centrality of personal and group welfare and survival. But prior to the advent of British colonial administration, the traditional societies that made up what is today called Nigeria had their different administrative and centralized political systems and orientations, and functioned as such in protecting the community welfare and assisting social development. Some of those societies had of course standing administrative blocs that made up of native Kings, Obas and Emirs. The three major blocs include the Kanem-Borno Empire in the North, Oyo and Benin Empire in the West and the Kingdom of Nri in the East. These formations later originated into regional formation that is to be vividly analyzed in this work, and have come to be identified in the contemporary times as the major ethnic groups in Nigeria.

4.1.1   Regional/Ethnic Formation

Regional formation has been fundamentally the underlying cause of sociopolitical cohesions and disparities in culturally and politically heterogeneous state like Nigeria. This formation is mainly based on resurgent interests of different ethnic nationalities in the struggle for autonomy. The starting point was the emergence of a tripolar regional structure of North, East and West in 1939-64 according to geo-historical, ethnic and clientele-based institutional compositions, and its politicization with the introduction of broad based electoral politics. In this formation, Anikpo notes that "the division of the country into three Regions [i.e. East, West and

104

North] by the 1947 Richard's constitution and the internal class conflicts of the emerging political leaders as they struggled for the privileged class positions to be vacated by the British, gave rise to class induced ethnic confrontations and fragmentation expressed structurally in ethnic political parties."[3] In this division, the Hausa-Fulani dominated the North with the largest population, followed by the Yorubas in the West and the East predominately Igbos. The other minority ethno-linguistic groups exist within these major divisions. As the nation struggle for independence, this characterization formed the pattern of ethnic identity and solidarity bound-up by primordial affiliations. Thus, the fight for ethnic dominance became the tool for political and social mobilization after independence.

However, in 1967 the three regions of Nigerian were abrogated. In its place came the creation of twelve states after the civil war, blurring the correspondence of region and ethnicity of the British three state systems which encouraged ethnic sentiments in nurturing peoples' differences rather than their similarities. In 1976, seven more states were created increasing the number to nineteen, then the number rose to twenty-one in 1987, to thirty in 1991, and finally to thirty-six in 1996; all with the intention to achieve national integration. Unfortunately, the intrinsic reason for the creation or multiplication of states was rather understood principally for ethnic interest and mobilization than for collaborative development as it was initially aimed. In this perspective, Mustapha observes that "far from curbing ethno-regionalism, the state creation process simply restructured it. Without their regional institutional backbone and now split into many states, hegemonic ethno-regional elites adopted other symbols and rituals as rallying points, leaving the old three regions almost intact. Meanwhile, some minority ethnic groups secured states of their own, sometimes in an uneasy alliance with other minority groups, leading to the emergence of 'majority' minority groups in some states [...]."[4] It follows that ethno-regionalism also gave rise to a situation where certain

---

[3] Anikpo, Mark (1985): 'Nigeria's Evolving Class Structure'. In: Ake, Claude (ed.): Political Economy of Nigeria, New York: Longman Inc., p. 45.

[4] Mustapha, Raufu A. (2006): 'Ethnic Structure, Inequality and Governance of the Public Sector in Nigeria'. In: United Nations Research Institute for Social Development: Democracy, Governance and Human Rights Programme. Paper Number 24, Geneva, p. 7. http://www.unrisd.org/Mustapha.pdf [accessed: 24.03.2009]

minority ethnic groups remained submerged in the majority, defining their status through alienation, and creating uneasiness in the polity and with the quest for more state creations. Nevertheless this phenomenon of state creation has turned into a political jamboree in which each region or the later geopolitical zone is angling and tabling a state creation bill on the floor of the National Assembly in demand for what may be termed 'equity and progress'.

But many Nigerians have continued to question the rationale behind these unending demands, judging from the fact that the outcomes of state creation exercises so far have failed to assuage the very forces that instigated their demands. Rather, the state has continued to be a device of appropriation and political domination by stronger ethnic nationalities. Even though the creation of states is not a bad policy, but when the intention is defeated by formalizing inequality, then it becomes problematic. Here Idowu rightly notes that, "whenever the state is subject to the control and domination by a single ethnic group, it often renders other groups weak, fragile and excluded. Such exclusionary policies are the very stuff or push factors which revive ethno-nationalism in a multi-ethnic setting. Given this state of things, the process of state-formation becomes increasingly difficult since the primary allegiance and loyalty that ought to be transferred from the nation, i.e. ethnic groups, to the state becomes unsuccessful."[5] Then in an effort to strengthen their allegiances and protection of their interests, some ethno-nationalities have mobilized themselves into pressure movements such as: Odua People Congress (OPC), Arewa People Congress (APC), Movement for the Actualization of the Sovereign State of Biafra (MASSOB), and Movement for the Emancipation of the Niger Delta (MEND) etc. Some of the ethnic movements in Nigerian history were however transformed into political organizations and the fate of the present ones are yet to be known. As more other new ethnic-movement groups or sub-groups are gradually emerging. In this regard, ethnic inclination is presently beginning to assume stronger form of allegiance over state coercive authority.

---

[5] Idowu, William (1999): 'Citizenship Status, Statehood Problems and Political Conflict: The Case of Nigeria'. In: Nordic Journal of African Studies Vol. 8, No. 2. Nordic Association of African Studies, p. 80.

On the other hand, the politically constructive role of ethno-nationalism and power struggle as Lonsdale postulates, transforms ethnicity into political tribalism or what is often called clientelism that flows down from high political intrigue. But both ethnicity and political tribalism however constitute the distinctive feature of cultural pluralism.[6] As a pluralistic society, personal and ethnic interests demonstrate the pattern of political formation in Nigeria. Thus the holders of state power maximize the opportunity and use the state apparatuses to achieve their patrimonial interests. In the same way, the majority groups continue to dominate the political structure against the minorities. This domination could as well manifest in the sharing of political offices and resources, whereby the majority groups would deny the members of minority ethnic groups the specific opportunities that may be opened to all. In fact, this attitude worsens the relationship between the ethnic groups. However, the domination of one ethnic group against the other either by the control of state or by ethnic allegiance becomes the ground for ethno-nationalism and power struggle. Hence the relationship between the minority and majority groups initiates a contradictory scenario in the construction of autochthonous political ideological that is compatible to national development.

Furthermore, the complexity of ethnic formation in Nigeria is said to be grounded on the ideological misinterpretation of the socio-cultural relationships by the colonial administrations through mere assumption without in-depth studies. According to Davidson, "colonial rule had worked on the assumption, dividing Africans into tribes even when these 'tribes' had to be invented. But appearances were misleading. What rapidly developed was not the politics of tribalism, but something different and more divisive. This was the politics of clientelism. What tribalism had supposed was that each tribe recognized a common interest represented by common spokespersons, and there was thus the possibility of a 'tribal unity' produced by agreement between 'tribal representative'. But clientelism – the 'Tammany Hall' approach – almost at once led to a dog-

---

[6] Berman, Bruce/Lonsdale, John (1992): Unhappy Valley: Conflict in Kenya & Africa, Book Two: Violence & Ethnicity. Oxford: James Currey, pp. 466-467. See also: Chabal, Patrick/Daloz, Jean-Pascal (1999): Africa Works, p. 59.

fight for the spoils of political power."[7] Castells further comments that "this redefinition of ethnic identity by colonial powers mirrored the structure of the colonial state, in a way that would reverberate in the long term for independent nation-states."[8] Based on a 'false foundation' through colonial legacy, the ethnological matrix that is responsible for the process of state formation became crystallized with variability of socio-cultural and political systems. This, of course aided the pursuit of ethnic and clientelistic interests instead of national interests. But I will later elaborate more on this point.

In fact, the nation-state lacked national consensus and the integration of different ethnic nationalities became problematic. The country as a nation became politically alienated with different ethnic and regional interests competing for supremacy. The political elites used this lack in personalizing the state power and instituting their own clientelistic networks. As a dominant factor in Nigerian political sphere, the political elites always insist on protecting this formation for the fear of losing power and then relevance in the future political equations. As it were, the policies of governments which tend to reflect ethnic interests in environments of strong inter-ethnic competition are usually promoted by the political elites in order to sustain and build their own political machineries and thereafter increase their clientelistic or neo-patrimonial networks.

Finally, Paul comments that; "in as much as the state itself leant on clientelistic networks and ethnic groups, it became not only the agent of special factions but also became 'infected' with an already distorted logic of reciprocity against which bureaucratic rationality had and has very slim chances of taking hold."[9] In that perspective, given the strong ethnic influence on Nigerian economy and politics and given various interests on resources, the state that functions as the neutral arbiter finds it difficult to constitute bureaucratic institutions independent of interferences by different forces both internally and externally. Therefore, the emerging

---

[7] Davidson, Basil (1992): The Black Man's Burden: Africa and the Curse of the Nation-State. London: James Currey, pp. 206-207. See also: Castells, Manuel (2010): End of Millennium: The Information Age: Economy, Society, and Culture Vol. III, 2nd Edition. Oxford: Wiley-Blackwell, p. 106.

[8] Castells, Manuel (2010): End of Millennium: p. 106.

[9] Paul, Axel T. (2008): pp. 223-224.

reality is that regional and ethnic formation in Nigeria as a politicized solidarity redefines the collective identity and weakens capacity of the state in exercising its functions in a democratic environment.

4.1.2   Subtle Demarcation between State and Civil Society

State and civil society are the two delimiting spheres that enlighten one's mind over the discourse on the history and development of social and political systems. But the relationship between the two concepts in the Nigerian context has been a subject of deep controversies among many scholars, without having much common consensus among the scholars. Whereas the civil society as a concept has gained considerable debates in the modern normative sciences as well as in the practical rationalism, the issue of its relationship with state on the other hand has continued to generate a lot of contradictions in the recent times. Mentan understood this fact when he proposed that, "it must be recognized that neither state nor civil society be idealized or conceived of as a homogeneous entity with consensual political direction. Rather plurality, polarization, contradictions, and conflict of interests are all aspects of the existence of state and civil society."[10] But how the divergences between the two concepts operate in Nigeria depend on the articulation of competing interests and balance of social forces significantly embedded in a particular society configuration. Hence I will attempt here to explore and examine the structure and dynamics of state and civil society and how they relate or interact in the Nigerian context.

The state is generally conceived as a regulating institution that represents the common interest. It is separate from the operation of the civil society. Civil society on the other hand constitutes the instrument of productions, and the empowerment of social interactions between the private and public spheres towards collective objectives. It simply implies that the effectiveness of the state depends on the procedural functions of the civil society. But in a marked distinction between the two operations, Pelczynski broadly states that "the distinction between state and civil society was first made by Hegel in print in his Philosophy of Right published in 1821. Within the philosophical mode of exposition which he adopted in his

---

[10] Mentan, Tatah (2010): p. 298.

work, civil society (bürgerliche Gesellschaft) represented a 'stage' in the dialectical development from the family to the state which contradicts the kind of ethical life found in the human micro-community in order to be itself contradicted and overcome (i.e. cancelled and preserved, aufgehoben) by the macro-community of the politically independent, sovereign nation [...]. The conceptual separation of the state and civil society is one of the most original features of Hegel's political and social philosophy although a highly problematic one."[11] The problem is because of the criticisms against Hegel's idea of separation of state and civil society that is based on state domination of the civil society or the attribute of the state as "Instanz des Allgemeinen,"[12] which is insufficient in understanding the proper distinction between them. In other words, the domination makes the state the prime route of accumulation and instrument of domination against civil society.

In his position, Diamond argues that "civil society is distinct from 'society' in general in that it involves citizens acting collectively in a public sphere to express their interests, passions, preferences, and ideas, to exchange information, to achieve collective goals, to make demands on the state, and to hold state officials accountable."[13] It follows that when the citizens collectively realize their objectives and how those objectives could be achieved towards the development of the state, then the civil society has important functions in state structure. But this, of course depends on the autonomy of the civil society. However, civil society in Nigeria is not clearly autonomous or separate from the state because of the difficulty in accommodating opposing social forces by the state. As dependent on material and social conditions, the state is not well institutionalized to guard the autonomy and existence of harmonious civil socie-

---

[11] Pelczynski, Z. A. (1984): 'Introduction: The Significance of Hegel's Separation of the State and Civil Society'. In: Pelczynski, Z. A. (ed.): The State and Civil Society: Studies in Hegel's Political Philosophy. Cambridge: Cambridge University Press, p. 1.

[12] See: Kößler, Reinhart/Wienold, Hanns (2001): p. 224. Kößler and Wienold opine that "die Problematik des Allgemeinen Interesse wird hier daher nicht einfach negiert, sondern als Problem von Staaten und Staatsapparaten kenntlich gemacht, die ein solches Allgemeines nicht unmittelbar, sondern nur in der Form der Klassenherrschaft zur Geltung bringen können" (Kößler, Reinhart/Wienold, Hanns (2001): p. 225).

[13] Diamond Larry (1999): Developing Democracy: Toward Consolidation. Maryland: The Johns Hopkins University Press, p. 221.

110

ty. Instead, what may be attributed to as civil society in Nigeria is significantly segmented, comprising of various interest/ethnic groups that compete for state resources and power in order to build up respective clientelistic networks.

Given the prevalence of ethnic nationalities in the pursuit of interests, Bayart warns that "the existence of 'ethnic' associations, which are the integrating factors within a region and between town and country, must not be allowed to disguise the proliferation of other forms of association which articulate economic or professional interests on a trans-ethnic or trans-geographical basis: directors' unions, lawyers' or architect's associations, and so on."[14] Nevertheless, these embryonic trans-ethnic or trans-geographical formations could be seen by some as a new phase of civil society crystallization in Nigeria. But in actual sense, they do not seem to constitute such; rather reiterate what Bayart referred to as 'civil society within political society'[15]. This development of course is as a consequence of state powers, non-institutionalization and informalization of politics, and societal disengagement through reciprocal assimilation by dominant class or state elites. These phenomena make one to question why the country has not been able to build and sustain a fundamental ideology of development that is nationalistic and capable of transcending the hegemonic dominance by the state.

Chabal and Daloz then suggest that "the emergence of a properly institutionalized civil society, led by politically independent citizens, separate from governmental structures, is only possible where there is a strong and strongly differentiated state."[16] By that, the state will act conjointly with the civil society in addressing legitimate matters that concerns the interests of the public. But the predominant attribute of state in Nigeria is its centrality and repressiveness, and that interferes with the regular productions of power that suppress the civil society. Consequently, civil society development has been in a restrictive and suppressive margin due to the

---

[14] Bayart, Jean-Francois (2009): pp. 161-162.
[15] Bayart notes that "institutions such as parliaments, parties, trade unions and the several consultative commissions, 'represent', in one way, civil society within political society. Despite their autonomy, structures of power do not escape the infiltrations of civil society [...]" (Bayart, Jean-Francois (2009): p. 163)
[16] Chabal, Patrick/Daloz, Jean-Pascal (1999): Africa Works, p. 21.

centralization of state power. Thus, a critical review of the socio-political history of Nigeria reveals that the development and organization of civil society was altered by the advent of colonialism, which practically suppressed the rights and freedom of the citizens as a way of fostering the British control of the state.

Giving an instance during the colonial era, Falana observes that "pursuant to the 'Public Order Ordinance' the right of assembly was limited as any meeting of more than five people required a police permit. Several persons were killed by the police during the Aba Women's Protest of 1921 and the Iva Valley worker strike of 1949 for taking part in demonstrations without authorization. In the same vein, many nationalist politicians, youth leaders and trade unionists were tried and jailed for allegedly making seditious statements or inciting the people against the colonial regime. A few traditional rulers were deposed and banished to some remote islands for daring to challenge the foreign exploitation of the resources in their domain."[17] The situation later empowered the state to repress other opposing groups or organizations that might constitute a hindrance to her authority, creating a dichotomy between the citizens and the state. Every activity was centred on the state as the instrument of power that dictates the tune of socio-political and economic events.

Paradoxically, the dichotomy between state and civil society continues to persist in the contemporary Nigerian society. This is as a result of the character of the postcolonial state, which was built and nurtured by the colonial administrations. The colonialism did not accord the civil society the required autonomy and participatory role, which also persisted after independence. According to Nwosu, "the postcolonial state that emerged at independence retained the trappings of the colonial order. The end of colonialism brought about a change of government personnel without a reconstitution of the state. The postcolonial state in Nigeria thus circumscribes the participatory latitude of civil society, especially on critical issues of democracy and governance. As in the colonial order, the postcolonial order controls significant economic resources in the state. State power offers opportunity for embezzlement. A result is the common quest

---

[17] Falana, Femi (2010): Civil Society and the Challenge of Anti-corruption Struggle in Nigeria. In: Sahara Reporter, Sunday, 16 May: http://www.saharareporters.com/

112

to personalize public power, making the state unduly coercive."[18] Transcending this colonial formation became a problem for the postcolonial state of Nigeria. This is due to the fact that the affairs of the state continued to be influenced by the state elites and also the Western world or neo-imperialists either directly or indirectly in order to retain their relevance in the colonized country.

Consequently, the state is personalized by the state elites that form the dominant political class, using state powers to build their own neo-patrimonial networks and influence the functions and activities of the civil society. In this perspective, Nwosu aptly comments that "personalizing state power brought about the client-patron relationship between state officials and their loyalists. Supporters of the government are rewarded with perquisites such as contracts, gifts, and public appointments, whereas the opposition is hounded and punished. This trend has so deeply pervaded social consciousness that civil society virtually worships power. Various types of people's organizations make solidarity visits to the government in power, no matter how it emerged. Such visits do not reflect goodwill or genuine support, but rather the political economy of corruption [...]. Such an environment can hardly foster the sort of sustained civil society necessary for electoral mandate protection or democratic transformation; it can generate only episodic agitations that yield piecemeal and inconclusive ends."[19] As a result, civil society in Nigeria, to the extent that it exists, has been in constant conflict and domination by state, and sometimes has been transformed into agencies of the government regimes. That implies that the civil society is the victim of the state power, in the sense that its operational mechanisms are curtailed by its development.

Fundamentally, the complexity of state-civil society relationship is another way of saying that the opposing forces of the civil society in Nigeria

---

[18] Nwosu, B. U. (2006): 'Civil Society and Electoral Mandate Protection in Southeastern Nigeria'. In: Bates, Stephen (ed.): The International Journal of Not-for-Profit Law Volume 9, Issue 1. Washington D.C.: The International Center for Not-for-Profit Law, p. 24. http://www.icnl.org/knowledge/ijnl/vol9iss1/ijnl_vol9iss1.pdf [accessed: 23.02.2010]

[19] Nwosu, B. U. (2006): p. 24.

are suppressed by the coercive force of the state.[20] In other words, at their whims and caprices, the so-called existing civil society, whose strengths amount only to bargaining or negotiations for the share of the spoils and rarely for common interests, is willy-nilly the victims of the power play in the state-civil society dichotomy. Therefore, civil society in Nigeria must be redefined to account for the participation and empowerment of individuals and groups in the state, which can result to effective and responsive democratic governance. This, of course could be gradually achieved by dismantling some of the repressive structures put in place during colonial period as well as by strengthening public participation in the democratic processes. This action can then significantly aid in the formation of a stable state in Nigeria that will accommodate and properly empower the civil society.

4.2   Political Evolution and Democratization

After independence in 1960, Nigeria was faced with the challenge of political development and nation-building. It was an enormous task by the country to fashion a political ideology that could suit the socio-cultural environment of the indigenous population, and in the same way, be able to integrate the nation into world politics. The imperative of this task was to realize a political system that could be said to be idealistic and practicable. Prior to this effort, it was believed that the political evolution of Nigeria was still on the scale, characterized by inherited structures of the colonial periods. Coupled with ethnic allegiances and elites accumulation of power, the state was said to be over-centralized and authoritative and was quite unsuitable to the contemporary needs and aspirations of the population. This situation manifested itself shortly after independence in the various conflicts of opposites that rocked the na-

---

[20] According to Chabal and Dolaz, "the history of Nigeria, with its recurring cycles of unity and discord, is exemplary of the dilemmas of modern politics in Africa. It demonstrates clearly how, since independence, political leaders aspiring to national office have found themselves torn between their need to transcend the country's social divisions and their inability to operate politically outside. Any serious analysis of the country demands that we reject a simplistic bi-polar view, opposing a single state to a notional civil society, and take into consideration the complexities of the political interaction between the countless socio-economic sub-systems which constitute Nigeria" (Chabal, Patrick/Daloz, Jean-Pascal (1999): Africa Works, p. 28).

tion's political space and the various arms of government. In confronting this impasse, one would be compelled to ask; to what extent has the political structure been reformed after the independence? This question then assists us in ascertaining the configuration of political evolution and democratization in Nigeria.

At the end of colonial regime in 1960, Nigeria chose to establish its government under a republican constitution with a democratic structure. But according to Diamond, "it was a structure fraught with tensions and contradictions, [...] contradictions between socio-economic and political dominance, which fed a reciprocal insecurity between North and South."[21] In fact, it became a critical moment for nation-building, whereby the nation was faced with undesirable conspiracies and dichotomy between the North and South. This attitude led to the emergence of military intervention that took power in 1966 and shortly thereafter, the civil war broke out lasting from 1967-1970. The military continued in power until the transition to civil rule in 1979, when the American type of Presidential system of government was adopted, bound together by a federal republic comprising the Executive President at the center, Governors at the state level and Chairmen at the local level. Moreover, the Executive together with the Legislative and the Judiciary form the three arms of government, exercising their duties through separation of powers provided by the constitution. These arms also operate in the three tiers of government, which comprise the Federal, the State and the Local governments as the federating units.

Furthermore, the constitutional provisions of federalism, which bind the arms and tiers of the government, are to foresee that each federating unit operates independent of the suppressing powers of the central government. On this note, Natufe identifies two fundamental premises of federalism to include: "First, both levels of government – the central government and the states (federating units) – are independent and coordinates, but never subordinate to one another. Second, the relationship between the central government and the federating units is horizontal and not vertical [...]. When any of these elements are vitiated, federalism is com-

---

[21] Diamond, Larry (1988): Class, Ethnicity and Democracy in Nigeria: The Failure of the First Republic. New York: Syracuse University Press, p. 71.

115

promised and the basis of good governance under federalism is eroded."
[22] In fact, the realization of these premises of federalism is geared towards renewed political consciousness and enthronement of good governance and power decentralization that can bind the nation to proper
unity and democratic development. But whether the political structure of
Nigeria met these standards becomes the question of nation-building and
good governance.

The yearning for 'good governance' has rather remained perennial in
practice and still a quest in the Nigerian political context, as well as in
most other Sub-Saharan African political system in general. In other
words, due to the nature of political institution, good governance has
remained unattainable. It follows that the issue of weak institutional arrangement as a result of colonial formation coupled with the absence of
strong nationalistic movements within the indigenous cultural institutions, has constituted a delimiting factor in political development. The
affirmation of weak formation continues to manifest in the turn of events
in recent times. Asserting to this situation, World Bank has observed that
"at the end of colonial rule, the euphoria of independence disguised the
reality that (beyond a consensus in favour of independence) support for
many African regimes was drawn from a narrow base, often with quite
weak roots in the society at large. At the same time, the starting point for
many African governments was a precarious combination of overex-
tended mandates, weak revenue bases, and low capacity."[23] In that case,
the state political structures were hardly constructed to meet with the
vicissitude of society as well as the expanding needs of the people. This
means that the independence of the state was mainly on the principle not
in actual sense, due to non-consolidation of the structures that could boost
its strong formation, and that has constituted a great challenge to democratic formation.

---

[22] Natufe, Igho (2006): 'Governance and Politics in Nigeria'. A Lecture Delivered on
November 21, 2006 at The Staff and Graduate Seminar Department of Political Science &
Public Administration University of Benin, p. 11. http://www.okpenation.org/doc/ gov-
ernance_and_politics_in_nigeria.pdf [accessed: 28.09.2009]
[23] World Bank (2000): Reforming Public Institutions and Strengthening Governance: A
World Bank Strategy November 2000. Washington D.C.: The International Bank for
Reconstruction and Development/the World Bank, p. 73.

In contextualizing the process of democratization, particularly in the light of weak foundation and in the throes of decolonization, the political system in Nigeria is indeed characterized by over-centralized state power with weak roots in civil society. This development has affected the political evolution and democratization in Nigeria. The significance of this development is the various changes in political structures, which have not yielded much positive results. On the contrary, it continues to question the legitimacy of the government and how new possibilities could be devised in transcending the socio-political and economic logjams of the Nigerian state. This phenomenon is then of compelling interest in investigating the three tripartite routes to political development in Nigeria.

4.2.1 The Heritage of Colonial Indirect Rule

The political evolution in Nigerian can fundamentally be analyzed by examining the colonial emergence in the country's history and development. No doubt, colonial rule as a historical phenomenon had both positive and negative influences on the political formation of Nigeria. The European exploratory and exploitative invasion in Africa in the nineteenth and twentieth centuries was an historical watershed. It redirected and redefined the socio-political history and landscape of the continent. As it affected the continent, so also it did to its component units. This side-by-side changeable influence is what Mentan referred to as 'colonial globalization'. According to Mentan, "the advent of colonial globalization was tsunamic for Africa [...]. She became embroiled in a dynamic that would change her structure, her culture and her future forever. The former league of tribes coagulated into pseudo-states, as a result of colonialism. Strange bedfellows became fellow citizens overnight. Consanguine relatives found themselves facing each other as citizens of different countries."[24] As it were, colonialism integrated as well as disintegrated different cultural groups and traditions. It exposed the continent to the rest of the world, which positively introduced new way of life and political orientations. But on the other hand, some native cultures were ravaged and replaced with foreign cultures that initiated both the disorientation from the native customs, as well as the loss of cultural identity.

---

[24] Mentan, Tatah (2010): p. 28.

As the starting point of colonialism; the 1884/85 Berlin Conference and later at Brussels (1890) presented a forum for uncoordinated scrambling and partitioning of the continent by the Europeans. The conference ushered in the beginning of 'conquered nation' with creation of new boundaries, which subjected the culturally related folks to tensions and conflicts. According to Oborji, "many African peoples or ethnic-groups were split as the new and often arbitrary boundaries drawn by the foreign powers came into effect. In most cases, many ethnic-linguistic groups sharing the same language and culture were often separated into different countries, and those with different cultures and languages were often merged with fractions of dismembered groups."[25] This development however was an attempt at peaceful possession and occupation motivated by mutuality of interests. But it rather exposed the continent to external aggressions and political litigation, in which hitherto European occupation or usurpation of African territories became the desire for economic exploitation and political competition.[26] This invasion also awakened the consciousness that the import of colonialism was meant to facilitate both political and economic influence on the African states.

Specifically in the case of Nigeria, identifying the historical advent of Europeans, Kolawole notes that "the first British penetration of the Niger Delta was by Sir George Goldie in 1885 under the Royal Niger Company. Suspicion in Britain as to the real intention of Sir George, led to the withdrawal of the Charter in 1897 and Lord Fredrick Lugard was sent to protect British interests against French encroachment."[27] The coming of Lugard to Nigeria introduced what was called the 'indirect system of

---

[25] Oborji, Francis A. (2005): Trends in African Theology since Vatican II: A Missiological Orientation. Rome: Leberit SRL Press, p. 30.

[26] Young notes that "colonial rule, assumed by its initiators to be perpetual, later proved to be a mere interlude in the broader sweep of African history; however, the steel grid of territorial partition that colonialism imposed long appeared permanent. Although possibly threatened by the patterns of disorder and state collapse that emerged in the 1990s, the stubborn resilience of the largely artificial boundaries bequeathed by the colonial partition is surprising" (Young, Crawford (2000): 'The Heritage of Colonialism'. In: Harbeson, John W. /Rothchild, Donald (eds.): Africa in the World Politics: The African State System in Flux, 3rd Edition. US: Westview Press, p. 23).

[27] Kolawole, Dipo (2005): 'Colonial and Military Rule in Nigeria: A Symmetrical Relationship'. In: Pakistan Journal of Social Sciences Vol. 3, No. 6. Grace Publications, p. 864.

rule' (i.e. using Africans to subdue Africans) that initiated new class culture and authoritarianism. The intention of the indirect rule include: i) easy reach to community supervision due to insufficient colonial officers, ii) preservation of the existing traditional political system and more importantly, iii) to guarantee the acceptance of the colonial lords by the traditional communities. This system however empowered the appointed traditional native authorities in exercising powers on behalf of the colonial masters but not without their supervisions. The underlying assumption of this development was to ensure a continued hegemonial influence against the captured territories through an indirect means. Meanwhile, different new districts were also created and districts heads were appointed as colonial machineries, mainly for the collection of taxes and enforcement of law and order through the native courts.

With the above development, the colonial administration according to Njoku introduced what is referred to as the 'system of unbalanced sociopolitical landscape' in the polity, "placing the public officers over their communities and reducing the power of the people to exercise a meaningful pressure on their public figures or calling them to order. The warrant chieftaincy which was introduced by the British in South Eastern Nigeria as an administrative apparatus, is an example of how colonialism fundamentally altered not only the perception of public office in an African community but also destroyed the local dynamics of checks and balances [...]."[28] It followed that the warrant chiefs were invested with authorities over the local communities, which gave them the feeling that they were above the community and were there more of to serve the colonial masters than to protect the community interests.[29] There were no standing

---

[28] Njoku, Uzochukwu J. (2006): 'Corruption and Social Change in Nigeria's Public Service: The Agency-Structure Debate'. In: Adibe, Jideofor (ed.): Is It in Our Stars? Culture and the Current Crises of Governance in Africa. The Journal of African Renaissance Vol. 3, No. 6, p. 80. http://www.hollerafrica.com/pdf/nov-dec-06.pdf [accessed: 28.06.2009]

[29] Okere comments that "the colonial era imposed the idea of ruling as a full time job, the idea of government as just the government of a state, the idea of state apparatus with forces of law and order, and involuntary taxations taking over services like public works, public health and education. Above all it introduced the idea of dictatorship. For the first time people saw that unjustly, militarily imposed colonial rule could be sustained with force and with impunity against the wish of the people" (Okere, Theophilus (2005): p. 173).

criteria in their appointments; only those the colonialists felt could function as their 'eye' in the community. This practice mainly in the Southern
Eastern Nigeria (because of the complex nature of its traditional society
composition that was not so open for a centralized political system), became more of a deal between the traditional chiefs and the colonialists.
On the one hand, protecting the colonial political and economic interests
and on the other hand, protecting the warrant chiefs against the community attacks (because of their exploitations) and sustaining their positions
(because only the colonial authorities have the power to depose them).

Furthermore, when Frederick Lugard later discovered some complexity in
diverse administrative methods between the North and South, and the
difficulty in maintaining control of the two different protectorates, he
recommended for an amalgamation of Northern Protectorate and the
Southern Protectorate on January 1, 1914. This amalgamation was to be
governed under one Governor-General in order to form a unified colonial
government. The period saw the introduction of various acts such as Native Authority Ordinance, Native Revenue Ordinance, and Public Lands
Acquisition Ordinance etc. The acts were later guarded by the various
constitutional provisions that were enacted such as the 1922 Clifford
constitution, the 1946 Richards Constitution, and the 1951 Lyttleton Constitution. In short, all was in an attempt to establish a modern state of
Nigeria and still maintain a hold of the state through indirect means. But
this development left also fundamental disparities between different geographical regions (creating one nation where there is no oneness and
shared ideology) that have been the cause of the country's woes in the
present political configuration.

In other words, the imprint of the colonial influence still remained on the
life-wire of the society especially on the political elites, who inherited
authoritative means of exercising political powers. Certain laws were
imposed on the communities and individuals against their wishes. The
crucial implication of the impositions accounted for the enthronement of
corruption and nepotism in the political system, which also implanted
unpatriotic attitudes upon the Nigerian elites. Succinctly put, the political
elites schooled by the colonizers' imperialistic formations and attitudes (a
way of teaching African elites how to be Africans in European clothes),
later used their acquired powers to corruptly amass their own personal

wealth, land, and establish their own patronage networks of sustenance. In effect, they tried to emulate the European way of life, which Paul rightly describes thus: "often traveling or even moving to the capital. They, or their children, went to school and learned about the cultural superiority and impressive deeds of conquerors. They became involved in business activities, earned money and stored riches in formerly unknown quantities."[30] These phenomena brought in corruption and cultural debasement, and alienated Africans especially their elites from their indigenous cultures[31], devalued their local traditional customs and fundamentally upturned the traditional societal network structures.

Finally, the colonial formation certainly had its profound influence on the Nigerian political development and still has continued to shape its essential structures. Hence after independence, the very problem that confronted the new state was how to reconcile the colonial political ideology with the existing trend of traditional formation in order to build a formidable and emancipated modern state. Although the colonial regime made effort in transforming the pre-colonial political organization into modern society, yet whether it helped in sustaining a bureaucratic and democratic formation becomes a question for further enquiry. Nevertheless, this supposition does not imply a total blame on colonialism for the deplorable conditions of state formation in Nigeria. Rather, it laid the foundation to what the country is experiencing in this recent time, by not absolutely championing the course for an integral development of an independent and sovereign state.

4.2.2 Military Interventions and Dictatorship

No less important than an obstacle in arriving at a balanced insight into the political system in the post-independence era was the intrusion of the

---

[30] Paul, Axel T. (2008): pp. 217-218.

[31] Here Paris emphasizes that; "as a principal tool for alienating Africans from their indigenous cultures, the goal of colonial education was to effect a profound loss of self-esteem and self-identity among a new African elite. The process by which that loss occurred is graphically evidence in Alioune Diop's tragic remembrance of his history classes in which he and his peers were taught to recite references to their Gallic ancestors as having blond hair" (Paris, Peter J. (1995): The Spirituality of African Peoples: The Search for a Common Moral Discourse. Minneapolis: Fortress Press, p. 8).

military to power and intervention in politics, which was the beginning of a 'systematic dismantling of federalism' in Nigeria, in favour of a military system of governance. The first military government came into power in January 1966. This was headed by Johnson Aguiyi-Ironsi and was later deposed in August 1966 by Yakubu Gowon, who ruled till July 1975 and was over-throne by Murtala Mohammed and Olusegun Obasanjo in February 1976. It was only until October 1979 that the military returned to the barracks, handing over to a democratic elected civilian president. Then barely four years after, the military struck again in 1983 by over-throwing a legitimate government through coup d'état headed by Muhammadu Buhari. And thereafter, three successive military dictators namely Ibrahim Babangida (1985-1993), Sani Abacha (1993-1998) and Abdulsalami Abubakar (1998-1999) ruled the country until they were compelled to relinquish power to civilian government in May 1999. With their successions and method of governance, the military regime is described as authoritarian with regard to its denial of public participation and its ultimate dictatorial character and personalization of power.

In specific context, it was alleged that military intervention in Nigeria owed its origin on the one hand, to the inability of the political elites to grapple with the crises of under-development and unemployment, and on the other hand, the failure of the dominant class (having both civilian and military backgrounds) to overcome the crisis that eclipsed the public socio-economic interests through unequal distribution, corruption and accumulation of state resources. According to Agbese and Udogu, the armed forces "depicted themselves as patriotic citizens who were forced to intervene in politics to save ordinary people from the greed and rapaciousness of civilian politicians. The military sold the idea that the involvement in politics was essentially a surgical operation to remove the political blight caused by bad civilian leadership."[32] But to what extent they achieved these noble objectives still constitute a major paradox to military interventions. Instead, the military governance in Nigeria has produced more political and economic confusions than the dilemmas

---

[32] Agbese, Pita O./Udogu, Ike E. (2005): 'Taming of the Shrew: Civil-Military Politics in the Fourth Republic'. In: Udogu, E. Ike (ed.): Nigeria in the Twenty-first Century: Strategies for Political Stability and Peaceful Coexistence. Trenton: Africa World Press, p. 16.

created by the various civilian governments, which the military over-
threw.

Similarly, Kolawole aptly states that "the military which intervened as a
corrective regime with messianic fervor only opened the Pandora box for
instability, ethnic rivalry, abuse of human rights and societal mistrust
between the military establishment and the civil society."[33] It could be
asserted that within the military regime due to its repressive nature, the
civil society either existed undergrounds or their role in the state was
debunked by the military presence. The military era in short witnessed
unprecedented abuse of powers and human rights. Unfortunately, it was
the very factors the military tried to intervene that they rather profusely
instituted. According to Agbali "it is no wonder that apart from institu-
tionalizing massive corruption, the Nigerian military, with a 'few exceptions', became a mimesis of symbolic nausea, agents of the degradation
and denigrators of the quality of life. The Nigerian military symbolically
embeds as a retrogressive and destructive force, mitigating the progressive essence of nationhood and socio-economic development."[34] In fact,
their use of force and violence made the state power to be centralized
only on the rulers. And given that their mandates were not constitutional
and the situations that brought them in were not really justified, they attempted every possible means in legitimizing their positions of power
either by force or violence.

Therefore, the failure of military rulers to keep to their numerous promises became a bane and betrayal of their intervention. In other words, Kieh
asserts that "[...] military intervention has not led to the promotion of
holistic democracy and development. Instead, it has helped foster authoritarianism and its associated vagaries of repression, suppression, exploita-

---

[33] Kolawole, Dipo (2005): p. 864. He further notes that "the class antagonism is promoted
more by the contempt with which the military holds the civil society. It assumes an air of
superior patriotism that imbibes it with a sense of paternalism over the civil society. Yet,
the civil society sees it as a hollow patriotism erected on enlivened self-interest of state
exploitation. But the civil society is driven to a level of helplessness as a result of the
military's monopoly of the coercive weapons of state" (Kolawole, Dipo (2005): p. 865).
[34] Agbali, Anthony A. (2005): 'A Reflection on Afigbo's Writings on Nigeria'. In:
Afigbo, Adiele Eberechukwu/Falola, Toyin (eds.) Nigerian History, Politics and Affairs:
The Collected Essays of Adiele Afigbo. Trenton: Africa World Press Inc., p. 44.

tion and marginalization."[35] Unfortunately, the military regimes failed to correct the anomalies in the society, and the military juntas were also unable to relinquish power either through their own judgment or through vociferous public demands as when due. And then when they were compelled to hand-over, they shrewdly used "their wealth and positions to shape the content and contours of the transition programs."[36] This attitude was in an effort to suit their interests and relevance. But all these notwithstanding, the military can as well play a determinant role in the process of political stability and peaceful coexistence in a developing country. But this can only be possible if deemed necessary, within the context of a civil-military relational archetype in which the military ought to be truly subordinate to elected leaders as obtainable in many developed countries of the world.

4.2.3 Democratic Transition vis-à-vis Political Liberalization

Analyzing the transition to democratic rule and the present political liberalism in Nigeria are of compelling interest in political development. This, of course aids in highlighting the processes of democratic formation and the various new changes experienced in the Nigerian political structure, consequent of the current wave of globalization. Through globalization, democratic formation across the world has witnessed its fastest widespread due to increased interaction and integration of different peoples and culture. The global interconnection in fact has facilitated the transformation of many authoritarian regimes into democratic governments with renewed participation, but also has drawn attention to the unevenness and different categories of international relationships. The categories of relationships have initiated spatial reorganization of social order that may have strengthened the international sovereignty at the expense of the declining capacity of state regulating bodies especially in developing

---

[35] Kieh, George K. (2004): 'Military Engagement in Politics in Africa'. In: Kieh, George K./Agbese, Pita O. (eds.): The Military and Politics in Africa: From Engagement to Democratic and Constitutional Control (Contemporary Perspectives on Developing Societies). England: Ashgate, p. 53.
[36] Agbese, Pita O. (2004): 'Soldiers as Rulers: Military Performance'. In: Kieh, George K./Agbese, Pita O. (eds.): The Military and Politics in Africa: From Engagement to Democratic and Constitutional Control (Contemporary Perspectives on Developing Societies). England: Ashgate, p. 59.

nations. As an interrelated process that is spatial and uneven, globalization has initiated 'new world order' in political landscape, whereby the national sovereignty is in the verge of collapsing and the existing gaps between nations have widened to the exclusion of many. Thus the systems of interconnectedness, interrelationship and internationalization periodically coexist to form often complex irreversible political process in a nation.

The process of democratisation in Africa has been a conventional route to capitalism, propelled by the concept of 'new world order' consequent of the end of the Cold War and the collapse of communism. On the other hand, liberalization process through democratization is seen by many as a necessary condition for good governance, and by others as a process that gear towards global inequality through the ascendency of hegemony over the developing countries.[37] For instance, the autonomy and sovereignty of states in Africa has been weakened by neo-liberalism, and as such the democratisation practices especially the citizens' participation in political processes have been hitherto hindered as consequent of global political and economic interests that have polarized the states. This phenomenon has initiated and/or still initiating political changes and developmental patterns that seem to have been the outcome of foreign policy considerations, which has endangered good governance in many African countries.

Specifically, democratization is even more difficult in a pluralistic society like Nigeria, where the state is divided along ethno-regional, cultural and religious lines. In this instance, reducing and/or unifying the pluralistic differences and political inequalities become the challenge of democratic practices. From the objective factors on the ground, it is clear to observe

---

[37] Ibanu opines that "it is not difficult to see that [...] Africa is one of those areas that are 'unfamiliar' with democratic practices to which democracy will inevitably spread by diffusion according to Western conception. It is true that global factors, for instance, the end of the cold war, the resurgence of liberal democracy in the former Soviet bloc countries and demands of political conditionalities by the Bretton Woods institutions, have had an effect on democratization in Africa. However, they have only served as a fillip to popular discontent with economic stagnation and political repression that had become pervasive on the continent" (Ibeanu, Okechukwu (2000): Ethnicity and Transition to Democracy in Nigeria: Explaining the Passing of Authoritarian Rule in a Multi-ethnic Society. In: African Journal of Political Science Vol. 5, No. 2, p. 46).

that the quest for democracy and development as yearned for by the populace can neither be served nor advanced by the prevailing new political order introduced by globalization and its imminent inequality in the country. Here Leftwich notes that "such inequalities, the class and regional conflicts they have generated, and their implications for politics have been the stuff of which the desperate cycles of authoritarianism and democracy have historically been made. Economic liberalization and democratic politics in this instance are highly unlikely to reduce these quickly; indeed they can be expected to deepen."[38] And on the other hand, the failure of the state to tackle the problems on ground has introduced various variations in politics, which, instead of harnessing the public demands, has pitched the society in conflicts with the external demands and pressures from international communities.

In a prevailing condition and quest for stable state formation with minimal external intervention, Leftwich posits that "democracy is unlikely to be the political form which can generate such a state or system of governance: quite the opposite. Furthermore, historical evidence shows that faith in the economic and political liberalism of the minimal state as the universally appropriate means of development is deeply flawed. Successful modern transformative episodes of economic development, from the 19th century to the present, have almost always involved both a strong and an active state to help initiate, accelerate and shape this process."[39] Perhaps, the Nigerian state is yet to attain the required autonomy in policy implementations/outcomes in developing and accelerating the democratization processes. Therefore, the problem with neo-liberalization vis-à-vis democratization is actually on the structural limitations to which it has demeaned the state's sovereignty through policy manipulations rather than on the process of democratization itself. What is needed is national consensus on policy formulation and then institutional orientation that can confront the perils of neo-liberal policies, which are detrimental to political development.

---

[38] Leftwich, Adrian (1993): Governance, Democracy and Development in the Third World. In: Third World Quarterly Vol. 14, No 3, p. 618. Available at: http://www.jstor.org/ [accessed: 12.04.2009]
[39] Leftwich, Adrian (1993): p. 620.

4.2.3.1 The Antecedents of Civilian Administration

The civilian political phase in Nigeria, by virtue of the involvement of the citizens in political affairs and the election of candidates from different political parties could be ascribed as democratic. Thus, as a presidential system of government, it applies representative democracy, which allows election of delegates beginning from ward levels to federal levels within the constitutional separation of powers among the executive, legislative and judiciary. But unfortunately, the system as observed seemed to be highly dominated by the executives, through their hegemonic influence on the legislative and judicial processes. Thus the president of the country is both the head of state and chief executive head of government, with the governors and local government chairmen at the state and local levels respectively. The legislative is composed of the Senate and House of Representative at the federal, House of Assembly at the states and Council at the local governments. On the other hand, the Judiciary is headed by the Supreme Court of Justice. Moreover, Nigeria as a Federal Republic has had four different Republics since independence, which include: the First Republic (1960-1966), the Second Republic (1979-1983), the abrogated Third Republic in 1993 and the current Fourth Republic since May 29, 1999. These Republics have been periodically intercepted with a prolonged and protracted military interventions and dictatorship. The current Federal Republic has so far seen the growth of political parties, which have grown from five in 1999 to over 50 political parties during the 2011 elections; even though not more than 10 parties won positions after the elections.

However, the transition to democracy and the subsequent civilian administrations in Nigeria in the midst of political, cultural and economic deprivation against many citizens are attributed with many difficulties and challenges. Besides, the most telling indictment against the civilian political actors has been their failure to keep faith with the tenets of democracy that they have purported to champion. Many of the political office holders assumed their respective positions in an illegitimate and illegal process of electioneering. In practice, more often than not, rather than the politicians submitting themselves to the democratic choice by the electorate, most of them prefer the skullduggery of rigging, thuggery, fixing, and patrimonalism in surmounting the processes and staying in office. As such, the electoral processes have so far witnessed series of malpractices and violence.

As a violence generator, the Human Rights Watch rightly observes that: "in a situation where there was absolutely no confidence that the polls themselves would be free and fair, those who felt frustrated by the existing systems for dividing up power (and thus wealth) then turned to violence. Of course those leading the violence do not necessarily have any commitment to a more equitable distribution of resources beyond securing their own share; but they are able to draw on an inexhaustible well of alienation from the current regime and its corruption, and frustration at the impossibility of changing government through peaceful means, in recruiting those who will fight for them."[40] In this formation, the political environment is burdened with the struggle for interests against the development of the political system. In that scenario, the political parties and their elites have capitalized on the weakness of the system in enthroning thuggery and rigging in electioneering in order to achieve their personal interests. This phenomenon has not only put the democratic ideals into question especially as the tenet of free and fair election has not met up with its standards, but also making some to lose faith in democratic governance. Some Nigerians have come to the feeling that the promise of democracy seems to be eluding them.

On the other hand, the true practice of federalism in Nigeria as the system of the government has remained a contending issue among the political analysts, and most state elites wittingly or unwittingly have no zeal in its defense. Unfortunately, the present scenario in the country seems to suggest a unitary government instead of federalism. Suffice it to say here that since the advent of the Fourth Republic in 1999, the weakness of federalism has been engineered by the actions of the elected political elites especially under the ruling political parties. In effect, the political practice in Nigeria is the concentration of authority and power in a single central government, having legal omnipotence over all national territories. Thus the center dictates the tune and modality of exercising powers on the peripheries. For instance, the interference of the presidency on the running of

---

[40] Human Rights Watch (2003): The Warri Crisis: Fueling Violence. Human Rights Watch Vol. 15, No. 18 (A), p. 15.

the state governments and the dependency of the states on the federal government especially on capital projects questions the premise of the federal system.

Likewise, Natufe observes that "these anti-federal characteristics that define federal-state relations are also replicated in state-local government relations across the country, where a local government council is considered a division of the governor's office. In fact, a chairman of a local government [...] holds his seat at the mercy of his state governor. These levels of dependency akin to a unitary system hinder the practice of federalism, and thus compromise good governance in the polity."[41] Often the situation is intensified by various conflicts that exist between the executives and the legislatives over political influence on the one hand, and on the other hand, over resource allocation.

Moreover, another characterizing factor in the present civilian dispensation is the issue of zoning of political offices. According to Banjo, "zoning is an undemocratic formula used by political parties to distribute power according to loosely-defined geographic 'zones' that are neither clearly explained nor sanctioned by the electorates. It is used to goad the citizens and railroad them into perpetual subservience to political elites."[42] In other words, it could be said to be a way of 'balancing' the power equation in the country with the view of accommodating different ethnic groups, geographical regions, constituencies, states, religious affiliations etc. But whether it has achieved its purported intention becomes the dangerous aspect of its formation. Instead, the formula has instituted mediocrity, division and confusion in the political system. In addition, the very modality of zoning principles has also in-tuned the crisis of political rotation among ethnic regions. In fact, Iroegbu was right when he argued that the zoning system paradoxically institutionalizes "ethnic and regional autonomies and separation in an attempt to reduce them."[43] For instance, the 2011 presidential election was a case at point that nearly put the coun-

---

[41] Natufe, Igho (2006): p. 15.
[42] Banjo, Lanre (2010): Zoning of Elective Offices is Destructive and fosters Disunity! In: SaharaReporters Online, 16 March 2010, http://www.saharareporters.com/
[43] Iroegbu, Pantaleon (1996): Communalism: Toward Justice in Africa. Owerri: International Universities Press, p. 113.

try into a state of collapse as to where power should be zoned or rotated. As a result, various elections have been mutilated by this development and when confusion in the zoning formula arises, the system is always endangered to crisis. On the other hand, the recent crisis rocking the country especially in the Northern region has been the consequence of the presidential election that produced a southerner as the President against the wish of the northerners who believed that it was their turn to produce the President. And it is obvious that the problem will continue to reoccur, as each region will consistently be clamoring to be on the top of the nation's affairs, if not well checked.

Finally, in evaluating the performance of the civilian administration; many may believe that the system is yet to achieve the required results expected. The economy remains virtually stagnant; inadequate government policies, weak institutions, and pervasive corruption have continued to undermine investments and productions. Personal security and national stability are threatened by rampant social conflict among ethnic, religious, partisan and criminal groups in various parts of the country. Some even conjecture that the return to civil rule has not yet allayed the fears of possible military re-emergence into Nigerian politics. However, some others may also believe that the civilian regime is gradually delivering some dividends of democracy seen in the improved human rights records and freedom of expression. Nevertheless, civilian government remains preferable to authoritative government, though substantial demands and renewed efforts on the part of the government are also expected in addressing and improving the general welfare of the population especially for the poor masses.

4.2.3.2 The Endemic Culture of Neo-patrimonialism

The culture of politics in Nigeria manifests itself in various dimensions, which are predominantly occasioned by the struggle for profit inclinations that suit the immediate needs of the actors against the common goods. The most significant aspect of this dimension is the culture of neo-patrimonialism, which is perceived today by many as one of the main complementary and persistent instrument of political development in Nigeria. It is an attempt by the political elites to informalize politics as their institutions of patronage using the formal structures of the state.[44] As a 'distinctive institutional hallmark' of African politics, Bratton and Van de Walle contend that "in neo-patrimonial regimes, the chief executive maintains authority through personal patronage, rather than through ideology or law [...]. Relationships of loyalty and dependence pervade a formal political and administrative system, and leaders occupy bureaucratic offices less to perform public service than to acquire personal wealth and status. The distinction between private and public interests is purposely blurred."[45] In essence, there is hardly clear-cut distinction between the formal institutions of state and informal private institutions. In other words, the system of neo-patrimonalism is sustainable because the political elites control power and use the state as the mobilizing engine for acquisition. They dominate the polity and use their acquired powers as means of survival, self-enrichment and sustenance of clientele networks.

With the indirect integration of the neo-patrimonial system into state institutions, the struggle for political power is primarily sought as a result of the opportunity that it can provide for illegal private enrichment and building of patrimonial networks. As a system of power struggle, neo-patrimonialism has dominated the political landscape of the country. The political elites in Nigeria through their actions and inactions have continued to compromise the formal structures of the political system by way of systematic informalization of political institutions occasioned by neo-patrimonialism. In this instance, the most notable configurations include: i) the extreme personalization of the state power by the political elites, ii) the use of national resources for political ends and legitimation, and iii) systematic clientelistic formation. Forsyth on this configuration comments that, "in Africa as elsewhere political power means success and

---

[44] For Chabal and Daloz, "the logic of neo-patrimonialism is focused on the proximate: the local and the communal. Its legitimacy depends on the ability to deliver to those who are linked with the political elites through the micro-networks of patronage and clientialism. There is no scope within such a perspective for deferring to a larger but less immediate macro-rationality, most significantly to the greater good of the country as a whole" (Chabal, Patrick/Daloz, Jean-Pascal (1999): Africa Works, p. 161).
[45] Bratton, Michael/Van de Walle, Nicholas (1994): 'Neopatrimonial Regimes and Political Transitions in Africa'. In: Journal of World Politics Vol. 46, No. 4. John Hopkins University Press, p. 458.

prosperity, not only for the man who holds it but for his family, his birth place and even his whole region of origin. As a result there are many who will go to any lengths to get it and, having got it, will surpass themselves in order to keep it."[46] More often than not, it is a matter of life-and-death that involves every possible means, even to the use of violence in order to achieve, acquire and retain power. Consequently, it encourages political domination and over-concentration of power in the hands of few individual elites, and then hampers democratization especially the public participation in politics.

In fact, Petithomme observes that "given the over-domination of the executive branch, African political systems are predominantly presidential. While the well-spread authoritarian nature of the postcolonial state has led to high concentrations of power at the top of the political system, the legislative and the judicial powers are mainly subordinated. Power is centralized around a single individual, who ultimately controls most of the clientelistic networks and can exert discretionary powers over state resources."[47] In other words, Chabal and Daloz suggest that "the aim of the political elites is not just to gather power. It is much more fundamentally to use that power and the resources which it can generate, to purchase, as it were, the 'affection' of their people or within what Hyden (1980) called an 'economy of affection'."[48] To sustain the economy of affection and maintain political influence, wealth and resources are essential prerequisites, which imply that political elites will always strive and apply every possible mechanism on their disposal in order to exploit the state as a resource for self and for supporters. In the actual sense, the political goal becomes how to nourish and sustain the economy of affection (neo-patrimonial networks) rather than entrenching democracy. It follows that Nigerian politics has come to be identified as a matter of the interests of a 'cabal of godfathers' rather than public interest. Indeed political and public offices are mostly shared and allocated to cronies, kith and kin, or clients in a manner that subverts and threatens the fledgling democracy.

---

[46] Forsyth, Frederick (1977): The Making of an African Legend: The Biafra Story. New York: Penguin Books, p. 25.
[47] Petithomme, Mathieu (2007): p. 14.
[48] Chabal, Patrick/Daloz, Jean-Pascal (1999): Africa Works, p. 158.

Furthermore, the powerlessness of the populace is shown by the influence been wielded by the political elites. This implies that the majority of the citizens are being dominated by the few political elites that control both the economic and political structures of the state. Aptly Durotoye observes that the "[...] well being of the citizenry is secondary in the consideration of the ruling elite in Africa and political manifestoes are just a ruse to deceive the electorate whose votes do not matter in the final analysis as long as the ruling party remains in control of the electoral apparatus."[49] This condition rightly points to the fact that what actually counts during electioneering is the number of strong men in the name of godfathers that are behind the political candidates. These strong men or financiers control and determine the tune of governance after elections.

Similarly, Okere notes that, "in African 'democracies' the people who effectively rule may just be the parties dominated by the elite. But more accurately, and in the long run, it is the financiers who manipulate, patronize and control them [...]. The charade of elections and representatives is often used to provide a smoke screen as the people are forced to legitimize those sponsored and imposed on them as their representatives by some faceless gnomes."[50] In that case, the patrons or godfathers constitute themselves as another arm of the government that install and demote candidates. Typically, 'god-fatherism' serves as a masked controller of the government, with its attendant advantages for the patrons. This kind of situation often leaves open the political violence and conflicts in the struggle for dominance. Incidents believed to be connected to political assassinations are widespread, while politically masterminded attacks on political opponents are a commonplace.

As already mentioned, Nigerian political elites have a history of doing whatever it takes to stay in power and to hold on to the wealth that this power has given them against the popular wishes. On the other hand, most Nigerians are covered under the 'veil of ignorance' and some others tend to tolerate this 'noble-peasant' system of Nigerian politics, which

---

[49] Durotoye, Adeolu A. (2008): Weathering the Storm/Reaping the Harvest? Democratic Dividends in Africa. In: All Academic Research. All Academic, Inc., p. 13. http://www.allacademic.com/ [accessed: 28.09.2009]
[50] Okere, Theophilus (2005): p. 184.

could therefore be attributed to low literacy level and disempowerment. Many others are yet to realize the tune of political process or how to make their impact felt in the process of change. Others still believe that there is no need to try in so far as their contributions cannot be of any value, and the fear that the resultant effects of their opposition may lead them to political woes. Even though many citizens will be clamoring for change, yet nobody will be ready to be a victim. But as long as this pa-tron-client system of neo-patrimonialism continues to assume the culture of politics, there is therefore the tendency that the marginalized majority will still remain isolated, and the future of democracy in Nigeria will as well be clouded with uncertainties.

4.3   Institutional Paradox of State Formation

In analyzing further the state formation in Nigeria, this study presents new dimensions of enquiry, especially when one looks at the internal components of the society. These internal components constitute part of the institutional make-up of the state. Usually, research attention is not properly giving to those institutions while examining the formation of state in Nigerian. Thus overlooking the relevance and the heritage of other conventional institutions of the state could be part of contributing factors to the complex nature of the Nigerian society. I will then investi-gate the roles such institutions like traditional rulers, religions and interest groups play in the formation of state in Nigeria.

4.3.1   The Role of Traditional Rulers

Fundamentally, the institution of traditional rulers is considered not based on seniority but rather on economic prowess, hereditary composition and the ability to influence changes in the local community. Due to diverse ethnic and cultural formations in Nigeria, there is hardly harmonious configuration of traditional rulers. However, this thesis will not bother to address the differential patterns of traditional institutions, because each region or ethnic group has its own formative processes. One basic princi-ple is that the cultural institutions of the society in Nigeria are predomi-nantly and deeply structured, and as such constitute two major classes: ruling class at the highest echelons and the subordinate class. The tradi-tional rulers are among the ruling class in the local context. This exami-

134

nation will then dwell more on the general notion of this composition and the role of traditional rulers in the society formation.

Although the role of the traditional rulers is not well specified by the constitution, yet they have played and continue to play vital roles in influencing local community development. On that basis, Blench et al note that Nigeria has traditionally had a large number of traditional authorities and rulers who have played an important role in community coherence and traditional systems in Nigeria. As such, they argue that "it has been observed that in parts of Nigeria, because traditional rulers' long establishment and the respect in which they are held makes them more effective in conflict resolution than 'official' mechanisms. They are also able to take pre-emptive action through their familiarity with the different sections of the community, where the government has been observed to be reactive. Even some traditional rulers work extremely hard with little official recognition of their efforts."[51] Historically, the existence of the traditional rulers in the pre-colonial times was significantly marked with ideological and juridical responsibilities, as a traditional institution for order and progress, where cases of deviance were referred to for punishment and settlement. As a result, the traditional rulers mostly encouraged the community towards public engagement, collective responsibility and protection of the local customs. Unfortunately, the dominant nature of the institution was majorly created during the colonial era, where the traditional rules were used as agents for slave-trade and an institution for indirect rule by colonial hegemony.

At the time of colonialism, the statutes of traditional authorities were recognized; including the creation of new more chiefs to harmonize the existing colonial political system. In that instance, local rulers had to be co-opted to act for the British authorities, hence the use of 'indirect rule', the governance of a region or district through existing institutions. It was a unique factor in Nigeria when compared to other Sub-Saharan African

---

[51] Blench, Roger/Longtau, Selbut/Hassan, Umar/Walsh, Martin (2006): The Role of Traditional Rulers in Conflict Prevention and Mediation in Nigeria. A Final Report prepared for Department for International Development (DFID) Nigeria, p. I. http://rogerblench. info/Development/Nigeria 2006.pdf [accessed: 11.10.2010]

countries.[52] Indirect rule thus made a certain kind of impact, and many of its features persisted long after it has formally ended with colonialism. Such that the impact was implanted in the minds of most political elites to the extent that they could maintain power and use their acquired powers to mime and intimidate their opponents. These methods of power application and their influence on the society were carried over to the new political construction of the modern state.

Against this backdrop, Sklar states that "any serious inventory of African contributions to the theory and practice of government in our time would necessarily include the modernized indigenous institutions [...]. The durability of traditional authority in Africa cannot be explained away as a relic of colonial rule. African agency in the construction of colonial institutions was largely responsible for the adaptation of traditional authorities to modern systems of government and the legitimacy they continue to enjoy among ordinary people."[53] He further argues that "the existence of traditional kings, councils, and courts do not greatly affect whether or not the sovereign government is democratic in form. But traditional political identity could prove to be a bedrock of political order for whatever system of government does possess legal sovereignty."[54] Consequently, the traditional chieftaincy institution plays underground role in political for-

---

[52] Blench et al note that "a rapid comparison with the situation in other West African countries reveals that the situation in Nigeria is unique. Although there were comparable chiefdoms and emirates, especially in the Sahelian countries, in pre-colonial times, the French system of governance treated them very differently, effectively downgrading their power to that of entirely ceremonial rulers. In a useful comparison of the two systems written shortly after the era of Independence, Crowder (1964) compares their functioning, noting that the French essentially converted traditional rulers into 'chefs de canton', turning them into tax collectors and making them administer boundaries arbitrarily different from their traditional domains. In many Anglophone countries a system of 'Indirect Rule' was adopted, at least in the early colonial era. Further east, the situation is somewhat different, as in Northern Cameroun and Chad, the problems of governance in the early colonial period mean the colonial authorities reached a similar solution to Nigeria by allowing rulers to maintain power, as long as the justice they administered was considered by colonial standards as not too transgressive" (Blench, Roger/Longtau, Selbut/Hassan, Umar/Walsh, Martin (2006): p. 7).
[53] Sklar, Richard L. (2003): 'The Premise of Mixed Government in African Political Studies'. In: Vaughan, Olufemi (ed.): Indigenous Political Structures and Governance in Africa. Ibadan, Nigeria: Sefer Books Ltd., p. 4.
[54] Sklar, Richard L. (2003): pp. 8-9.

136

mation, but it is also in one way or the other being paradoxically integrated into the political system either as an adversary body or internal regulative unite of the government. The formalization of this institution by its integrative roles has re-opened the debate on its constitutional relevance in Nigeria. Though some of the rulers enjoy the legitimacy as the traditional authorities aiding in promoting their traditional communities as well as in representing the interests of the people they serve before the government, yet the system has become another class formation and a quasi-political institution meant for the exploitation of the community resources and the domination of people.

Nevertheless, the interaction between the traditional institutions and the state bureaucratic institutions constitutes a fundamental niche towards fragmented society, class conflicts and the increased struggle for regional and ethnic interests. In fact, Vaughan contends that "the main concern of regional political classes has been to protect their interests by seeking refuge behind traditional structures, themes and symbols that are summoned to validate local aspirations. In this context, state structures are hardly used as effective institutions of administration and governance. Rather, they function largely as mechanisms for allocating patronage and ensuring political domination. Thus, chieftaincy structures – as communal and ethnic-based institutions – partly reinforce a rentier state dominated by ethno-regional commercial and bureaucratic classes."[55] It follows that the traditional institutions function in such a way that they aid in mobilization of ethno-regional struggle, which gives the political elites more ground to control the power of the state. It is not surprising to observe that the roles of the traditional authorities and what they represent appeal to the political elites who use them just like the colonial masters, in achieving their personal feats.

However, one fundamental area which makes the traditional institution so appealing to the political elites is the prestigious honorary traditional titles it confers. The rate of increase in the quest for chieftaincy titles in Nigeria has assumed another dimension, in the sense that it has become

---

[55] Vaughan, Olufemi (2000): p. 12-13.

another form of status symbol.[56] Paradoxically, it has turned out to be not necessarily a meritorial conferment, but the question of who can afford the bidding cost with the traditional rulers. It has also initiated an avenue for the traditional rulers to reward wealthy donors in order to attract more donors. In fact, the conferment provides the political elites the leverage to use the awarded title to legitimize their positions in the society. On the other hand, the relationship between the traditional rulers and the political elites manifest especially during electioneering. Hence, during the elections, the political parties tend to use the traditional rulers for their political purposes especially in the mobilization of voters. This however puts a question mark on their non-partisan role in the political affairs and their traditional statute. Therefore, the traditional rulers are relevant as long as their services are required by the political rulers and they could also be deposed by the political rulers when their bids are not met. This practice has weakened the serenity in which the institution of traditional rulers had formerly enjoyed as a reputable social force in the local communities especially during the pre-colonial periods.

4.3.2   The Role of Religion

In Nigeria, about 50 per cent of the population is Muslim, mostly concentrated in the Northern savanna of the country where Islam first appeared between the eleventh and fourteenth centuries and later took hold after the jihad of Usman dan Fodio that led to the establishment of the Sokoto Caliphate in the early nineteenth century. On the other hand, roughly 40 per cent of the population is Christian, concentrated most heavily in the South and Middle Belt where Christianity first came through the European missionaries in the nineteenth century. The rest of the population, about 10 per cent practices indigenous religions based on natural phe-

---

[56] Blench et al rather state that "a particular trend from the 1990s onwards has been the widespread upgrading and creation of chieftaincies either to reinforce ethnic agendas or to reward wealthy political donors. As a result, the position of these 'new' chiefs is regarded with skepticism by the general population and they do not command the allegiance essential to effective functioning. The sheer numbers of created chiefs inevitably contributes to the dilution of the authority of traditional chiefs as well as reducing the extent of their domains" (Blench, Roger/Longtau, Selbut/Hassan, Umar/Walsh, Martin (2006): p. 106).

138

nomena and ancestor worship.[57] But each of these three major religious formations has in one way or the other a profound influence on its believers. In that perspective, religion as a spiritual phenomenon influences the patterns of interaction in the society. It affects many aspects of peoples' lives including socio-cultural, economic, and political relationships.

However, religion has played a fundamental role in the political development in Nigeria. On the one hand, Akinade observes that "shortly after independence, the Northern People's Congress (NPC) adopted a grand policy of Islamization. The Premier, Alhaji Sir Ahmadu Bello, who was the Sardaunna of Sokoto (the center of the former Islamic Caliphate) 'asserted himself as the Apostle of Islam, and Islam became the gateway to Northern political fortunes and the sole criterion of who was a true Northerner'. In 1961, the Sardauna established the 'Jama'tu Nasril Islam' to coordinate the systematic Islamization of Nigeria. The society was designed to carry out the missionary task of the Umma and to 'establish and run schools, hospitals, dispensaries, public enlightenment through seminars, lectures and conferences, and so on'."[58] With the utmost submission to Islamic customs and laws, it follows that the Muslims view politics as a vigor that links them to the wider world. That is why most of

---

[57] See: Falola, Toyin/Heaton, Matthew (2008): A History of Nigeria. Cambridge: Cambridge University Press, pp. 4-5.

[58] Akinade, Akintunde E. (2002): The Precarious Agenda: Christian-Muslim Relations in Contemporary Nigeria. Duncan Black Macdonald Center for the Study of Islam and Christian-Muslim Relations: Hartford. http://macdonald.hartsem.edu/articles_akinade.htm [accessed: 21.06.2010]. See also: Turaki, Yusufu (1997): 'The Social-Political Context of Christian-Muslim Encounter in Northern Nigeria'. In: Studies in World Christianity, Vol. 3, No. 2, p. 133; Kalu, Ogbu (2000): Power, Poverty and Prayer: The Challenges of Poverty and Pluralism in African Christianity, 1960-1996. Frankfurt am Main: Peter Lang, p. 142. According to Loimeier, "the foundation and the development of Jama'at Nasr al-Islam (JNI, Association for the Support of Islam) can be regarded as the most important effort to unite the Muslims in Northern Nigeria under one umbrella. In contrast to the Kaduna Council of Malamai and the Usumaniyya, the JNI has survived a number of crisis. It was the only religious organization with a supraregional orientation in which religious scholars and religious movements of different and opposing tendencies have come together in order to discuss and determine their political and religious aims and to present them to the Nigerian public" (Loimeier, Roman (1997): Islamic Reform and Political Change in Northern Nigeria. Evanston, Illinois: Northwestern University Press, p. 135).

them believe that there is only a subtle distinction between religion and politics in defense of faith.

On the other hand, apart from introduction of Christianity in Nigeria, its legacies are quite important to the formation of state. The Christian missionary activities in the Southern part of Nigeria significantly influenced the structure of the society through the introduction of Western education as a powerful instrument of development. This arrangement created developmental dichotomy between the North and South. According to Subero, "the most poignant expression of this dichotomy was the huge historical southern head start over the North in virtually every aspect of modernization, including education, per capita income, urbanization, wage employment, commerce, and industrialization."[59] It made the Christian South to have dominant role in civil service and economic sectors as against the North, who only dominated the political structure after independence. In other words, the Muslim northern elites dominated the politics, which could be attributed to the colonial balanced-method of integration, as well as an avenue of empowering the less-endowed Muslim North in the political equation of the country. These political elements of religion have demonstrated a power struggle not only on religious bases but also on socio-political and economic control that have influenced the state structures.

In fact, the dichotomy between the North and South in Nigeria has been the consequence of the politicization of religion. In 1976, the Christian Association of Nigeria (CAN) was formed in order to unite all Christians in one umbrella. By 1988 CAN has embraced almost every Christian church and has become so politicized that it is almost an unofficial opposition to the government regime and a force against the Islamic dominance of the national politics. However, the enlisting of Nigeria into the Organization of the Islamic Conference (OIC) in 1986 and introduction of strict Shari'a law in Muslim states in 1999 helped to spark off yet another feeling of mistrust and anxiety among the Christians against the Muslim believers. Subero then notes that "since the OIC imbroglio, Nigeria appears to have degenerated from a religiously peaceable to a reli-

---

[59] Suberu, Rotimi T. (2001): Federalism and Ethnic Conflict in Nigeria. Washington, DC: United States Institute of Peace, p. 22.

140

giously polarized federation. Aside from the bloody interreligious riots that have convulsed many northern cities since 1987, clashes which eventually provoked reprisal killings in the Igbo southeast during early 2000, a key manifestation of this polarized climate has been the increasing mobilization of religious identities behind the sectional struggles [...]."[60] This religious mobilization is more prominent especially in states where the population of Muslims and Christians are relatively similar, with the insistence on the equal distribution of the economy or political offices based on religious lines. Indeed, such mobilization has resulted to crises either motivated by political reasons, economic struggle or on religious differences.

Moreover, in various states of the country, religious mobilization plays out in three different levels: in an area predominantly Muslim, in an area predominantly Christian and in a mixed area. And because the traditional and other religious sects are the minorities, their influences are not well felt except when it comes to the use of charms and other magical powers, which may also be beneficial to both the Muslims and Christians irrespective of their beliefs. Some even believe that no leader can gain or maintain power without strong magical assistance from a Juju man or other spiritual powers. Some leaders and their lieutenants even commit themselves to those powers before taking up assignments. It is unfortunate that most of the political leaders are strongly committed to the oaths they secretly sworn to the spiritual oracles than to the constitution of the republic in which they were sworn in.

Finally, religion can significantly aid in state transformation if it remains truth to its preaching. On the contrary, Falana states that "the manipulation of religion by some powerful individuals who hide under the guise of religion to pursue selfish interests remains one of the negative effects of religion on the polity."[61] On that note, one cannot therefore neglect the influence of religions in the formation of state in Nigeria taking into ac-

---

[60] Suberu, Rotimi T. (2001): p. 17.
[61] Falana, Femi (2010): Religion and Political Reforms in Nigeria. A public lecture delivered at the 51st birthday anniversary of Rt. Rev Alfred Adewale Martins, Catholic Bishop of Abeokuta, Ogun State on Saturday June 5, 2010. In: SaharaReporter Online. http://www.saharareporters.com [accessed: 6.06.2010]

count the far-reaching cleavages and political polarization as its major consequences.

4.3.3 The Role of Interest Groups

The organized interest groups have continued to play significant roles in the Nigerian socio-political and economic development. The growing pressure at international level for the promotion of democratization and participatory processes of governance in Nigeria has seen an increasing involvement of organized interest groups in programme designs meant for building up the socio-political strengths of the state. Such groups are predominantly Non-Governmental Organizations (NGOs). Thus the following organizations are categorized as organized interest groups: Trade Unions (such as Nigerian Labor Congress (NLC), Academic Staff Union for Universities (ASUU), Nigerian Union of Teachers (NUT), Civil Liberties Organization (CLO) etc.); Professional Organizations (such as Nigerian Bar Association (NBA), Nigerian Medical Association (NMA), Nigerian Society of Engineers (NSEs) etc.); Student Associations (such as National Association of Nigerian Students (NANS)); and the Media.

However, many of what people may regard today as civil society movements in Nigeria are conferred on the various interest groups representing community and individual interests. Through their different vital roles, the activities of the interest groups have shaped and exerted considerable influence on the political and economic trends in the history of the country. For instance: they range from the anti-colonial nationalistic movements to the struggle against military dictatorship towards restoration of democracy, and the involvement in public policy making either in defense of the human rights or for protections of public goods. They also assist the government in providing information and strategies on relevant issues such as reform initiatives and their mode of implementations. Other roles include: fight against social disparities and discriminations in employment opportunities especially on gender and minority levels, enhancement of workers' welfare through equitable wage distribution as against stagnant salary structure, creating awareness on AIDs infections and the resistance against government's repressive policies.

From the above conception, we shall now pay greater attention on the organized Trade Unions especially their development and influences.

142

Historically, it is noted that "the organized Trade Union Movement in Nigeria dates back to 1912 when the workers in the Civil Service under the then Colonial administration organized themselves into workers representatives. This then became known as the Nigeria Civil Service Union. This became a pivot with which workers in other sectors began the agitation for the formation of Trade Unions before and after independence in 1960."[62] Thus it is not common today to find organizations, institutions or government parastatals in Nigeria without an umbrella that unifies them. The aim is primarily on public policy issues affecting workers and the society at large especially in the struggle against exploitation of the poor and the minority. During the military regimes, the movements were suppressed through the imposition of limitations on their capacity in negotiating or dialoguing with the military dictators. However, they contributed significantly in enthronement of democracy and civilian government in 1999.

Furthermore, the Trade Unions have since continued to heighten the consciousness of the general public towards socio-political and economic development in the form of campaigns and public awareness programmes. This consciousness is particularly based on pluralistic conception that advocates shared interests among interest groups in pursuit of common good either by way of dialogue or through conflict engagement. If positive agreement is not reached, the groups may embark on industrial actions or strikes and instigate others to join suit as have been evident in various strikes embarked by such movements like NLC, ASUU etc. And in some cases, such interest groups may initiate direct actions against the government or by way of civil disobedience. Perhaps one of the major loopholes associated with the movements' actions is that in some instances, some political elites can take advantage of the movements either to achieve their personal goals or as political weapons against their opponents. Thus, the ruling government often finds it very difficult to contend with the activities of such groups, because of the consequences they may have on social order and political stability.

---

[62] Nigeria Union of Petroleum and Natural Gas Workers (NUPENG): History of Trade Union in Nigeria. Lagos-Nigeria: NUPENG House, p. 1. http://nupeng.org/id17.html [accessed: 21.09.2010]

Hence one major setback on the activities of the interest groups is the government intervention and interference. For instance, the agitation of the Unions against the implementation of the Structural Adjustment Programme under the military junta of General Ibrahim Babangida in 1988 made the government to overtake the supervision of the Nigerian Labor Congress. The same authoritative attitude by the government was also carried-over by the civilian government. In that instance, Alalade notes that "under the current Civilian Democratic dispensation in Nigeria, government bases its relationship with Trade Unions on absolute authority. The ruling class strives to brandish the doctrine of sovereignty on all groups within and outside the country. Thus, threat of strikes notwithstanding, at the bargaining (or negotiating) table, government retains the power to accept, select or modify agreements between union representatives and government representatives."[63] In that case, the interference of the unions by the government has constituted the major obstacle in their operations. Therefore, unless a conducive environment is created so that the interest groups could function effectively and meet with the complex requirements and challenges in nation building and state formation, the groups will continue to be subjugated and in some instances, will remain an extension of government's institutions.

4.4   Conclusion

In this section, we have succeeded in analyzing the formation of state and political legacy in Nigeria before and after independence. Thus the state and political formation in Nigeria has been punctuated with different phases, ranging from colonial hegemony, military interceptions and the political elites 'indifference' to political integrity. Unfortunately, these phases have failed to guarantee stable political relationships; rather the bone of contention is the struggle for state power or may be referred to as privatization of state. On the one hand, I have argued that the ethnic formation and cultural pluralism in Nigeria portray a condition of violence and conflict that form political weapon in the struggle for power and supremacy. The high point of this struggle was the outcome of the Nigeria-Biafra civil war between 1967 and 1970 that left many wounds on na-

---

[63] Alalade, F. O. (2004): 'Trade Unions and Democratic Option in Nigeria'. In: Journal of Social Sciences Vol. 9, No. 3. Kamla-Raj, p. 201.

tional unity, and subsequently, the current political violence rocking the nation.

However, the problems of ethnicity, neo-patrimonial interests and religious inclinations coupled with the colonial legacies have thus far defined the foundation of institutional ineffectiveness in Nigeria. At this point, one must acknowledge the fact that the nature of state in Nigeria is composed of different interests, priorities and objectives. The harmonization of the different interest groups and ethnic identities has remained a major challenge to nation-building. On the other hand, I have also argued that the state remains the basic instance of accumulation that sustains different interests. It means that an access to the state power implies also an access to its resources. Hence to gain access to power becomes not necessarily on individual class identity struggle but on political mobilization either on regional, ethnic, or religious lines. Invariably, these appropriation lines are also compromised by the ruling classes in such a way that their patron-client structures are rightly promoted, thereby making them unable to see beyond immediate interests.

Finally, overlapped by significant influences of both internal and external forces, the fact remains that alienating the majority from political participation suppresses the basic tenets of liberal democracy. Instead the political conditions have widened the gap between the state elites and the common people. The truth is that the government should well define its political policies especially the unbalanced participations that exclude the larger percentage of the citizens. An important understanding of these facts is the unidentified boundary between public sphere and private sphere in institutional configuration. Therefore, if the political elites could isolate themselves from the state resources and attempt to build an environment of equal participation, that can ultimately aid in balancing the political landscape and creating more room for all-inclusive development of the state.

5   ECONOMIC DEVELOPMENTS AND GLOBAL INFLUENCE

In the last chapter, we x-rayed how the formation of state in Nigeria came to be an object of interplay between two major interests namely; the colonial hegemony and political elites' and ethnic's interests. This, of course has created diverse interests in the struggle for accumulation of wealth and power. In this chapter, we shall empirically focus on economic interests as the major determinant factor of global integration and domination of the state and its apparatuses. Although the development of a country's economy is considered as an important enterprise in promoting the general living condition of the populace, yet if the present economic policies in the country do not favor those they are meant for, then the organizational framework must be reconsidered. However, one could suggest that the advancement of modern economy in Nigeria is still on the process of evolution. Thus the formation and transition to modern economy is usually linked to the period of colonialism. Even though, prior to this period, the traditional economic structure, though not well developed according to the western conception, made some significant impacts in achieving local needs and domestic sustainability. Nevertheless, the integration of the Nigerian economic into capitalist modern economy, which started as a colonial legacy, served predominately the economic ends of the colonial powers as the source of raw materials for their industries. This economic provision of the colonial powers through capitalism unfortunately projected the colonial states to be the major source of profiteering and accumulation for the state elites.

Following the above conception, the colonial states became the avenues of capital accumulation for the would-be ruling elites. As a result of global integration that made the state the subject of accumulation, Paul rightly points out that "the state was never an economically neutral institution but rather the main actor and principal profiteer of an anything but free economy. And because it had to rely on local collaborators, be it for the recruitment of labor, the cultivation of cash crops, exploitation of mine or the levying of taxes, it became mixed with private interests, or 'patrimonialized', right from the beginning. The state, rather than a non-existent, or not yet existing, capitalist economy, became the main route for accumulation."[64] In fact, this primordially clandestine economic appropriation of the state was inherited by the post-colonial state elites, who increasingly continued to use the state to accumulate resources in pursuit of personal ends. Unfortunately, this economic arrangement seems to have exposed the Nigerian state into rent-seeking economy rather than achieving its developmental objectives on the well-being of the population. Hence analyzing the Nigerian economic development and its global influence basically portrays the relational crisis between the state elites or dominant classes and the majority poor in the bid for the struggle of state resources. This formation is consequent of the nature of institutional arrangement of the state. Thus, in this analysis, the result of the historical pattern of economic development and global influences is of compelling interest.

5.1   Incorporation into Global Economy

The incorporation of the Nigerian economy into global economy brought in new changes in the trends of trade and capital flow, which have continued to produce various impacts on the society development. Thus global economy and capitalism are seen as two sides of one and the same coin, where the purpose of production is basically for the possible realization of market profits.[65] In this perspective, the incorporation of most local (or subsistence) economies into global economy is predominantly influenced by Western market interests and trade contacts, which were aided by international economic policy interventions epitomized by the Bretton Woods institutions (i.e. International Monetary Fund and World Bank) in the 20th century. This process of integration extends beyond national boundaries, although it has since begun as early as 17th century with the introduction of slave trade, as well as the economic imperialism of the 19th century in the name of colonialism. However, it is truly after the fall of Soviet Union in the late 80s and early 90s that the global economy really ushered in a new phase of capitalist world economy.[66] In this

---

[64] Paul, Axel T. (2008): p. 219.

[65] See: Zündorf, Lutz (2008): Das Weltsystem des Erdöls: Entstehungszusammenhang, Funktionsweise, Wandlungstendenzen. Wiesbaden: VS Verlag für Sozialwissenschaften, S. 29.

[66] Akindele et al express that "it is germane to adumbrate that the collapse of the Eastern bloc in the late 80s and early 90s led to the emergence and ascendancy of a global econ-

new phase, many developing economies suffered losses (especially with the introduction of Structural Adjustment Policy), as trade and capital inflows continue to flourish and benefit some particular segments of world, leaving the others in a disadvantaged opportunity.

According to Callaghy, "in the 1980s Africa became more tightly linked to the world economy in two major respects: 1) by an extreme dependence on external public actors, particularly the IMF and the World Bank, in the determination of African economic policy; and 2) by the liberal or neoclassical thrust of this economic policy conditionality, which tried to push the continent toward more intense reliance on and integration with the world economy."[67] As a result, the Nigerian political elites willingly accepted the conditionalities of the global actors and then traded off the local entrepreneur in order to promote economic contacts with the global capitalists. Having become victims of the attractive global market and having realized that it was a quicker way of appropriation of state resources, there was no other choice rather than to maintain the trade contact even to the detriment of the economy and the local population. On the other hand, the dependence on the external economic actors especially the global institutions became a dominant factor in virtually every local economic policy interventions.

---

omy that is primarily structured and governed by the interests of Western behemoth countries, thus, facilitating the integration of most economies into the global capitalist economy. With the demise of the Eastern Europe in the early 90s, capitalism as an economic system now dominates the globe more than it had been at any time in its history. Even, China, by far the largest non-capitalist economy, has undergone dramatic changes in its international economic policy orientation, and, is today the recipient of almost one-half of all foreign direct investments that go into developing nations – this is a country that essentially blocked all foreign investments until the 1980s" (Akindele, S. T. /Gidado, T. O./Olaopo, O. R. (2002): 'Globalisation: Its Implications and Consequences for Africa'. In: Globalization Vol. 1, No. 2. Pueblo, USA: Colorado State University, pp. 1-20 (Published Online by the International Consortium for the Advancement of Academic Publication (ICAAP)). http://globalization.icaap.org/content/v2.1/01_akindele_etal.html [accessed: 28.06.2010]).

[67] Callaghy, Thomas (2000): 'Africa and the World Political Economy: More Caught Between a Rock and a Hard Place'. In: Harbeson, John W. /Rothchild, Donald (eds.): pp. 47-48.

148

The origin of dependency as illustrated by Chabal and Daloz lie within three distinct areas: "the continuation of economic connections with the former colonial powers; the place of Africa's economies in the world trade system; and the growth in international borrowing."[68] This dependency was thus "one of the chief instruments which enabled African elites to obtain the means to continue to feed the patrimonial system on which their power rested."[69] On the other hand, African governments through these patrimonial interests exploited the chance not minding the consequences such actions may have on the country's future economic development. Chabal and Daloz moreover identified two evidences to this very fact: "i) the ruling elites took a short-term economic view, seeking to maximize returns immediately rather than invest for future development [...]. They continue to rely for revenues on export of their traditional crops or minerals, thus merely increasing their country's dependence on outside markets and ii) they did not seriously pursue policies likely to diversify their economies, and thereby lessen their reliance on single exports."[70] This lack of diversification of the economy illustrates the very fact of Nigeria's heavy reliance on oil economy. This reliance on oil as the main foreign exchange (which shall be fully investigated later in this section) has constituted one of the major woes of the country's economic development.

In fact, studies have shown that the interests of the Multinational Oil Companies (MOCs) on the Nigerian oil and gas reserves have been the main facilitator of the nation's embrace to global market. Through the process of market expansion, the multinational corporations, who mainly represent the interests of their transnational states, exploit and control the local economies as well as wield much influence on the government economic policies.[71] Categorically, the exploitative activities of those trans-

---

[68] Chabal, Patrick/Daloz, Jean-Pascal (1999): Africa Works, p. 112.
[69] Chabal, Patrick/Daloz, Jean-Pascal (1999): Africa Works, p. 115.
[70] Chabal, Patrick/Daloz, Jean-Pascal (1999): Africa Works, p. 113.
[71] Anugwom observes that "the past two decades in Nigeria have witnessed a gradual but considerable control of the economy by foreign or multinational concerns representing largely external interests. Moreover, nowhere is this more pronounced than in the oil and civil construction industries where all the giant firms are multinational enterprises. Even where it appears as if Nigerians are in charge, they are nothing but the surrogates for the foreign owners" (Anugwom, Edlyne E (2007): Globalisation and Labour Utilisation in

national corporations provide a powerful framework in explaining the emergence of political and economic violent conflict hunting most African countries especially the case of Niger Delta region of Nigeria as an instance. Therefore, the implication of this formation is that the integration of Nigerian economy into global capitalist economy mostly driven by the oil sector of economy has fundamentally defined its trade contacts and policies, with the international trade interests taking precedence over the developmental interests of the state. At this point, this study will attempt to examine two propelling factors of global integration as it affects developing economy, namely: free market economy and structural adjustment.

5.1.1   Free Market Economy

The global economic integrations of local economies through trade contacts and financial flows have been the main characteristic of globalization. The dominant actor in this process of globalization is the policy changes occasioned by free market forces (or trade liberalization) that limit the state interventions to market principles. Here Chase-Dunn emphasizes that "under conditions of increased economic globalization, the ability of national states to protect their citizens from world market forces decreases. This results to increasing inequalities within countries, and increasing levels of dissatisfaction when compared to the relative harmony of national integration achieved under the Keynesian regimes."[72] Although the achievement of Keynesianism has not much to do with the global integration of the local economies, which gave rise to its abandonment in other to allow market regulation through the process of monetarist macro-economic policies and interplay of market forces. Yet this development later encouraged free market interaction as a fiscal policy and capital mobility that created more spaces for international investments. On the other hand, the Bretton Woods institutions, through their stringent free market policies such as deregulation, privatization, struc-

---

Nigeria: Evidence from the Construction Industry. In: Journal of Africa Development Vol. 32, No. 2. Council for the Development of Social Science Research in Africa (CODESRIA), p. 129).
[72] Chase-Dunn, Christopher (2000): p. 127.

tural adjustment etc. imposed conditionalities predominantly on the developing countries.

The imposition of free market policies on the developing economies came as a Marshall plan in deploying monetarist ideas and constraint, anything but prevalence of global capital investment, whereby the African countries for instance have minimal or no influence on free market capitalism. In this sense, free market is then conceived as a market economy driven by the profit orientation, which increasingly alter and decrease the traditional market forces. Thus, the comparative economic advantages and promises that the free market intended to achieve are rather punctuated with unequal market freedom and unequal rewards. In this way, Weiss and Thakur categorically state that "the rapid growth of global markets has not created a parallel development of social and economic institutions to ensure that they will function smoothly and efficiently, labor rights have been less assiduously protected than capital and property rights, and the global rules on trade and finance are unfair to the extent that they produce asymmetric effects in rich and poor countries."[73] Therefore, under the conditions of unequal market relationships and global asymmetries, the local economy is rather subjected to developmental deficiencies that deter the creation of wealth for the national population. In the end, the greater advantages of integration go to the money managers or the capitalists who control the global market economy under the framework of free trade.

5.1.2   Structural Adjustment Programme

Structural Adjustment Programme (SAP) as driven by the neoliberal economic approach to development was the major face of globalization especially in the developing World countries. It is aimed at transforming productivity measures and increasing market competitions through devaluation of currency, deregulation of market policies and exchange rates, and privatization of government and public utilities. Thus the programme was explained by Leftwich as "the generic term used to describe a pack-

---

[73] Weiss, Thomas G./Thakur, Ramesh C. (2010): Global Governance and the UN: An Unfinished Journey (The United Nations Intellectual History Project Series). Indiana: Indiana University Press, p. 35.

age of economic and institutional measures which the IMF, the World Bank and individual Western aid donors – singly, but more often in concert – sought to persuade many developing countries to adopt during the 1980 and 1990 in return for a new wave of policy-oriented loans."[74] With the introduction of SAP, it is projected that it will aid the increase of economic efficiency, market competition as well as help in achieving long-term economic development, though not without its stringent constraints on the local economies.

Specifically, structural adjustment was first introduced in Nigeria under the Economic Stabilisation Act of 1982. But it was only in the mid 80s that the federal government under the regime of General Ibrahim Babangida quickly embraced the SAP policy in its fullness, which may be explained in terms of pleasing the international community in order to legitimize the military junta. This is also not minding the restrictions the policy may impose especially on domestic economic distribution. The policy however brought in austerity measures as dominant market forces, which profoundly affected the cost of living, and also led to sharp cuts in public sector welfare, retrenchment of workers and cuts in employment capacity.

Paradoxically, the SAP instead of promoting economic growth rather opened up the doors for the military junta and political elites to loot the resources of the country through dubious means. It factionalized the political environment, initiating new identity politics and competition that subjected the country into economic crisis. In that way, Jega notes that the Nigerian state "[…] came to be afflicted by a devastating economic crisis, manifested in declining revenues from oil (e.g. from N10,915 million in 1985 to N8,107 million in 1986), a heavy debt burden, of about 20 billion US dollars [which rose to around 30 billion dollars in 1994], and a generalised crisis of production and the rapidly declining purchasing power of the incomes of the Nigerian workers due to inflation and a general decline in the production of goods and services in the Nigerian econ-

---

[74] Leftwich, Adrian (2000): pp. 109-110

152

omy."[75] In fact, the policy created new form of consumer dependency on the foreign goods with little or no corresponding local market to meet with the global market competition. This phenomenon was what plunged the country into external debt crisis with the fall of gross national product (GNP) per capita from $1,160 in 1980 to about $564 in 2005.

In addition, the adjustment policy also affected various sectors of the economy and different population groups. On the one hand, the impact was more evident in the production capacity and the reduction in operation input of the local manufacturing industries. On that note, Onyeonoru vividly observes that "in terms of size, the Food, Beverage and Tobacco industry experienced contraction in its structure in the SAP era, from 80 companies in 1986 to 69 in 1992 [though only 26 were identified as thriving on account of their after-tax profit and return on capital employed] with intermittent rises and falls. In the industry, the beverage sub-sector was worse hit with the survival of 25 companies in 1992 compared with 40 in 1986."[76] On the other hand, studies have shown that the inability of the adjustment programme to produce intended results affected mostly the women in urban and rural sectors. According to Pereira "the effect of the economic crisis and of SAP, whilst debilitating for the majority of the population, women as well as men, have been more punitive for most groups of women than for men, given the multiple demands and responsibilities facing women."[77] These multiple demands really show that most domestic inputs and outputs are carried out by women and as such the tension created by the programme subjected most of them to poverty and exposed them to socioeconomic vulnerability. Consequently, it increased women trafficking, which is associated with international prostitutions in the bid to earn a living. On that basis, quite numbers of women are de-

---

[75] Jega, Attahiru (2000): 'The State and Identity Transformation under Structural Adjustment in Nigeria'. In: Jega, Attahiru (ed.): Identity Transformation and Identity Politics under Structural Adjustment in Nigeria. Stockholm, Sweden: Elanders Gotab, p. 29.
[76] Onyeonoru, Ifeanyi P. (2003): 'Globalisation and Industrial Performance in Nigeria'. In: Journal of Africa Development Vol. 28, No. 3 and 4. Dakar: Council for the Development of Social Science Research in Africa (CODESRIA), p. 58.
[77] Pereira, Charmaine (2000): 'National Council of Women's Societies and the State, 1985-1993: The Use of Discourses of Womanhood by the NCWS'. In: Jega, Attahiru (ed.): Identity Transformation and Identity Politics under Structural Adjustment in Nigeria. Stockholm, Sweden: Elanders Gotab, p. 109.

ported annually, constituting also a social burden to the society. This implies as well that their integration into the society amounts to great social problem not only for the government who has no concrete plan for them, but also for their relatives who may be subjected to all sorts of moral litigation associated with prostitution.

Therefore, the unsuccessful implementation of SAP was predominantly based on its imposed conditionalities, which were not suitable in the Nigerian context in accelerating immediate economic growth. Also the weak economic structure of the Nigerian state neither guaranteed economic interventions when it was needed nor withstood the policy impositions. The policy was also not able to limit the accumulation routes of the state elites. Instead of transforming the economy, the structural adjustment rather created uneasiness in the economic transformation. Hence according to Stein, "while structural adjustment has exacerbated the underlying weaknesses of African economies, its greatest crime is located in its inherent inability to structurally and institutionally transform African economies. The major reason can be found in its roots that lie in neoclassical economic theory with its misplaced emphasis on balancing financial variables in a hypothetical axiomatic world. Adjustment is simply incapable of either assessing the nature of Africa's problems or putting in place the policies that will put the continent on a trajectory of sustainable development."[78] It follows that the policy agenda of SAP was regrettably never open for negotiation and debate among the general public due to the authoritarian military regime that saw it as an opportunity for legitimation (i.e. an avenue of appeasing the West in order to say in power), coupled with the problem of corruption that bedevilled the policy's implementation. As such, the organized civil society groups that either ventured to protest or agitate against the implementation of structural adjustment programme were either intimidated, suppressed, or humiliated. These are all consequences of globalization. Thus far, in a more specific instance, this mode of global integration leads us to examine the performance of the Nigerian economy in the recent times.

---

[78] Stein, Howard (2006): 'Rethinking African Development'. In: Chang, Ha-Joon (ed.) Rethinking Development Economics. London and New York: Anthem Press, p. 153.

5.2   Economic Performance since Independence

The development of Nigerian economy since independence has been marked with instability and lack of proper policy agendas to swing up the pendulum for sustainable growth. This deficiency is majorly characterized by the non diversification of the economy or rather put as consequence of dependency on one major sector of the economy especially for foreign exchange and fiscal development. Focusing particular attention on the basic structures and the policies and events which have contributed to economic development and vice versa, this analysis with the features of the economy in the era of globalization serves as a useful background for the construction, estimation, and simulation of the model of the Nigerian economy.

However, there have been number of attempts to expand and diversify the economy through series of developmental economic plans, which fed well at initial stage of implementation with strong potentials and promises for long-term growth, but unforeseeably went into crisis formation since the discovery of oil in commercial quantity. Thus, given the conditions of the economy after independence, and given the phenomena that characterized its heavy dependency on oil and dominant character of the global capitalism through policy reversals and lack of proper state regulatory framework, it has become increasingly clear that the economic growth in Nigeria is relatively poor as evidence in the growth of GDP per capita when compared to other countries.

Table 2.1: Comparing Average Annual Growth Rate of GDP per Capita (PPP), 1980-2006

Countries	% Growth Rate
Nigeria	0.0
Indonesia	3.6
Pakistan	2.5
East Asia and Pacific	6.6
Sub-Saharan Africa	0.0
World	1.6

Source: World Development Indicator (WDI) 2008.

Empirically, when one compares the economic growth in Nigeria with other countries of relative economic strength and population, it shows that the growth rate of Nigeria's GDP per capita remains very low as an indicative of poor economic development (see Table 2.1). Between 1980 and 2006, table 2.1 indicates that a country like Indonesia had annual growth rate of 3.6% and Pakistan 2.5% respectively, with Nigeria showing no impressive growth within the two decades but has only remained stagnant. When this is compared with the previously GDP annual growth which stood at an average rate of 6.9% per year between 1965 and 1980, it indicates that the Nigerian economy was initially very variable. The recent decrease in development however is evident in the decline in agricultural productivity, increase of domestic prices and high population growth. Or that could also be attributed to the consequence of the country's economic concentration propelled by the oil dependency at the expense of the development of the other sectors of the economy that would have sustained the growth rate.

Figure 2.1: Comparing Average Annual Growth Rate of GDP per Capita (PPP), 1975-2005

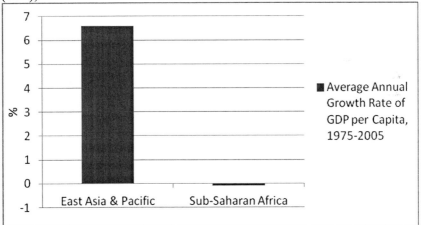

Source: World Development Indicator 2008.

Similarly, figure 2.1 shows the average annual growth rate of GDP per capita from 1975 to 2005 in comparative terms between East-Asia & Pacific and Sub-Saharan Africa. The time frame of this indicator is within the period in which most nations in Sub-Saharan Africa gained their in-

156

dependence as well as integrated into global economy. Whereas East Asia and Pacific countries have made progressive changes of about 6.6% GDP growth within the period, Sub-Saharan African countries have remained redundant with average annual growth rate of -0.1%. However, this wide developmental gap between East Asia/Pacific and Sub-Saharan African is described by some analysts as East Asian 'miracle' and the Sub-Saharan African 'debacle'. It is not surprise to note that the structure of Sub-Saharan African economies has probably not allowed a progressive development. This indicator is also very significant in understanding the structure of Nigerian economy. Even though it was not only Nigeria that suffered economic decline within the given period, yet, this illustration is quite importance, because Nigeria stands as one of the major economic growth determinants in the Sub-Saharan regions due to her highest rate of population and natural resources.

Figure 2.2: Nigeria GDP - Real Growth Rate (2000-2010)

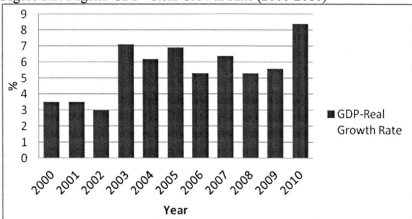

On the national basis, there seem to be some progressive indications of growth of GDP currently in Nigeria as a result of increased performance of the non-oil sector, especially in agricultural sector and service deliveries. But the greatest challenge of the growth is its sustenance through the process of investments that can widen the economic horizons. Thus figure 2.2 illustrates the GDP growth on an annual basis adjusted by inflation as expressed in percentage. The real growth rate is illustrated here in order to show the economic progress since the return to civilian administration in 1999. Although when the economy is generally measured by the Real GDP growth rate on a cumulative basis from 2000 to 2010, it shows that the economy has been relatively unstable and inconsistent. However, between 2000 and 2002, there was absolutely no real growth of the GDP, but it experienced comparatively greater changes during the periods between 2003 and 2005 with an average of 6.73% growth rate, slide in 2006 to 5.3% but increased again to 6.4% in 2007 with slight decrease in 2008 and 2009. In 2010, the GDP real growth increased to 8.4%, indicating its highest point in the decade. Hence this growth could be associated with the moderate weather conditions that improved the agricultural harvests, and relatively reduced the cost of local food supply on total aggregate. But when this GDP growth is considered on visible levels especially its impact on the living conditions of the population, then, it is where one begins to have much misgiving on the economic development. In that sense, the visible outcome of the growth has rarely significant manifestation on the general economic welfare.

Table 2.2: Percentage Distribution of Sectoral Contribution to GDP in Real Terms (at 1990 basic prices), 2001-2006

Sectors	2001	2002	2003	2004	2005	2006
Agriculture	34.32	43.89	42.60	40.98	41.19	41.72
Oil and Gas	31.49	24.47	27.50	25.72	24.26	21.85
Distributive Trade	12.39	10.87	10.43	12.90	13.75	14.95
Manufacturing	4.18	3.79	3.64	3.68	3.79	3.91
Others*	17.61	16.97	15.83	16.71	17.00	17.56
Total	100.00	100.00	100.00	100.00	100.00	100.00

*Source: National Bureau of Statistics (Note: *Others include Solid Mineral Mining, Utilities, Hotels & Restaurants, Transportation, Communication, Finance & Insurance, Business Services and Government Services. Since 2003, there has been a decline in the contributions of these sectors to real GDP)*

Moreover, table 2.2 shows the percentage distribution of sectoral contribution to GDP in real terms from 2001 to 2006 based on 1990 prices. The contribution to growth in 2006 was driven primarily by the non-oil sector, which is attributed to increase in distributive trade sector and agricultural sector. On the other hand, oil and gas sector that fed relatively well in 2001 continues to fall from 2002 due to changes in crude oil prices as well as crisis situation in Niger Delta region. Currently, oil and gas input

158

has made comparative progress as a result of the amnesty programme that seems to have restored peace in the Niger-Delta region, as well as slight increase in oil production within the period. Nevertheless, there is also the tendency and speculation that with the emphasis on macroeconomic development of non-oil sectors such as agriculture, tourism, telecommunications, domestic trade etc. it could improve the economic performance that could also accelerate constant drop in the rate of inflation. Though the needed attention required for significant changes in the share of non-oil sectors of the economy in total GDP in the recent times has not been impressive, since much concentration has been paid on oil foreign exchange income as against improving the domestic income productions.

Figure 2.3: Average Rate of Inflation (1980-2011)

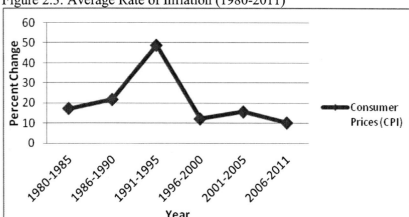

Source: International Monetary Fund – 2011 World Economic Outlook

In addition, average rate of inflation as shown in Figure 2.3 based on changes of commodity prices and the corresponding changes in trade policies is officially placed at about 10.8% in 2011 as against 9.97% in 1980. There was visible improvement to single digit in 1982, but rose continuously from 1983 after the military takeover of the government and the subsequent introduction of SAP that affected the consumer price index. However, the statistics are based on a comparative term between the military regime that ended in 1999 and the return to civilian dispensation. The commodity prices were higher before the democratic government, affecting the rate of inflation; but relatively stabilized from 2006 and with the tendency for much improvement in the value of trade, though the rate of inflation still remains high. On the other hand, unenviable status of the naira as a currency with indeterminable value continues to be a 'hydra-headed problem' pushing high the rate of inflation, budget deficit, and generally stagnant and vulnerable economic activities. The Nigerian currency is constantly depreciating against the US Dollar in the last two decades in exchange market. In other words, a strong and extended downward movement of the exchange rates through reforms can basically reduce inflation, most especially since Nigeria depends mainly on import of finished goods which has also strong implications for the foreign reserves and economic growth.

Be that as it may, the fundamental attribute of the Nigerian economy is that majority of the population are still very poor, with the household income per capita among the poorest in the world. This attribute, which will be fully examined in the next chapter, suggests an unequal distribution of economic resources and poor policy choices that have hindered redistribution of the economy. However, there have not been much serious signals at the moment to show that the future economic options will perform significant miracles. This is judging from the present structure of economic and political trends, particularly the mismanagement of the economy by the corrupt leaders, the constant threat by political instability as well as the exploitation of the market inflows by the global capitalists.

Following that perspective, one can suggest that what might be the root cause of poor economic development in Nigeria is consequent of its weak foundation. On the one hand, the economic structures that were inherited from different colonial regimes were fashioned mostly to satisfy the colonial's accumulation interests and that of the political elites. As such, the economy was not diversified, concentrating majorly on raw materials for export and for few industries with little manufacturing capabilities. This undiversified economy diminished the participation of the country in the flow of direct foreign investment. On the other hand, most of the policy choices of the colonial administration did not lay strong foundation that could aid future economic options coupled with the inability of the political elites to withstand the enormous challenges in pushing for lasting economic policies within the specific time frame. Even the later efforts of the government to rebound the economy through embracing and implementation of the structural adjustment programme also went into dead-

160

lock due to the unfavorable environment to contain the conditionalities imposed by the policies. Therefore, the numerous economic failures of the federal government are predominately linked with poor policy implementation combined with instability, poor governance and corruption, and the external economic influences associated with capitalism. Thus, we shall further attempt to examine empirically certain significant and major sectors of the economy, both formal and informal as well as some aspects of the Nigerian economy that can aid in establishing an appropriate framework to the topic of discussion.

5.2.1   Oil and Gas Economy

The oil and gas sector plays a determinant role in the Nigerian economy, overwhelmingly accounting for major foreign exchange earnings. In a brief historical development, the exploration of oil in Nigeria began in 1938 with the 'Royal Dutch Shell' and the British Petroleum (BP). But it was only discovered in commercial quantity in the Niger-Delta region in 1956. It was after the independence that the Nigerian government granted licenses to other oil companies. From 1958 more than 1,481 oil wells have sprung up, producing about 159 oil fields. With about 13 oil companies in operation, there are more than 7,000 kilometres of pipelines and flow lines, and 275 flow stations, with up to seven terminals for export.[79] By 1965, the Nigerian government established a 'Joint Venture' with Shell and BP and expanded production to the export market. With the Organization of Petroleum Exporting Countries (OPEC) resolution in 1968, that each oil-producing country is obliged to uphold greater share of production, the Nigerian National Oil Corporation (NNOC) was founded in 1971 to control the sector.

Since the oil-boom in the late 1970s, much of the particular colour of events have principally been shaded by the impact of oil revenues accruing from exportation of crude oil from the Niger Delta lands and deeper water offshore, controlled by the Nigerian National Petroleum Corporation (NNPC) (founded in 1979) in joint venture with other major oil

---

[79]See: United Nations Development Programme (2006): Niger Delta Human Development Report. Garki-Abuja: UNDP Nigeria, p. 75. http://web.ng.undp.org/reports /nigeria_hdr_report.pdf [accessed: 08.02.2009]

companies. Presently, the Niger-Delta region is the main base of oil and gas reserve in Nigeria. The region covers an area of about 70,000 kilometers, which comprises of the nine oil-producing states: Akwa Ibom, Bayelsa, Delta, Rivers, Cross River, Edo, Abia, Imo and Ondo; of which Rivers, Bayelsa, Delta and Akwa Ibom constitute the major oil-producing states.

Figure 2.4: Nigerian Crude Oil Production, 1980-2004 (includes Lease Condensate)

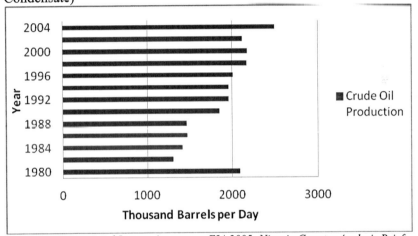

Source: Environmental Impact Assessment EIA 2005: Nigeria Country Analysis Brief

As one of the largest producers and exporters of crude oil in the continent and in the world, with proven reserves of about 25 billion barrels, Nigeria plays a predominant role in the global oil market and one of the leading members of the OPEC. Figure 2.4 indicates the crude oil production from 1980 to 2004 within the range of OPEC regulations. It shows a constant increase in production from 1990 but experienced slight decrease in 2002, which may be attributed to pipe line vandalization and the routine maintenance of production equipment. Besides, billions of Dollars have been generated as revenue in the last three decades due to high demand of oil in the world market. Williams notes that "today, production exceeds two million barrels per day, or 60.3 million per month, making Nigeria, a member of OPEC, the world's sixth-biggest oil provider. The majority of the Nigeria's crude oil is exported to Europe, Asia and the USA. The low-sulphur content of much of Nigeria's oil makes it especially desira-

162

ble in a pollution-conscious world. At present oil revenues constitute over 95% of Nigeria export earnings, 90% of foreign-currency earnings and 85% of total government revenue (over US$50 billion in 2006)."[80] Besides, statistics indicates that the greater number of oil production are exported for foreign exchange, leaving just little for local utilization.

Unfortunately, Nigeria's production and exportation capacity in crude oil, which have substantial increased, have not impacted significantly on the life of the poor population due to corruption and unstable price of crude in the world market. In other words, the amount of revenues generated from crude oil has not really translated into social development. In fact, the negative impact is particularly visible in the living conditions of people in the oil producing areas, causing crisis of resource struggle. Though there is currently concerted effort on the part of the federal government to address the situation through the resolution of the crisis and the introduction of amnesty developmental programme for the Niger-Delta.

Figure 2.5: Nigerian Natural Gas Production, 1980-2002

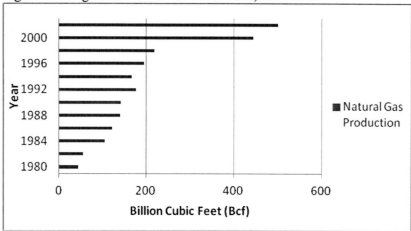

Source: Environmental Impact Assessment EIA 2005: Nigeria Country Analysis Brief

On the other hand, harnessing the natural gas has been a great challenge to economic reform in Nigeria. Over the years, there has been constant

---

[80] Williams, Lizzie (2008): Nigeria: The Bradt Travel Guides 2nd Edition. USA: The Globe Pequot Press Inc., p. 27.

increase in liquefied natural gas (LNG) production as illustrated in figure 2.5. The figure however shows that since 1980, billions of cubic feet (Bcf) production of gas has been explored reaching its peak in 2002. However, from Oil and Gas report of 2005, Nigeria is estimated to have about 176 trillion cubic feet (Tcf) of proven natural gas reserves mainly located on Bonny Island. With this estimation, Nigeria is expected to be one of the largest producers of natural gas on the global rating. But this expectation depends on the proper utilization of the gas reserves, which can also reduce drastically the greater quantity of gas-flared, as well as minimize environmental hazards. As such, the Nigerian government through the Nigeria Liquefied Natural Gas Corporation (NLNG) is expected to increase the production capacity of natural gas both for local and export earnings.

Subsequently, at the downstream petrochemical industry, there are four refineries and hydrocarbon productions in Nigeria located at Eleme, Warri, and Kaduna. Nevertheless, due to poor maintenance, improper operation and lack of adequate power supply, the production output of these refineries has considerably reduced. The implication of the refineries inefficiency has been frequent importation of finished petroleum products even at very expensive prices. As a result, it predominantly affects and reduces the foreign direct investment and exchange rate. Currently, the government is campaigning for the full removal of petroleum subsidy for the local consumptions in order to improve the efficiency of the refineries and other developmental needs of the country. But whether that can achieve its purpose and not another way of subjecting the poor population to more hardship becomes the burning question.

5.2.1.1 The Scale of Dependency on Oil Economy

The paradox surrounding oil discovery in Nigeria has played out with many analysts questioning the rationale behind oil economy. In analyzing such controversy, Joseph points out that "there is a well-known story that is regularly acted out in many countries of the world. An individual suddenly wins a large fortune – from a lottery or horse race – and is catapulted from rags to riches. After a few years of dissipation, the money has been squandered, the physical and mental health of the 'nouveau riche' broken, and the glorious future of unlimited possibilities constricted into a bleak vista of regret and recrimination. At the moment of exhilaration, what the person concerned – understandably enough – failed to recognize was that the danger such sudden wealth represented was no less great than the dazzling promise. At this point the winner of the lottery might distinguish the mirage from the grudging reality and act to stem the downward slide."[81] This story could however be likened to the oil boom and scale of oil dependent economy in Nigeria. Since mid 1970s, the Nigerian economy has remained dependent on oil and gas with little diversification because of its quick revenues. Not surprisingly, this unhealthy dependence on oil as the major revenue base has consequences on other previously important sectors of the economy that initially accounted for both domestic and external earnings such as agriculture, mining and manufacturing.

In other words, Ihonvbere observes that "the export concentration led to the direct neglect of agriculture and of course, the rural areas and rural people. Thus, while crude oil account for 2.7 percent of Nigeria's exports in 1960 and non-oil exports accounted for 97.3 percent, by 1975 oil was accounting for 97.6 percent and non-oil exports 2.5 percent. By 1985, the situation had not changed much as oil accounted for 95.8 percent of total exports, while non-oil exports accounted for only 4.2 percent. In 1990, oil accounted for 97 percent and non-oil export accounted for only 3.0 percent."[82] Presently, there have not been significant changes in diversifying the export substitutes in order to avoid much concentration on oil. Due to heavy dependence on oil, the budgetary expenditures are majorly determined by the price of crude oil in the global market. This is quite significant in the sense that oil has become the most strategic commodity for Nigeria's international trade contact.

In a similar manner, oil price movement in the global market also determines the direction of the nation's GDP growth per capita. If the oil price contracts, the GDP growth contracts as well. This phenomenon was evidence during the height of the recent global economic/financial crisis between 2008 and 2009. In fact, the crisis had an immense impact on the

---

[81] Joseph, Richard A. (1978): Affluence and Underdevelopment: The Nigerian Experience. In: The Journal of Modern African Studies Vol. 16, No. 2. Cambridge: University Press, p. 221.
[82] Ihonvbere, Julius O. (1994): p. 22.

Nigerian economy because of the decline in global crude oil prices that affected the GDP growth. When we observe the GDP real growth rate as illustrated in figure 2.2, it affirms that there was significant decrease in real growth rate of the economy in 2008 and 2009, and the same period also experienced an increase rate of inflation consequent of oil price decline. This movement in prices had also adverse effects on the commodity price changes, which disadvantaged especially the poor in income distribution.

Moreover, dependency on oil-economy has large implications on social and economic development as well as the increase in vulnerability of commodity price shocks especially on rural households. Studies have shown that the greater the dependency on oil resources, the worse the socio-economic development. Many economists referred to that as the 'curse of oil' economy or the 'paradox of plenty' in comparative market economy. Unfortunately, the production capacity expansion over the years has not had much impact on socio-economic development especially on the rising trends of inequality and poverty. Instead it has plunged the country into crisis of development with continued increase in corruption and fall in the standard of living.

In fact, Karl may be right when he observed that "countries dependent on oil as their major resource for development are characterized by corruption and exceptionally poor governance, a culture of rent seeking, often devastating economic, health, and environmental consequences at the local level, and high incidences of conflict and war. In sum, countries that depend on oil for their livelihood eventually become among the most economically troubled, the most authoritarian, and the most conflict-ridden in the world."[83] These characteristics may be linked to the Nigeria's reliance on oil rent, which may be seen as a curse rather than a blessing. In short, the situation has pushed the country into a form of rentier state with weak structures, lack of accountability, lack of political will on the part of the state elites to drive the economy, security challenges and poor institutional arrangements. It is not surprising, judging from the fact that any incoming political regime would always try to consoli-

---

[83] Karl, Terry Lynn (2004): 'Oil-Led Development: Social, Political, and Economic Consequences'. In: Encyclopedia of Energy Vol. 4. Elsevier Inc, pp. 661-662.

date its powers and patronage protection through the resource accumulation from oil revenues to the detriment of the greater number of the population. Therefore, it will be a difficult task to improve on the economic performance if oil dependency remains undiversified, which implies that its consequences on socio-economic development will continue to be felt especially by the poor majority of the population.

5.2.1.2 The Strength of Multinational Oil Company

The foremost Multinational Oil Companies in Nigeria are known as Oil Majors which include: Shell Petroleum Development Company of Nigeria Ltd. (SPDC) that is a subsidiary of Royal Dutch Shell (with more than 40 percent of the total Nigerian oil production capacity and 14% of its total global operations), ExxonMobil, Chevron-Texaco, the Italian company Agip and France's Elf-Aquitaine (commonly known as Elf). There are also some other indigenous oil companies such as Dubril Oil Company, Peak Petroleum Limited, Atlas Petroleum International Limited, Consolidated Oil Limited, Amalgamated Oil Limited etc. that the federal government later gave operation license. This was in order to encourage local participation; though their production capacities are comparatively quite minimal.

The multinational companies operate in Nigeria under a joint venture with NNPC on behalf of the federal government. The joint venture implies that due to the capital intensive of the technological requirements for oil production, the government partners with the multinational oil corporations in the exploration by acquiring the major asset and liability. The joint venture began in 1973 with 35% share from all the multinational oil corporations by the NNOC, which later increased to 55%. In 1979, the share was increased to 60% by the federal government under the control of NNPC. All these were intended to minimize funding of the sector by the government and to have dominance over the oil, which aimed at regulating the market as well as avoiding the monopoly of the multinationals. Notwithstanding, only Shell controls almost half the production of oil in Nigeria with other companies sharing the remaining contract production arrangements with sizeable interests in dominating the export market.

The strength of the Oil Majors in influencing the economy of Nigerian state could be likened to the dominant nature of the core regions over the periphery regions in the world capitalist system. This is because; these multinational companies represent the economic interests of the core nations especially Europe and America. In other words, the main interests of the multinational oil firms consist of constant exploration to satisfy their economic needs and those of their native countries, with little or no consideration on the natural environment of the indigenous oil communities. Because they have the freedom to explore and then to exploit the environment, monitoring and control their operations by the federal government are usually limited. Again, judging from the fact that the government depends on their production for the national economic growth especially yearly budgetary allocations, they tend to operate at the whims and caprices of the host communities.

Table 2.3: Major Nigerian Oil Production Ventures

OPERATOR (%INTEREST)	OTHER PARTNERS (%IN-TEREST)	NNPC (%IN-TEREST)	MAJOR PRODUCING FIELDS	PRODUC-TION BPD(EST. 2003)
Shell (30%)	TotalFinaEl f (10%) Agip (5%)	55%	Bonny or Eastern Division- Nembe, Cawthorn Channel, Ekulama, Imo River, Kolo Creek, Adibawa and Etelelbou. Forcados or Western Division – Forcados Yorki, Jonas Creek, Olomoro,Otumara, Sapele, Egwa and Odidi.	950,000
ExxonMobil (40%)	None	60%	Edop, Ubit, Oso, Unam and Asasa	500,000
Chevron Texaco (40%)	None	60%	Meren, Okan, Benin River, Delta/Delta South, Inda, Meji and Robertkiri, Funiwa, Middleton, North Apoi, Pennenton and Sengana	485,000
Agip (20%)	Phillips (20%)	60%	Obama, Obiafu, M'Bede, Abugara and Oshi	150,000
TotalFinaElf (40%)	None	60%	Obagi, Aghigo, Okpoko, Upomani, Afia, and Obodo Jatumi	150,000

Source: Environmental Impact Assessment EIA 2005: Nigeria Country Analysis Brief

Table 2.3 shows the operational status of major oil companies in Nigeria as compiled by the US Government through Environmental Impact Assessment in April 2003. From the table, it indicates the interest shares of different oil companies with the NNPC holding 60% share of interests over the Oil Majors. But that notwithstanding, those companies continue to determine the mode of operations and production as well as having the control over the oil economy. Also due to transparency problem and corruption, it is quite difficult to estimate correctly the amount of revenue or income accruing either to the oil companies or to the Nigerian financial reserves. A lot of irregularities and thefts are associated with the oil production in Nigeria especially the incessant diversion of oil through bunkering.

Moreover, from the report by the Climate Justice Programme and Environmental Rights Action/Friends of the Earth Nigeria, it emphasizes that "the main hallmarks of the development of the Nigerian oil and gas industry over the last 50 years, apart from its internationally-notorious environmental and human rights record, have been two-fold: a) significant production by foreign oil companies – first of oil, and now increasingly of gas – the vast majority of which has been exported to the developed world for billions of dollars, and b) the fattening of a corrupt elite, as the vast majority of Nigerians fail to benefit which results to the fact that the country becomes one of the world's poorest. This has also deliberately eroded community values and systems which would have allowed communities to challenge company practices."[84] Likewise, because the majority of the country's foreign exchange is derived from oil, the federal government is not really eager to review the production policies of oil extractions. As a result, the Nigeria Extractive Industry Transparency Initiative (NEITI) bill that was passed into law in 2007 to account for transparency and accountability in extraction has neither prevented misappropriation of the oil revenues nor proper monitoring of the sector due to poor implementation. Similarly, the proposed Petroleum Industry Bill (PIB) since 2009 to review transparency, state participation and contractual agreement has not been passed into law. However, the bill has been vehemently opposed by the multinational oil companies and the big

---

[84] Asume, Osuoka/Roderick, Peter (2005): Gas Flaring in Nigeria: a Human Rights, Environmental and Economic Monstrosity (A report by the Climate Justice Programme and Environmental Rights Action/Friends of the Earth Nigeria). Amsterdam: The Climate Justice Programme, p. 8. http://www.foe.co.uk/resource/reports/gas_flaring_nigeria.pdf [accessed: 26.05.2009]

indigenous oil-dealers as a result of its new tax regime proposal. It is hoped that if the bill is passed into law, it can reduce government funding, increase production capacity and protect the environment against risks and pollution.

The oil benefits unfortunately go mainly to the multinational oil companies and the few corrupt political elites that use their accumulated wealth from oil to maintain their vertical patron-client relationships. Cooper aptly states that "instead of providing capital for the diversification and the industrialization of the Nigerian economy, oil revenues were used above all for the primary task of the political elites: patronage."[85] In other words, Zündorf categorically expresses that "dabei benutzen politische Machthaber den öffentlichen Sektor dazu, Ressourcen zugunsten von Partikularinteressen umzuverteilen, das heißt auf eigene Familie, die eigene Sippe, den eigenen Stamm, die eigene Ethnie, auf deren Loyalität sie ihre Herrschaft gründen."[86] This implies that the distribution of oil resources is usually governed by the interests of the political elites. On the other hand, the sharing or allocation of oil blocks to companies and individuals notwithstanding the introduction of open bidding in 2005, and then the associated oil revenues, which are mostly based on affiliation or compensation for political purposes, have also indicted government's transparency in economic development. Therefore, with the passage of the Freedom of Information bill into law in May 2011, there is also the hope that it can checkmate the government's financial misappropriations which have long been shrouded in secrecy.

5.2.2 Agricultural Sector

The role of agricultural sector in a nation's economic growth cannot be overemphasized. Nigeria is endowed with high potentials for agricultural activities with rich land, moderate weather conditions and human capital to propel sufficient production. Prior to the discovery of oil in Nigeria in larger quantity, agriculture was the main source of foreign exchange and domestic income earnings. Some of these agricultural products include crops such as cocoa, cassava, corn, yam, millet, groundnuts, rice, sor-

---

[85] Cooper, Frederick (2002): Africa since 1940: The Past of the Present. Cambridge: Cambridge University Press, p. 173.

[86] Zündorf, Lutz (2008): p. 155.

ghum etc.; trees such as palm oil, rubber, mango, trees for timber etc.; and Livestock such as cattle, pigs, goats, sheep, chickens etc. However, cash-crops were introduced during the colonial era by the Western economic regime in order to sustain local and foreign consumption. Though these according to Jarmon "suppressed traditional communalistic systems of subsistence agriculture and brought the indigenous economy into a dependent relationship with the modern world system. This had the effect of changing the traditional arrangement between production, distribution and consumption [...]. Yet, cash-cropping accelerated specialization and advanced it to such levels that between and within regions various locations became identified with the products which they produce. Lumber and plywood mills, for example, became identified with Sapele; groundnuts became identified with Kano and its environs; palm products became associated with the Ibadan-Ogbomosho environs."[87] In this period, Nigeria could boast of being self-sufficient both in consumption and distribution. Coupled with cash cropping, many subsistence farmers maintained their production, offering larger proportion of total food consumption requirements available to feed the growing population.

Unfortunately, the development of agriculture was short-lived due to the discovery of oil and industrial boom in the mid 1970s. The oil discovery however diverted the attention of the political elites from the development of agricultural sector as the main wealth of the nation.[88] The agricultural sector that initially accounted for the major export earnings has dropped drastically with low productivity and little expansion in the recent times. In other words, the low share of export earnings coming from agriculture reflects the heavy reliance of the Nigerian economy on single non-renewable resources. Most agricultural activities have remained un-

---

[87] Jarmon, Charles (1988): Nigeria: Reorganization and Development since the Mid-Twentieth Century (Monographs and Theoretical Studies in Sociology and Anthropology in Honour of Nels Anderson). The Netherlands: E. J. Brill Leiden, Publication 23, pp. 21-23.

[88] Diamond observes that "the central economic problems faced by Nigeria at Independence were that the agricultural sector was largely ignored by political leaders in their obsession with all things modern, and that growth would require a level of discipline, savings, and sacrifice that the people seemed little disposed to endure and the politicians had no intention of proposing in a political system that demanded immediate and tangible improvements" (Diamond, Larry (1988): p. 83).

derdeveloped with vast majority of farmers cultivating predominately for the immediate needs of their families. And because of the rapid growth of the population, the minimal indigenous production has remained unable to sustain the domestic needs, subjecting the country to rely on importation of most food products.

However, it has been observed that through proper funding, agricultural productivity could easily be diversified. This is because; it has the potential of involving greater number of the population through which employment opportunity could be created. On that note, the World Bank observes that "agriculture employs about two-thirds of Nigeria's total labour force, contributed 42.2% of Gross Domestic Products (GDP) in 2007; and provides 88% of non-oil earnings. The agricultural GDP is contributed by crops (85%), livestock (19%), fisheries (4%) and forestry (1%). More than 90% of the agricultural output is accounted for by small-scale farmers with less than two (2) hectares under cropping. It is estimated that about 75% (68 million ha) of the total land area has potential for agricultural activities with about 33 million hectares under cultivation. Similarly, of the estimated 3.14 million hectares irrigable land area, only about 220,000 ha (7%) is utilized."[89] In fact, the main challenge that faces the sector is on how to utilize the available agricultural land and develop the method of production to enhance commercial mechanized farming activities. On the other hand, the major constraint to agricultural development is that the mode of agricultural productivity has virtually remained the same old methods without much commitment and investment on the part of the government. Even most of the agricultural installations such as farming machines are now dilapidated due to lack of maintenance. As a result, productivity has not grown sufficiently and which could as well be attributed to underinvestment and slow adoption of modern agricultural technology to boost growing demands.

---

[89] World Bank (2008): Project Appraisal Document on a Proposed Credit In The Amount of SDR 100.7 Million (US$150million Equivalent) to the Federal Republic of Nigeria for Commercial Agriculture Development Project. Report No: 46830-NG, p. 1. http://cadpnigeria.org/documentation/Project%20Appraisal%20Document.pdf [accessed: 16.02.2010]

Similarly, the World Bank broadly explains that "the vast majority of farmers produce mainly food crops using traditional extensive cultivation methods, while commercial agriculture based on modern technologies and purchased inputs remains underdeveloped. The capacity of the agricultural research system has eroded in recent years, as has that of the agricultural extension service. As a result, even when improved technology is available, often it fails to reach farmers. Farmers' lack of technical knowledge is compounded by deficiencies in distribution systems for purchased inputs, which limit the timely availability of improved seed, fertilizer, crop protection chemicals, and machinery. Where inputs are available, farmers' ability to acquire them is often compromised by a lack of production credit, because rural financial institutions are in general, poorly developed. Farmers who produce marketable surpluses lack reliable access to market outlets, and the high cost of transporting produce to distant buying points over bad rural roads reduces their competitiveness."[90] All these phenomena constraint the development of the agricultural sector, and the poor farmers are mostly discouraged by these unfavorable conditions. In view of the importance of this sector of the economy, it becomes pertinent that the federal government should pay much attention to its development. This is because; any little improvement in the agricultural sector can have a considerable positive impact on the national economic growth, and as such can also reduce the importation of food products as well as the poverty rate.

5.2.3   Manufacturing Sector

The manufacturing sector is composed of small-scale and large-scale sub-sectors. The industrial development in Nigeria in its early stages began as a small-scale sector but with significant artisanal crafts works, which today still accounts for vast employed majority of the population mostly regarded as self-employed. However, during colonialism and after independence, manufacturing sector grew progressively from raw material production to what became a medium and large-scale industry (with the Nigeria's earliest manufacturing firms such as United Africa Company (UAC) and John Holt) contributing up to 80% of the total value-added in manufacturing. The medium or large-scale industries are however capital-

---

[90] World Bank (2008): Project Appraisal Document, p. 29.

intensive and have high growth prospect for the economy but accounts for lesser number of work forces.

The medium and large-scale industries were predominantly monopolized by the foreign investors until mid 1970s when the indigenization decree was promulgated by the federal government, offering the state and local investors the opportunity to share in the asset and liability of the manu-facturing companies. As a developmental plan, it was a radical restructur-ing of the manufacturing sector in order to sustain economic growth and ensure price stability. Again, with the idea of import substitution, it gave rise to granting license to many local and foreign investors and provided them with opportunities in establishing manufacturing industries. It was a measure by the federal government to reduce the amount of importation of finished products and a way of conditioning the foreign industries into production rather than exploring raw materials only for export. Although this revolution did not significantly achieve its main aim because most of the industrial equipments are imported to sustain the regular production input of the manufacturing industries. Yet, Nigeria could at the moment boost as one of the major industrial country in the West African Sub-Saharan region. The manufacturing sector hence produces a range of finished and feeder goods both for export and domestic utilization with high income elasticity.

Some of the major sections in the manufacturing sector include: food and beverages, rubber and plastic, iron and steel, hide and skin, timber and furniture, textile, floor mill, chemicals and pharmaceutical etc. However, most manufacturing industries are located in the big cities especially where there are more accesses to business transactions. According to Ajayi, "the pattern of the distribution of manufacturing industries at the city level indicates that there is a marked concentration of manufacturing establishments in the southern part of the country, and especially Lagos, Ibadan and Benin in the southwest. Other locations of relative high con-centration of industrial establishments are Kano in the North; and Enugu and Port Harcourt in the southeast."[91] These cities are strategic due to

---

[91] Ajayi, Dickson D. (2007): 'Recent Trends and Patterns in Nigeria's Industrial Devel-opment'. In: Journal of Africa Development Vol. 32, No. 2. Dakar: Council for the De-velopment of Social Science Research in Africa (CODESRIA), p. 139.

relative availability of basic infrastructures, raw materials and easy link to other major cities. Thus these logics of concentration are usually explained in terms of specific principles of industrial revolution and development.

However, Nafziger observes that "whereas manufacturing increased rapidly during the 1970s, tariff manipulations encouraged the expansion of assembly activities dependent on imported inputs; these activities contributed little to indigenous value added or to employment, and reduced subsequent industrial growth."[92] It follows that the relative contribution of manufacturing sector to GDP in real terms stood at 32.4% in 1972, which declined to 9.2% in 1981 and 5.5% in 1993 respectively. Table 2.2 above indicates that the share of the manufacturing sector in GDP decreased drastically from 4.18% in 2001 to 3.91% in 2006. In addition, Ajakaiye and Fakiyesi observe that "the average manufacturing capacity utilization rate, estimated at 52.6% in 2008, fell by 3.1% and 0.2% below the level in the preceding half year and the corresponding period of 2007, respectively. The decline in manufacturing production could be attributed to poor facilities and services; especially electric power supply, which remains sporadic, as well as the constant increase in the pump price of diesel and then the poor road networks. Other constraints to increased production include unfair competition from imported finished products, which constrained the demand for locally produced goods."[93] As it were, many manufacturing industries in Nigeria function as assembling plant of imported goods due to lower tariff placed on imported inputs especially in automobile industries. Thus the government's effort in reforming and restructuring this sector has encountered many difficulties over the years as trade deficits continue to increase as well as lack of investors' confidence consequent of poor working conditions and infrastructures.

Similarly, due to high cost of production, market competition and inadequate infrastructural development, the country's manufacturing capacity

---

[92] Nafziger, Wayne E. (1992): 'The Economy'. In: Metz, Helen Chapin (ed.): Nigeria: A Country Study 5th Edition. Washington: GPO for the Library of Congress, p. 184.
[93] Ajakaiya, Olu/Fakiyesi, 'Tayo (2009): 'Global Financial Crisis Discussion Series Paper 8: Nigeria'. In: Overseas Development Institute (ODI). London, p. 3. http://www.odi.org.uk/resources/download/3310.pdf [accessed: 22.03.2010]

utilizations still remain very low. According to Ajayi, "the revitalization of the industrial sector to promote the development of other sectors and the entire economy has been a major consideration in the National Rolling Plans, as policy objectives include the achievement of maximum growth in investment and output, and expansion of employment."[94] Consequently, with large spending on manufacturing sector without impressive results, the government is recently propelled to regenerate the sector through privatization especially the state owned industries. Finally, in this globalization era, manufacturing sector assumes a definitive position as one of the fastest link to trade contact with the global society. Therefore, the development of manufacturing sector depends on the number of foreign investors the government is able to attract as well as engaging the private sectors and supporting them through partnership. But this depends heavily on providing adequate environment conducive for investments.

5.2.4 Services

Service delivery is an integral aspect of economic development that requires paramount attention and consistent advocacy in order to attract both local and foreign investors. However, the high cost of doing businesses in Nigeria has often hindered the input of service delivery to the economy. Lack of essential infrastructure, the threat of security and associated crime rate, insufficient credit loans from financial institutions and non-transparency in business contracting constitute some of the major impediments in the economic environment since the beginning of early 1980s. In this section, we shall concentrate only on two major aspects of service delivery in Nigeria which include: Electricity and Communication as well as Import and Export services. Banking and finance will be considered later under the current reform agenda of the government.

5.2.4.1 Electricity and Communication

The contributions and importance of electricity and communication to the economic breakthrough of a country provide the basis through which other sectors of the economy could be effectively harnessed. Thus they

---

[94] Ajayi, Dickson D. (2007): p. 146.

determine the pace of innovation and investment as well as enhancement of production efficiency and capacity utilization towards modern industrial development. Unfortunately, notwithstanding various policy interventions taken by the federal government in Nigeria, the provision of essential infrastructure such as electricity and communication networks to assist business environment has continued to experience major set-backs.

Table 2.4: The Physical Infrastructural Shortage in Nigeria

Infrastructure	Macro Dimension			Micro Dimension						
	Nigeria	Region	Income	Small	Medium	Large	Exporter	Non Exporter	Domestic	Foreign
Number of Power Outrages in a typical Month	26.7	5.3	9.8	26.6	27.1	29.5	27.0	26.7	26.7	32.8
Value lost due to Power Outrages (% of Sales)	8.9	3.7	6.8	9.1	8.5	6.8	4.0	9.0	8.9	9.8
Delay in obtaining an Electrical Connection (days)	7.7	24.3	33.3	8.0	6.5	6.3	8.4	7.6	7.7	-
Delay in obtaining a Mainline Telephone Connection (days)	7.6	26.0	32.6	8.0	7.2	4.5	4.2	7.6	7.6	5.5
Products shipped to supply Domestic Markets lost due to Breakage or Spoilage (%)	3.2	1.3	1.3	2.5	4.6	7.4	4.0	3.2	3.3	1.5
Firms using the Web in Interaction with Clients/Suppliers (%)	9.7	29.4	13.2	4.2	22.6	73.5	64.9	9.0	9.3	48.7

Source: World Bank Enterprise Surveys Online (2009)

For instance, table 2.4 summarizes the challenges of poor infrastructure which is one of the greatest constraints of service deliveries in Nigeria. In the energy sub-sector, studies have shown that inefficient power generation specifically assumes the greatest limitation in doing business in Nigeria, which has resulted to numerous economic losses. The table indicates that the number of power outages in a typical month in Nigeria was 26.7 in 2009. In comparative terms with other developing countries, the situation in Nigeria remains very appalling. However, of the total number of typical monthly power outages in Nigeria, the foreign micro-dimension was mostly affected. As one can aptly infer from the table, the poor power generation reduces production output, which affects market costs as well as discourages new investors in sustainable industrial development. For example, the value lost due to power outages in Nigeria stands at 8.9% in 2009. It is expected to rise if much attention is not paid on power and energy sector. Presently, the domestic power plants in Nigeria consist of three hydro-based and five thermal plants, which are poorly maintained with other unharnessed renewable energy resources such as hydropower, biomass, solar and wind.

Moreover, energy supply is also regarded as one of the major sources of social and economic development in any country. Every other sector relies on it for its growth. In other words, the growth of the other sectors of the economy depends on the amount and quality of energy generated and distributed for utilization. It influences not only industrial production but also domestic utilization. Inefficient electricity generation in Nigeria has continued to retard economic growth and improved livelihood, with more than 55% of the population having no access to electricity. From about 23 million megawatt-hours (MWH) of electricity generated in 2004, which also decreased to about 21 million megawatt-hours in 2008, thermal supply plant contributed more than half of the generation. This generating capacity is an indicative of poor facilities and inability of the government to expand the power sector. In fact, Nigeria operates below its installed generating capacity of 5,900 megawatts, an indicative of lack of maintenance and improper servicing of the power sources. Most industries and firms have resorted in spending huge amount of resources in acquiring electric generators as alternatives for their private power generation. With the constant increase in the tariff without electricity, does the government hope to improve power generation? Nevertheless, the issue has remained so politicized that each government coming into power will continue to make empty promises to improve capacity generation without much result, notwithstanding billions of naira being allocated for the investment yearly.

On the other hand, the telecommunication sub-sector has significantly improved in Nigeria since 1999 and seems to be presently the fastest growing market in Africa. There are evidences of rapid growth in demand, usage, density and coverage. The available services include Fixed Telephone, Mobile Telephone, Internet Services and other basic value added services. Through the privatization of the telecommunications industry in Nigeria, which started with the awarding of licenses to Global System for Mobile communication (GSM) operators at the end 2000, it introduced quite healthy competition and an increase in quality service delivery in the industry.

However, the deregulation of mobile telephone services, which relatively reduced cost of communication and increased also the communication efficiency, has been one of the advantages of privatization. But unfortunately, the methods of billing and the constant rise in tariff have become another form of exploitation by the mobile telecommunication industries. Some of the main providers include Mobile Telephone Networks (MTN), Airtel, Globacom, Etisalat, Intercellular, Visaphone, Multilinks, M-tel, Reltel etc. These companies also provide Internet services but often quite inefficient for subscribers' benefits due to much congestion. On the other hand, the fixed telephone networks that would have been an alternative for the masses have remained stagnant and unreliable as indicated in the figure. However, this could be attributed to the inefficiency of the government to maintain the Nigerian Telecommunication Company (NITEL) which is the major telecommunication network own by the government. Finally, there are still the necessities to increase and strengthen the government incentives to the communication industries in order to improve service delivery designed for suitable economic development.

5.2.4.2 Import and Export

The importance of import and export services as the major link to international trade is based on their role as the engine of developmental processes of a country's economy. Import and export have been the utmost interest of many economic and sociological researchers. The key element of this exercise is expansion and sustainability of direct investment through trade contacts. Empirical evidences have shown that more increase in the volume of export against relative lower volume of import substitutes accelerates the value and balance of trade and at the same time create a healthy economic competition. Nations engage themselves in import and export to maintain what is called 'comparative advantage'[95] that can ensure balance of trade. And more importantly, comparative advantage facilitates and ensures stability of mutual economic benefits.

One of the essential elements that promote comparative advantages and then drive the competitive trade contact is openness. This significantly allows flexibility, innovation and promotion of foreign investments. According to Alan Winters, "[...] openness brings advantages not only on its own but also as part of a constellation of policies designed to ensure efficiency and competition in markets, and transparency and predictability in policy-making."[96] Nevertheless, the foreseeing difficulty is that if the economy is not growing or only gives advantages to one party, then the chances of competitiveness are narrowed down, to the extent that the result would be a lopsided global trade relationship, as evident in most African countries.[97] In fact, unequal trade relationships have been the burden of most developing countries, as they rely on importation of manufactured goods for their domestic utilization without corresponding ex porting powers.

Contextually, the increase in the export of primary products or raw-materials, which do not commensurate with the constant increase in the import of finished goods has generated a new pattern of consumption among Nigerians, whose taste for Western commodities have continued to attract the attention of expatriate entrepreneurs. For the elites, anything

---

[95] Richardson emphasizes that "exports are important when they are the necessary means to obtain unique or uniquely desirable imports. Exports are the quid pro quo for imports in the classic account of gains from international trade. They are the main cream of the nation's competitiveness exchanged for the cream of overseas competitiveness" (Richardson, David J. (2001): 'Exports Matter ... And So Does Trade Finance'. In: Hufbauer, C. Gary/Rodríguez, M. Rita (eds.): Ex-Im Bank in the 21st Century: A New Approach? Washington, DC: Institute for International Economics, p. 59).

[96] Winters, Alan (2002): 'Trade Policies for Poverty Alleviation' In: Hoekman, Bernard/Mattoo, Aaditya/English, Philip (eds.): Development, Trade and the WTO: A Handbook, Washington DC: World Bank, p. 31.

[97] Chabal and Daloz state that "it is generally accepted that the continent's reliance on the exports of a few primary products, its lack of competitiveness, its vulnerability to the price fluctuation of essential imports and its marginalization in the world economy all militate against its development potential"(Chabal, Patrick/Daloz, Jean-Pascal (1999): Africa Works, p.110).

that is locally produced by Nigerians is inferior. Consequently, the exchange of products and goods in terms of import and export between the West and Nigeria has been one of the colonial legacies, which were monopolized by the Western indigenous companies. For example, Cohen observes that; "Giant expatriate firms, notably the United Africa Company (a subsidiary of Unilever), John Holt's, and the Union Trading Company, had long held a grip on the export of Nigeria's primary products and on the import of manufactured goods from the industrialized world. By the late 1930s the UAC alone as responsible for more than 40% of the import-export business though it is worth noting that the metropolitan-satellite axis was not so rigid as to prevent penetration of the Nigerian market by non-British firms which in 1939 and 1949 respectively accounted for 37% and 40% of her imports [...]. This situation persisted to a large extent into the post-colonial period."[98] Perhaps, this could be attributed to the fact that there were scarcely indigenous manufacturers or domestic industries. And wherever they are found, they may not be well-developed and/or effective to compete in the global market with other foreign firms. This situation brought the idea of import-substitution in the mid 1970s in the bid to revolutionize the monopolized import market. But Nigeria is yet to meet up with the challenges of global competition in the world market, notwithstanding the current market reforms.

However, poor competition of the Nigerian market economy in the world trade could also be attributed to many factors such as insufficient industries, poor infrastructure and inadequate power supply, lack of maintenance culture, insecurity, corruption etc. These factors militate against industrial development, in the sense that Nigeria depends on foreign importation mainly from Europe, America and Asia for most domestic and industrial goods such as machines, electrical and electronic equipment. In fact, the recent unbanning of some hitherto banned import items such as; textile, rice, used electronic etc by the federal government gives reasons to question some of the economic policies of the government towards economic growth.

---

[98] Cohen, Robin (1974): Labor and Politics in Nigeria 1945-71. London: Heinemann, p. 38.

Table 2.5: Nigeria's Top Import Partners (2008)

Countries	% of total Nigerian Imports
China	10.7
United States	8.4
Netherlands	6.2
United Kingdom	5.8
France	5.6
Brazil	5.1
Germany	4.5

Source: Library of Congress, Federal Research Division. Country Profile: Nigeria (2008)

On the other hand, the table 2.5 shows the countries that dominated import market in Nigeria based on 2006 statistical reports. The analysis of imports on country basis indicates that China is leading the import market in Nigeria with the total value of 10.7% of the total imports, and then followed by United States with 8.4% and other European countries. It is not surprise that China is gaining the market in Nigeria. This is because; China attracts and feeds the country with anything but cheap and inferior commodities such as electronics, textiles, chemicals etc. as a result of poverty and inability to afford expensive goods from America and Europe, China is now the strong alternative for the growing population. For instance, if one could buy a handset phone from China at $5 that could serve the same purpose with a handset phone from America that costs $50, then the market option becomes clear for the poor population in choosing less expensive goods. Unfortunately, this condition has also negative impact on the local economy, because it limits foreign investment as well as patronization of indigenous goods.

Table 2.6: Nigeria's Top Export Partners (2008)

Countries	% of total Nigerian exports
United States	48.9
Spain	8.0
Brazil	7.3
France	4.2

Source: Library of Congress, Federal Research Division. Country Profile: Nigeria (2008)

From the other perspective, Nigerian export capacity has been unstable. Nigeria exported about US$62 billion of goods in 2007 according to the Library of Congress report. The main export commodities are petroleum and petroleum products, cocoa and rubber. However, only oil accounted for 95 to 99 percent of merchandise exports, and cocoa and rubber accounted for the remainder.[99] This phenomenon thus points once more to the undiversified nature of the Nigerian export goods that relied on high level of petroleum export. Table 2.6 shows the average percentage of 'export partner concentration'[100] in Nigeria. From the table, it indicates that the trade partner with largest percentage of concentration is USA, which accounted for an average of 48.8 percent of Nigeria total export and predominately crude oil. Other countries with major stake include Spain, Brazil and France. Already, the earnings from export trade have been affected in the recent years due to price fall in some raw-material goods and also due to unstable crude oil prices as consequence of global economic crisis.

Although the value of import and export transaction in Nigeria has continued to increase over the years, yet there have been lesser visible balances in terms of impact on the developmental strategies. The positive balances of trade that may have been experienced in the recent times were significantly driven by the upward increase in import merchandise, mostly cheap consumer products from Asia. But this increase may on the other hand deter economic development and may also affect local production utilization of the indigenous goods. Altogether Nigeria has also experienced visible balances over the years due to crude oil demand in world market, but unfortunately, most of the trade surpluses are again recycled into foreign exchange, which on the one hand discourages market innovation and on the other hand limits the foreign reserve for eventual economic recovery in time of crisis.

---

[99] Library of Congress (2008): Federal Research Division. Country Profile: Nigeria, p. 14. http://lcweb2.loc.gov/frd/cs/profiles/Nigeria.pdf [accessed: 23.02.2009]
[100] The ratio of the value of the exports to the largest trade partner to the total exports of a country (Chase-Dunn, Christopher (2000): p.124).

Figure 2.6: Export and Import Levels 1988-2008 (US$ mill.)

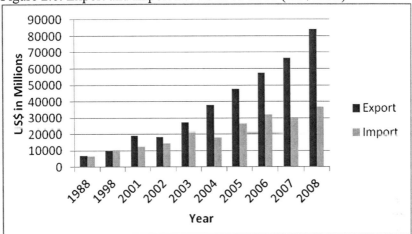

*Source: The World Bank Group (2009): The Developmental Economic LDB database—
Nigeria at a glance*

On the other side, figure 2.6 illustrates the exports and imports levels in Nigeria from 1988 to 2008. The time frame is based on the difference developments between the military government and democratic government. It however shows that there is a constant increase in export and export within the time frame. In 1998, the debit items of import equally corresponded with credit items of export, but there was progressive difference in improvement in the subsequent years especially in 2008 where there was a significant differential in the balance of trade between import and export. Consequently, it implies that the value of export continues to grow over the import merchandise; an indicative of a healthy economy? Unfortunately, that is not quite so in the Nigerian context as a result of mono-cultural economy or non-diversification as well as much dependence on import of manufactured goods especially domestic commodities which could ordinarily be manufactured locally.

Nevertheless, creating business environment and sustaining local production can enhance economic growth as well as reduce a lot of risks and cost implications involved in importation. Investigation by the US Department of State for African Affairs shows that "Nigeria inspects all imports on arrival, rather than at ports of origin; as a result, about 95% of containers are physically examined. This procedure, along with Nigeria's uneven application of import and labeling regulations and poor infrastructure, complicates the movement of goods through Nigeria's notoriously congested ports and increases the cost of doing business. The government has promoted foreign investment and encouraged reforms in these and other areas, but the investment climate remains daunting to all but the most determined."[101] On the other aspect of market relationships, clearing of goods on the Nigerian seaports is regularly delayed, which predominantly accumulates demurrage that discourages especially the foreign investors' interests. In this regard, committed efforts in improving business environment especially in infrastructure, institutions and market orientation become a basic necessity of the country in attracting more foreign investments.

Finally, another important area in transforming import and export is proper transportation networks. As an engine of growth, transportation plays a vital role in social and economic development of a nation, particularly in facilitating movement of people, goods and services. Unfortunately, investigation also indicates that "Nigeria's publicly owned transportation infrastructure is a major constraint to economic development. Principal ports are at Lagos (Apapa and Tin Can Island), Port Harcourt, and Calabar. Docking fees for freighters are among the highest in the world. Of the 80,500 kilometers (50,000 mi.) of roads, more than 15,000 kilometers (10,000 mi.) are officially paved, but many remain in poor shape [...]. Four of Nigeria's airports – Lagos, Kano, Port Harcourt and Abuja – currently receive international flights. There are several domestic private Nigerian carriers, and air service among Nigeria's cities is generally dependable. The maintenance culture of Nigeria's domestic airlines is not up to international standards."[102] Therefore, the improvement of Nigeria's transportation industry would be an important gateway to import and export development, by which sustainable economic growth could be achievable. This, of course can go a long way to improve the financial inflows and foreign exchange, as well as attracting expertise in ensuring a continual growth of the economy.

---

[101] US Department of State (2010): Bureau of African Affairs November 1, 2010. Background Note: Nigeria. http://www.state.gov/r/pa/ei/bgn/2836.htm [accessed: 6.11.2010]
[102] US Department of State (2010): Bureau of African Affairs.

5.2.5 Informal Sector of the Economy

With the increase of rural poverty rate consequent of the oil wealth and decline of other economic sectors especially agriculture and manufacturing, informal sector of the economy has grown extremely in the recent times. Informal sector is categorized under unregistered private sector businesses, and it is estimated that its economic activities account about 75% of the Nigerian economy and contribute a sizeable share of the GDP. It comprises of all unrecorded and unregulated economic activities that function alongside with the institutionalized economic framework of the formal sector. In other words, informal sector's activities according to Coate et al "take place outside the framework of corporate public and registered private sector establishment."[103] The most commonly used definition is contained in the International Labor Office report, which states that it is "a way of doing things, characterized by its ease of entry, reliance of indigenous resources, family ownership of enterprises, small scale of operations, labor-intensive and adapted technology, skills acquired outside of the formal school system and unregulated and competitive markets."[104] However, informal sector can play a dynamic role in economic growth, especially as an integral enterprise in the developing economy. It generates employment (especially self-employment) and accounts for major household income-earnings.

On account of insufficient set-up capital, the inadequate method of costing and the inability to compete with the formal sectors, the informal sector consists mainly of small-scale business transactions and service delivery such as trading, agriculture, mechanics, furniture making, lending services, transportation etc. These establishments account for the major labor forces in both rural and urban areas. Due to low rate of employment as well as the increase of migration, vast majority of the population engage themselves in this sector as an alternative opportunity to earn a living and reduce poverty.

---

[103] Coate, Bromeyn/Handmer, John/Choong, Wei (2006): Taking Care of People and Communities: Rebuilding Livelihoods through NGOs and the Informal Economy in Southern Thailand. In: Shaw, Rajib (ed.): Disaster Prevention and Management: An International Journal Vol. 15, No. 1. Emerald Group Publishing Ltd., p. 137.

[104] International Labor Office (1972): Employment, Incomes and Equality: A strategy for Increasing Productive Employment in Kenya. ILO Geneva, p. 6.

Meanwhile, informal sector can be an engine of economic growth, but that requires other mechanism of economic supports. In that perspective, Akintoye emphasizes that "[...] informal sector cannot operate effectively at this task without the support of other key players, which is basically the availability of credit, as the best of ideas may never translate to reality without the wherewithal to make it happen [...]; hence the availability of credit to finance the informal sector cannot be under estimated."[105] That is the reason way it is very necessary to initiate microfinance schemes that can drive the sector sustainability such as credit unions, moneylenders, cooperative groups etc. This, of course can provide capitals that will ensure adequate servicing of the sector's operations.

Finally, a striking feature of the informal sector in Nigeria and elsewhere is that it does not reflect in macro-economic indicators, and that may also have a negative consequence on the economic growth. Because the activities are unreported, informal sector does not often comply with market regulations such as taxes, monetary policies and licensing requirements. The challenge of sustaining this sector for economic growth becomes how its activities could be incorporated into general economic indicators in order to enhance competitiveness and ensure social security. This in fact requires government involvement and assistance through partnership and proper policy framework and implementation without diminishing the grassroots economic mobilization in which the informal sector businesses tend to foster. Therefore, in order to achieve needed economic progress and long-term fiscal sustainability, the government would also be able to promote informal sector as well as diversify and decentralize the oil economy.

5.3   Current Economic Reform Agenda

Since the last three decades, several attempts have so far been made in order to reform the Nigerian economy. The austerity measures of the early 1980s, the Structural Adjustment Programme (SAP) introduced in

---

[105] Akintoye, Ishola R. (2008): 'Reducing Unemployment through the Informal Sector: A Case Study of Nigeria'. In: European Journal of Economics, Finance and Administrative Sciences, Issue 11. EuroJournals, Inc., pp. 102-103. http://www.eurojournals.com/eje-fas_11_10.pdf [accessed: 12.08.2010]

1986 and then the recent economic reform policies. These have unfortunately not yielded satisfactory goals and aspirations. The goals and aspirations are quite essential in formulating guidelines and policy framework that can achieve growth especially in this period when inflation rate is souring higher, the poverty rate on the increase and high rate of unemployment is increasing.

In May 2004, the federal government launched an economic reform agenda called the National Economic Empowerment Development Strategy (NEEDS), which as a macro-economic framework, aimed at tackling the underdevelopment and the related inadequate infrastructures. It is also a process that will allow diversification of the economy away from over-dependency on oil. The state governments were also encouraged to design a complementary program: the State Economic Empowerment Development Strategy (SEEDS) as well as a related local government initiative known as Local Economic Empowerment Development Strategy (LEEDS). The NEEDS is however based on the principles, which "stipulates that public policy must be directed to balance the objectives of efficiency, effectiveness, and equity in order to ensure a broad-based poverty reducing growth and development strategy, the dividends of which will be distributed fairly among all classes [...]. Its focus is wealth creation, employment generation, poverty reduction, corruption elimination and general value re-orientation."[106] These enumerated initiatives are to ensure sustainability of policy interventions and self-rediscovery with comparative advantage of the various stakeholders in the multifaceted fight against poverty and inequality.

In addition to the NEEDS, an economic policy agenda known as Vision 20-2020 millennium goal was introduced in 2006. The objective of this agenda is to transform the Nigerian economy into one of the world's top-20 economies by 2020. Vision 2020 envisaged the enactment of a 'Seven Point Agenda' initiated by President Umaru Musa Yar'adua in May 2007. This agenda consists of the following points: 'power and energy infra-

---

[106] National Planning Commission (2004): Nigeria: National Economic Empowerment Development Strategy (NEEDS). Abuja: The NEEDS Secretariat/Federal Secretariat, pp. 28-29. http://www.cenbank.org/out/publications/guidelines/rd/2004/needs.pdf [accessed: 16.09.2009]

structure; food security and agriculture; wealth creation and employment; mass transportation; land reform; security (including bringing stability to the Niger Delta); and education.'[107] The strategic plan of this agenda is to enable proper integration of Nigerian economy as a promising economy for foreign investments through consistent advocacy and stability. The procedures though a gradual process, are aimed at diversifying the economy away from primary sectors and initiating a long-term financial innovation.

Moreover, the economic agenda has so far given rise to relatively positive result in its renewed efforts in consolidating and transforming the economy towards Vision 20-2020 and debt cancelation. The US Department of State on African Affairs affirms that "arguably Nigeria's biggest macroeconomic achievement has been the sharp reduction in its external debt, which declined from 36% of GDP in 2004 to less than 4% of GDP in 2007. In October 2005, the International Monetary Fund (IMF) approved it's first-ever Policy Support Instrument for Nigeria. In December 2005, the United States and seven other Paris Club nations signed debt reduction agreements with Nigeria for $18 billion in debt reduction, with the proviso that Nigeria pay back its remaining $12 billion in debt by March 2006."[108] This agreement has rated Nigeria high by the credit rating agencies especially the IMF. But unfortunately, the debt has started once again to accumulate as a consequence of non-continuity problem and unguarded directions of government policies.

Furthermore, the financial sectors such as banking, insurance and capital markets have been the main inspiring visions and targets of the economic reforms. Oshikoya has observed that "Nigeria's financial sector has undergone major restructuring with the number of banks reduced from 89 to 25 and with minimum capital requirements increased ten-fold. The financial sector reform process has been widely and acknowledged as one of the most far-reaching in the world. As a result of the reforms, Nigeria now has the fastest growing banking sector in Africa, attracting over $1.5 billion of foreign investment since 2005. Before the reforms, there was no Nigerian bank among the top global 1000 banks. By 2006, 12 Nigerian

---

[107] Library of Congress (2008): p. 11.
[108] US Department of State (2010): Bureau of African Affairs.

banks were in the top global 1000. The financial sector, however, remains under-developed relative to the size of the economy. For example, South Africa's largest bank, Standard Bank Group, in 2004 had about the same capital base and three times the combined assets of all the current 25 banks in Nigeria. Mortgage loans represent less than one percent of GDP in Nigeria compared to 20 percent of GDP in South Africa."[109] Moreover, after financial auditing of the banks in 2009, it was also discovered that 10 out of the 24 capitalized banks were running into liquidation as consequence of unchecked, unmonitored and poor lending processes. As a result, six billion dollars were carved out by the Central Bank of Nigeria in order to bail the banks, and subsequently, their management teams were sacked and replaced with new teams. But the Nigerian financial institution is yet to meet up with the set targets consequent of instability and proper monitoring schemes.

In spite of the positive economic transformations already recorded, many challenges still lie ahead over the policy agendas. This is pertinent especially at this moment when the economy in per capita income is not stable, and also the very task of enhancing the quality of living conditions of the population. On the other hand, due to poor policy implementation and lack of proper regulative institutions, most of the policies are yet to achieve desired results. Nevertheless, though still an ongoing process, but judging from the trends of things at this period of time, there is slight possibility that the Vision 20-2020 will be attained; majority of the population are still very poor, inadequate and inefficient infrastructure are also to be contended with, fights against corruption are strongly hindered by ineffective institutions and political interferences, and the promise and drive of economic growth through reforms have so far seen poor political will. Therefore, for a renewed integration into the global economic competitiveness, the Nigerian state must ensure that its economic priorities are well set in view of its prominent role in Africa and for the sustenance of democratic formation.

---

[109] Oshikoya, Temitope W (2008): 'Nigeria in the Global Economy: Nigeria's Integration into the Global Economy is below its Potential'. In: Business Economics Vol. 43, Issue 1. UK: Palgrave Macmillan, p. 36.

5.4   Consequence of Global Economic Integration

The ideology of global economy as an integrating factor has initiated and continues to initiate unequal trade relationships and barriers between regions and nations. It is an integration that involves one-dimensional overhead start, which conditions the turn of events and the boundary-line of market freedom and productivity. Rodney was right to observe that "when Europe and Africa established close relations through trade, there was therefore already a slight edge in Europe's favor – an edge representing the difference between a fledging capitalist society and one that was still emerging from communalism."[110] In this composition, the capital inflow between industrialized nations and developing nations plays an important role in an integration process. Interestingly, economic integration has continued to evolve in this way through a long process of capital accumulation, which has not only opened market doors but also increased global inequality.

Conceptualizing globalization through the process of integration unveils what Meyer and Geschiere referred in their work as the 'dialectic of flow and closure': that is, whereby the process of 'integration' masks a deeper route to fragmentation. According to this idea, "the more current the notion of globalization becomes, the more it seems to be beset with vagueness and inconsistencies."[111] Thus, the consequence of economic integration as a changing process on the one hand, reveals how the developing economy of Nigerian state is unprepared to meet up with the global competition and on the other hand, how the global economic forces have dominated the local economy for anything but becoming the prey by which the new imperialistic hegemonies feed on. In either case, it is another way of saying that the new configuration of the capitalist economy has not in the real sense been to the advantage of the developing economies.

---

[110] Rodney, Walter (2012): p. 70.
[111] Meyer, Birgit/Geschiere, Peter (eds.) (1999): Globalization and Identity: Dialectics of Flow and Closure. Oxford: Blackwell, p. 1.

5.4.1 Comparative Market Decline

The changing structure of global market formation through trade contacts has been ascribed as the major cause of comparative decline of market investment in the developing world. According to Rodney, "one of the common means by which one nation exploits another and one that is relevant to Africa's external relations is exploitation through trade. When the terms of trade are set by one country in a manner entirely advantageous to itself, then the trade is usually detrimental to the trading partner."[112] In this apparent situation, one discovers that industrialized countries subdue equal concessions in bilateral trade partnership with developing countries through unilateral policies. This dichotomy gives rise to unbalanced outcomes and comparative market disadvantages. Thus the free trade arrangement has not really promoted comparative advantages for all economies, which can allow global mobility of goods and services without interference or undue preference to one party in the process. The right idea is that what one country exports ought to be relatively concurrence with its total imports in order to promote local entrepreneurship. Although globalization has opened the door for foreign inflow of goods in the Nigerian market, yet the local market interaction to the external trade is still limited.

On the other hand, due to the increasing business mobility around the world, the transnational corporations (TNCs) invest in most of the developing countries. This is majorly for economic accumulation generally propelled by low taxation, cheap labor and poor environmental protection in those countries. Even though the investments in some instances could intensify competitive market activities and promote development, yet the direct foreign investors could on the other hand frustrate and hinder the local corporations who may be unable and incapable of competing in the global production process. This investment method has also continued to foster economic inequality as well as increasing poverty in Nigeria.

Nevertheless, the technological development of market substitutes or alternative methods of production of the primary goods through modern sciences has bracketed most market opportunities in Nigeria and other

---

[112] Rodney, Walter (2012): p. 22.

192

developing countries. For instance, Stein enumerates that "advances in biotechnology and material sciences are leading to synthetic substitutes for primary products such as vanilla and sugar. Products such as cocoa and palm oil [that were before the major Nigeria foreign exchange earnings] are also being challenged by Western firms as they undertake genetic research to develop outright synthetic substitutes or alternatives methods of production. Natural resources like copper are being replaced by optical fibres or microwaves, contributing to the downward pressure on prices from the demand side."[113] From another perspective, because many big machines and equipment built for industrial uses and household utilities are not locally produced, they are mostly fashioned in a manner that can lead to their rapid irrelevance in the fast changing technology. Even the availability of their spare-parts or their maintenance is locally very difficult. This strategy by the industrialized world has vehemently propelled the developing countries to continuously import the new technologies. This has as well compelled the invitation of the foreign expatriates to assist in the technical operations with exorbitant wage salaries, or alternatively importing those foreign commodities that would have required the use of those machines to manufacture in high import tariffs.

Hence, the massive importation of finished products has altered the structure of many traditional patterns of production, which could not withstand the modern market forces. The significant manifestation of this formation is the issue of import concession with low tariff given even to certain goods that could ordinarily be produced locally. The consequence remains that most of the indigenous manufacturing companies are on the verge of collapsing. Because one can buy cheaply in the global market, the local market suffers the defeat that could have promoted economic growth. Therefore, the integration of the local economies into the global sphere calls for equal participation and to maximize the opportunity in which the process offers for effective and efficient growth of the local economy.

---

[113] Stein, Howard (2000): p. 156.

5.4.2 Deceleration of Economic Growth by Global Financial Crisis

The global financial crisis affected and continues to affect every country but the developing countries of Africa are mostly put at the receiving ends of its consequences. Apart from the fact that the projected economic growth rates in many of those countries are tremendously affected, the price hike of commodities in the domestic market affected largely the poor majority. This is because the economic structures of those countries are not well organized to promptly absolve the shocks of the financial meltdown. In the report submitted by the Committee of African Finance Ministers and Central Bank Governors to the G20 in London on 'Impact of the Crisis on African Economies', it presents that "Africa is now suffering from a virulent financial bug brought about by the recession in the West. The Continent's woes now include: worsening macro-economic balances with countries facing widening current account and budget deficits, expected shortfall in export revenues with oil exporters suffering the largest losses, reduced trade, declining capital inflows, depleted foreign reserves, reduced capacity to import even basic commodities such as food, medical supplies and agricultural products, shortage of liquidity in international markets, cancellation of projects and, refusal of international banks to issue lines of credit or to confirm pre-committed ones."[114] In the midst of these reported cases, Nigeria is still faced with the challenge of responding to the problem as well as stabilizing the financial market. For instance, the bubble burst of the Nigerian Stock Exchange (NSE) market that experienced a drastic decline from December 2008 after impressive performance in the previous months has been a major consequence of the global financial crunch. The all share index of about 283 listed companies with $125 billion total market capitalization that recorded a peak value of about 66,371 points in March 2008 is yet to recover fully from shocks with the dip current value of 20,359.23 points as at November 2011.

---

[114] A report from the Committee of African Finance Ministers and Central Bank Governors established to monitor the crisis (March 17, 2009): Impact of the Crisis on African Economies – Sustaining Growth and Poverty Reduction: African Perspectives and Recommendations to the G20. http://www.londonsummit.gov.uk/resources/en/PDF/africa-recommendations [accessed: 12.04.2010]

Generally, the global financial crunch created in the local economy the crisis of confidence and weak consumer demand of commodities. On the one hand, it occasioned massive reduction in consumer purchasing power as a result of drastic cut in public sector spending, and on the other hand, it affected the demand for goods and services as well as the consumption pattern of the populace. Finally, the consequence of the meltdown also deterred the budget implementation due to massive decline in oil revenue as the major source of government spending. Mostly affected was on the area of social spending such as health, education and social services. Therefore, for the immediate response to the persistent decline in economic growth, the federal government is obliged to build a formidable economic policy with effective implementation, in order to meet with the challenges of the global integration in all ramifications.

5.4.3   Environmental Degradation

As one of the major consequences of globalization, Nigeria is now facing many environmental problems especially through ecological exposures that have affected and continue to affect both the natural habitats and the well-being of the citizens. For instance, constant deforestation has had a disastrous consequence on biological and ecological substances as a result of damages occurring from ever-increasing industrialization and urbanization. Williams aptly observes that "a century ago there were five million hectares of trees and in 1897 two-thirds of Nigeria was covered by rich tropical rainforest. Today, only 4% of this original rainforest remains, with most of the deforestation having happened since the 1980s – between 1981 and 1994 Nigeria lost 3.7 million hectares of rainforest [...]. Causes include fuel wood gathering, conversion of natural forest to commercial tree plantation, oil exploration, mining and urbanization. And of what's left, over 3% is lost annually, and only a third is in protected areas, either under the protection of forestry department or in national parks."[115] Subsequently, it is also surprising to know that most of the wildlife is nearing extinction; while many of them are being carried away mostly to the Western countries. Some others are slaughtered for food and domestic purposes. This is unfortunate taking into cognizance the

---

[115] Williams, Lizzie (2008): pp. 4-5.

number of tourist this would have attracted as a means of economic development.

However, addressing the issue of oil exploration in Nigeria is of utmost important to the discussion on environmental degradation. Thus oil exploration by the multinational oil companies has extremely exposed the environment and the natural habitats to environmental risks such as pollution, biodiversity, sea-level rise etc. The region where the extraction is carried out is the major recipient of the unjust catastrophic pollution. According to Agbola and Alabi, "the development of petroleum resources by the Nigerian State and its allied multinational corporations, multilateral organization and local elites has brought about clear examples of environmental injustice where the vulnerable ethnic minorities of the Niger Delta region bear the heaviest burdens."[116] This attitude is a sheer neglect of the environment both by the Nigerian state and the multinational oil companies on account of their mutual understanding to the detriment of the host communities. Such corporate romance between them was never a new phenomenon in economic productivity. This sometimes "unholy alliance" operates at an official as well as in an unofficial levels, but it all boils down essentially to the same thing in terms of their multiplier effects in fostering mutual rewarding to the neglect and social exclusion of communities where the resources are extracted.

In this scenario, Karl observes that "the environmental dimension of oil exploration is a chief cause of social dislocation. Hazardous wastes, site contamination, and the lack of sufficient protection of surface and subsurface waters, biodiversity, and air quality (both in the immediate vicinity of the oil project and in relation to global concerns such as ozone-depleting substances and greenhouse gases) have endangered the health of local populations near oil installations and pipelines; local livelihoods such as farming and fishing have been destroyed."[117] In fact, the Niger Delta environment is characterized with continuous oil spills and gas

---

[116] Agbola, Tunde/Alabi, Moruf (2003): 'Political Economic of Petroleum Resources Development, Environmental Injustice and Selective Victimization: A Case Study of the Niger Delta Region of Nigeria'. In: Agyeman, Julian/Bullard, Robert Doyle/Evans, Bob (eds.): Just Sustainabilities: Development in an Unequal World. London: Mit Press, p. 279
[117] Karl, Terry Lynn (2004): p. 670.

flaring. UNDP has noted that the "available records show that a total of 6,817 oil spills occurred between 1976 and 2001, with a loss of approximately three million barrels of oil. More than 70 per cent was not recovered. Approximately six per cent spilled on land, 25 per cent in swamps and 69 per cent in offshore environments."[118] These oil spills have widespread implications for livelihood, range from health risks to increase in poverty rate as consequent of unfit environment for farming and fishing.

For these neglects of the environment to have lingered for decades indicates on the one hand, the strength and the dominant nature of the multinational oil companies in Nigeria, and on the other hand, the inability of the government to design a proper legislation and ensure its enforcement to check the activities of those companies. Although the Federal Environmental Protection Agency (FEPA) was lately established by the federal government in 1988 to supervise environmental management and compliance, yet the agency still lacks the required expertise to monitor the environmental activities. This is because the agency and other monitoring departments are less equipped with the modern technological devices and techniques to carry out the assessment.

Finally, flaring the gases other than conserving them for further utilization in the course of oil production has much cost implications. In other words, the multinational oil companies usually shy away from embarking into such projects that will consume them sizeable capitals at the expense of the environment. Thus the report released by the Amnesty International in June 2009 states emphatically that, "Government's failure to protect the human rights of its people does not absolve companies from responsibility for their actions. Oil companies such as Shell are not free to ignore the consequences of their actions just because the government has failed to hold them to account. The international standard is not 'whatever a company can get away with' – there are international standards for oil industry operations, and in relation to environmental and social impacts that oil companies in the Niger Delta are very well aware of. Despite its

---

[118] "The Niger Delta has experienced two major oil spills: the Funiwa oil well blowout in 1980 and the Jones Creek oil spillage in 1998. These resulted in the greatest mangrove forest devastation ever recorded worldwide" (United Nations Development Programme (2006): p. 76).

public claims to be a socially and environmentally responsible corporation, Shell continues to directly harm human rights through its failure to
adequately prevent and mitigate pollution and environmental damage in
the Niger Delta."[119] Therefore, environmental protection boils down to
combined effort of the government and the multinational oil corporations
in having corporate responsibilities for the Niger Delta environment and
infrastructural development. This action can give the region the feeling of
self-belonging as well as creating awareness of mutual interest and understanding for some who have taken up arms and engaged in
vandalization of oil installations and disruption of oil production. Not
only in the Niger-Delta region that environment protection is a necessity
but also in the whole Nigerian society especially this period climate
change and global warming is threatening every human ecosystems and
biological existence.

5.4.4 Emergence of Conflicts and Grass-Root Movements

Global integration of local economies has fueled conflicts in many regions of the world. It has been argued that environmental injustices and
much dependency on oil economy are most likely to lead to violent conflicts. The manifestations of such conflicts in Nigerian context include:
conflicts over resource control among communities, conflicts between
host communities and multinational oil corporations on the one hand, and
between host communities and federal government on the other hand.
Thus, conflicts as structural disagreements due to resource struggles are
explained by conflicts theorists as "the scarcity and value of resources in
society [...] as groups struggle to gain access to and control those resources."[120] This phenomenon is quite peculiar to the situation in Niger-
Delta region, where it has taken the character of crisis-ridden region due
to environmental injustices and the struggle for resource control. This has
also culminated into institutional crisis, in that when accounting for the
volatilities in democratic governance, global integration and distribution
of resources, the federal government in collaboration with multinational
companies becomes the main actors of the conflict generation.

---

[119] Gaughran, Audrey (2009): 'Petroleum, Pollution and Poverty in the Niger Delta'. In:
The Guardian Newspaper Online, June 30.
[120] Giddens, Anthony (2006): Sociology, p. 1010.

In the same perspective, Abrahamsen and Williams note that "the conflicts in the Delta are numerous and complex, involving multiple political and economic agendas and actors. The oil companies, and their installations and employees, are at the centre of these conflicts for a number of reasons. Oil production has sometimes caused environmental damage and social dislocation, leading to protest and discontent among the effected local communities who reap few benefits and whose share of oil-based revenues has for decades been eroded by the federal government. Over the years, the activities and practices of the oil companies have also contributed to inter-communal conflict, as payments for land rent, compensations or other company benefits such as development programmes and social funds have become spoils to be fought over."[121] Thus as the different interest groups struggle for the spoils, the oil economy has turned into a 'distributional crisis'[122] – on the one hand, between the federal government and the Niger Delta region and on the other hand, between the multinational oil companies and the host communities. In both cases, exclusion from resource accumulation has governed the thoughts of Niger Delta region and manifests itself in violent conflicts that has dislodged and continues to dislodge investments as well as loss of thousands of barrels of crude oil. And at that same time, it has constituted impediments to development in Niger Delta over the years.

It is regrettable to note that the oil exploration has had little impact on the socio-economic development of the population especially on the people whose soil the oil is extracted. The widespread poverty in the region constitutes a deeper sense of contradiction in the midst of plenty, which has fostered violence and tension. This situation has not only changed the pattern of social relationship, but has also instigated the emergence of socio-political and resistance movements in recent years. These move-

---

[121] Abrahamsen, Rita/Williams, Michael (2005): The Globalization of Private Security, Country Report: Nigeria, p. 12. http://users.aber.ac.uk/rbh/privatesecurity/countryreport-nigeria.pdf [accessed: 26.09.2009]. See also: Abrahamsen, Rita/Williams, Michael (2011): Security beyond the State: Private Security in International Politics. Cambridge: Cambridge University Press, p. 133.
[122] Beck asserts that "the distribution of socially produced wealth and related conflicts occupy the foreground so long as obvious material need, the 'dictatorship of scarcity', rules the thought and action of people (as today in large parts of the so-called Third world)" (Beck, Ulrich (1992): Risk Society, p. 20).

ments which assumed the key oppositions to the perceived environmental and economic injustices perpetuated upon the people operate either through mass protests or violent attacks. Hence, the formation of the 'Movement for the Emancipation of the Niger Delta (MEND)' is a brainchild of this struggle. This is an armed militant group devoted to the struggle against injustices meted through resource control and environmental degradations. Their main targets are usually the multinational oil companies through the disruption of their operations and the onward demand for compensations. This situation affects peace and security in the region.

Even though the federal government is making frantic effort to address the problem in the Niger Delta through developmental amnesty to the militants, yet there should also be more committed effort to a people-oriented development programme. This effort will not only provide the basic infrastructures but also aids in alleviating the rate of poverty in the region. In response to this, the effort needs political will and proper supervision in order to reach the targeted local population. Therefore, there is also the constant need for a renewed dialogue in the Niger Delta, between the federal government and the oil communities on the one hand and on the other hand between the government and the multinational oil corporations. This is in consideration of the importance of the region as the economic cradle of the nation, and the necessity of peace and security towards stability in the Nigerian polity.

5.5   Conclusion

In this section, we have empirically reviewed the stand of economic development and global influence of Nigerian economy. Through global incorporation that began with colonialism, I argue that whereas many emerging economies of the developing countries have comparatively benefited from globalization, there is the concern in many spheres that the impact on Nigerian economy is yet to assume a turning point in its economic development. The economic potentials have not really manifested visibly in the general livelihood of the growing population judging from the fact that majority of the citizens are still very poor and the social indicator of the country is ranked among the lowest in the world. The agricultural sector that would have decreased the rate of poverty and social inequality has been neglected consequent of oil discovery that enrich mostly the capitalists elites. In fact, the economy was plunged into global capitalism without strong structures to participate in its gains. In other words, large segment of the economy is yet to withstand and meet up with the institutional challenges and the pressure of the global capitalist economy. Thus lack of strong institutions, over-centralization and policy failures were all the delimiting factors in this process of market liberalization.

Finally, globalization itself could enhance development, if its asymmetrical affiliation is evenly distributed to maximize equal opportunities and simultaneous formation. Unfortunately, Nigeria remains on the periphery of the global players. Interacting with external institutional arrangements demands proper understanding of their principles and operational mechanisms. Thus Nigeria can achieve this feat only through strong state that has the potentials of policy interventions, which can translate the advantages of globalization into proper economic transformation. Therefore, taking advantages of globalization requires both regional and global efforts in working out a suitable modality that is negotiable and open to equal participation. On the other hand, the fundamental trust of each region becomes how to fashion its own developmental trajectory through key policy programmes, which will be an absorber to the global influence, but at the same time borrowing some leave from the global framework for its innovations. And this is what Nigeria requires at this critical time of deeper penetration of global capitalist influences.

PART III

SOCIAL STRUCTURAL ANALYSIS AND INEQUALITY

6   TOWARDS CONTEXTUAL STUDY OF THE SOCIAL STRUCTURE

Having examined extensively the political and economic developments and their impeding capacities to effective growth in chapters four and five respectively, I will move on in this chapter to articulate and relate the already discovered results to the social structural changes eminent in the Nigerian society. These changes affect both the endogenous and exogenous components of the society. The changes also offer insights into the criteria of social positioning in the society especially in terms of exclusion and inclusion from the developmental processes, and the resultant crises associated with global formation. Apart from various attempts so far made by the government through policies and laws on economic distribution as well as in decreasing the magnitude of inequality gaps, the structural dichotomies that exist both within and among regions, classes and between genders continue to persist. The gaps, of course are not unconnected with various forces both internal and external that struggle to take control over the state through the unending accumulation of resources. Our investigation into this matter is quite important in observing how globalization has positively as well as negatively affected the structural development of Nigerian society. The theoretical contents drawn from part one of this work, will assist the empirical examination in this present part, by giving the contextual framework the needed body of knowledge towards proper sociological inquiry.

6.1   Configuration of Social Networks

Social network as a form of communal relationship and mutual interdependence is a common concept in the traditional African society, which constitutes an important aspect of the social structure. In Nigeria, the family and kinship dominate the social structure as its fundamental endogenous units. They assume the centre stage in providing the basic needs of life, both material and moral assistances. Both systems embrace the socio-economic, cultural and environmental conditions of the people's life. The family is regarded as the commonly close knit community of blood relatives that share life and destiny together. That is to say, it is a uniting element which ideally provides social, economic and psychological security to all its members. It goes beyond the ordinary accentuation of the term which makes it more extensive, inclusive and encompassing.

Thus the family system operates basically in two different dimensions, namely: extended and nuclear family systems. The extended family system is a larger corporate unit that extends across generations, which consists of parents, grandparents, aunts, uncles, brothers, sisters, nephews, nieces, cousins, etc. with common ancestral lineage. Though the component of this system is separated in terms of residential togetherness, yet it is united by communal origin and mutual responsibility. On the other hand, the nuclear family consists of members of the immediate hereditary link that embraces the household unit of husband, wife and their children. This system of nuclear family, which was not original to the African traditional social structure, seems to be the very outcome of modernization. Nevertheless, extended family system still remains the most important aspect of Nigerian society structure.

Chabal and Daloz rightly emphasize that, "the basic reference unit in Nigeria, as elsewhere in Africa, remains family-and kin-based: it is the fundamental 'circle of trust' within which individuals operate."[1] It follows that the circle of trust constitutes the basic form of social relation, which includes lineages that are based on descent through common ancestry and other forms of adoption. The identity of individuals in this relation centers primarily on kinship and family links, but does not negate the individuals' importance in the society. However, family and kinship are differentiated from other institutions of relationship based on the various forms of intimate ties among their members. Succinctly put, kinship refers to a social relationship founded on a biological or putative blood relationship that lays emphasis on the social character of the relationship more than its biological character. As a regulatory unit of family relationship[2], kinship system constitutes the paramount social reality for the Afri-

---

[1] Chabal, Patrick/Daloz, Jean-Pascal (1999): Africa Works, p. 27.
[2] Mbiti explains that "the deep sense of kinship, with all it implies, has been one of the strongest forces in traditional African life. Kinship is reckoned through blood and betrothal (engagement and marriage). It is kinship which controls social relationships between people in a given community; it governs marital customs and regulations, it determines the behavior of one individual towards another. Indeed, this sense of kinship binds together the entire life of the 'tribe', and is even extended to cover animals, plants and non-living objects through the 'totemic' system. Almost all the concepts connected with human relationship can be understood and interpreted through the kinship system. This it is which largely governs the behaviour, thinking and whole life of the individual in the

205

can peoples. It provides for the family needs and welfare such as healthcare, education and social development. On the other hand, the cases of deviance are also addressed through the kinship relationship. That is why it is not uncommon for the kin to invoke a restorative penalty in dealing with problematic behaviors of individuals against the community and social orders.

Furthermore, Kayongo-Male and Onyango aptly describe the importance of kinship and the nature of its familial reciprocity thus: "The most significant feature of African family life is probably the importance of the larger kin group beyond the nuclear family. Inheritance was commonly the communal variety wherein the entire kin group owns the land. The members of the extended family are linked in strong reciprocal aid relationships which entail complex rights and responsibilities."[3] Nevertheless, it is good to note that the idea of communal variety of kinship relationship is quite unconnected with communist's conception of 'collective will' that surmount the place of individual in the community. Against this backdrop, kinship operates as a principle of mutual reciprocity among individuals through the distribution and preservation of community values. It means that what affects one kin-member affects the others, and what affects all can only be surmounted through one's contribution to the communal responsibilities. Thus the individual in the community sees him/herself not as an individual per se, but as part of the living community with mutuality of purpose. This conception does not imply that the individual has no definitive role in the community; rather the individual finds his/her meaning and relevance in that community in which he/she belongs. This reciprocity is of course regarded as a fundamental aspect of African cultural value.

On the other hand, community is made up of individuals who constitute its essence but however find their meanings in its corporate unit. The individual as an important member of the community builds upon his personal identity and moral perception through the corporate relationship

society of which he is a member" (Mbiti, S. John (1989): African Religions and Philosophy 2nd Edition. Oxford: Heinemann Educational Publishers, p. 102).
[3] Kayongo-Male, Diane/Onyango, Philista (1984): The Sociology of the African Family. London/New York: Longmans, p. 6.

in the community. In fact, this relationship tends to determine and influence the behavioral outcomes with the other members of the community. In that sense, the individual participates in the community of relationships that is governed by a shared life, mutual action and mutual benefits. It follows that the family and kinship ties as a community-base social structure play a major role in linking the individuals to the community through which the vertical power structure of the society is introduced and sustained.

Subsequently, Kabeer notes that "one of the key organizations associated with kinship and family is 'the household', usually based on shared residence and/or shared budgets."[4] Following this idea of household, Nigerian traditional practice places emphasis on one's lineage through the male head of the household, which is regarded as patriarchal and at the same time hierarchical. In addition, the emphasis on lineage system through descent is usually accompanied by the intergenerational linkages which generally sustain the 'inheritance'[5] formation. This system assures of lineage continuity; and it is believed that lineage does not die but its members die and are replaced or regenerated through birth. This is because each new birth in the lineage is regarded as providing a vehicle for its expansion. And the desire to perpetuate the lineage results in the large kinship network.

Likewise, marriage which is considered as a community affair through the consent of both families involved is seen as a way of producing more children in order to perpetuate the kinship network. In other words, marriage is not merely a contract between two individuals; it is an alliance between two communities, families or descent groups. Such alliances are contractually sealed for the indefinite future through the dowry or 'bridewealth' paid by the groom's family to the bride's family. Therefore, these

---

[4] Kabeer, Naila (2003): Gender Mainstreaming in Poverty Eradication and the Millennium Development Goals: A Handbook for Policy-Makers and Other Stakeholders. London: Ashford Colour Press, p. 48.

[5] An inheritance implies according to Caldwell et al "a system whereby property, which is usually communal, remains within the lineage or clan and normally passes between members of the same sex" (Caldwell, John/Caldwell, Pat/Quiggin, Pat (1989): 'Disaster in an Alternative Civilization: The Social Context of AIDS in Sub-Saharan Africa'. In: Population and Development Review Vol. 15, No. 2, p. 188).

familial connections, which serve as the foundation for one's social identity, form vast network of relationship whereby the perpetuation of descendants is sustained.

The network of relationship nevertheless draws the background link to African conception of communalism. This conception accounts for mutual responsibility and interdependence as the main articles of human relationship. Unfortunately, the cultural value of communalism is being endangered by the process of globalization. The emerging order of social formation is becoming individualism or neo-patrimonialism in its extended formation. Consequently, the system of the extended family as a form of traditional social safety network especially in providing social security (that is: care and support) for the elderly and the young ones continues to be deformed in many respects, thereby simultaneously being replaced by the modern nuclear family system network of direct parents and children.[6] In other words, the emphasis boils down to social responsibility only on immediate generation of parents and children at the expense of the extended scope of traditional network of social sustainability. Thus the diagram below indicates that changing pattern of the social network, which has pitched a social and physical distance in the family setting, is significantly transforming the social structure.

---

[6] Ajomale notes that, "there is an observable progressive shift in function away from the traditional family. Traditional functions of the family, like care and social support to older family members, have gradually decreased in the recent past due to economic problems, migration and influence by foreign culture. Family members however are unable to effectively cope with the challenges of daily living. Emphasis is now on the nuclear family of 'me, my wife and my children' at the expense of other members of the wider family network, especially the older ones who look to the younger generation to provide them with economic security in old age [...].These changes in family structure in Nigeria have caused gradual disintegration of the extended family and of the communal sense of living in Nigerian society" (Ajomale, Olayinka (2007): 'Country Report: Ageing in Nigeria – Current State, Social and Economic Implications'. In: Hoff, Andreas (ed.): Summer Newsletter 2007 of the Research Committee (RC11) on the Sociology of Aging of the International Sociological Association (ISA). Oxford: Oxford Institute of Ageing, p. 16. http://www.rc11-sociology-of-aging.org/system/files/2007Newsletter.pdf [accessed: 12.04.2010]).

Diagram 3.1: Social Network Formation

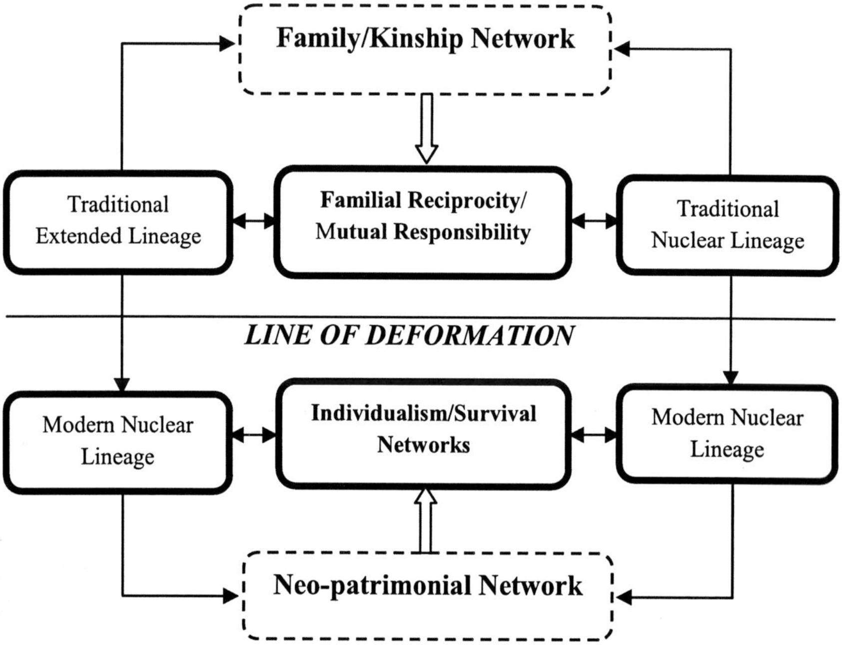

```
          ┌ ─ ─ ─ ─ ─ ─ ─ ─ ─ ─ ─ ─ ─ ─ ─ ─ ┐
      ┌──►│      Family/Kinship Network      │◄──┐
      │   └ ─ ─ ─ ─ ─ ─ ─ ─ ─ ─ ─ ─ ─ ─ ─ ─ ┘   │
      │                    ⇓                      │
  ┌───────────┐    ┌──────────────────┐    ┌───────────┐
  │Traditional│◄──►│Familial Reciprocity/│◄──►│Traditional│
  │Extended   │    │Mutual Responsibility│    │Nuclear    │
  │Lineage    │    └──────────────────┘    │Lineage    │
  └───────────┘                            └───────────┘
```

Traditional Extended Lineage ◄──► **Familial Reciprocity/ Mutual Responsibility** ◄──► **Traditional Nuclear Lineage**

LINE OF DEFORMATION

Modern Nuclear Lineage ◄──► **Individualism/Survival Networks** ◄──► Modern Nuclear Lineage

```
          ┌ ─ ─ ─ ─ ─ ─ ─ ─ ─ ─ ─ ─ ─ ─ ─ ─ ┐
      └──►│      Neo-patrimonial Network     │◄──┘
          └ ─ ─ ─ ─ ─ ─ ─ ─ ─ ─ ─ ─ ─ ─ ─ ─ ┘
```

From the diagram, one can deduce that the traditional extended family structure is assuming new formation especially in the urban regions, where the influence of modernization is more severe. This changing formation draws a major line of demarcation as indicated in the diagram between what is 'traditional' and what is 'modern'. By that it implies that the traditional orientation of family relationship is coming in conflict with the modern society formation that lays more emphasis on individual capacity of survival as against communal responsibility. That means that the extended family structure is in danger of being uprooted from its communal and familial belonging and then being exposed to an alien environment of humiliation and deprivation by the modern network of sustainability. The modern network structure is now based on individual interests and the ability of building a network of patronage that gives individuals assurance only to the immediate personal interests. Instead of kinship circle of trust, the individual as the centre of welfare association takes the position of a patron, and tries as much as possible to convert many clients as he/she wants to a vertical network of personal interest.

Significantly, the network formation in this sense may be attributed to idea of self preservation (or expressed as 'Spinoza's Conatus' – striving), as well as a mechanism towards adaptive arrangements.

Consequently, in the concerted bid for the formation of new network of adaptation or belonging in the changing family social structural system that is being influenced by the current wave of globalization, the Nigerian society is now being trapped into a neo-patrimonial system. In such new configuration of network according to Chabal and Daloz, "the pressures of modern political competition demand that political leaders surround themselves with an ever larger number of dependents. These dependents will enable them continuously to widen their support base. This leads to clientelistic and factional politics, the foundations of which are inevitably more precarious, the further removed they are from the 'circle of trust'. Political elites seek to establish principles of mutual aid, patron-client reciprocity, based on the model of kin and family relations."[7] Following this model of network, the modern Nigerian society instead of being liberated from traditional constraints of free choices is rather deepened by the personalization of interests that makes social inequality more visible. Furthermore, the bane of the socio-economic development therefore remains the yawning gap between the rich and the poor, and the threat of the cultural values. Even the political system is corruptly structured because it is only the few elitist (rich) class that controls the system to the detriment of the vast majority. Because of that configuration, the fundamental rights and privileges of the greater majority of the citizenry are not adequately protected. It follows that the country's socio-political system is in fact punctuated with human right abuses, political oddities and instability as a result of changing pattern of social structure.

---

[7] Chabal, Patrick/Daloz, Jean-Pascal (1999): Africa Works, p. 27. Paul also notes that "the precondition for the emergence of clientelism is the weakening and disruption of kinship ties as the oldest and historically most common form of social organization and solidarity. Through clientelism, [...] state actors accumulated, on the one hand, the coercive means to rule over people who are not their kin, to found dynasties and to institutionalize a new 'class' difference between rulers and ruled. On the other hand, clientelism embraced aspects that linked it to older forms of horizontal reciprocity, and that made the legitimacy of the new order of social inequality at any rate a possibility" (Paul, Axel T. (2008): pp. 212-213).

With these premises, our survey of the social structure in Nigeria attempts to clarify questions of relevance and proposes explanations as to the nature of socio-economic and political transformation in this era of globalization. Basically, it is a historical 'transformation from traditional to modern'[8], which manifests itself in societal changes and most eminent in the developing world. These changes have influence on the cultural traits, and are also exposing the Nigerian society into many precarious dangers of modernity. The changes are also remarkable in the complex nature of social structural composition in the society.

Through an empirical lens, this study investigates the structural and cultural dynamics in Nigeria's social developmental processes as a consequence of modernity as well as the structural transformation that has taken place over the time. This investigation will aid in producing a contextual framework for an eclectic approach in understanding the institutional and social elements, which have profound influence on the society development. But suffice it to say at this point that the socio-economic and political history of Nigeria could indicate the appearance of institutional lapses and the unending quests for state control by different interests groups. Nevertheless, as an important tool for our discussion, I will firstly examine the imports of social structural indicators as well as their changing consequences on distributional outcomes in order to determine how they contribute to inequality changes.

6.2 Indicators of Structural Differences

The main subject matter in this section is to examine empirically the tendencies of structural differences consequent of the mode of distribution of basic life chances. It suffices to say that the distributional impasse has been the major contributor to inequality trends in Nigeria. Hence inequality has been and continues to be a problematic niche in social structural formation in Nigeria. Discussing the trends of inequality in Nigeria by analyzing the measures of economic, political and socio-

---

[8] Giddens says: "sociologists have often discussed the transition from the traditional to modern world in term of the concepts of 'differentiation' or 'functional specialization'. The movement from small-scale systems to agrarian civilizations and then to modern societies, according to this view, can be seen as a process of progressive inner diversification" (Giddens, Anthony (1990): The Consequences of Modernity, p. 21).

cultural opportunities, one would first of all question why are some groups and individuals more privileged or favored than their counterparts? Or to put the question in another way; why has the structure of the society given undue advantage to some groups as we shall see in wage differences, and why are the manifestations of inequality differences becoming more visible in this present period of global integration? These questions are generally considered in relation to the changing pattern of the distributional incomes and wealth, and the underlying forces of those changes attributed to the systems and processes of globalization.

In this examination, Gini coefficient will be applied as the measure of inequality trends, and the tendency of changeable in the social structure. However, the trends of inequality in Nigeria, comprising income differences, places of residence, inequalities existing within and among sociopolitical groups, as well as exclusion from political participation are to be empirically examined in this section. In a study of this manner, attempt will be made to analyze inequality differences by way of historical antecedence, as well as to understand why income distributions and other accessibility to human developmental goods are the way they appear to be in a culturally pluralistic society such as Nigeria. The investigation is carried out through the correlation of different pieces of information made available by existing statistical data, their shortcomings notwithstanding.

But before scrutinizing the inequality trends, it is pertinent to overview first of all the social indicators in Nigeria, which are the essential instruments for productive capacity, efficiency and creativity in a society's poverty and inequality indices. This overview goes down to expatiate if there are significant changes before and within the periods of global transformation, by comparatively analyzing some selected statistical data. It will of course elaborate what was the condition of social development before independence and what has changed thereafter. As the determining factors to the quality of life, social indicators (comprising of population growth, life expectancy, mortality rate, human literacy level etc.) in a given society on the basis of epochal divergences foreclose fundamentally the overall development of human and material resources. Due to the mode of distribution of incomes, poor service deliveries and lack of infrastructural facilities as we shall observe, the indices of social development in Nigeria are negatively being affected in comparison with other developing countries.

Table 3.1: Social Indicators in Nigeria and some Comparator Countries (2007)

Social Indicators 2007	Nigeria	Bangladesh	Indonesia	Pakistan
Population (million)	147.98	158.57	225.63	162.48
Life Expectancy at Birth	47	64	71	65
Infant Mortality (per 1,000 live births)	97	47	25	73
Mortality rate under 5 (per 1,000)	189	60	31	90
Total Fertility Rate	5	3	2	4
Adult Literacy	72	53	92	54
Gloss Primary School Enrolment	97	103	114	84
Gloss Secondary School Enrolment	32	44	66	33

Source: The World Bank, WDI Online.

Table 3.1 shows the social indicators in Nigeria and some comparator countries in 2007. It indicates that Nigeria is behind such countries like Bangladesh, Indonesia and Pakistan in the overall core social indicators especially on the mortality rate. Due the increase of poverty line, more than 42% of Nigerian children are malnourished, contributing to 18.9% mortality in every 1000 children under the age of 5 years as against 6% mortality rate in every 1000 children under the age of 5 years in Bangladesh or 3.1% in Indonesia respectively. Although the adult literacy in Nigeria is little above average as compared to Bangladesh and Pakistan, yet the rate of educational enrolment remains comparatively low as it favors mostly the rich population to the detriment of the poor majorities. In fact, this observation could be attributed to the inability of the federal government to match up with the challenges driven by the population growth, as well as inadequate policy strategies to improve the human development indices through resource redistribution mechanisms and inclusive development.

Table 3.2: Nigeria Core Welfare Indicator by Zones, 2006 (%)

Household Infrastructure	North East	North West	North Central	South East	South West	South South
Secure housing tenure	40.2	58.0	68.4	60.3	73.1	58.0
Access to water	88.5	93.5	81.0	64.4	94.3	79.2
Safe water source	30.7	50.6	48.9	40.8	73.5	45.9
Year round water source	37.7	38.8	31.5	54.3	42.6	56.7
Water treated before drinking	4.6	7.5	14.1	11.4	20.4	5.8
Safe sanitation	45.4	61.6	46.6	69.5	62.1	55.0
Improved waste disposal	6.2	10.7	8.8	9.0	36.0	13.2
Non-wood fuel used for cooking	3.5	7.1	16.8	24.0	58.3	33.7
Has electricity	30.7	37.7	44.6	65.4	79.1	62.2

Source: NBS (2006): Core Welfare Indicators Questionnaire Survey.

Moreover, the method of distribution of key household infrastructure affects also the social indicators in Nigeria. The redistribution mechanisms so far have not equitably embraced the core welfare provisions especially when one observes the household infrastructures available in different geopolitical zones. Specifically, table 3.2 shows that the Nigeria core welfare indicator according to geopolitical zones generally ranked the southwest as relatively higher in 2006 when compared to other zones, with northwest trailing lowest in core welfare provisions. This indicator proves that the provision of basic household infrastructure is not equitably distributed according to geopolitical zones. The major deficiency that is shared by all the zones is on the area of inadequate provision of treated water for drinking. This basic problem exposes the majority of the population to various water borne diseases such as cholera and malaria that continue to account for high mortality rates. Apart from that, poor conditions of health services in Nigeria also contribute to decline in life expectancy. It has also been observed that the federal government has not been keen in providing enough basic health facilities. Most general hospitals are poorly funded as well as inadequately equipped by the government. And then the exorbitant hospital bills without proper treatments also scare the poor patients. It implies that as a result of inept healthcare system, and precisely the absence of functional health insurance schemes that can guarantee the security of life, the financial burdens involved in caring for

214

the sick are for the growing poor population the major barriers of good healthcare.

Figure 3.1: Nigeria's Human Development Index by Zones 2008

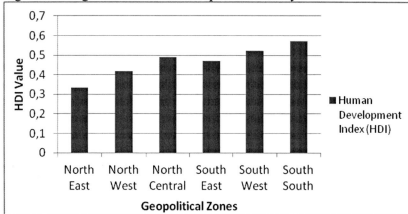

Source: NBS & UNDP (2011)

On the other hand, when we observe the human development index (see: figure 3.1) according to geopolitical zones in terms of people's well-being and life chances, it highlights the disparities among the various zones. Though the index does not account for a comprehensive measure of human development that may include equality of right and freedom, yet it provides a broad measure of living standards in terms of basic amenities, employment opportunities, adult literacy and life expectancy. It has been observed that the human development index has been significantly very low in Nigeria when compared to other developing countries. According to UNDP HDI report 2011, Nigeria is ranked 156 out of 187 countries as a low human development country. The national index value was 0.446 in 2008, but increased slightly to 0.459 in 2011. This little increment is not yet enough to improve the life chances of the growing population. If we then observe the development index differences among the geopolitical zones as shown in figure 3.1, it indicates that north-east was ranked the least, with south-south occupying the highest HDI in 2008. Unfortunately, the living opportunities offered by the government have not been sufficient to account for a higher measure of human development in Nigeria. The disaggregated index of human development especially educational attainment and how the social goods and wealth are distributed will be analyzed later in this study in order to show the inequality disparities between urban and rural regions, among geopolitical zones, genders and classes.

As a background instance, we shall first of all examine comparatively the measures of economy and inequality in Nigeria among some selected countries. This comparison, in relation to social indications already observed, is to assist in determining certain forces that constitute a hitch to the national distributional outcomes, as well as to discover the changing impact of globalization on inequality differentials in Nigeria. It follows that the proper analysis of inequality trends in Nigeria will come to reveal the day-to-day intolerable differentials in socio-political and economic structures that govern social interactions. These differences are evidence when one compares the Nigerian life opportunities with other countries characterized under similar human development index, and some even less endowed with economic resources than Nigeria.

Table 3.3: Measures of Economy and Inequality of Selected Countries 2007

Countries	Population (2007 Mil)	Population (2020 Mil)	GDP per Capita (US$)	Share of Income or Expenditure		Inequality Measures	
				Poorest 10%	Richest 10%	Richest 10% to Poorest 10%	Gini Index
Nigeria	147.7	193.3	1,118	2.0	32.4	16.3	42.9
Ghana	22.9	29.6	646	2.0	32.8	16.1	42.8
Bangladesh	157.8	185.6	431	4.3	26.6	6.2	31.0
Pakistan	173.2	226.2	879	3.9	26.5	6.7	31.2
India	1,164.7	1,367.2	1,046	3.6	31.1	8.6	36.8
Indonesia	224.7	254.2	1,918	3.0	32.3	10.8	39.4
Egypt	80.1	98.6	1,729	3.9	27.6	7.2	32.1

Source: UNDP Human Development Report, 2009

Hence table 3.3 illustrates the measures of economy and inequality of selected countries as compiled by the United Nations Development Programme (UNDP) in its Human Development Report (HDR) 2009. The inequality measure is basically determined by the overall social indicators in terms of life expectancy, literacy level, income opportunity etc. as

216

already illustrated in table 3.1 above. However, the index report in table 3.3 was calculated based on the ratio of the income and expenditure per capita share of the 10% richest group to that of the 10% poorest group in a particular country. This ranking, of course is aimed at determining the inequality differences between the two groups as a measure of national inequality. It is striking to observe that the Gini index of Nigeria stood at 42.9 from 2000 to 2010, worst than other comparator countries. This index gap in fact indicates high inequality rate in Nigeria in the midst of rising population growth. Although India has more population and lesser GDP per Capita than Nigeria in 2007, yet the inequality measured by Gini coefficient shows that Nigeria has about 6.1 index differences as compared to India. This trend is an indicative of poor economic and human development planning goals to improve the general household living standards.[9] Consequently, the poverty incidence and inequality index in Nigeria are mostly observable in the life patterns of the vast majority of the population.

Figure 3.2: National Poverty Incidence from 1980-2010

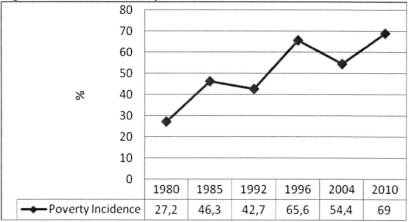

	1980	1985	1992	1996	2004	2010
Poverty Incidence	27,2	46,3	42,7	65,6	54,4	69

Source: National Bureau of Statistics, 2011

---

[9] Levis opines that "the failure of Nigerian development in terms of reduction of inequality differences stems above all from the absence of a political and institutional center to serve as a principal of economic change. Nigeria's elites, divided along communal and factional lines, have not consolidated stable political regimes or fostered capable state organizations" (Lewis, Peter M. (2007): Growing Apart; Oil, Politics, and Economic Change in Indonesia and Nigeria. Ann Arbor: University of Michigan Press, pp. 77-78).

It is evidence to note that the majority of Nigerian population still lives below the poverty line. This manifests mostly in the rural areas where there are limited availability of social goods. However, the dichotomy between the poor (below poverty line) and the non-poor (above poverty line) is usually determined by various indicators. Using the Nigeria Living Standard Survey (NLSS) which was adopted by the National Bureau of Statistics, this study broadly identifies many indicators of poverty such as human development index (see table 3.1/figure 3.1), per capita income and expenditure, household welfare (see table 3.2), as well as employment opportunities (see figure 3.6 below). Figure 3.2 then shows the national poverty incidence from 1980 to 2010. This time-frame represents the period from the second civilian republic to the present civilian government (fourth republic). Even though there were several interceptions by the military dictatorships within the period, yet the same period saw the major economic transformation in Nigeria especially in terms of integration of the local economy into global capitalism. Unfortunately, the table significantly indicates that there has been a constant increase of poverty rate in Nigeria in comparative estimation with other developing countries, reaching its peak in 2010. It follows that the poverty incidence in Nigeria negates the outcome of the GDP real growth rate of the economy within the same period, which explains the fact that the 'said-economic growth' has not benefited the poor household majorities in Nigeria. Nevertheless, what is actually needed for poverty reduction is a reform agenda that will target social spending to the poor especially in the rural areas. That implies that any effort in improving the social indicators will also check the growing rate of inequality both within and among groups and individuals in the Nigerian society.

In order to understand and estimate the trends of inequality in Nigeria, it is necessary to observe inequality manifestations within and between groups. Using statistical data, Gini Coefficient will be applied in measuring the inequality differences. However, the computation of inequality index in Nigeria is usually based on wage differences that contribute to the poverty profile between the non-poor and the poor within the same period, as well as unequal opportunities in social goods or living chances and the mode of distribution of incomes within and among individuals and groups. Even though the determination of the exert inequality measure has remained quite difficult due to divergences in the collection of

218

statistical data, yet the overall estimation is very important in analyzing and studying the level of inequality in Nigeria. The estimation is based on the changes in inequality differences that emanated before and after the democratization as well as the integrating role played by the liberalization process within the same periods.

Figure 3.3: Lorenz Curve Showing Inequalities in Nigeria (2004)

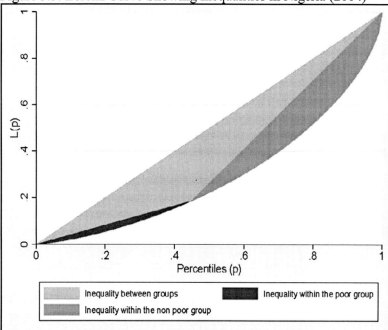

Source: Araar, A/Taiwo, A (2006:13)

However, Araar and Taiwo illustrate the overall tendency of inequality in Nigeria both between groups as well as within the poor and non-poor groups using Lorenz curve.[10] From the graph in figure 3.3, it shows that the trends of inequality can be more evident within the non-poor groups (i.e. those living above the poverty line) than within the poor group (i.e. those living below the poverty line), and also between groups such as

---

[10] Araar, Abdelkrim/Taiwo, Awoyemi (2006): Poverty and Inequality Nexus. Illustrations with Nigeria Data: p. 3 & 13. http://www.cirpee.org/fileadmin/documents/Cahiers_2006/ CIRPEE06-38.pdf [Accessed: 12.04.2012]

gender, regions as well as among the geopolitical zones and classes. These tendencies will assist us in this study towards understanding the manifestations of inequality in the Nigerian society.

Figure 3.4: National Inequality Trends 1985-2010 (Gini Coefficient)

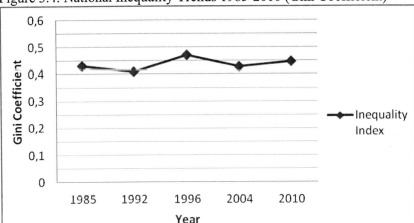

Sources: FOS (1999) Poverty Profile for Nigeria 1980-1996 & NBS (2011) Poverty Profile for Nigeria.

The inequality trends as shown in figure 3.4 are based on the life changes of the population according to the human development index such as access to educational and employment opportunities, income distribution etc. When one vividly observes the trends of inequality in Nigeria between 1985 and 2010 as indicated in the figure, one notices that inequality index has been on the increase since 1985, especially when the Federal Government first implemented the liberalization policies. Although there was a little positive development between 1985 and 1992, yet it was not sustained due to poor implementation of the adjustment policies. The improvement between 1996 and 2004 was the outcome of the transition to democratic government that opened more opportunities for socio-economic and political participations. However, the movement of inequality index has continued again to increase from 2004 despite the real growth of the economy within the same period. Between 2004 and 2010, inequality in Nigeria rose from 0.4296 to 0.447, making Nigeria one of the most unequal countries in the world. It is doubtful from the look of things whether there will be much improvement in the future outcomes.

But be that as it may, it all depends on government policy programmes that can ensure distributive justice and economic empowerment.

Empirical findings from part two of this work have already revealed that the Nigerian government is not sufficiently taken the chances offered by the global interaction especially on income revenues accruing from oil market to improve the social and physical infrastructures of the society. For instance, the deteriorating rate both in quantity and quality of social amenities and poor human capital developments are indications of the fact that the political and economic systems are dysfunctional. Besides, even the existing facilities are poorly maintained with insufficient personnel to handle the operations as well as limited accessibility to those facilities available by the poor majority. This deficiency questions the positive impact of globalization on social development. And because the rich and the political elites could have easy access to improved facilities such as in healthcare services and education elsewhere outside the country, the local facilities have remained underdeveloped. In this sense, inequality could be conceptualized as the rational outcome of inadequate household infrastructures, poor income redistribution as well as limited living opportunities. As the important determinants of inequality among individuals and groups in the society, we shall then move forward to examine different inequality determinants in Nigeria.

6.2.1 Income Distribution

Allocation of resources either in terms of social amenities, capitals, labor or wages has been one of the major developmental challenges facing the Nigerian government. Income or wealth distribution accounts for dynamic movement of government fiscal and welfare policy agendas aimed at accelerating social and economic growth. Income distribution is simply described as the share of available resources of a nation among its populace. But in this section, we shall analyze income distribution from the point of view of how labor, wealth, and resources of the country are redistributed. In that sense, it becomes necessary to understand the relationship between income growth in terms of availability of resources and their redistribution to achieve sustainable development. Taking a look at the trends of demands among classes, regions and ethnic groups in the struggle over available resources, the mode of distribution of incomes remains very essential in determining the system of socio-economic development. The pattern of distribution is also important in accounting for those welfare mechanisms through which resources could directly or indirectly affect the living conditions of individuals and groups in the society. It follows that the wider range of distribution of income explains both the general welfare as well as the measures to forestall or regulate the changing patterns of consumption towards sustainable development. But because the mode of distribution of income in Nigeria does not sufficiently sustain the general welfare of the population, the key factor of the distributional outcome is for immediate survival of the individual.[11]

With regard to distributional outcomes, Stewart and Berry distinguished primary incomes from secondary incomes. They propose that "primary incomes are those generated by the economic system (e.g. wages or dividends) and these are affected by the impact of changes in the structure of the market on the incomes people earn. Secondary incomes on the other hand, consist of deductions from individuals' primary incomes (e.g. through taxes), or additions to income such as through pensions provided by the state, or remittances from other family members, or public goods, provided by the state, but also by non-governmental organizations (NGOs) and families. Secondary incomes are thus affected by changes in government taxation and expenditure policies and by access to publicly provided goods and services."[12] But usually the production profile of low income countries in terms of 'what they produce and what they export' is significantly influenced by the impact of liberalization, making distribution of primary incomes more unequal. This inequality manifests significantly on the wage difference between the public and private sectors.[13] The high unemployment rate contributes also to insufficient access to primary incomes. Besides, the secondary incomes in most developing countries are neither sufficiently harnessed to balance the distribution outcomes nor able to promote the declining household expenditures due

---

[11] The traditional structure of the kinship network that gives credence to redistribution of resources to kith and kin within intra-family and inter-community lines is usually the source of immediate survival of individuals in the community.

[12] Stewart, Frances/Berry, Albert (1999): 'Globalization, Liberalization, and Inequality: Expectations and Experience'. In: Hurrell, Andrew/Woods, Ngaire (eds.): Inequality, Globalization, and World Politics. New York: Oxford University Press, p. 153.

[13] Simply put, public sectors are those enterprises under the control of the government, whereas private sectors are the economic investments owned by individuals or groups.

to limited access to public goods. Even the remittances are limited to particular set of families that have sons and daughters, who are well-to-do outside their home country. And due to changes caused by capitalist economic policies, there are rapid increases of domestic expenditures, which have continued to affect the general incomes.

It is a fact that capitalist market policies affect income distribution of a country either positively or negatively, depending on how the economic system of that country is developed. Liberalization policies however emphasize more on high productivity and expansion of market profits for the capitalists than proper attention to equitable redistribution of incomes for the local development. Thus the developing economies are mostly affected as a result of policy changes occasioned by globalization influences. The policy changes, of course, vary with the nature of the economy causing the distributional outcomes either to rise or decrease. In the Nigerian case, the decrease in per capita income continues to affect the quality of overall growth. Here Kaplinsky observes that "Nigeria displays a picture of falling per capita incomes over time and of rising inequality."[14] It follows that the policy interventions against rising inequality have not yielded positively on overall growth. On the other hand, the restrictions in government policy interventions caused by neo-liberal principles have also contributed to the hindrance towards equitable income distribution in Nigeria.[15] In that case, the neo-liberal principles benefit mostly the multinational corporations and the corrupt-ridden public enterprises that play the underlying determinant role in the economic structure.

On the general assessment, the system of allocation and of distribution of resources in Nigeria usually results to contentious phenomenon of debate in the pursuit of nation-building. The absolute criterion or formula for

---

[14] Kaplinsky, Raphael (2005): Globalization, Poverty and Inequality: Between a Rock and a Hard Place. Cambridge: Polity Press, p. 40.

[15] Forrest emphasizes that "in Nigeria, as elsewhere, political and social processes and the institutional structure of the state have profoundly conditioned economic activity, state policies and forms of intervention. In this way they affect the allocation and use of resources, patterns of accumulation and the growth and development of the economy" (Forrest, Tom (1986): 'The Political Economy of Civil Rule and the Economic Crisis in Nigeria (1979-84)'. In: The Review of African Political Economy Vol. 13, No. 35. London: Routledge, p. 4).

national distribution of resources remains more political than socio-economical, giving rise to undue competitions among various interest groups. It has been observed that "so contentious has the matter been that none of the formula evolved at various times by a commission or by decree under different regimes since 1964 has gained general acceptability among the component units of the country. Indeed, the issue, like a recurring decimal, has painfully remained the first problem that nearly every incoming regime has had to grapple with since independence."[16] In addition, the debate continues to foment various types of conflicts in the polity such that each coming regime will be struggling not to favor one particular zone against the others. As a result, the system of distribution is such that it has structured the state in a preferential conflict, given the degree of inequality and distributional difference among the geopolitical zones.

In a specific instance, the intense struggle for distribution or sharing of federal revenues by the government was the by-product of cross-subsidization, which was introduced during the colonial era. In this conception, it has been noted that "at the root of the amalgamation of the Southern and Northern Protectorates by Lord Lugard in 1914 was the issue of cross-subsidization – the richer South would subsidize development endeavors in the poorer North. The level of cross-subsidization was not clearly specified. The first attempt to write down the basis and levels of sharing revenues among the component units (or regions, as they were then called) of the Nigerian Federation was in 1946, when the Phillipson Fiscal Commission, set up by the Colonial Administration, proposed the derivation principle as a basis for fiscal federalism. The idea was that revenue should be shared, among other things, in proportion to the contribution each region made to the common purse or central government. Derivation became the only criterion used to allocate revenues among the regions in the 1948-1949 and 1951-1952 fiscal years."[17] However, before and shortly after independence, the derivation formula was still maintained, which also encouraged enterprising competition among the regions. Within those periods, each region was noted for specific economic

---

[16] Federal Republic of Nigeria (1987): Report of the Political Bureau. Lagos: Federal Govt. Printer, p. 169.

[17] United Nations Development Programme (2006): p. 13.

ventures especially on the area of agricultural productivity in order to improve regional revenues and per capita incomes. But the situation took another turn after the discovery of crude oil in commercial quality that put the federal government in total control of the petroleum resources. It saw to the radical review of the sharing formula that majorly put the producing regions on disadvantaged positions.

Table 3.4: Federal and State Shares of Petroleum Proceeds 1960-1999

Years	Producing State (%)	Distributable Pool Amount or Federation Account (%)
1960-67	50	50
1967-69	50	50
1969-71	45	55
1971-75	45 minus offshore proceeds	55 plus offshore proceeds
1975-79	20 minus offshore proceeds	80 plus offshore proceeds
1979-81	-	100
1982-92	1.5	98.5
1992-99	3	97
1999 -	13	87

Source: Modification of Sagay 2001.

For instance, the table 3.4 shows the derivation formula, indicating the shares of petroleum revenues between the producing states and federal government from 1960 till date. Between 1960 and 1975, the shares of the petroleum proceeds were approximately equal between the producing states and the federal government but started to increase in favor of the federal government from 1975 during the oil boom. This sharing culminated to its worse formation during the military regime between 1983 and 1999. Presently, one can observe that federal government has centralized and usurped the major revenues accruing from oil production against the backdrop of the earlier derivation principle based on fiscal federalism. The process of derivation has remained so politicized that the producing states, which belong to the minority ethnic groups, have been so marginalized by the distributional policies. It is indeed a paradox that the region with the wealth of the nation seem to be neglected, why the majority of the region's population live in abject poverty without properly benefitting from the oil revenue in order to augment the comparative deprivations such as good agricultural land farming.

The political shift from geographical regional formula to state revenue allocation in 1967 through the decree on state creation has not yielded the desired results either, consequent of inefficient institutions to regulate the national economic planning and fiscal decentralization of the resources. Thus the key distribution instance remains the government at the center,[18] and it controls more than half of the revenue from the federation account and distributes the remainder to states and local governments. Although the creation of more states in conjunction with the intention to decentralize power and governance under the military regimes shifted the focus of distributional debates on revenues away from the geographical regions to some extent, yet the major debate is currently based on geopolitical competitions that culminated in ethnic mobilization and struggle.[19] As a country majorly dependent on one-commodity revenue, ethnic mobilization has altered the nationalistic-will and has become the strategic means to resource struggles and accumulation. As a result, the political elites continue to act in defense of their own ethnic-nationalism. It suggests that income distribution has created major gaps between urban and rural regions, among states and classes. The high rate of unemployment, growing

---

[18] Gerhard Hauck stellt fest: „Entsprechend ungleich ist die Einkommensverteilung. Sie ist es in nahezu allen afrikanischen Staaten – eine Spitzenposition nimmt hier Nigeria ein, wo der Gini-Index der interpersonalen Einkommensverteilung schon 1976 einen zwischen 0.7 und 0.8 liegenden Wert aufwies, ein Ungleichheitsniveau, das auch weltweit nur noch von Brasilien und Honduras annähernd erreicht wurde [...]. Der Staat ist und bleibt deshalb die primäre Allokationsinstanz, die über Art und Umfang der Akkumulation der Bourgeoisie entscheidet." (Hauck, Gerhard (2001): Gesellschaft und Staat in Afrika. Frankfurt am Main: Brandes & Apsel, pp. 25-26).

[19] In that sense, Bienen rightly states that "although Nigeria had periods in its history when welfare politics were salient, the primary meaning of distribution was in terms of the division of public resources among territorial units [that is to say in terms of revenue distributions between regions and then states]. The factors that led to the ascendancy of ethnic-territorial criteria for distribution were: general poverty; the introduction of electoral politics; the attempt to mobilize support by appeals to communal blocs; the weakness of class groups, given the relative lack of differentiation within the Nigerian economy of the 1950s and 1960s; and the ideas of welfare which stressed raising absolute levels rather than interstrata comparisons" (Bienen, Henry (1985): Political Conflict and Economic Change in Nigeria. London: Frank Cass & Co, p. 65).

poverty and the persistent inequality clearly manifest in the various ethnic cleavages and political violence.

Furthermore, this analysis is incomplete if it fails to examine the income distribution in relation to labor market principles, which is also a quick root to persistent inequality. In that case, the social, political and economic context of inequality among and within individuals or groups in relation to the larger social system manifests itself majorly in the labor market. In fact, the analysis of the labor market in Nigeria indicates the level of income inequality that exists in the country. With little and competitive employment opportunities, the labor forces are subjected to various forms of risks such as uncertainty, insecurity and low remuneration. Indeed, another reality of labor market under the risk condition is that many Nigerian work-forces are confronted by new market principles created by globalization, which have resulted to job losses. This phenomenon also manifests in the job insecurity in most of the public-private firms and informal enterprises, which greatly reduces the employment chances both for the skilled and unskilled workers. For instance, the recent recapitalization of the banking sub-sector in Nigeria gave rise to many workers in the bank industry losing their job positions. Consequently, many disengaged workers have remained in depressive conditions whereas some have engaged themselves in pitiable occupations in order to eke out a living.

On the other hand, the structural differences in the labor market with regard to its distributions according to ethnic origins, classes and genders are often the subject of prejudices and stereotypes that often lack legal protection and security.[20] The differences manifest themselves in various exploitive ways but mainly in wage differences and domestic input whereby some work harder but earn lesser and vice versa. Besides, the distribution of income between urban and rural dwellers is quite unevenly distributed. As we shall see later in this study, findings indicate that the urban areas have more access to basic infrastructures and more advantaged in finding high-paid jobs. This tendency implies that urban income earners have more advantage over the rural paid workers in terms of opportunities to maximize their incomes. But nevertheless, the existence of

---

[20] I will still elaborate on this point later in the study.

inequality in income distribution may be more pronounced in the urban areas as a result of high cost of living and rapid rate of urbanization. In that case, the rural dweller may have advantage because most of them are subsistence farmers and have the possibility of engaging in mini-enterprise for their sustenance. As a follow up, I will then examine in more details the tendencies of income inequality both within and among various groups.

6.2.2 Minimum Wage and Maximum Difference

Analyzing the movement of wage differentials in a given society makes it easier to determine the distributional outcomes and the level of consumption patterns from time to time. This, of course takes into consideration number of factors such as market options or principles, policy interventions, labor utilization, social infrastructures etc. These factors may either be externally or internally induced, resulting to their varied modes of consequences on the wage differentials. From a country perspective, globalization through trade liberalization constitutes the main external induced factors. Some scholars suggest that globalization through liberalization process appears to have a significant de-equalizing effect on developing countries as a result of policy interventions, as well as importation of new technology that renders the local entrepreneur less active and irrelevance in the labor demand and supply. It follows than that the changes in commodity prices are also associated with new technological inversion, but could as well influence positively the wage floors through direct foreign investments. On the other hand, internal factors include the country's economic policies, political instability and wealth redistribution through minimum wage legislations. The distributional impacts on the wage differentials create economic variations that mostly give rise to the increase of income inequality.

However, wage differentials are conveniently addressed in this section in terms of minimum wage and maximum difference. Minimum wage is explained as the wage-floors between the low income and high income earners in the public and private sectors. Its aim is to cover the basic minimum needs of workers adjusted to purchasing power of the local currency and commodity price-increase within a given period. In Nigeria, the legislation on minimum wage originated "as a means of closing the gaps between the two extreme groups of lower and upper wage earners in the public sector, minimum wage legislation has been on debate since the late 1970s of the Udoji minimum wage award. Since then 'wage floors' have always come as welcome and genuine economic policy; and immediate and quick measures to close income gap or as palliative against changing prices or for a particular economic policy."[21] In fact, the harmonization of the wage floors initiated by Udoji commission has had positive impacts on low-income workers' welfare in the late 1970s, but minimally started to change in the early 1980s as consequence of structural adjustment policies. It followed that the action of the government in the 1980s to downsize the public sector at federal, state and local council levels due to unpaid wages rather worsened the conditions of the low-income earners and thereupon many workers were retrenched from their jobs during the austerity periods.

There are also other evidences to point an increasing level of wage differences in Nigeria, which have continued to be the most challenging socio-economic problem and concern to policy makers. For instance, changes in the Gini-coefficient during the structural adjustment regime were indicative of income inequality, which affected mostly the rural dwellers and low wage earners. However, to determine the actual wage differential in Nigeria has always been a difficult task, because of the variations in data collections that make the analysis more sensitive, as well as due to unrecorded incomes coming from informal sector of the economy. But the present survey is based on already-published data reports especially on earnings and welfare packages in the public and private sectors. Though certain assumptions will also be made concerning the outcomes of wage differentials on the daily life experiences of the population.

---

[21] National Bureau of Statistics (2007): The Middle Class in Nigeria Analysis of Profile, Determinants and Characteristics (1980-2007). [Produced under the Auspices of the Economic Reform & Governance Project, ERGP] Federal Republic of Nigeria, p. 16. http://www.nigerianstat.gov.ng/ [accessed: 03.04.2009]. Here Wage floors or minimum wage means "a transfer of resources from the high income to the low income earners, thereby helping to act as a push factor from the low wage group to the emergence of the middle income group. The net effect is a decrease in income inequality between the low and high income groups" (National Bureau of Statistics (2007): The Middle Class in Nigeria, p. 17).

Table 3.5: Some Federal Government Policies on Minimum Wage from 1974 to 2011

Year	Commission/Act/Budget	Minimum Wage Recommendations per Month
1972/1974	Udoji Commission	N60
1981	Minimum Wage Act	N125
1990	Minimum Wage Amended Act	N250
1993	Federal Budget	N363
1998	Government Directive on Wages	N3,500 (Fed. Workers) N3,000(State Workers)
2000	Minimum Wage Act	N7,500 (Fed. Workers) N5,500(State Workers)
2010	Minimum Wage Amended Act	N18,000

Sources: Federal Ministry of Finance/Central Bank of Nigeria/International Labour Organization

Table 3.5 shows some of the federal government policies on minimum wage from 1972 to 2010. The first National Minimum Wage Act in post-independent Nigeria came into law in 1981 with N125 per month as the national minimum wage. This act, of course was to account for all workers in the public sector as well as in private sectors that had up to 50 workforces. The act was later reviewed in 1990, which then fixed minimum wage at N250 per month. Through the amendment of National Minimum Wage Act in 2000, the Federal Government subsequently proposed national minimum wage floors of N7,500 per month at the Federal level, and N5,500 at both Private (formal sector) and State levels respectively. But due to the rising consumer price index that affected the rate of inflation, the salary structure of 2000 was again reviewed by the Federal Government in 2010, approving the new salary structure of N18,000 per month with the intent harmonization in various state levels and parastatals. But the implementation of the new federal minimum wage, which was passed into law on the 23rd of February 2011 by the National Assembly, has been a tug of war and big debate between the Federal and State Governments on the one hand, and on the other hand, the government and the labor unions. Even as that, many private sectors have remained adamant in the full harmonization of the new minimum wage. Consequently, the poor implementations have resulted to warning strikes and eventually industrial actions in various parastatals of both state and federal governments.

Table 3.6: Federal Minimum Wage (1980-2007)

Year	Nominal Minimum Wage			Real Minimum Wage		
	Federal Minimum Wage (N)	Federal Minimum Wage ($)	Federal Wage Rate (N)/hr	Federal Minimum Wage (N)	Federal Minimum Wage ($)	Federal Wage Rate (N)/hr
1980	100	183.02	0.63	10.10	18.49	0.12
1981	125	227.27	0.78	16.23	29.52	0.18
1991	250	31.09	1.56	19.23	2.39	0.01
1992	363	36.63	2.27	25.03	2.53	0.02
1999	1300	14.08	8.13	196.97	2.13	0.01
2000	4000	39.33	25.00	579.71	5.70	0.04
2003	4500	34.82	62.19	397.18	3.07	0.02
2007	11132	82.46	69.58	1008.33	7.47	0.05

Source: National Bureau of Statistics 2007

Besides, table 3.6 shows federal minimum wage from 1980 to 2007 that differentiated between nominal and real wages valued in Naira with the corresponding US Dollar exchange rate within the periods. This differential is fundamental in determining the actual changes in wages. It is interesting to note that from 1980 to 2007, there is about 11,032% change of minimum wage, but if we compare the wage sum with the dollar equivalent, it indicates about minus 100% increase within the periods. Again, when we compare the nominal minimum wage (i.e. the lowest wage floor per month) with the real minimum wage (i.e. the consumer price index of the wages), it shows the very poor purchasing power of the wages and the worst when the real wage rate is calculated per hour. The implication of the statistics is that the wage increase in Nigeria does not actually indicate the improvement of living standard of the population due to inflation, and it also shows that all the workers within minimum wage range live below one dollar per day and therefore below poverty line. It is unfortunate that the salary increment in Nigeria does not account for the purchasing power of the domestic commodities, as well as the differences among the income groups. This situation explains the cause of rising inequality index as we have observed in figures 3.3 and 3.4 above.

On the other hand, the minimum wage bracket in Nigeria is yet to counter the income differences between the two levels of federal and state wage income earners due to some additional allowances enjoyed only by the federal workers. As a result, many job seekers aspire more to gain employment in the federal civil service than in the state civil service, diminishing the productive outputs of the state governments. From all indications, it is obvious that most economic activities are concentrated on the federal level to the disadvantage of the state governments who depend on the federal government for their monthly allocations. This trend is often more difficult for some states with little internally-generated incomes to fund their financial demands, both for recurrent and capital projects. In other words, some states spend most of their monthly allocations in paying workers' salaries, leaving little or nothing for developmental projects. Some other states have also placed embargo on employment as a result, causing the increase in unemployment rate. The unemployment rate is however illustrated in figure 3.6 below, which indicates constant increase in the rate of unemployment especially among the rural households.

Table 3.7: Approximate Comparison of Monthly Salaries of Selected Public Sectors (2007)

Maximum Difference	Armed Forces	Police/ Other Paramili-tary Forces	Academic Staff of Fed. Tertiary Inst. & Teaching Hospitals	Non-Academic Staff of Fed. Tertiary/ Research Inst. & Teaching Hospitals	Other Fed. Civil Servants	State Civil Servants
Minimum Wage	N7,500	N7,500	N7,500	N7,500	N7,500	N5,500
Lowest Level	N21,600 (Private)	N5,250 (Recruit) & N24,400 (Constable)	N57,800 (Level One)	N12,600 (Level One)	N12,000 (Level One)	
Highest Level	N220,000 (Brig. Gen.)	N205,000 (Ass. Insp. General)	N266,000 (Highest Paid)	N239,000 (Level 17)	N190,000 (Level 17 Director)	

Source: Revenue Allocation and Fiscal Mobilization Commission (2007)

Nevertheless, inequality in Nigeria is also explained in terms of the dichotomy between wage groups, i.e. the high earners (highest levels or

232

level 17 in the civil services) and the poor earners (lowest ranks or level 1) or may be described as those who live in affluence and those who live below poverty line. A closer look at the monthly wage salaries of different public workers on similar grade levels as illustrated in table 3.7 indicate wide wage margins. The comparison is considered based on the consolidated salary structure of 2007 that may be susceptible to changes. As vast majority fall under the low income level, the inequality difference widens the more. However, when one also considers the trend of disparity between the federal employees and state employees, one discovers that the onward compliance to the federal structure of the monthly salaries by the state governments differs from one state to another. Because of the wage differences, it is difficult to collectively account for wage floors at the state level, which constituted the reason why it was not highlighted on the table 3.7. Thus the state civil service employee wages depend on the financial capability of the individual states. This tendency implies that richer states pay more wages and the poorer states pay lesser, justifying the incidence of poverty among the states of the federation.

Figure 3.5: Average Sectoral Monthly Wage 2009 and 2010 (Naira)

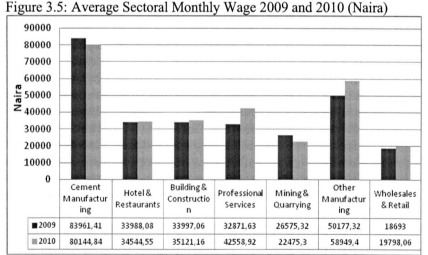

	Cement Manufacturing	Hotel & Restaurants	Building & Construction	Professional Services	Mining & Quarrying	Other Manufacturing	Wholesales & Retail
2009	83961,41	33988,08	33997,06	32871,63	26575,32	50177,32	18693
2010	80144,84	34544,55	35121,16	42558,92	22475,3	58949,4	19798,06

Source: *National Bureau of Statistics 2011*

If we also look at the monthly wages in some branches of the formal sectors (both public and private) as illustrated on figure 3.5, it indicates differentials on the wage benchmarks. Hence the statistical data shows that cement manufacturing has the highest monthly wage, and wholesale and retail sector has the least average wage between 2009 and 2010. There was a little upward movement of monthly wage in 2010 that favored mostly the professional services and the other manufacturing sectors. But the general trend is that wage movement has strong influence on consumption pattern of the workers. Also by comparing the public and the private (formal) sectors' wage differences, one discovers varied income gaps that breed inequality outcomes. Although the wage remuneration of the public sectors stagnated between 1981 and 1998 against the private sectors according to NBS reports, but comparatively, the public sectors continue to enjoy wage increase. This increase is not regularly observed in the private sectors (although some earn more than the public sector) when compared to the amount of time the private sector workers engage in productive activities.

Furthermore, when one compares the monthly remuneration of the political office holders with the other paid-workers in the government and public-private (formal) sectors, it is shocking to notice the yearning gaps of difference. Unfortunately, the monthly wages of the politicians and appointed government officials are not determined by the official fiscal commission of the federal government. As a result, what the least political office holder in the Local Council earns is almost equivalent to the highest grade level worker's salary in public sector as shown in table 3.7 above. For instance, "an average political office holder in Local Government administration with primary six as highest educational attainment, earns a minimum of N62,500.00 per month against the 2007 National minimum wage of N5,500.00."[22] This dichotomy evidently shows the huge income disparity between political office holders and members of their former closed associates in the same class, making a political office a juicy enterprise and a gateway to accumulation. That is also why politics has remained a 'do or die' affair as many desire to have the share of the national largesse.

Subsequently, in order to understand more the growth of income inequality, it is essential to take into consideration both shifts in the demand for and in the supply of skilled and unskilled workers, which are the conse-

---

[22] National Bureau of Statistics (2007): The Middle Class in Nigeria, p. 40.

234

quences of changes in fiscal wage institutions. In other words, the visible impact of the upward wage differential is observable because of the changing patterns of labor demands and supply. In fact, due to the growing number of unskilled labor-workers mainly migrating from rural to urban areas in search of employment, it affects the wage floors, in the sense that the unskilled labor-workers accept any wage condition in so far as they could be gainfully employed. In some instances, some unskilled employees have become the substitutes for the skilled labor forces because of their cheap welfare maintenance. It requires only giving the unskilled workers some little training to enable them to perform, especially in some mechanical fields that do not require much sophisticated technique or theoretical competence. It then follows that engaging vast number of unskilled labor in wage-employment could also affect the labor chances of the skilled labor as well as rendering some of them jobless. This tendency is also evident in the number of unemployed trained graduates roaming the streets in search of gainful employment.

Figure 3.6: National Unemployment Rate (2000-2011)

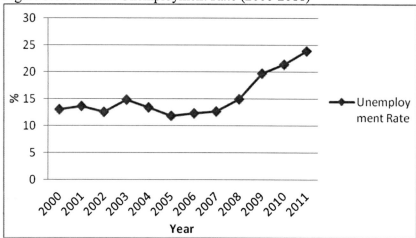

Sources: National Bureau of Statistics

Consequently, the rate of unemployment in Nigeria is growing rapidly. Because of low availability of reliable statistics, this examination dwells more on unemployment condition since the return to the civilian government in 1999. Figure 3.6 however illustrates the trend of national unemployment rate from 2000 to 2011. From the statistics, it shows that the rate of unemployment, which stood at 13.1% in 2000, increase at the rate 0.5% between 2000 and 2001. There was relative improvement in 2002 but then experienced 2.2% shock rise in 2003. Thus it has been a constant upward movement since 2005, reaching its peak at an average increase of 2.5% increase between 2010 and 2011. The deregulation of the communication and banking industries that initially created jobs in 2002 and 2005 respectively went into crisis that made many workers to lose their jobs. It is also good to note that the increasing rate of unemployment does not match with the real growth rate of the economic as observe in figure 2.2 of the previous part. It means that 'economic growth that is jobless'[23] is only ill-conceived measure of inclusive development.

Perhaps one could also argue that the main contributing factor of unemployment is the liberal market forces as well as the inability of the government to match the unemployment situation with proper policy advocacy. Unfortunately, the vast majority of the unemployed falls within the age of 15 and 35 years, and women constitute the greater percentage. Then, reducing unemployment in Nigeria becomes a great challenge to the policymakers of which their major priority ought to be job creation and enhancing more domestic productivity. In the normal circumstance, minimum wage legislation should aid productivity and create more employment opportunities, but the Nigerian case is quite difference. Instead wage increase gives rise to retrenchment of workers and subsequently, the placement of embargo on employment as has been the case.

Finally, minimum wage laws from the empirical findings so far benefit mostly a small portion of Nigeria's labor force leaving the majority in abject poverty. The major issue is not just the increase of wages; but whether it matches with the existing cost of living that should also be considered in line with the national rate of inflation. In other words, the demand and supply shift in wages should also be viewed in terms of induced productivity that could aid economic growth. Therefore, by creating a better balance between the supply and demand of skills, it can also

---

[23] Olesin described the Nigerian economic growth as jobless growth (Olesin, Ayo (2011): Nigeria's Jobless Growth. In: National Mirror, 19. September, 2011. http://nationalmirror online.net/index.php/business/business-and-finance/matrix-with-ayo-olesin/20978.html [Accessed: 14.03.2012]).

help in reducing within the country's income inequality, preventing the spikes in income that are believed to be related to a shortfall in supply of certain skills. In effect, the balance will enhance a favorable environment for economic growth and equal distribution.

6.2.3   Education as a Structural Determinant

The education system in Nigeria has undergone many developments and transformations as a result of much influence coming from different phases such as the colonial period, the period of the military rule in Nigeria and then the influence of democratic formation. Historically, the progress of western-style education which marked the beginning of the formal education in Nigeria was the Christian missionary legacy around the mid-nineteenth century. Cohen and Goldman on this, note that "by 1950 the country had already developed a three-tiered system of primary, secondary, and higher education based on the British model of wide participation at the bottom, sorting into academic and vocational training at the secondary level, and higher education for the destined elite for leadership."[24] However, this educational formation was first developed in the southern states of Nigeria because of their earlier contact with the Christian missionaries during the colonial period[25] that uplifted the face of education in Nigeria and opened up many possibilities of human development.

A closer look at the evolution of educational system in Nigeria indicates as Ajibola rightly affirmed that "the type of education imported to Nigeria under British control reflected the needs of the colonial government. Thus, Nigeria had the 7-5-4 which represents 7 years of primary educa-

---

[24] Cohen, Ronald/Goldman, Abe (1992): 'The Society and its Environment'. In: Metz, Helen Chapin (ed.): Nigeria: A Country Study 5th Edition. Washington: GPO for the Library of Congress, p. 142.
[25] Nugent notes that "whereas the preservation of the emirate system in Northern Nigeria had sealed off the North from outside political influences and restricted access to education, the South-West had enjoyed a long acquaintance with mission education and was fast being caught by the South-East" (Nugent, Paul (2004): Africa since Independence: A Comparative History. UK: Palgrave Macmillan, p. 29).

tion, 5 years of secondary education and 4 years of 'tertiary education'[26]. While in some regions, it was 6-5-4 across the three tiers respectively. This system was later replaced for the entire country in 1983 by the 6-3-3-4 system, that is, 6 years of primary education, 3 years of Junior Secondary School (JSS), 3 years of Senior Secondary School (SSS) and, 4 years of tertiary education. The difference is the additional one year to the secondary education and its split to 2-tiers: junior and senior secondary. This system sought to correct the structural imbalances in the colonial system of education."[27] On the other hand, the educational transformations in Nigeria were also accompanied by Universal Primary Education (UPE) programme established in 1972 by the Federal Government in order to increase access to primary education and later the Universal Basic Education (UBE) programme adopted by the National Policy on Education that began in 1999. The focus of this programme was on compulsory free education for the first nine years of school curriculum. But amidst all these innovations and reforms, there have not been significant positive results in term of qualitative outcomes due to inadequate learning materials, insufficient qualified teachers and poor policy implementation within the various levels of educational system.

Education is typically seen as a means of narrowing inequalities, but at the same time represents a medium through which the worst forms of social stratification and segmentation are created. The inequality that exists within and among groups in Nigeria manifests significantly as one examines the level of educational attainment. It is observed that the na-

---

[26] In Nigeria, "there are three major categories of higher or tertiary education. One is postsecondary, which is non-university level training in technical and vocational fields. Students receive certificates of training for completing work-oriented courses. The second type of higher education institution consists of higher technical, but non-university level programs offered at technical colleges, polytechnics, and colleges of education. They usually offer a variety of options for students that lead to a National Diploma (ND) for two years of study or a Higher National Diploma (HND) for four years of study. The third type of tertiary institution is the degree-granting institution offering bachelor's and higher degrees" (Nigeria - Educational System—overview: Education Encyclopedia. http://education.stateuniversity.com/ [accessed: 12.09.2009]).

[27] Ajibola, M. A. (2008): Innovations and Curriculum Development for Basic Education in Nigeria: Policy Priorities and Challenges of Practice and Implementation. In: Research Journal of International Studies, Issue 8, p. 53. http://www.eurojournals.com/rjis_8_05.pdf [accessed: 23.02.2010]

tional adult literacy in Nigeria between the age of 15 and 24 remains very low with an average rate of 72% between 2000 and 2007, but with differences in gender and places of residence. This rate is based on the number of people who can speak and understand the English language as the official language, and it is even worse when we consider adults above the age of 24. Thus the level of educational attainment is also visible in such phenomena as employment opportunities, income availability, class formation, place of residence, gender disparity etc. As one of the contributing factors of production, those who are not better placed or opportune to benefit from the means of capital production through education are often the subjects of structural arrangement that situates them in conflict with the reality of class competition.

However, findings reveal that it was through the historical method of educational system that regional and ethnic inequalities were significantly created in Nigeria. In this perspective, Iroegbu opines that "educational inequality is at three levels. There is first the historical fact that the Northern Muslims for instance were initially reluctant to embrace Western education and have today come to win the title of an educationally backward area. The second factor is ethnic. While some ethnic groups or states have, others do not have free educational programmes for their members. The third factor follows from this: In the latter case, only those families who are wealthy can afford to pay for the education of their members. In other words, there is a total absence of equality of opportunity in (educational) life-chances right from the start."[28] These factors however summarized that the disparities in educational accessibility were seriously influenced by historical, socio-cultural, economic and family backgrounds. Hence the privileged ones have the opportunities to attain to any level of education and stand the better chance than the disadvantaged ones, who have minimal opportunities and then become targets of systematic exclusion from societal goods.

The NBS reports that the average national adult literacy rate between the age of 15 and 24 in 2006 stood at 64.2%. The North has average of 50.2% adult literacy and 76.5% in the South in same survey period, comprising of 26.3% difference. Hence table 3.8 illustrates the dichotomy

---

[28] Iroegbu, Pantaleon (1996): p. 38.

between the North and South in the secondary school output between 1912 and 2005. It also shows the historical development of education in Nigeria. For instance, Cohen and Goldman observe that "[...] in the late 1950s, Nigeria had gone through a decade of exceptional education growth leading to a movement for universal primary education in the Western Region. In the north, primary school enrolments went from 66,000 in 1947 to 206,000 in 1957, in the west (mostly Yoruba areas) from 240,000 to 983,000 in the same period, and in the east from 320,000 to 1,209,000."[29] Irrespective of the exceptional growth in educational development in Nigeria, the primary school range at present in terms of regional gaps has remained almost the same due to economic constraints, as well as religious bigotry affecting mostly children in the North.

Table 3.8: Secondary School Output in Northern and Southern Nigeria, 1912–2005

	Northern Nigeria		Southern Nigeria	
Year	No. of schools	No. of pupils	No. of Schools	No. of pupils
1912	0	0	10	67
1926	0	0	18	518
1937	1	65	26	4,285
1947	3	251	43	9,657
1957	18	3,643	176	28,208
1965	77	15,276	1,305	180,907
2004	4,252	2,600,680	6,661	3,678,784
2005	4,252	2,879,606	6,661	3,517,737

Source: Adapted from Adamu (1973)[30] /Federal Ministry of Education, Abuja.

Similarly, there are prominent changes in the secondary school output from 1912 to 2005 as indicated in table 3.8. The rate of transformation within the period has been impressive, though there is still significant gap especially when one considers that the population in the North is more than the South. However, the number of secondary schools in the North rose from 1 in 1937 to 4,252 in 2005 with significant increase in the number of enrolment. The Southern Nigeria as the head-start in education

---

[29] Cohen, Ronald/Goldman, Abe (1992): p. 142.
[30] Adamu, H. (1973): The North and Nigerian Unity. Zaria: Gaskiya Press, p. 51.

also experienced significant development within the same period. According to NBS welfare report in 2006, 41.5% children in the North have access to secondary school and 49.2% children in the South. This statistics indicates a closing gap between the North and South in educational accessibility, and it is also significant in affecting the rate of inequality between the two regions.

Table 3.9: Primary and Secondary Schools Statistics 2004-2008

	Primary School Enrolment			Secondary School Enrolment			Dropout before Secondary
Year	Male	Female	Total	Male	Female	Total	%
2004	11,824,494	9,571,016	21,395,510	3,539,708	2,739,745	6,279,462	70.7
2005	12,189,073	9,926,359	22,115,432	3,543,425	2,854,718	6,397,343	71.1
*2006	12,575,689	10,441,435	23,017,124	3,642,871	2,893,167	6,536,038	71.6
*2007	11,683,503	9,948,567	21,632,070	3,460,146	2,608,014	6,068,160	71.9
*2008	11,483,943	9,810,575	21,294,517	3,682,141	2,943,802	6,625,943	68.9

*Sources: Universal Basic Education Commission/Federal Ministry of Education (Note: * Provisional)*

In comparing the enrolment movements between primary and secondary schools from 2004 to 2008, the statistics as shown in table 3.9 generally reveal poor enrolment increase especially in the primary schools. The primary school enrolment unfortunately recorded in 2008 minus 0.24% increase when compared to the 2004 enrolment figures. In the same way, secondary school enrolment only increase by 1.76% in 2008 when compared to the 2005 total enrolment. Another significant observation from the data is that the total number of male enrolment both in primary and secondary schools levels remains higher than female, an indicative of gender disparity in education. Moreover, more than half that enrolled in the primary school were not able to enroll in the secondary school after six years. For instance, 70.7% of pupils dropped out before secondary school in 2004 and the percentage further increased to 71.9% in 2007.[31]

---

[31] Meredith indicates that "in about one-third of African countries, less than half of the child population received primary education; in only six countries were more than 20 per cent of the age group attending secondary school" (Meredith, Martin (2006): The State of

Thus the high drop-out rate could be attributed to financial predicaments. Consequently, due to high cost of educational attainment, many poor families especially those who do not have stable incomes find it difficult to send their wards to school. It is not surprising to observe that rich families are more educated than poor families in Nigeria. It is obvious that vast number of school children from poor families drop-out of school especially after primary education to engage in apprenticeship or mini-trade as the only means of survival.

From another perspective, as at 2010, there were about 104 universities (excluding Polytechnics and Colleges of Education), of which 41 were private universities owned by individuals and organizations. This is following the announcement of the federal government in 2010 for the establishment of six more universities at the six geopolitical zones to complement the existing ones. Yet, the increase in number does not guarantee easy and free accessibility since they are measured by cost of sponsorship. The high rate of tuition is sadly not affordable by many families. It has become the norm that education is only for those who can afford it, widening the gap between the rich and the poor. Even some poor intelligent students who may have loved to obtain university education may not because of the financial involvements. This condition contributes significantly to social inequality that varies according to different population groups and individuals.

The World Bank however notes that "the re-emergence of civilian government in 1999 raised hopes of an educational renaissance and teacher, leading to higher levels of coverage and quality and ultimately to improved educational outcomes that are rewarded in the labor market and in the increased esteem with which educated people are regarded."[32] Unfortunately, these hopes are yet to be materialized judging from the turn of events, and also lack of educational materials and conducive teaching environment in the schools. Under these conditions, as well as the issue

---

Africa: A History of Fifty Years of Independence. Reading: Cox & Wyman, p. 283). This similarly shows the low advancement of education in Africa.

[32] World Bank (2003): School Education in Nigeria: Preparing for Universal Basic Education. Human Development III: Africa Region, p. 21. http://siteresources.worldbank.org/AFRICAEXT/Resources/no_53.pdf [accessed: 12.08.2010]

242

of poor working state for the teachers such as under-rewards and delays in their salaries; most teachers both in the universities, primary and secondary schools have abandoned their duties in search of greener pasture elsewhere in order to earn a better living.

Figure 3.7: Total Number of Teachers in Federal Universities, 2001/2002 – 2005/2006

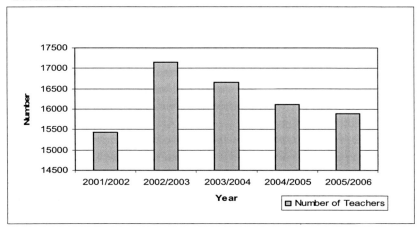

Source: National Universities Commission (NUC)

Figure 3.7 indicates that the number of teachers in the federal universities has continued to decrease since 2003 and there is the tendency that it will continue in that direction if not adequately checked. Many university lecturers have switched over to other employment sectors that could earn them more income and some others combine their teaching profession with other business ventures. Some others as well have migrated to other countries that could give them more opportunities of service and earning. This situation has however weakened the educational input, which would have sustained the increase in social indicator and human development in Nigeria.

From the available statistics, one could conclude that although the gross enrolments into primary, post-primary and tertiary schools are on the increase in Nigeria, other indicators of child well-being and qualitative education show the precarious situation in which the Nigerian pupils and students continue to find themselves. This situation is because of the poor conducive environment for studying, lack of textbooks, inadequate basic infrastructures and poor education funding when compared to other countries' budgetary allocations on education. On the other hand, the budgetary allocations are often not quite sufficient to charter for the general maintenance and advancement of the educational system. The shrinking and plummeting economic development has also constituted another constraint to educational funding by the Nigerian government. In that sense, the absolute cost of qualitative education in Nigeria renders especially the poor families obsolete and handicap.

On the other hand, the poor educational system could also be one of the causes of various violence crimes in the society. Inadequate provisions of equal educational opportunities for all school-age citizens indicate government's unpreparedness to meet up with the challenges imposed by low rate of literacy in this contemporary period, consequent of poor planning and financing. Instead, the current socio-political structure is destabilizing the development of education by creating undue advantages to the rich, thereby widening the disparities between the poor and the non-poor. Therefore, the system of education in Nigeria still remains dysfunctional and needs more innovations and improvements in order to achieve a substantive structural development. Hence the process of reconstruction and development of education must of course take into account primary studies and skills acquisition as priorities, in order to limit unequal life chances within and among regions and classes, as well as an avenue in minimizing the tendencies of social deviants among the younger population.

6.2.4 Urban and Rural Dichotomy

In analyzing the dichotomy that exists between urban and rural areas, this study empirically examines the decomposition of inequality among urban and rural households as consequence of urbanization. Thus urbanization as the bridge to development and human settlement is also one of the major causes through which social structural changes and differences are endorsed. In Nigeria as an instance, urbanization has weakened the extended family welfare system through which individuals could find a definitive means of human security. It has pitched a divide among families as well as alienated communities from their indigenous cultural values. As a structural changing mechanism, Shorter defines urbanization as "the social process by which people acquire material and non-material elements of culture, behavior and ideas that originate in, or are distinctive of, the city or town. It can affect rural areas through the 'rural-urban continuum' or interdependence of rural and urban areas. It is a major example of structural change [...]."[33] The structural change accounts for differences that exist between urban and rural areas. This, of course gives credence to loss of traditional values in the urban settings as well as developmental neglect of the rural communities.

However, a typical description of the rural community dwellers in Nigeria is people living in clusters of small houses mostly with common ancestral origin and ideology. Cohen and Goldman here note that "it was among these people that ways of life remained deeply consistent with the past."[34] But the idea ('consistent with the past') does not imply living in the past, rather it means that the people still retained those essential values of the culture such as communal responsibility. Hence about 64.7% of Nigerians were rural dwellers in 1990 according to UNDP Human Development Reports 2010, but decreased to 50.2% in 2010. Though there is constant increase of urban population in Nigeria, yet the greater number of the population as at 2010 still lives in rural areas, mostly in poor farming villages that have little access to basic amenities and life chances. But the reason for the continuous decrease in rural population is not far removed from socio-economic needs and migration, which will be later addressed in this section.

Nevertheless, the rate of urbanization has continued to increase in this recent period of global integration. The urban population in 1990 was 35.3% of the total population and then rose to 49.8% in 2010, experiencing about 14.5% growth within 10 years against the projected 2.5% national growth rate. Some of the urban areas in Nigeria such as Lagos, Kano, Ibadan, Port-Harcourt etc are densely populated. In the same way, other new urban cities have sprung up in the last four decades. Thus the current rapid growth of urban areas in Nigeria has continued to negate the corresponding growth in the rural communities.[35] Through the phenome-

---

[33] Shorter, Aylward (1998): p. 34.
[34] Cohen, Ronald/Goldman, Abe (1992): p. 112.
[35] Simmel, Georg, a German sociologist in his work, 'The Metropolis and Modern Life (1903)' argued that "city life bombards the mind with images and impressions, sensations and activity. This is 'a deep contrast with the slower, more habitual, more smoothly flowing rhythm' of the small town or village.' In this way, Ferdinand Tönnies argued that

non of urbanization associated with radical societal changes, urban development and management in Nigeria has been expressed by many in terms of loss of communal living (Gemeinschaft), cultural values and increase in migration. These factors have increased social seclusion in the urban-rural interaction, as well as constrained the access to strategic resources by the rural communities. In fact, the changes are relevance in determining the rate of poverty and the corresponding social inequality that have been a major challenge to urbanization in Nigeria.

Figure 3.8: Trends in Poverty Levels between Urban and Rural Areas 1980-2010 (%)

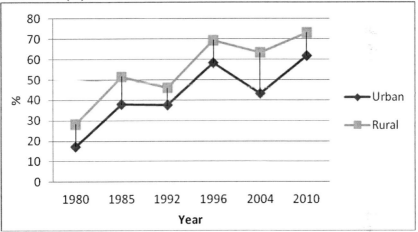

Source: National Bureau of Statistics 2011

At this point, it is imperative to note that there are visible socio-economic disparities, which exist between urban and rural households. In the first instance, the percentage trends of poverty between urban and rural areas as shown in figure 3.8 is to be vividly examined. Here the major determi-

---

'urbanization, which occurred with the industrial Revolution, irredeemably changed social life. He charted with sadness the gradual loss of what he called 'Gemeinschaft' or community (1887), which he characterized as based on traditional, close-knit ties, personal and steady relationships between neighbours and friends, and a clear understanding of one's social position" (Giddens, Anthony (2006): Sociology, p. 896). The Gemeinschaft however goes beyond social goods and service delivery. It is all-embracing, in the sense that people's whole livelihoods and their pattern of relationship are put into consideration.

nant of poverty is the social indicators such mortality rate, literacy rate, employment rate etc. In that way, we could define poverty as closing the opportunities through which people can liberate themselves from the life difficulties. From the available statistics, the urban poor rose from 17.2% in 1980 to 61.8% in 2010, and at the same time the rural poor rose from 28.3% in 1980 to 73.2% in 2010. The differences in poverty rate within the time range from 1980 to 2010 have shown an average of 44.6% increase in the urban areas and 44.9% increase in rural areas respectively. The figures generally indicate that the rural households are poorer and the rate of poverty continues to increase more than the urban households. As most of rural populations engage themselves in agricultural productivity, it contributes to their poverty due to shortage of land, capitals and regular low returns from agricultural productivity.

Furthermore, one can observe from the above figure that there was a rapid rise of poverty in 1985 as a result of austerity measures caused by the liberal economic policies that affect both areas. For more than three decades, the poverty level differentials have remained constant, culminating in 2004 with more than 20% difference between urban and rural sectors. Hence the rural poor remains above the national poverty rate, which stood at 69% in 2010. One other observable fact is that the trends in poverty lines in both urban and rural areas have been on the steady increase, except in 1992 and 2004 that experienced slight drop, which more or less favored the urban households. Thus the main factor that explains the poverty differentials between urban and rural areas is consequence of income distribution and employment chances. For instance, the unemployment rate, according to the NBS general household survey 2011, remained higher in the rural areas (25.6%) than in the urban areas (17.1%). One of the contributing factors could be the more availability of wage labor in the urban regions than in the rural areas. It means that the urban households have more advantages over the rural households especially in having better chances to society goods and wage-employments. Also, there are great margins in urban and rural per capita income ratios, which explain why the urban households are more favored than their rural counterparts in terms of life chances. As the rural poor continue to grow, it is the responsibility of the government to increase investment on agriculture (as a means of poverty reduction), which is the commonest rural employment opportunity.

On the other hand, inequality is determined by comparing the poor and the non-poor in a given society. According to Araar and Taiwo, there is a link between poverty and inequality both in static and dynamic settings by arguing that inequality is more within the non-poor group than within the poor group.[36] In that instance, figure 3.9 shows the trends of inequality among the urban and rural households from 1985 to 2010 as measured by Gini coefficient; and within the period, the poverty rates were more among the rural dwellers. Thus the inequality index within the urban household was 0.49 in 1985, which was higher than the inequality index of 0.36 within the rural household at the same period. The urban sector rise in inequality index in 1985 could be attributed to the consequences of structural adjustment programme that had worse impact on the urban households within the period. This is because more opportunities that were created by the austerity measures favored mostly the urban workers than the rural workers.

Figure 3.9: Inequality Trends by Urban and Rural Sectors 1985-2010 (Gini Coefficient)

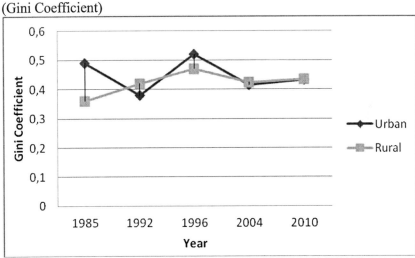

Sources: FOS (1999) Poverty Profile for Nigeria 1980-1996 & NBS (2011) Poverty Profile for Nigeria.

---

[36] Araar, Abdelkrim/Taiwo, Awoyemi (2006): p. 3.

Moreover, figure 3.9 also indicates that there was a slight change in 1992 in which the inequality trends among the rural households surpassed that of urban households. But whereas Gini indices both for urban and rural sectors rose simultaneously, inequality remained higher among urban households in 1996 and 2004 respectively. In 2010, the inequality index within the urban region slightly rose to 0.4328 and with only 0.95% increase within rural sector from 0.4239 Gini Coefficient of 2004. In fact, the general findings reveal that the trends of inequality are higher in urban sector than in rural sector. Then following Araar and Taiwo illustrations of 'poverty and inequality nexus' in figure 3.3 above, it means that because the majority of the rural dwellers in Nigeria are poorer than the urban dwellers, the inequality that exists within the rural population becomes lesser than the urban population. This difference could be explained in terms of unusual falls in some urban real income-wages, and sometimes attributed to fairly improvements in some rural incomes accruing from better agricultural harvests and prices. Also it could be as the consequences of migration driven by greater influx of population from rural to urban areas in search of better livelihood. Such influx can be characterized as 'push and pull factors'[37], based on the perception of urban attractions by the rural households.

Historically, people migrate as a result of socio-cultural, economic and political factors. Urban migration in Nigeria is seen by many as a possible strategy in solving most of the socio-economic and political problems befalling the society. The current globalization factors have also contributed to the unprecedented rate of rural-urban migration. Unfortunately, most of the urban cities in Nigeria are presently over-populated with an increase rate of crime, traffic congestions and pollution. These situations could be as a result of urban growth that does not correspond with the socio-economic development. In other words, one of the most serious adverse effects of rapid urban growth as witnessed in Nigeria in the re-

---

[37] According to Giddens, "'Push factors' referred to dynamics within a country of origin which forced people to emigrate, such as war, famine, political oppression, or population pressures. 'Pull factors' by contrast, were those features of destination countries which attracted immigrants: prosperous labour markets, better overall living conditions and lower population density, for example, could 'pull' immigrants from other regions" (Giddens, Anthony (2006): Sociology, p. 524).

cent times is the problem of matching the provision of urban infrastructural facilities and services with their levels of demand. As such, most urban cities are in chaotic form consequent of poor planning, insufficient housing and inadequate amenities to harmonize with the rate of population growth. The high cost of living, low income-wages and high unemployment rates in the urban areas have also implications on the trends of inequality.

Figure 3.10: Nigerians in US Diaspora 1961 2008

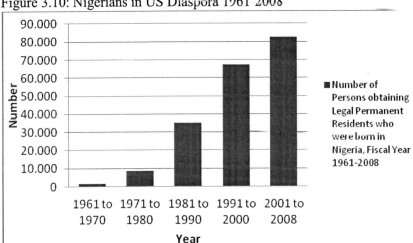

Sources: US Department of Homeland Security, Office of Immigration Statistics, 2008 Yearbook of Immigration Statistics.

On the other hand, due to hardships and increased competition for wealth and other means of survival, vast majority of the population continues to sort out other new possibilities to make the ends meet. In this dimension, migration is considered by many as essential in achieving success, and young people who do not migrate or commute to towns or abroad are often labeled as idle and may become object of ridicule in their community. Hence the migration phenomenon is no more limited to rural-urban but transcends the borders to other countries. Just for an emphasis, from the investigation carried out by the US Department of Homeland Security, Office of Immigration Statistics, 2008, it shows that the number of Nigerians seeking permanent residence only in the United State of America continues to rise every year. From 1961 to 2008 more than 80,000 Nigerians have obtained permanent residence as indicated in figure 3.10.

In fact, many professionals and students have migrated to foreign countries in search of better living conditions. This migration increase has indeed necessitated several brain-drains in the country.[38] Thus, it is a clear sign that urbanization exercise in Nigeria is yet to achieve the desired results that can create conducive environment through which the growing population will benefit. Instead, it has placed a big dichotomy between the rural and urban dwellers.

Finally, the country is faced with the challenge of improving on the social service delivery through provision of basic infrastructural facilities, as well as opening up of business partnership between rural and urban areas. Tackling this challenge can necessitate a balanced developmental outlook both in the urban and rural areas. As a renewed effort, the intervention of the government is basically required in formulating new policy programmes and ensuring their implementations in order to reduce the rate of urbanization. This intervention will therefore assist in limiting the influx to urban cities and also making the country more attractive for the Nigerians in Diaspora in order to sustain the country's human capital development.

6.2.5   Regional Differentiation

The trends of inequality in Nigeria can also be explained in terms of its strong regional concentrations and development. Mostly, economic and power distributions are linked to regional ethnic struggles and identification, and expressed in terms of differentials in the composition of the six geopolitical zones that make up the Federal Republic of Nigeria.[39] These

---

[38] Stiglitz observes that "developed countries do, of course, allow the migration to their countries of high-skilled labor, because they see clearly the benefits to themselves of doing this [...]. This amounts to taking the developing countries' most valuable intellectual capital without compensation: after the developing countries have invested their scarce dollars in education, the developed countries, often inadvertently, try to skim off their best and brightest" (Stiglitz, Joseph E. (2007): Making Globalization Work. New York: W. W. Norton & Company, Inc., p. 89).

[39] Mustapha notes that "each zone can be given a broad ethnic identification, based on the majority of the population in that zone. In this regard, the northwest zone is the core Hausa-Fulani area, while the northeast zone contains a mixture of Hausa-Fulani, Kanuri and many northern ethnic minorities. Both zones are regarded as the 'far north', with overlapping cultural and Islamic attributes. The north-central zone is traditionally regard-

include: the southern regions of South-South, South-East and South-West, and the northern regions of North-Central, North-East and North-West. These regional compositions constitute power blocs, giving rise to struggles as well as deprivations, which have historically been the main grounds of inequality formation in Nigeria. Even the infrastructural developments of those regions are unevenly distributed due to the economic concentration in some particular regions and the political dominations by other regions.

In analyzing the regional concentration in Nigeria, Aka states that "regional inequality and polarization of activities have persisted in Nigeria despite its quest over many decades for socioeconomic and political development and modernization. This condition contributes to serious distributional problems such as hyper-urbanization, spatial concentration of population and modem activities, unemployment and underemployment, income inequality and poverty, persistent food shortages, deteriorating material conditions of farm populations, and external dependency."[40] These enumerated conditions by Aka are not quite strange considering the fact that unequal economic distribution has militated against sustainable and equal development of the geopolitical zones. Hence the regional differentiation in this section is viewed in terms of economic, social and political deprivations that have increased the rate of inequality trends among the geopolitical zones.

---

ed as the zone of the non-Islamic northern ethnic minorities, many of whom are Christian. Though this zone was equally involved in the political construction of a monolithic Northern regional identity against the South in the 1950s, it is also a zone of resistance against alleged Hausa-Fulani 'domination' and cultural oppression in the colonial and immediate post-colonial periods. The culture of this 'lower north' is different from that of the far north. The southwest zone is made up of the old Western Region, the heartland of the Yoruba, while the southeast is made up of the Igbo heartlands of the old Eastern Region. The last zone, the south-south, is the zone of southern ethnic minorities, from the peripheries of the Igbo core of the old Eastern Region, and the whole of the old Mid-West Region" (Mustapha, Raufu A. (2006): pp. 10-11).
[40] Aka, Ebenezer (1995): 'Regional Inequalities in the Process of Nigeria's Development: Socio-Political and Administrative Perspective'. In: Journal of Social Development in Africa Vol. 10, No. 2, p. 64. http://archive.lib.msu.edu/DMC/African Journals.pdf [accessed: 25.03.2010]

Figure 3.11: Spreads and Trends in Poverty Levels by Zones 1980-2010 (%)

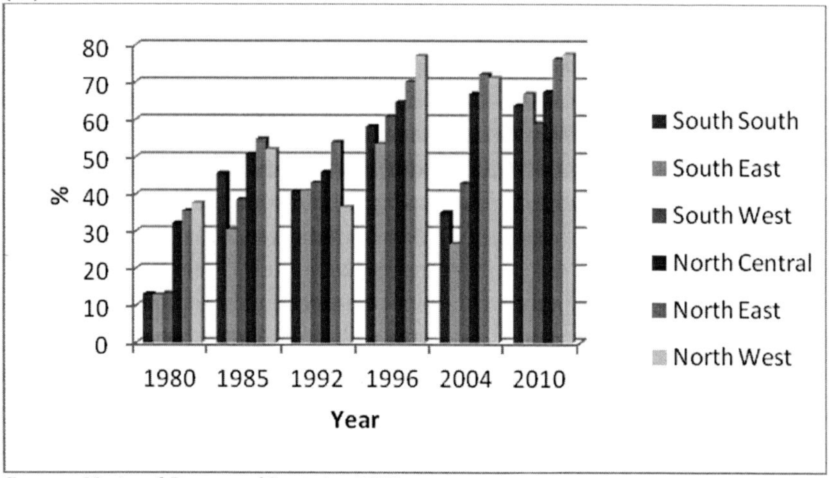

Source: National Bureau of Statistics 2011

The determinant of the spreads and trends in poverty levels by geopolitical zones as shown in figure 3.11 is based on the dimensions of human development indices in terms of living chances as we have already seen in figure 3.1 above. The people that live below the threshold level of development index are regarded as below poverty level. The statistics however show the percentage spreads and trends in poverty levels by geopolitical zones in Nigeria from 1980 to 2010. However, as we saw in figure 3.2, the overall national poverty incidence increased from 27.2% in 1980 to 69% in 2010, which indicates about 41.8% increase of poverty nationwide in the last three decades. One important fact about the poverty increase in Nigeria is that, as the population increases, so also the poverty rate increases.

From the geopolitical consideration, the above statistics generally indicates that the poverty levels in the southern regions are relatively lower than the northern regions, also supporting the HDI report between the North and South. That means that the majority of the poor population resides in the northern part of the country. One could suggest that there is a historical undertone towards this development. Because the southern regions are head start in education and vast majority are self-employed and engage also in trading and farming, it explains the basis for the poverty differences between the North and South. Notwithstanding the differences between the regions, there exist also differentials in poverty incidences within the regions especially among the various states of the federation that make up the geopolitical zones.

Comparatively, southeast zone according to the above figure has the least average poverty level because of the fact that most people in the zone engage in mini-trade and subsistence farming, but rose to 67% in 2010 as an indicative of its lowest share of per capita income among other zones, as well as unfavorable business and farming environments such kidnapping, poor rainfall etc. Thus the zone was formally noted for palm production as its main economic resource; but due to poor production and insufficient demands in the foreign markets, it was quick enough to seek other alternative means of income production mostly in commerce industry and retail trading. But within the southeast zone, Ebonyi state is regarded as the poorest, with limited life chances in comparison to other states in the zone. The south-south on the other hand has the highest per capita income and is noted as the key oil producing zone, generating the major economic income of the country. Although the level of poverty in the zone is relatively low with Bayelsa state having the highest percentage of non-poor, yet vast majority in the area still suffer economic neglects and environmental disaster as a result of the exploration activities of the multinational oil firms. As the zone with the highest economic activity, southwest recorded the lowest poverty line in 2010. But the economic activities in the zone are mostly concentrated in the major cities, giving rise to hyper-urbanization that affects the development of the hinterland states such as Ogun and Ekiti states. For instance, the zone was initially noted for cocoa production and concentrated the earnings mainly on the development of new towns, leaving most of the villages impoverished. This concentration is also as a result of the region's methods of economic distribution and land-tenure system, which gave much advantage to particular towns and income groups.

However, the abolition of slave-labors in the late 19th century contributed to the economic setback for the Hausa farmers and Fulani aristocrats in the northern regions. Consequently, the Fulani-aristocracy later became an extension of the colonial administration and formed the background to the region's political hegemony. Unfortunately, the northeast and north-

254

west, which are regarded as the 'far north' and predominantly Muslims, remain the poorest despite the fact that both zones have remained more than other zones in the seat of governance in Nigeria. And that could not be far-fetched from the cultural and religious attitudes that influence the zones' entrepreneurship in business as well as unfair redistribution of wealth. In particular, northwest is the most populous zone and remains the zone with highest poverty rate, affecting mostly the states such as Sokoto, Jigawa and Katsina. As I have already noted, the population growth in the zone contributes to its poverty levels. The other two zones of northeast and north-central have also high poverty incidence with Gombe state leading the table. Nevertheless, the general trend is that poverty in Nigeria has been on the increase and it has major impact on the inequality trends.

Figure 3.12: Inequality Trends by Geo-Political Zones 1985-2010 (Gini Coefficient)

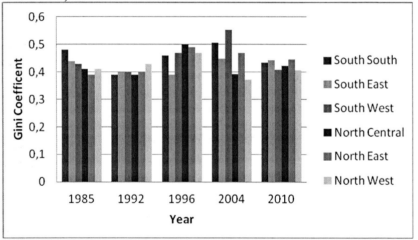

Sources: *FOS (1999) Poverty Profile for Nigeria 1980-1996 & NBS (2011) Poverty Profile for Nigeria.*

The level of inequality among the geopolitical zones is the outcome of the limited opportunities to socio-cultural, economic and political goods. One sees here the relationship between poverty and inequality in Nigeria, such that one affects the other. Figure 3.12 concisely shows the trends of inequality from 1985 to 2010 measured by Gini coefficient according to geopolitical zones. It is observable to note that the differentials in regional inequality index have been on regular increase since the inception of austerity measures in 1985. There was relative stability in 1992, but experienced again more differentials from 1996, which culminated in 2010. From an average index calculation of inequality from 1985 to 2010, it indicates that among the geopolitical zones, south-west and south-south zones have the highest Gini inequality with an approximate index of 0.45, followed by the north-east zone with 0.44. The north-west has the average lowest inequality index of 0.417 and north-central and south-east have 0.423 and 0.425 respectively. In reference to the argument by Araar and Taiwo (See: figure 3.3), it follows that there are more inequality increases within the non-poor groups. This tendency justifies the fact that south-west and south-south being the more affluent zones (i.e. south-west with the largest economic activities and south-south with the highest per capita income due to oil derivation), have the highest Gini inequality, whereas the north-west as the poorest zone has the least Gini inequality.

However, the inequality imbalances within and among the zones have been the failure of the macro-economic policies of the country to intervene on the politico-economic and social structural distributions. It follows that the reduction of inequality in one zone with the poverty increase in that zone does not favor the overall growth of society. Instead, what is required is a balanced system of development that can account for inclusive participation in the society goods. Such in-depth factors of inclusion may consist of the method of industrial investments, employment rates, household expenditures and revenue allocations according to states and local governments. For instance, as most of the states and local governments are unable to generate internally enough per capita income and then depend monthly on the federal government for allocation, it means that the region with more states and local governments have advantage over the others. In other words, the northern region has more than 60% of the states and local governments and has more allocations every month. That means that balancing the federal structure could also assist in development.

Furthermore, the differentials in economic distribution in Nigeria affect the trends of inequality among zones and regions, and they are capable of injecting anger and resentment that could fuel crisis in those zones that majority of the population is disadvantaged. On the other hand, the oil-dependent economy driven by the unbridled capitalism has perhaps rendered the regional economic reserves powerless, causing undue advantage of the stronger regions over the weaker ones. Within the context of the above examination, regional disparities and inequalities in Nigeria in part can be explained in terms of over-concentration of the power and economic activities in some regions. And on the other hand, over-concentration manifests in the level of income distribution in different geopolitical zones that is governed by the utility of those who are meant to protect the laws and rights of the citizens (especially the political elites). Nevertheless, there is a substantial opportunity for inequality reduction if much resources and essential infrastructural facilities are equitably distributed to enhance equal outcomes, as well as the ability of the states and local governments to remain independent of the federal allocations through the building of strong economic generation platforms rather than engaging in political struggle for economic and power control in order to protect regional and ethnic interests.

From another point of view, as a dominant political parameter in Nigeria, regional struggles, as well as disparities in politics have become the bane of democratic principles and governance. The regional rivalries and interests have debased the democratic ideals, as different geopolitical zones continue coming up with demands of their own share of resources and political positions mainly for ethnic and regional protection. It is not uncommon to hear people clamouring for southern president or northern president based on ethnic nationality in one country in the bid to have control over the state and its wealth. For instance, in this conflict situation Diamond observes that "in every election in Nigeria, ethnic mobilization has become the calculated strategy of dominant-class elements locked in bitter competition for control of state, power and resources. If not consciously a mask for class action, such tribalism was certainly a manifestation and tragic consequence of it."[41] As a result, it is no more strange to realize that all the presidential elections conducted in Nigeria since independence have been based on regional and ethnic divide (i.e. the southerners voting strongly the southern candidates and the northerners voting also the northern candidates); all in an effort to control the national econ-

---

[41] Diamond, Larry (1988): p. 300

omy, as well as a strategy of selfish accumulation of wealth. But whether that has actually aided development of the nation-state becomes the question for the colonial amalgamation of the North and South, as well as the inability of the government in realizing the uneasiness between the state and its citizens in the pursuit of common ideals.

Map 3.1: Presidential Election Results by Geopolitical Zone 2011

Source: Independent National Electoral Commission 2011

Furthermore, the northern and southern dichotomy that usually manifests in the poverty lines and inequality trends is also visible in the struggle for political distribution. For instance, the recent 2011 presidential election was a case in point that polarized the country along northern and southern divide as illustrated on the map 3.2. Within the three political parties under investigation, two candidates were of the northern extraction and one candidate was from southern part. Apart from the north-central zone that is regarded as non-core north, all other states in the northern zones voted massively for the Congress for Progressive Change (CPC) party with a northerner as its presidential candidate. On the other hand, the southern zones voted amass for People Democratic Party (PDP) with a southerner as its candidate. For the third party Action Congress of Nigeria (ACN), which is believed to be southwest dominated party, had only in-route in one state of the geopolitical zone. But because the presidential candidate was a northerner, he was abandoned for the southern candidate of the PDP. This formation however raises many questions on regional composition and national unity. It sees elections into political offices as an access to the nation's wealth, and constitutes a ground for regional struggles, inequality and conflict generation. Therefore, the regional differentiation in Nigeria has showcased a number of variables of inequality and could only be reduced through appropriate structural reforms that can account for equitable redistribution of life chances.

6.3   Inequality in an Intersectional Perspective

The questions: "Who are you? What are you? Or where do you come from?" capture the intrinsic nature of inequality dynamics that exist in social interaction and as such, keep one apart from the other. The use of the concept: 'Intersectional Perspective' is merely to portray the interplay of the categories of inequality in the social structure. Thus the basis of social structural formations corresponds to identity differences and social positioning through which the social categories collide in producing inequality relations. The outcome of this formation is usually an absolute or relative deprivation, exclusion or what could be termed as marginalization. Under this analysis, the idea of marginalization is viewed as a simultaneous process of socio-economic and political positionings that inform unequal participation, suppression or discrimination within and among individuals or groups. It is a process of conflicting interest that victimizes the margin in a particular context and locations to the advantages of the center. Exploring the production of this process involves not only taking a range of social factors such as struggles and negotiations into account but more importantly, by paying closer attention to gender, class or ethnic differences and the autonomous ontological meanings that each social relation tends to produce.

In other words, the social categories of inequality are understood through varying degrees of marginalization that manifest themselves in diverse conditions of inequalities, but also consistently across various social groups and individuals. In the recent times, the phenomenon of marginalization has continued to be a major contention in different dimensions of relationships, ranging from political, social and economic disparities in Nigeria. The situation has continued to assume not only a general concern, but also, frightening dimensions that have occasioned the emergence of ethnic mobilizations, political instability, gender struggles and religious extremists. It follows that each of the six geo-political zones or various states as well as each ethnic group in the country has one claim or the other, to have been marginalized either politically, economically or socially. Marginalization has become a major tool of political bargaining in the Nigeria ever since the independence. The main bone of contention is; who is marginalized and who is not?

Empirically, this discriminatory contention is evident in analyzing the interaction within and among groups understood within the context of inequality differentials. Generally speaking, within the ascribed gender characteristics, class antagonisms or belonging to a minority social group is associated with a certain amount of deprivation, operation and vulnerability. Evidence of vulnerability tends to be of a structural nature ranging from statistics on illiteracy levels, poverty rate, accessibility to social goods, unemployment rate, income distributions, power relations, and so on. However, poverty and illiteracy could actually be characterized as the supreme structural risk factors in these categories that bring out the existing contradictions and ambiguities of inequality. On the other hand, the minorities and the disadvantaged or underprivileged groups tend to suffer from sociopolitical and economic deprivation not because they are apart from developmental system but due to their limited access in comparison to the national accessibility, sometimes as a result of repression and assimilation policies.

As a paradigmatic approach to the study of inequality, the intersectional dynamics of social categories play an important role in analyzing different structures and formations in human relationships. To understand these phenomena demand distinguishing between privileges and power differentials, and how they are experienced within different circles or groups. Thus the nature of power relates to influences and controls in which it is exercised, resulting to either oppression on the other or dominance by those who possess it. On the other hand, privilege is based on personal identities that support the domination of one group against the other. At that level, the underlying categories of inequality respond to the relationships that exist within the measures of power and privilege that create a comprehensive outlook towards individual and group interactions.

Hence in a cultural pluralistic society like Nigeria, the compounding relationships that make a group difficult to accommodate the other subgroups continue to expose the nature of subordination and inequality within the society. In this examination, the mode and process by which inequality categories manifest themselves, both within and among different associations that structure the relative positions of a group or individual in Nigerian society will form the key-point of analysis. This is to be done by empirically examining the social categories, and how they create a discriminatory pattern of relationship that keep one apart from the other.

6.3.1　Class Distinction

Class study is a broad area of inequality investigation, which inquires into structural relations and organizational changes in a society. Reflecting on the social relations that take place in the society and as a result of class consciousness, people are led to the awareness of their life situations. This awareness touches not only on the economic sphere but also on the mentality of individuals and groups towards their perception of reality that usually manifests in social interactions. In Karl Marx's view, the central identification of social class is not actually wealth but the availability of the means of production and how different groups interact in such availability through their class consciousness. However, the Marxist assumption may be considered as exhibiting some complexity in understanding the structure of classes in Nigerian society. Hence in Nigeria, both the mode of production and material wealth contextually assume the functional method of class analysis. In other words, class formation in Nigeria is mostly linked to political power and wealth accumulation. This idea reveals more the clear cut class distinctions that are though founded on means of production, yet manifest empirically on wealth and power accumulation. In that sense, the ultimate source of income and power determines the class consciousness and as such, wealth and capital are considered only if they contribute directly to class differences that separate the poor from the rich and the privileged from the dominated.

The economic structure of the Nigeria is build under a 'class' of capitalists whose economic interests and mode of productivity are sharply in conflict with those of the other population, who are subjugated to oppression and pauperization. In analyzing the social class in Nigeria, Ifidon aptly identifies two broad categories that go beyond the classical Marxian classes, which include: dominant social classes' or 'privileged classes', and 'oppressed classes' or 'underprivileged classes'.[42] The political elites and the wealthy bureaucratic elites belong to the dominant classes, who enjoy fabulous wealth, control the economy, make political decisions, allocate public funds and then misappropriate the funds.[43] The rest of the other population constituting more that 80% falls under the oppressed classes such as the artisans, students, unemployed youths, rural farmers, retired workers etc. But in the actual sense, the dominant or upper classes only consist of the small segment of the society, whereas the vast majorities that make up the oppressed or lower classes live in abject poverty.

Consequently, there is considerable existence of inequality margins that is evident between the two major class-groups of super rich and the very poor. In that circumstance, it is always very difficult for the lower class to transcend to another higher class because of the centralized institutional arrangements, lack of opportunities and poor educational attainments. On the other hand, the majority of the lower classes live in poor rural areas, whose domestic incomes are derived mainly from agricultural produce with little or no access to capital, social security and infrastructural amenities. In fact, the rural sector is either devoid of economic opportunity or

---

[42] Ifidon, Ehimika A. (1999): 'Social Rationality and Class Analysis of National Conflict in Nigeria: A Historiographical Critique'. In: Journal of Africa Development Vol. 24, Nos. 1 & 2, p. 150.

[43] Diamond rightly states that "the total misappropriation by the political class must have amounted to a significant portion of the capital available for development spending. Federal Ministers' official salaries and allowances alone amount to one per cent of the Federal Budget. When one considers that this was only a fraction of their total take: that others were helping themselves up and down the political and bureaucratic ladders; that contracts were let at hugely overpriced sums, often to wholly incompetent firms; and that the portion of the budget spent on official salaries and benefits was particularly large in relation to that for productive investment; the accumulated drag on the development process looms large indeed. And this does not include the other elements of waste, the unproductive expenditures on prestige projects and buildings, which did little to improve peoples' lives or to stimulate economic growth" (Diamond, Larry (1988): p. 311).

simply an exporter of productive resources to urban areas without much economic gains in return.

Nevertheless, the existence of middle class in Nigeria has been a popular discourse and a topic of long debate. Some analysts are simply of the opinion that in Nigeria you are either on the top class or down below, the existence of intermediary group as the stabilizing element is yet to be fully manifested. That notwithstanding, there seem to be some little signs of emerging middle class groups in Nigeria mainly in the financial institutions and communication industries, but they relatively constitute a mini-portion of the society. Thus the middle class is determined through the analysis of the household incomes that identify some groups on the upper class level and some others at lower class level. Then there may be other groups, who may not be considered as in the upper or lower classes groups, but stand within the middle quintile or between two extreme quintiles in the household incomes. As a result, the National Bureau of Statistics subdivided the economic class groupings in Nigeria as follows: lower class, lower-middle class, upper-middle class, lower-upper class and upper-upper class.

Table 3.10: Economic Grouping by Class 1996 & 2004

Classification	1996		2004	
	Population %	Population (million)	Population %	Population (million)
Lower Class	50.00	51.12	50.00	63.16
Lower-Middle Class	8.44	8.63*	1.20	1.52
Upper-Middle Class	21.57	22.07*	28.79	36.37
Lower-Upper Class	7.84	8.02*	3.68	4.64
Upper-Upper Class	12.14	12.42	16.32	20.61

*Source: National Bureau of Statistics, 2007 (*slight modification)*

From the table 3.10, it identifies the number and percentage distribution of five economic groupings by class in 1996 and 2004. These divisions are determined by wage difference among the groups. The table indicates that about 50% of the populations are in the lower class mainly in the rural areas and mostly self-employed, and the other remaining 50% are distributed among the other economic groups, who are mostly wage earners. Between 1996 and 2004, there was no significant change in the lower class formation, an indicative that the socio-economic and political environments have not given room for lower class transformation. This tendency also questions why the influence of global economic integration has not made positive impact on the lower class formation since the adjustment policy. Instead, the lower class has remained suppressed in the economic scheme of the country. However, there were notable changes in middle and upper class groupings in Nigeria from 1996 to 2004. The statistics reveal that about 7% of the lower-middle class transcended to upper-middle class, and about 4% climbed up to upper-upper class from lower-upper class from 1996 to 2004 respectively. This positive development could be explained as a result of transition to democratic government in 1999 that relatively opened the economy as well as allowed the increase of participation in the political and economic processes. But unfortunately, this positive impact has gradually started to disappear especially in the middle class formation. For instance, in 2010 the economic class trends indicate that the overall middle class groups decreased to 14.3% of the population against the overall estimate of 29.9% in 2004, resulting to an average of 15.6% difference. Even though there was about 16.1% growth in the population from 2004 to 2010, yet the general trend is that the middle class, which would have been the driving force of the economy, is in developmental crisis causing the constant growth of the lower class group. As we have already noted, within the period of 2004 and 2010 many middle class workers lost their jobs due to deregulations in the banking and financial sectors as well as poor policy advocacy to sustain the growth of the middle class. The deregulation exercise has rather given much advantage to the upper class to the detriment of the lower class majority.

Finally, in the general trends of class struggle, there is the tendency that the lower class in Nigeria will continue to stay unchanged in the midst of few weak middle class that still strives between labor demands and capital availability. Hence, the upper class that owes the means of production continues to alienate the rest of the classes as the dictator of demand and supply, which give them advantage over others. From the empirical evidence so far, it shows that the existing disparity between the upper class and the lower class will persist all the more, if there are no adequate social developmental mechanisms and policies in place to forestall the structural changes. Therefore, balancing the class structural differences demand more provision of basic facilities, and conducive and better working environments that could enhance the chances of middle class as the bridge to class stability and economic development.

6.3.2   Ethnic Identity Struggle

Ethnic identity is another major factor that contributes to inequality and social differentiation in Nigeria. This is constructed by various categories of interaction, represented by clusters of groups and sub-groups that have the same culture, language and dialects, shading into one composite unit. In Nigeria, ethnic identity plays a predominant role in socio-political and economic relationships that set one group or individual apart from the other. There are about 374 ethnic groups divided along different linguistic and cultural lines. These ethnic groups are also divided into major ethnic groups and ethnic minorities.

Map 3.2: Major Ethnic Groups in Nigeria.

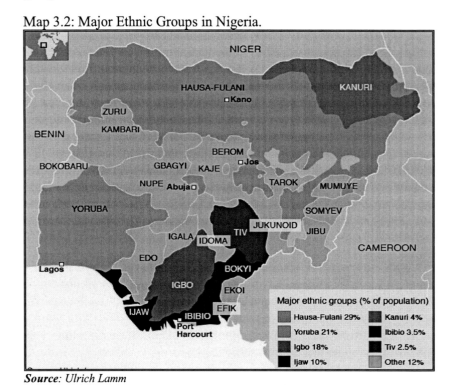

Source: Ulrich Lamm

Map 3.2 shows the percentage distribution of the population among the major ethnic groups and other minority groups in Nigeria with their boundary locations. It indicates that the Hausa-Fulani in the north, the Yoruba in the southwest and the Igbo in the southeast constitute the largest ethnic groups in their respective order and are regarded as the three ethnic majorities in Nigeria. From the statistics, it reveals that the major ethnic groups are made up of about 68% of the total population; the rests consist of the minor groups. Within the minority groups, there are also other subdivisions. Such ethnic groups like Ijaw, Kanuri, Ibibio and Tiv are regarded as larger minorities with a total of 20% of the population, the others 12% are the small minority groups. In fact, these classifications have major influence on the distribution of power and economic resources in Nigeria.

The distribution of socio-political and economic resources either through social infrastructures, employment, sharing of administrative positions or political powers are usually based on ethnic identity struggle. For instance, there are evidences to show that in some recruitment exercises whereby a southerner or northerner is in charge or in control; either of them will always struggle to fill any vacant employment opportunity with a member of the same tribe or ethnic group not minding whether the employee is qualified for the post or not. This principle disregards merit and people get employed based on affinity with people on top or in good positions of authority. It is on this note that Nnoli comments that "once the members of a particular group gained access to the best jobs and other resources, they used their positions to find jobs for others or at least to pass on news of job opportunities to them. The repercussions were felt in unequal levels of unemployment, income and in differing degrees of social status among the communal groups. Attempts by each group to escape the negative consequences of this phenomenon led to the further strengthening of communal associations."[44] This phenomenon as a result of socio-economic and political competitions breeds such terms like – state of origin, federal character, quota system, catchment area etc. being applied in selection/employment of worker. The aftermaths of these sys-

---

[44] Nnoli, Okwudiba (1995): Ethnicity and Development in Nigeria. Aldershot: Avebury, p. 40.

tems are often competence failure, loss of productivity and morale declination.

On the other hand, ethnic identity protection lays the foundation for ethnic inequality, as the dominant groups continue to suppress the minority groups. On this, Mustapha notes that, "ethnic inequalities are pervasive in Nigeria, affecting not just the public sector, but also the private sector. Invariably, the senior management and professional cadre of industries and businesses reflect the patterns of inequalities in educational and professional achievements, with the southwest and southeast having the largest numbers of private sector professionals. The character of private sector businesses and civil society organizations are also shaped by these inequalities."[45] Thus it has become a norm that the ethnic groups will try to utilize any opportunity whenever, in order to protect their respective ethnic interests. This protective attitude leads to ethnic struggle and subsequently diversities that has continued to poison the minds of the people, shaping their social, economic and political perceptions.

There is no gainsaying the fact that the structures, which have proliferated ethnic contradictions and diversities, were not unconnected with colonial configuration. Chabal and Daloz subscribe to this fact by say that "the colonial state which formalized the ethnic map and conspired to define the relationship between ethnicity and politics – both of which influenced directly the complexion of post-colonial politics."[46] They also resulted to ethnic contradictions which Nnoli also affirms that they "have an objective basis in the social structure of society. As an element of the ideological superstructure of society, ethnicity rests on, is functional for, and is determined by the infrastructure of society the mode of production."[47] In building on this functional mode of production through associations, this idea strengthens the ethnic mobilization in contradictory terms as each group collides in the struggle for scarce resources. This process of coalition will continue to persist in so far as the struggle for limited resources gears towards the demand for autonomy; and yet the

---

[45] Mustapha, Raufu A. (2006): p. 31.
[46] Chabal, Patrick/Daloz, Jean-Pascal (1999): Africa Works, pp. 57-58.
[47] Nnoli, Okwudiba (1978): Ethnic Politics in Nigeria. Enugu: Fourth Dimensions Publishers, p. 11.

267

fierce competition for socio-economic interest as a functional mode of production will then continue to deepen the ethnic contradictions.

Finally, the contradictions in interethnic relations have been the bane of underdevelopment in Nigeria, giving rise to ethnic cleavages, different power blocs and political instability. Mustapha here states that "efforts to reform interethnic relations in Nigeria and the attempts to create inclusive institutions have had limited success. It has been relatively easier to broaden ethnic representation in the executive and legislature than to create genuine structures of social inclusion. Even in the context of increased ethnic representativeness, hegemonic impulses of particular ethnic groups are not totally suppressed in the executive. This problem is even more obvious in the organization of political parties, where efforts at wider representation remain subject to manipulation by the more powerful ethnic groups, involving such tactics as the recruitment of lightweight politicians from particular areas to meet federal character injunctions."[48] Therefore, while reforming the interethnic relations may fundamentally transform the Nigerian state to an extent, it will still be a hard knock in engaging the ethnic mobilization and solidarity towards progressive change. This is because; mobilization and solidarity constitute the collective member interests in the struggle for economic and political distributions.

6.3.3   Gender Disparity

Gender simply refers to ascribed roles based on different social and cultural institutions that periodically manifest among males and females. Gender roles are socially and culturally constructed and influenced by such factors like sex orientation, ethnic origin, location, class and age. On this Sen opines that "gender inequality is not one homogeneous phenomenon, but a collection of disparate and inter-linked problems."[49] This is because other forms of inequality have great effect on the situational outcomes of gender inequality. It appears that there are often new formations

---

[48] Mustapha, Raufu A. (2006): p. 43.
[49] Sen, Amartya (2008): 'Many Faces of Gender Inequality'. In: Webber, Michelle/Bezanson, Kate (eds.): Rethinking Society in the 21st Century: Critical Readings in Sociology 2nd Edition. Toronto: Canadian Scholars' Press Inc., p. 201.

in gender inequality, which depends not only on income distribution but also on deprivation of social goods, as well as the outcome of disintegration of family value systems by capitalist market forces. In identifying several faces of gender inequality, these new forms of disparity constitute a spatial force in which the traditional culture has not been able to withstand.

With the significant changes in social formation, gender inequality continues to exhibit its worsening configuration on the male-dominated society like Nigeria. Thus the patriarchy system of the society relations seems to place the women as second class citizens. In other words, the present status of women in Nigeria illustrates an overwhelming cumulative process of ever-increasing male ascendancy. This structured-domination forms the important context of long-standing historical process. As an instance, most married women belong to backward classes, and are regarded as possession and subject to their husbands. On this Chiegboka opines that "the cultural situation have in addition rendered women complacent since owing to economic protection and indispensable need to marry at all costs, women have been found to desire still the position of second and even seventh wife of a man."[50] In addition, most women lack the autonomy and political will to dissociate themselves from this domination because of the inability of mediation between the contending economic and socio-cultural forces that enhances this phenomenon.

For instance, the traditional preference of the male genders as the heirs of the family categorically suppresses the opportunities of the female genders especially in overall domestic distribution. According to Sen, "there are systematic disparities in the freedoms that men and women enjoy in different societies, and these disparities are often not reducible to differences in income or resources. While differential wages or payment rates constitute an important part of gender inequality in most societies, there are many other spheres of differential benefits, e.g. in the division of labour within the household, in the extent of care of education received, in liberties that different members are permitted to enjoy."[51] It follows that

---

[50] Chiegboka, C. A. (1997): Women Status and Dignity in the Society and the Church: A perspective from Gal. 3, 36-39. Enugu: Pearl Functions, p. 33.
[51] Sen, Amartya (1995): Inequality Reexamined, p. 122.

women lag far behind men in most indicators of socio-economic and political welfare. As a result, opportunities and representations both in the family and in the society are more accessible to male gender.

Table 3.11: Gender Disparity in Core Development Indicators 2006 (%)

Gender Stratification within the Overall Economy & Private Sector		
Development Issue/Sector	Men	Women
Below Poverty Line	35.00	65.00
Fed. Civil Service	76.00	24.00
Mgt. Staff	86.00	14.00
Medical Doctors	82.50	17.50
Informal Sector	13.00	87.00
Access to Bank Loan	78.10	21.90
Land Ownership	90.00	10.00
Agricultural Work	30.00	70.00
Animal Husbandry	50.00	50.00
Food Processing	10.00	90.00
Marketing Inputs	40.00	60.00
Properties Disposable at	95.00	5.00

Source: National Bureau of Statistics – CWIQ, 2006

However, table 3.11 presents the gender stratification within the overall economy and private sector in 2006. It indicates that in the core development indicators, women are mostly disadvantaged. With lower adult literacy, about 65% of Nigerians that are below the national poverty line are women in 2006. It is imperative here to note that different forms of gender inequality culminate in poverty and literacy levels, which manifest in various means such as in lack of basic access to common goods, social services, property disposal and ownership rights etc. Thus only few women are engaged in high paid jobs when compared to men population. On the other hand, the majority of women are involved in informal sector of the economy mainly petty-trade and other domestic-based works as the only available means to cope with life situations. Although only 10% of women have land ownership rights, yet more than 70% engage themselves in agricultural productivity majorly to carter for their immediate families and other domestic needs. Besides their significant contribution

270

to children upbringing and domestic functions, women are also subjugated and suppressed by cultural impositions such as in right of ownership.

Moreover, empirical findings reveal that women are majorly subjected to exploitive domestic positions that make them over-represented in low-paid employment, chiefly because of the traditional role-stereotyping of men domination and unequal access to resources. However, in analyzing the employment statistics from a gender perspective, it gives insight into the existing gaps between women and men in different categories. In addition, when the amount of time spent on doing work is considered, it also reveals a lot more than mere inequality. Rather it exposes the excessive work burden and exploitation women are subjected to, both in the rural and urban households.

Figure 3.13: Percentage Rate of Labour Force Participation by Gender 2009

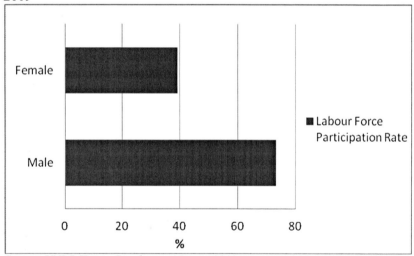

Source: UNDP Human Development Report 2011

Figure 3.13 shows the percentage rate of labor force participation in 2009 among male and female. It indicates that only 39.2% of the female population is engaged in labor force in Nigeria as against 73.4% of the total number of male population in the year 2009. There was absolute null improvement from the previous year assessment, where the population of female participation was 39.5% and male 74.8% respectively. Comparatively, a country such as Ghana has higher human development index than Nigeria, with 73.8% population of female participate in labor force and 75.2% of male population in 2009. The implication of this development is that either the majority of female are unemployed in Nigeria or they are limited to domestic works and other unrecorded work domains, which also consume more energy and time than wage-employment. But both cases have serious consequences on inequality formation.

Furthermore, the issue of direct or equal inheritance constitutes also a major disparity between males and females. Generally, females have limited rights over inheritance in Nigeria. As already shown in table 3.11 in term of properties disposable at Will, the table vividly indicates that only 5% of women have the right of inheritance. It is basically and traditionally considered that inheritance is a male affair notwithstanding the legal right the women also have to inheritance. In most ethnic and cultural groups in Nigeria, inheritance is passed on to the males in the family after the death of their father regardless of their age. In a case where the man has no son, the male relatives such as brothers or uncles take possession of his inheritance. Though there may be some exceptions to this rule with regard to cultural differences and modernization influences, yet women are by and large subdued in inheriting property in most Nigerian cultural settings.

Moreover, the cultural constraint in some communities also contributes to unequal access to the means of production, particularly lack of power to purchase and own land. In some cases, mostly in southern part of the country, whereby women are beginning to exert comparative influence both in political and economic environment, the situation is relatively quite different. But on the other hand, the condition varies in the northern Muslim states where polygamy is a major practice. Thus most women are secluded from public views, lack educational opportunities and political participations, and have little or no chances in engaging with income-earning ventures. Most of them often depend only on their husbands for their daily upkeep.

Figure 3.14: Enrolment Distribution in Nigerian University by Gender 2003-2010 (%)

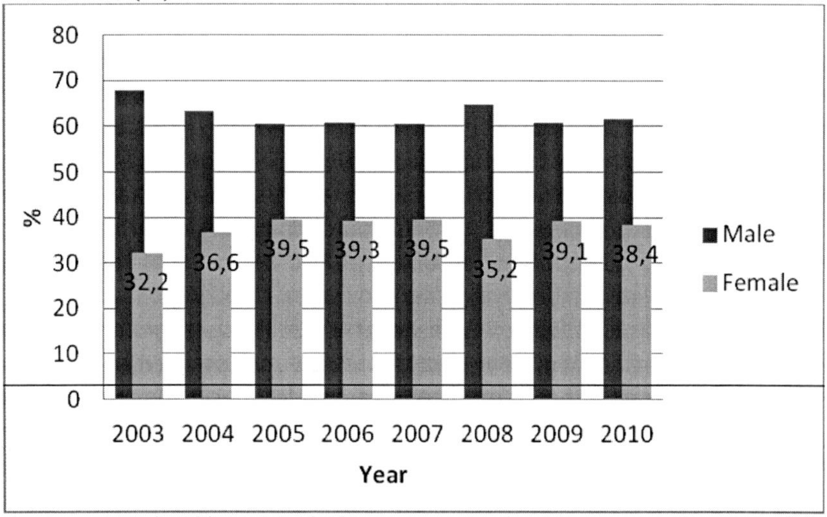

Sources: *JAMB/NUC/Ministry of Education, Digest of Statistics 2010*

In the educational attainment, males continue to dominate the females both in the primary, secondary and tertiary institutions. As already observed, the overall statistics indicate that the greater percentage of males enrolls in the various schools when compared to female enrolments. As further evidence, figure 3.14 shows the percentage enrolment distribution of gender in the Nigerian University from 2003 to 2010. In average terms, about two third of the total enrolment are males. Although there was a little progressive shift on female enrolment in 2010 as compared to 2003, yet the general outcome indicates a major disparity between male and female in the university enrolment. It suggests that due to inadequate financing, most families especially in the rural areas believe that sponsoring a woman in the university is a waste of resources, because at a certain time she will be married out from the household. At some other instances, young girls are forced into marriage in their early age to give better opportunity for the education of the males.

Table 3.12: Distribution in National Assembly by Type, Year & Gender
1999-2011 (%)

Legislators	1999	2003	2007	2011
SENATE				
Men	97.2	96.3	91.7	93.6
Women	2.8	3.7	8.3	6.4
HOUSE OF REPS.				
Men	96.7	94.2	92.8	95.0
Women	3.7	5.8	7.2	5.0
BOTH HOUSES				
Men	96.8	94.7	92.5	94.7
Women	3.2	5.3	7.5	5.3

Source: Independent National Electoral Commission (INEC)

Furthermore, there are also evidences to show imbalances in gender participation in political positions and seats in Nigeria. For instance, table 3.12 illustrates the percentage distribution of seats held in both upper and lower houses of the National Assembly according to gender, from the time of transition to democratic government in 1999 to 2011. In the Senate, out of 109 available seats, women had only 3 seats in 1999; the rests were taken by men. There was marginal change in 2007 after the elections, where women constitute 8.3% of the senate positions but again suffered decline to 6.4% after the 2011 elections. The same trends are also observed in the House of Representatives, where 92.8% of the 360 available seats in 2007 were occupied by men and increased to 95% after the 2011 elections, leaving only 5% seats to women. When one observes both houses, the general tendency is that women have little or no voice in the law making process in the country.

Although the visibility of women in elective offices in comparison with the previous years is steadily improving, yet the male dominance both in the local, state and federal levels is still significantly affecting female position in the societal affairs. Perhaps, this is an expression of absolute gender difference that is more noticeable in the rural areas. It implies that if women have minority voices both in the parliaments and executive arms of the government to take decisions in the matters that affect their well-being, then it is obvious that they will continue to experience socio-economic and political deprivations. In that case, the dominant position of men in the society especially in the decision-making is not unconnected to power centralization and the socio-economic structure of the state that give them undue advantage over women. Therefore, since most of the gender inequality manifests within the economic and power differentials, it is pertinent that policy programmes that will address better welfare opportunities become the ultimate priorities of the government.

6.4   Inequality and Globalization: Social Consequences

Investigating the social consequences of inequality would be a resource point in constructing various facts about globalization influence on developing countries such as Nigeria. There are many empirical evidences that have shown various facets of globalization impacts on social categories of inequalities such class, gender, residential location and ethnic origin. In other words, globalization impact on human development indicators as it were, carries along with it many features of risk factors, which are detrimental both to individuals and society. Thus globalization as underlying structure of inequality has heightened discrimination and oppression, and created sense of disillusionment on developing economy as a result of structural differences that have systematically disconnected many from the global participation, thereby aggravating exclusion, poverty and risks.

In fact, the neo-liberal policies have created a divide that dissociates and pitches one group against the other both locally and internationally. Viewed from the integral process of power differentials among various social groups, the divide indicates that unequal access to economic and political resources can result to violence and social conflicts. In that instance, high levels of inequality result to various risk threats such as insecurity, political instability, violence etc. that affect people differently, as people strive to challenge various dominant productions. And on the other hand, globalization has continued to shape the traditional patterns of family system and gender relationships, forming new structures of individualism with consequences on social inequality differences. Hence the following inquiries will specifically illustrate the dimensions of social changes that can illuminate the understanding of inequality and globalization.

6.4.1 Insecurity and Fear

Today, the significant changes in the world have initiated new fears, tensions and insecurities. Globalization has opened the doors and exposed the world into many security dangers such as nuclear annihilation and terrorism.[52] Many world leaders now begin their various speeches by remarking how 'dangerous' and 'risky' the society is becoming. According to Beck, "the movement set in motion by the risk society is expressed in the statement: 'I am afraid!' The 'commonality of anxiety' takes the place of the 'commonality of need'. The type of the risk society marks in this sense a social epoch in which 'solidarity from anxiety' arises and becomes a political force."[53] In this situation, insecurity and fear transcend borders and affect also those who did not initiate or propagate the risk factors. It implies that insecurity is felt by everyone, but the mostly affected are the poor and minorities, who are cut-off from the life securities by the global forces.

However, insecurity and fear are now assuming many ridiculous dimensions in Nigeria, producing ever new dangers to national integration. No day passes without one form of atrocity or the other that instigate fears and insecurity. For example, kidnapping (and its newest form of 'adultnapping') and armed robbery have remained unabated. Nobody is sure of the next day as every passing hour is full of anxiety and uncertainty. People's minds remain often in suspense, because anything can happen at any time. Unfortunately, it is no longer only the rich or the highly placed that are robbed and kidnapped; it has spread to all strata of the society: children, old men and women, rich and poor, now stand the risk of sudden kidnapping and then huge ransom that must be paid for their release. Most often than not, the situation handicaps the security agents, who, as a matter of fact unequipped to handle the matters and may as well fall as victims. In the words of Chinua Achebe, 'things are no longer at ease' with security situation in Nigeria.

---

[52] Stiglitz notes that "increased insecurity is one of the reasons that opposition to trade liberalism is so widespread. But while globalization has led to more insecurity and contributed to the growing inequality in both developed and less developed countries, it has limited the ability of governments to respond" (Stiglitz, Joseph E. (2007): p. 69).

[53] Beck, Ulrich (1992): Risk Society, p. 49.

Subsequently, the issue of insecurity could as well be viewed from an aesthetic level that linked it to dissatisfaction of the people in the state of national affairs.[54] When people's aspirations and feelings are not met, it results to deprivation and frustration, and the reality of insecurity and fear assume the defining factors. No doubt, the situation of insecurity and fear are also attributes of unequal access to political and economic resources. According to Ujoma, "the crisis of national security in the nation can be seen in the political and economic difficulties arising from both the struggle for state power among the national elite, as well as in the distribution and management of the society's wealth and resources. It has been noted that the problem of national security in Nigeria has been aggravated by the intolerance among the various ethno-cultural and religious groups. This situation has led to the engendering of mistrust and divisive tendencies in the society."[55] Thus the fact remains that vast majority of the population have not benefited from the wealth of the nation, which has remained in the hands of the very few, affecting equal participation and representation of class, gender and ethnic origins. In other words, majority of Nigerians live below the poverty line. This situation unfortunately

---

[54] Ujomu and Adelugba note that "the linking of security to satisfaction among the producers, users and observers is most clearly seen in the general state of dissatisfaction that members of the society have expressed about the state of affairs. Such objections have been varied but they underscore the same point that there is insecurity in the land and that the bulk of Nigerians are very uncomfortable with the existing situation. The whole idea of satisfaction at one level is tied to the concept of feelings. The point must be made that in the case of a feeling such as 'fear', there are clear physiological and social or normative aspects. The physiological aspect connects to the physical changes that the human being undergoes in the state of fear. These changes affect the mind and the body. At the social level, there are certain institutional frameworks that imbue fear or certain symbolic structures that deliver the message of fear. These can include agents and institutions such as rites and cults. The feeling of security is therefore largely tied to the feeling of satisfaction that things are going well or that one remains in control" (Ujomu, Philip Ogo/Adelugba, Dapo (2008): 'An Aesthetic Theorising of the Challenge of National Security in the Post-Colonial Context'. In: Adelugba, Dapo/Ujomu, Philip Ogo (eds.): Rethinking Security in Nigeria: Conceptual Issue in the Quest for Social Order and National Integration. Senegal: CODESRIA, p. 64).

[55] Ujomu, Philip Ogo (2008): 'The Bounds of Security Theorising: Envisioning Discursive Inputs for the Rectification of a Post-Colonial Situation'. In: Adelugba, Dapo/Ujomu, Philip Ogo (eds.): Rethinking Security in Nigeria: Conceptual Issue in the Quest for Social Order and National Integration. Senegal: CODESRIA, p. 42.

leads to complex inequalities, increased crime rate and general insecurity that hinder socio-economic growth and development.

However, insecurity threats have continued to increase by the day unchecked. Thus the Islamic group Boko Haram (meaning Western education is a sin) mostly in the northern part of Nigeria with its strong links to Muslim fundamentalists is a case in point. Since 2009, it has become unabatedly a national threat, causing sectarian violence, bomb attacks and clashes with security agents that have claimed many lives and properties. And it appears that the government has remained helpless in confronting adequately the situation. Hence this observation re-establishes the fact that the socio-political structure in Nigeria is not adequately in place and has subjected and positioned the greater number of the population to multiple relationships that engenders risks of physical and social insecurity.

On the other hand, the economic implications of insecurity cannot be overemphasized due to economic losses associated with crimes. From the findings, it reveals that the more security in place, the lesser the percentage of economic losses but paradoxically it can also give rise to increase of security costs. As a result of the high level of insecurity in the country, many public and private sectors have resorted to private security personnel. This, of course has become the security alternative for those who can afford the private security services. Here Abrahamsen and Williams observe that "the commercial sector is the main market for private security, and virtually all businesses of any size in Nigeria employ private security in one form or another, as do international organizations, NGOs and embassies. The most sought-after contracts are with transnational corporations, particularly with the oil companies and the various contractors and service companies associated with the oil industry."[56] But unfortunately, this security practice has continued to assume complex situations, in the sense that the main cause of insecurity is yet to be addressed by private security outfits. Thus the major issue is that vast majority of the population still lives in extreme poverty, and the resort to private securities is rather a form of suppression and dominance over the helpless population. Instead, the government should rationalize the security problem by put-

---

[56] Abrahamsen, Rita/Williams, Michael (2005): p. 5.

ting in place the required institutional development that can ensure equal opportunities and better living standards.

It follows then that the necessity of security demands a proper re-examination of the core idea of human development and the value of life. The integral solution to insecurity and fear should corroborate at least with other central principles and practices that influence their make-ups. Here Beck is of the opinion that "handling fear and insecurity becomes an essential cultural qualification, and the cultivation of the abilities demanded for it becomes an essential mission of pedagogical institutions."[57] In that sense, insecurity cannot be achieved merely by providing professional security outfits but through the government's proper policy interventions. Those interventions should therefore gear towards provision of necessary infrastructures, which can address developmental constraints, as well as promote the social security of life and property in Nigeria.

6.4.2   Emerging Individualism

In analyzing the notion of individualism as opposed to communalism or socialism, this work may not go as far as establishing a normative definition of the term, but rather view the notion as distinct character of individual in the commonality of relationships. Thus the communal relationship has come under serious threat with globalization influences. In this recent time, the wave of globalization according to Giddens, "is fundamentally changing the nature of our social relation and everyday experiences. As the societies in which we live undergo profound transformations, the established institutions that used to underpin them have become out of place. This is forcing a redefinition of intimate and personal aspects of our lives, such as the family, gender roles, sexuality, personal identity, our interactions with others and our relationships to work. The way we think of ourselves and our connections with other people is being profoundly altered through globalization."[58] Thus the new emerging formation of individualism occasioned by globalization process has continued to pitch conflict formation in the traditional social networks and social sustainability.

---

[57] Beck, Ulrich (1992): Risk Society, p. 76.
[58] Giddens, Anthony (2006): Sociology, p. 67.

The traditional African notion of human existence finds its root in community relationship, in which it is believed that the individual is not apart
from the community but finds his meaning therein. According to Mbiti,
the individual can only say: "I am, because we are; and since we are,
therefore I am. The existence of the individual is the existence of the
corporate; and where the individual may physically die, this does not
relinquish his social-legal existence since 'we' continues to exist for the
'I'."[59] In that sense, the living community offers the individual deep sense
of security and moral upbringing; and hence the individual depends on
the corporate group for survival.[60] Unfortunately, this traditional axiom of
communalism has been practically altered by the current wave of neo-
liberalism. In fact, the cultural value of African extended family system
as the fundament of communal living has been debased by this development. As such, the uncertainty of communality isolates groups and individuals from social networks.

Consequently, individualism is now understood as a historically contradictory process of explosive transformation of social relations. It is a
conflict between traditional culture and modern culture, depriving the
individual the opportunity to see beyond immediate self. Thus the growing trends of inequality associated with gender disparities, class differentials and ethnic protections have their root in the distinctive characters of
individuals in the pursuit of personal goals against common interests. In
other words, individual competitions have assumed a highly dominant
value, with the desire to satisfaction of personal demands and needs
against the community interest. According to Beck, "the tendency is towards the emergency of individualized forms and conditions of existence,
which compel people – for the sake of their own material survival – to
make themselves the center of their own planning and conduct of life."[61]
In effect, the traditional welfare systems that tend to sustain the aged and
minorities are disappearing through the process of individual thrusts. The

---

[59] Mbiti, S. John (1989): p. 141.
[60] In African perspective, individuals according to Chabal and Daloz, "are not perceived
as being meaningfully and instrumentally separate from the (various) communities to
which they belong [...]. This means that individual remains firmly placed within the
family, kin and communal networks from which (s)he is issued" (Chabal, Patrick/Daloz,
Jean-Pascal (1999): Africa Works, p. 52).
[61] Beck, Ulrich (1992): Risk Society, p. 88.

unprecedented number of separations and divorces in marriages has continued to split up the family bonds and keep the children apart from the parental cares, consequent of individual interests in conflict with the social community. Hence the changing pattern of social relationship is seriously altering the family system in the African context, which has assumed an exclusive features rather than inclusive features of individual commitments to the community networks. Therefore, as the danger of individualism increasingly constitutes a fundamental community burden, so does it extend significantly to nation-state; threatening the social formation and relational outcomes.

6.4.3   Clash of Interests and Violence

In a risk situation, a variety of new social differentiations and clash of interests commonly emerge as incompatible factors that both internally and externally undermine democratic institutional development. In Nigeria as elsewhere, struggle for personal interests and subsequent violence characterize the ever-growing polarization and antagonism between different social and political groups. The concept of interests is also synonymous with power struggles. In other words, Rajaee opines that "striving for power is related to some notion of 'interest', defined as security or preservation of one's wealth and position."[62] Apparently, wherever such conflicting interests manifest within or among groups as a result of unmet needs and failure of the government to address people's animosity due to inequality differences, violence is to be anticipated. This occurrence has been heightened by the structural changes initiated by modernization.

As a leading factor of differentiation, globalization has opened the doors to new types of fragmentations and differences, which have undermined efforts in creating a stable and democratic multi-ethnic society in Nigeria. As manifestations of inequalities, when differences such as in gender, class or ethnicity are neglected or ignored within or among individuals as well as groups, they frequently result to violent clashes. On this, Walby contends that "violence needs to be added to the conventional set of institutional domains of economy, polity and civil society, since it is so important in the structuring of gender, ethnic, national, and religious ine-

---

[62] Rajaee, Farhang (2000): p. 39.

qualities. Violence is not merely an instrument of power, but can also be constitutive of social relations."[63] It follows that when the dominant groups are not ordinarily able to achieve their goals, they resort to violent attacks on the oppressed groups. It becomes more troublesome when weaker groups or individuals have no wherewithal or power to face and withstand the violent attacks.

In fact, Abbink opines that "African social structure, ethnic communities and modes of governance in the post colonial era are not congruent, and they are not really in the process of becoming so [...]. Violence remains a widespread political means that elites and power holders can and do resort to without hesitation if their position is at stake. The global international system that props up their position largely aids and abets them, and has no other solution ready."[64] Thus the widespread of violence is evident in the growing number of political violence that is affecting the stability of the developing countries. Nevertheless, violence as a result of clash of interests is often so complex that it is hardly difficult to resolve or manage. It has been observed that almost 40% of reported cases of violence episodes in Nigeria were perpetuated with the use of weapon ranging from political, religious to ethnic violence, thus heightening the danger of risk in the society. These are predominantly fuelled by struggle for natural resources as the case in Niger-Delta region, so also other social, political and economic problems as well as ethnic and religious factors as it is the case in the northern Nigeria.

In specific terms, Kariuki observes that "Nigeria's two major religions, Islam and Christianity, are sometimes depicted as monolithic entities that confront each other in pitched battles, with formal implementation of the criminal aspects of the Muslim Sharia legal code (or the likelihood of implementation) providing the spark that touches off violence. Riots based (at least ostensibly) on religious affiliation and religious policies have indeed occurred, the worst such being the two confrontations that took place in Kaduna between February and May 2000. This poses a con-

---

[63] Walby, Sylvia (2009): Globalization & Inequalities, p. 20.
[64] Abbink, John (2004): 'Violence and State (Re)formation in African Context: Global and Local Aspects of Crisis and Change'. In: Westerfield, Robert E. (ed.): Current Issues in Globalization. New York: Nova Science Publishers Inc., p. 146.

stitutional problem because the Nigerian constitution guarantees a secular state, guarantees freedom of religion, and vests in states concurrent power to establish their own court systems. At both constitutional and practical levels, these guarantees are incompatible in light of the fact that Islam rejects separation of political from religious authority and proposes a unified theocratic system of governance."[65] And because there are religious diversities and ideological differences, it makes the socio-cultural phenomena more incompatible within a given group, thereby creating uneasiness and violent clashes. As a result, many lives have been claimed and many families displaced on account of such violence. Some of the conflicts, which have religious undertone, may be on the other hand politically motivated, as the case of ethnic conflicts in Jos-Nigeria and terror attack by the Boko Haram sect in the recent time.

In another instance, ethnic violence is one of the major aspects of clash of interests affecting most African countries. Nigeria being a multi-ethnic nation is deeply subsumed in this problem of ethnic violence, which is at the heart of her developmental crisis. The struggle for scarce resources by different ethnic groups has compounded the ethnic discords, and increased the experiences of inequality differentials among ethnic groups; pushing some groups to mobilize themselves for economic and political struggles. Berman et al however observe that "the combination of economic decline and state failure, exacerbated by the disruptive effects of neo-liberal reforms, has led to increasing conflict, insecurity and distrust which has, in turn, increased individual and collective reliance on clientelistic networks and the solidarities of ethnic communities."[66] Hence, within the unfettered arena of political and economic competition, ethnic mobilization and solidarity assumes the fundamental means of ethnic protection, which more often than not ends up in violent strife in which the Nigeria-Biafra civil war between 1967 and 1970 assumes here the paradigm instance.

---

[65] Kariuki, Angela (2010): Violence begets Violence: Nigeria's Deathly Religious History. In: Consultancy Africa Intelligence. http://www.consultancyafrica.com/ [accessed: 24.10.2010]

[66] Berman, Bruce/Eyoh, Dickson/Kymlicka, Will (2004): 'Conclusion: African Ethnic Politics & the Paradox of Democratic Development'. In: Berman, Bruce/Eyoh, Dickson/Kymlicka, Will (eds.): Ethnicity and Democracy in Africa. Oxford: James Currey, p. 318.

Finally, lack of shared beliefs, attitudes and values among the rulers and the ruled, as well as among the various segments and groups in Nigeria, are the major factors through which clash of interests still remain an endemic feature in the nation. In fact, the North cannot accommodate their southern brothers and vice versa. Day-in-day-out, one continues to experience one form of violence or the other. In that instance, the struggle for interest according to Ifidon was "between the East and the West on the one hand that is for posts and economic advantages, and on the other hand between the East and the North for political power. On another level, it was between the South (East and West) and the North [for the control of state]. Then there was friction between the Hausa-Fulani and the Ibo, and between the Ibo and the Yoruba on [ethnic protection levels]."[67] In fact, the struggle has also translated to a situation in which there is existence of fundamental rivalry of social value demands and needs among various interests and groups with regard to the proper meaning and approach to national integration, peace and stability within the polity. Therefore, globalization as an agent of social change has continued to intensify the forces of value among various segments of interest groups, and then opening more avenues through which people could obtain weapons of destruction. In the long run, the minorities especially the women and children are the majority bearing the risk consequences.

6.5   Conclusion

We have empirically attempted in this part to scrutinize the changes in social structure and inequality in Nigeria as consequence of globalization. We started by analyzing the changing structures of the value systems and network formations. We then identified that the traditional African cultural relationships emphasize such values as family, community, social control etc. In recent times, these traditional cultural values are being confronted with the new value systems initiated through globalization networks such as western music, videos, internets, cable and satellite television, advertisements etc that challenge and sometimes subsume the norms and beliefs of the original culture. These counter-cultural phenomena have consequently shifted the traditional African value system from their original formation. Here Ntibagirirwa however points out that this

---

[67] Ifidon, Ehimika A. (1999): p. 156.

shift has two aspects: "The first aspect is the fact that the leaders and scholars of the African independence and post-independence era have betrayed the African value system by analyzing it with socio-economic and political implications that are drawn from a different value system, namely Marxism. The second aspect is the fact that Africans are now engaged in the process of completely abandoning their value system by trying to embrace another value system, namely, liberalism which is articulated in Kantianism or/and utilitarianism."[68] In the first shift, it points to the fact that colonialism brought alone with it structural phenomena that forced the political elites to believe that their social and anthropological perceptions were deficient and must be transformed to suit the colonial intentions. And on the other hand, the Africans then went into cross-cultural crisis that left many value systems to be abandoned for the modern culture that could not whole guarantee their social safety networks. As such these shifts reinstate the changing pattern of the traditional culture and social formation occasioned by capitalism and the pursuit of wealth and power accumulation. Hence coping with these modernization influences have indeed continued to be a defining factor in the formation of socio-political ideology in Nigeria.

Nevertheless, the socio-political and economic order has been characterized by instability and policy failures due to the fact that the society has been diffused and not able to cope with the modern phenomena of change. Thus the gaps between the rich and the poor on the national level are still on the increase with the spread of liberalization. In fact, the social inequality, which has hitherto been affected by the changing value system of the social order, occasioned by the liberalization processes and translated in terms of the expansion of market values and the quest for more profits, have been a major threat to Nigerian society development. In fact, individuals are no longer defined by their community values but actually by their wealth, that is, by what they have acquired through whatever means in so far as their ends are met. For instance, many are no longer

---

[68] Ntibagirirwa, Symphorien (2001): 'A Wrong Way: From Being to Having in the African Value System'. In. Giddy, Patrick (ed.): Protest and Engagement: Philosophy after Apartheid at an Historically Black South African University, Cultural Heritage and Contemporary Change Series II, Africa, Volume 7. Washington, D.C.: The Council for Research in Values and Philosophy, p. 65.

after how people make their wealth, but how they could strongly influence the community with their wealth. They buy people over in order to actualize their various motives and maintain their patrimonial and clientele influences, be that social, political or economical. They monopolize the means of production and increasingly alienate the vast population through unending accumulation and unequal distribution of resources. These compositions have been the outcome of global integration.

Hence the desire for more profits has caused marginalization of certain groups and individuals in the distribution of incomes. The political elites and the rich business men, who have control over the means of production and capitals, determine the modality of distributions. This configuration analyzed within the last three decades, manifests in the trends of inequality both in educational attainment, urban and rural dichotomy, and regional differentiations. It is discovered from the analysis that most of the inequalities due to unequal chances exist among individuals and groups according to their place of residence, gender and geopolitical zones, but manifest a consequential effect within the groups mostly the non-poor groups. For instance, the disparities, which exist between urban and rural areas, are usually taken for granted. But when that is viewed within either urban or rural households, it reveals lot more of inequality differentials. Though it is more outstanding in the urban sector, where there are majority of non-poor groups. In that case, there are considerable chances for inequality reduction if much essential infrastructural facilities and economic opportunities are sufficiently well distributed. On the other hand, developmental policies that can encourage more population to stay in the rural household will also substantially reduce the level of inequality differentials in the urban areas.

The underlying features of social categories such as class, gender and ethnic origin were addressed in this analysis as the forceful determinants of inequality differentials and they intersect with each other in producing complex social relationships. The existence of class antagonism, which is linked with gender and ethnic differences, has ensured a difficult crossover from oppressed class to dominant class. The middle class formation has become insignificant in balancing the existing gaps between the upper and lower classes. However, this configuration was more evidence within the gender formations, where the majority of female gender occupied the lower class and has little opportunity to social goods. This, of course calls for a rethinking in the manner in which different genders interact and participate in the affairs of the state, in order to promote developmental outcomes.

In a nutshell, Nigerian state due to structural changes, socio-political differences, ethnic diversities and inability to create sufficient autonomous spaces for socio-political and economic participations, no doubt, contributes to the reproduction of structures of inequality, insecurity and violence. The political elites on their own part have continued to personalize the state structures, and sometimes have succeeded in limiting the formation of strong civil society groups that could withstand their excesses. In keeping with these phenomena, the Nigerian state is influenced by selfish individual chauvinism for self-aggrandizement and political usurpation. Therefore, the poor and the minority remain the prime targets of the assuming and emerging consequences.

PART IV

NIGERIA: THE FUTURE OF THE PRESENT

7.   CHALLENGES

One of the major impediments that have continued to characterize the process of state formation in Nigeria, as well as the concerted effort against the increase in social inequality since independence has been the institutional deficiency of the state. This deficiency has been persistently causing instability, corruption and policy failures both in the political and economic systems, thereby aiding the increase of social inequality. As the study has already substantiated in the previous chapters, the impediment of institutional formation has both external and internal features. The external features have to deal with the colonial heritage and the current influence of global integration; and the internal feature is majorly rooted on the system of neo-patrimonialism or so to speak, the personalization of the state by the ruling class. However, in this fourth part of the work, attempt will be made to x-ray some of the future challenges of the post-colonial state of Nigeria. The articulations of the challenges are not merely to-do lists but actually some critically drawn-up prerogatives needed for urgent action, as well as some set-up principles in tackling the changing patterns of social structural formation in this era of globalization. The challenges are to be addressed under two main headings: firstly, the different approaches needed for immediate action and secondly, the necessary axes of future plan.

7.1   The Approach for Immediate Action

There is no doubt whether globalization has come to stay. The major preoccupations and challenges of the moment remain chiefly on how globalization could be fashioned towards workability; and to improve the social standard of the majority poor population, who are mostly affected by its negative consequences. The main prerogative then implies putting into action those theories and/or those other necessary principles of development, as well as putting into practice those ever-sermonized good intentions of individuals and groups. The articulation of this idea may be related to Talcott Parsons' view on individual actions and behavior in the social system. However, our methodological approach goes beyond individual capability to collective actions towards the immediate needs of the people. In other words, it is an all-embracing mechanism that can account for the integration of diverse groups and individuals in the society scheme. Although the human society consists of individuals as the theorists of social action would argue, yet the goal of a rational society does not only base on the individual but on the nature of the institution that make up the society, which should also have purpose or motives and ends to enhance developmental outcomes. That means that to encounter the challenges by developmental actions requires corroborative efforts both on the part of the citizens, corporate organizations and the government in forming stable institutions. These three-fold entities must correlate in their various capacities in pursuing definitive goals. Having said this, urgent attention is required in the following directions:

7.1.1   Change of Mind-Set

More often than not, the visions and aspirations of people do not usually match with the life events especially when one experiences the current changes in the global formation. Certain traditions or norms could push over and dominate other viewpoints people might have. It is on this basis that the change of mind-set comes into play as a rediscovery of those creative potentials within the environment and beyond, which can give people the assurance of the way forward against the pessimistic thoughts. This idea entails a radical shift from the existing traditional mode of thinking in order to become engaged in more interactive and reflexive life norms. The change of mind-set demands of course, a new way of think-ing and acting, which ultimately recognize the fact that the future of any society lies on its citizens. And therefore the much preoccupation of some activists in blaming the woes of the present on the past colonial heritage should rather be less emphasized by paying much attention on the good future options for development. But this mind-set change does not actual-ly imply to forget or ignore entirely the past, because the past could be a propelling axle for future opportunities. In that case, the conscious reali-zation of the relationship between the past and present could be a push for alternative ideas that might transform the social system. That could also recognize those lost values that would be beneficial for system growth and overall societal development. In fact, this transformation must begin from within in order to aid the arrival into without. That is to say: the belief that history could also be re-written by way of freedom from the past failures and the responsibility of the present actions that will gear towards creative future insights.

To arise to this challenge demands putting into action those developmental frameworks that can positively and directly affect the living conditions of the people. The motive could be drawn from the integral processes of the essential components of development as well as the realization of the fundamental needs of the growing population such as social services, basic education, employment opportunities, financial management etc. Nevertheless, the change of mind-set which gears towards a new way of acting means that by knowing the priorities and defining the basic interests of the population, the action could create the right awareness of the global environment where people interact freely with each other. In elaborating this fact, Stiglitz states that "the greatest challenge is not just in the institutions themselves but in mind-sets: Caring about the environment, making sure the poor have a say in decisions that affect them, promoting democracy and fair trade are necessary if the potential benefits of globalization are to be achieved. The problem is that the institutions have come to reflect the mind-sets of those to whom they are accountable."[1] In other words, Stiglitz's idea further connotes that the local priorities have been misdirected by the intentions of global institutions. Hence the change of mind-set assists in this direction in building confidence and interest in the global system, through heuristic reflections on the interactions among the local, national and transnational powers as well as the creation of the ability of self-critic to societal problems by way of re-branding and constructive changes. In elaborating this viewpoint, the work will further address the issue of national consciousness and the idea of aiding Priority through Collective initiatives.

7.1.1.1 The Imperative of Patriotism

In the recent time, there has been an increase of negligent attitudes towards national duty or consciousness to the pursuance of personal and ethnic interests. This negligence has been the bane of national cohesion in Nigeria. Thus the basic notation of patriotic imperative ought to be the understanding that the state belongs to all and the growth of the nation is the growth of the individual and vice versa. But it is unfortunate that many especially the elites, who are to be looked upon as examples, are

---

[1] Stiglitz, Joseph E. (2002): Globalization and its Discontents. London: Penguin Books, p. 216.

rather disappointing in this direction. No one takes responsibility for failures, even the people at the helm of affairs. The ruling class and the elites believe and also instill in the minds of their subjects that being in authority is an opportunity to enrich oneself from the common purse. Nevertheless, the rhetorical question is on how the attitude of selfish interest could encourage the younger generations towards patriotic commitment to nation-building in so far as those at the top have different perspective or mind-set on national consciousness. Hence the pursuance of national interest is a sine qua non, and demands sacrifices and efforts in order to champion the spirit of patriotism.

As an instance, there are numerous professionals and academics from Nigeria living in the Diaspora especially in the United States and Europe. Many of them were sent overseas in those early days of the country through the community assistance or awarded scholarship by the government in order to learn and return home to help in building the state. There are also others who are still studying abroad, some may decide to return thereafter but majority would always like to remain without the intention of going back to their Fatherland in order to make their input to nation-building. This attitude is unlike what is obtainable from most other nationals especially from the Asian countries, who would return to their respective countries after their studies so as to make their contributions towards developmental processes. But for many Nigerians abroad, they would abscond from returning, looking at immediate benefits or remuneration rather than to future developmental outcomes. Some may even argue that the Nigerian system is not working properly or that the security threats and risks are enormous, and conclude that the country is not habitable. But who could impact changes and make the system work out if not through the citizens' patriotic feelings and commitments. As one of the Igbo proverbs states: "onye oku na-agba ulo ya, anaghi achu nta oke", meaning that he whose house is on fire does not hunt for the rat. It is better to keep the house in order before pursuing for other material and fame benefits. Therefore, a lot of sacrifices are demanded on the part of the citizens in being solutions to own problems through patriotic commitments rather than constituting problems that could prevent developmental outcomes.

From another perspective, patriotism is said to entail the identification with one's country especially in defense of one's identity. But it is also unfortunate that many Nigerians in the Diaspora live with a lost identity or are dispassionate about their country. They find it difficult to proudly say that they are Nigerians or do anything that may suggest to people around them that they are Nigerians. For instance, many other nationals on the contrary have some remarkable signs (such as in their houses, places of work, cars etc.) either national colors in the form of stickers, flags or some dressing codes to depict their nationalities, which are rarely obtainable on the part of Nigerians.

In a similar conception, the lack of patriotic feelings also spells out in the field of sports. For instance, for the majority of Nigerians, in order to depict their 'globality' usually abandon the needed support to the local football leagues by assuming strong fans of the football teams in Europe that they have never encountered and would never encounter closely except through media. Those fans can name all the teams in Europe and their players but may not be able remember any of the indigenous clubs not to mention of knowing the names of the players. On this basis, patriotism becomes an imperative. Therefore, patriotic spirit suggests the making of an individual dream the Nigerian dream. This spirit will continue to promote more loyalty to national government than to the tribal and religious consciousness.

7.1.1.2 Aiding Priority through Collective/Collaborative initiatives

It is not only the conscientious efforts and commitments on the part of the citizens toward nation-building that constitute one of the major challenges to state development, but also the interest to common interface towards problem solving. The normal thinking that what happens to the 'other' is not the concern of the 'another' in so far as it does not affect the 'another' personally should totally be abolished. As a part of mind-set change, here comes also the urgent need for change of attitude and mentality in addressing societal issues through collective initiatives. Thus, when the individual interests surpass the needs of the society and vice versa, it tends to play down on the corporate unity and collaborative responsibility. What is required here is a balance of interests that could recognize the dignity, rights and responsibility of the various segments of the society, be it individuals, groups or organizations. By recognizing that all has a contribution to make in one way or the other towards positive change in the society or what Parsons regards as 'collectivity of roles' in society formation; that could certainly aid priority settings.

In properly articulating the collective roles, the government should encourage individual and group initiatives through provision of necessary infrastructures such as basic education, social security, political participation etc. that can allow and support freedom of capability and competence to thrive. On this note, Obodoechina emphasizes that "unless people are involved in the process of their own development, motivated to grasp new ideas and skills, to develop their own sense of worth and autonomy, and are allowed the opportunity to do things which they alone can do well, no human society can reasonably develop in the true sense of the word."[2] This emphasis is basically a collective action towards nation-building as well as a way of defining the roles of individuals and community towards common goal.

From another perspective, collaborative initiative also demands the appreciation of the cultural values, which recognize the interests of the community as primary over the individual interests. In that perspective, the 'primacy of the community' as Ntibagirirwa noted, means that "the community alone constitutes the context, the social and the cultural space in which the individual can realize oneself. In other words, the community is prior to the individual in so far as it is the medium through which the individual person works out and chooses one's goals and life plans, one's values and ends. A person is constituted by social relationships in which one necessarily finds oneself."[3] But the primacy of the community should not negate the reality of the individuals and their important placement in the community participations. On the other hand, as a maxim for African socio-cultural interaction, Gyekye opines that "in the context of the relationship between the individual and the community, the analogical meaning of the maxim is that one individual person does not constitute a com-

---

[2] Obodoechina, Uchechukwu (2006): The Imperative of Self-Reliance for the Churches in Africa: A Study in Christian Social Ethics. Frankfurt am Main: Peter Lang GmbH, p. 47.
[3] Ntibagirirwa, Symphorien (2001): p. 69. See also: Gyekye, Kwame (1998): 'Person and Community in African Traditional Thought.' In: Coetzee, P. H./Roux A. P. J. (eds.): The African Philosophy Reader. London/New York: Routledge, p. 320.

munity. Just as we would not speak of a forest where there is only one tree, so we would not – cannot – speak of a community where there is only one person. According to the maxim, a community emerges, that is, comes into existence, with the congregation of individual persons [...]."[4] This community relationship is in fact predominant over the individual interests and modern accumulation systems offered by global capitalism.

Sustaining the community relationship through collaborative initiatives has been a critical challenge to the Nigerian society due to unending social changes fostered by globalization. Henriot on that note observes that "the fundamental fault with globalization as experienced in Africa is that it is not rooted in community but structured from above according to abstract economic laws. To counter this situation in an ethically authentic and creative fashion calls for the promotion of local communities that work for integral human development and are effectively linked with similar groups across national boundaries."[5] In this linkage, the major challenge demands closing link between the government policy formulations and the community intentions; by ensuring grassroots mobilization, development of infrastructure in the local communities, supporting the individual performance with community harmonization, and strengthening the democratic ideology through proper coordination between the local communities and federal government agencies. And exactly here is where the religious bodies and voluntary organizations could play a greater role in partnership with the government as forces for political changes. Although, the Churches in Nigeria are making visible efforts in this direction especially during electioneering, yet such efforts should be extended to other areas of social development such as fight against corruption, promotion of civil rights, environmental protection and the campaign against deadly diseases. Without taking official political roles, the religious bodies can in that way strongly influence the politics; that is by speaking out against the ills in the society and the demand for political accountability.

---

[4] Gyekye, Kwame (1998): p. 321.
[5] Henriot, Peter S.J (2003): 'Globalization: Implications for Africa'. In: Drischoll, William/Clark, Julie (eds.): Globalization and the Poor: Exploitation of Equalizer? New York: International Debate Education Association, p. 56.

Finally, the absence of proper class crystallization in Nigeria is drawn out from the boundaries of regional, tribal and religious differences that prevent the balance of relationships between gender and among ethnic origins and classes. As such, various institutions of the state and political parties also toe this line of demarcation, making impossible 'collective responsibility' towards the system development. These differentials are also configured by the socio-political formation of the state and the mode of economic distribution. The problem becomes on how to widen the relationship among classes, ethnicity and between gender in order to capture the deep changes in the society as well as the contextual specificity of those changes towards problem solving. As a male-dominated society that is mixed up with ethnic and class differences, collaborative initiatives from individuals and corporate organizations should then gear towards the protection of rights and duties of individuals. Unfortunately, most of the constitutional provisions remain in principle with little of their practicability or enforcement, or lopsidedly enforced for particular sets or groups. That means that certain laws may be applied to some but for the others, they are above those laws. For instance, one cannot imagine that someone could be sentenced to life imprisonment for stealing five thousand naira and the one that steals billions of naira in office is allowed to move freely around the streets and sometimes garlanded with national honors. It is here that one can appreciate the efforts of the human right activists, NGOs and the religious organizations as the voice of the voiceless. Therefore, more collaborative efforts and change of mind-settings are still urgently needed in the fight against human rights and social development.

7.1.2   The Need for Subsidized Education System

For the operational systems of a state (be it: social, political or economic) to work effectively, there is the need for the government to provide high-quality education to meet up with the global standard. As the study indicated in chapter six, education is one of the major structural determinants; its lack diminishes opportunities, and its availability uplifts the social standard. Education opens people's mind-set both theoretically and practically in embracing new changes and challenges in the society, as well as a means of empowerment. Qualitative and affordable educational system remains one of the prerogatives of development. In fact, education is seen "as a powerful factor in levelling the field of opportunity, as it provides individuals with the capacity to obtain a higher income and standard of living and enables those living in contaminated environments to over-come major health threats. By learning to read and write and acquiring technical or professional skills, people increase their chances of obtaining decent, better-paying jobs. As these facts indicate the importance of equal access to a well-functioning education system, particularly in relation to reducing social inequalities and creating a healthy society, cannot be overemphasized."[6] In other words, education essentially cultivates the ground for the integral development of the human capital, not only through the formal institutions of learning, but also through non-formal processes.[7] The non-formal processes of learning such as through socio-cultural contacts and interactions could also guarantee general knowledge especially on the areas of basic human rights, capability productions, economic capacity and the awareness of the new phenomena of societal changes. These knowledge bases could be very important avenues of narrowing the differentials and inequalities that exist in the society.

As it has been previously observed in this study, the disparities in educa-tional attainment especially in the formal processes contribute significant-ly both to individual and regional differentials. Unfortunately, the cost of formal education in Nigeria with the regular increase in level of poverty has created more division between the 'haves' and 'have nots'. Even the introduction of the compulsory education to certain school level by the government has not helped in diminishing the high cost of learning. It is not only the cost that matters, but also the standard of learning, which must be taken into consideration. It is unfortunate that most of the public schools owned by the government are below normal standard and the alternative qualitative provisions by private, religious and non-governmental organizations are mostly unaffordable by the majority poor masses. There seems to be a failed recognition by the government, in the

---

[6] United Nations (2005): The Inequality Predicament: Report on the World Social Situa-tion 2005. Department of Economic and Social Affairs, New York: Academic Founda-tion, p. 21.
[7] Sen emphasizes that through education, learning, and skill formation, people can be-come much more productive over time, and this contributes greatly to the process of economic expansion (Sen, Amartya (2001): Development as Freedom. Oxford: Oxford University Press, pp. 292-293).

sense that improper investment in the educational sector would have a long term negative impact on the socioeconomic and political development. The consequence has been the glaring inequality in income and power distributions. Hence, expanding educational opportunities is a sine qua non for capacity building and commodity production through government subsidization and proper monitoring. This expansion can fundamentally aid developmental project, as well as a measure in reducing inequality among locations, classes, genders and geopolitical regions.

For the onward improvement and sustenance, the provision and supervision of education in Nigeria should not be left for the government alone. This is where the social and religious organizations as well as private enterprises can come into as partners in progress. Of course, the present commitment of religious institutions and NGOs in education attainment through the building of schools, aiding researches and awareness campaigns cannot be deniable. But it is evident that most crises in the educational system in Nigeria began after the complete take-over of the mission schools in the early 1970s by government. This fact is not difficult to prove in the sense that those schools and colleges that are currently being controlled by some social and religious groups and NGOs are among the best in Nigeria. That means that the government effort should be to help and encourage those organs in their endeavor through adequate subventions. This is because most of those schools owned by social organizations and private investors lack sufficient capitals especially in maintaining the welfare of their teachers and building new structures. Unfortunately, in order to meet with the demands of their standard provisions, those private owned schools and colleges usually charge exorbitant fees that only give the rich the maximum opportunities to the detriment of the poor population who cannot afford the tuition fees. Hence the consequential effect is that most of the private schools and colleges that are owned by the religious and NGOs have become the root of exploitation and income generation. And even some that were established through financial aids from the foreign and local donors are no exceptions; thereby undermining the intention of their establishment for the assistance and social welfare of the poor population.

Therefore, in most countries where there are much progressive changes, the government provides opportunities through subsides or loans, in financing education. In some others, the government partners with the religious groups, private investors and the NGOs in the management of the schools either in the form of funding or curriculum planning. The most important priority should now be the promotion of education through collaborative efforts. On the other hand, due to the difficulties that may be associated with granting free education at all levels, offering scholarships to the poor could be another possible alternative to educational financing and motivation. Hence the government in collaboration with the private sectors' urgent intervention in education system in Nigeria is a big challenge especially at this modern time formal education and integral knowledge is mostly demanded. This intervention will greatly aid development and the reduction of social inequality.

7.1.3 Safety-Net for the Poor

Reducing unemployment through job creation is an important aspect of safety-net. Unfortunately, the continuous increase of unemployment rate in Nigeria as already indicated in the findings constitutes not only a danger to social security but also contributes significantly to extreme inequality and social disorder. For instance, when the greater number of the population has no means of survival and no hope of finding one, the consequence is always the breach of the social order. That means that the vulnerably unemployed and the welfare-disconnected population can always go to any length in finding means to sustain their immediate needs and that of their household, which may then result to an increase in crime and violence. In this instance, job-creation should definitely assume the mainspring of the government prerogatives in policy formulation and developmental project. It could as well be achieved through a joint effort with the private sectors. Although job does not materialize automatically, yet what is actually needed is an enabling environment that can encourage investment and then widen the space for job creation.

However, with the decline in the formal sector employment rate since the introduction of structural adjustment policies in the early 80s, much economic activities in Nigeria exist both legally and illegally in the informal sector, and then mainly on the area of subsistence agriculture, artisanship and retail businesses. Fervently, the informal sector of the economy has undeniably made some enormous contribution to economic growth since independence, yet its much dependency on the structure of the formal sector without being strongly protected from market shocks still deters its development. From the findings, it shows that notwithstanding that much of the activities in the informal sector are not captured in the national economy; it contributes greatly in employment opportunities and labor forces both in the rural and urban areas. That is why that the government's conscientious effort in developing and expanding the informal-private sector businesses as well as subsistence agriculture especially through availability of credits, loans with lower interest rates and entrepreneurship awareness can generate growth, reduce the rate of poverty and at the same time check the rate of inequality in Nigeria. This expansion implies that the private sector on the one hand should be supported and harnessed for effective production towards targeted commodities, and for entrepreneurial development through proper regulation of private sector's activities. This effort can ensure capacity building for income generation, employment creation as well as assisting the government in its strategic planning for development. On the other hand, the public sector should assume the innovative instance, aiding priority setting as well as partnering and assisting in the private sector investment. Understanding this corroboration can to a great extent promote the public-private partnership in the management of risks and to an effective and qualitative economic growth.

In addition, United Nations Reports has reaffirmed that "to reduce inequality in a sustainable manner and promote the development of a more just and equitable society, it is important to focus on expanding and improving opportunities for employment, with emphasis on both the quality and quantity of jobs."[8] The idea 'employment strategy'[9] as one of the

---

[8] United Nations (2005): The Inequality Predicament, p. 134.
[9] "An employment strategy aimed at promoting decent work under conditions of equality, security and dignity should be a fundamental component of any development strategy, and must be oriented to include employment creation in macroeconomic policy. Such a strategy also requires undertaking employment impact analysis as a basic criterion for macroeconomic policy and for policy decisions adopted in other areas. Furthermore, it calls for adopting specific measures to incorporate the informal sector in social protection programmes and for establishing incentive structures that promote employment creation by directing investment to sectors that are productive and labour-intensive, with a special view to promoting small- and medium-sized enterprises" (United Nations (2005): The Inequality Predicament, pp. 134-135).

primary focuses of the New Partnership for Africa's Development (NEPAD) can encourage not only new avenues of employment sustenance, but can also build integrated mechanism for more economic and social participation. Although a number of intervention policies are currently in place, yet a careful consideration should be given to integrated strategies through partnership with social, religious and private organizations as ways of ensuring positive social transformation. In that way, the advantages of responding to social security become visible to human development. These responses can fundamentally expand the choices that people have as well as a way of diluting the negative effects of globalization.

Addressing the issue of social-net from another perspective, it is good to note that the changing pattern of institutional structure of the global economy has become a threat to traditional essence and cultural values.[10] The basic notation of the modern institutional structure is the continuous accumulation processes that tend to negate the communal consciousness or collective concern, which usually recognizes the inclusive as well as exclusive natures of African identity. These patterns of identity function as a social safety-net especially for the poor. For instance, the traditional welfare system such as remittance seems to have depreciated over the years by the modern identity structures, and then endangers the individual link to the traditional social network of sustainability. The effect of that could be seen by the increase in the number of beggars along the main streets of the major cities in Nigeria. The elderly, widows and orphans are mostly affected by this development due to the fact that they normally depend on their extended relatives for social security in the absence of government provisions. As a communal response, attention should focus on: i) building a collective strategy for social protection sensitive to age and gender through social network and solidarity; ii) bringing out new guidelines on social services as well as a new social policy that can focus on issues of security of life and property.

As has been already indicated, the traditional social network system that is embodied with solidarity and communitarian consciousness plays a major role in the social structure as against individualism of the modern

---

[10] See: Stiglitz, Joseph E. (2002): p. 247.

network structure. It is a form of community solidarity that identifies both with the poor and the disadvantaged in forming a common scheme for development. The common solidarity is viewed here as distinct from communist's conception of 'collective will' that is rather against the freedom of the individual. The idea of community solidarity however aims at protecting both the interests of individuals and the community. It is more of a social bond, which Durkheim may rather refer to as an 'organic solidarity' towards shared views and common interest that is bound towards social stability. Thus the major challenge at hand becomes how to promote the community values and integrate them into the modern society structure. In fact, the communitarian structure, in as much as it gears towards common goods, it also account for individual endowment and empowerment in the social structure. It implies that through proper realization of individual potentials and rights in the community, communal consciousness could assist in promoting the sustenance of the society goods and interpersonal relationships. Therefore, for the Nigerians to participate fully in the global arena, they need to reenact their commitment to traditional solidarity towards global goals. This reenactment can then promote integral development, as well as re-appreciating individual contributions towards positive transformation of the society.

7.1.4   Matching Economic Growth with Sustainable Development

Bringing us back to the analysis in part two of this study, we can still ask: Why have the so-called statistical economic growths in Nigeria not had much significant impact on the sustainable development of the country? Or why have there not been efficient developmental outcomes from the economic policy advocacies so far? As already indicated in the work, the answers to these questions are not far-fetched from the following: i) based on the structure of the capitalist economy (that gives the political elites and the few business moguls ever the chances of surplus accumulation to the disadvantage of the poor population), ii) the lack of political will in the pursuance of developmental agenda and, iii) poor policy implementations.

It is arguable to say that the much revenues accruing from the huge deposits of natural resources in Nigeria have not been properly translated into sustainable development. On the other hand, it has become a big challenge to the nation in continuing and improving on the economic discoveries made during the colonial periods. It is here that one could appreciate positively the efforts of the colonial administrators towards economic expansion, though not without their country's economic interests in sapping the natural resources. But that notwithstanding, they significantly helped to open the four walls of the country to economic resources and infrastructural developments. But it is also unfortunate to observe that most of the physical infrastructures such as bridges, railways, housing, postal services etc., which were designed and built during the colonial period, have remained either under-maintained or now in dilapidated states. This negligence takes us to the issue of non-continuity of development plan by the subsequent regimes. Often whenever there is a new government, it comes with its own new agenda and policies. And many undergoing projects of the previous governments are usually abandoned thereby causing waste of resources.

Hence concerted actions especially on imbibing the culture of maintenance and policy continuity, as well as in supporting economic stability with functional regulatory bodies (especially against tax evasion, resource thefts) should assume the standard prerogative of any incoming government. What should really count in economic developments are not basically the statistical quotations of growth but the visible manifestations in form of job creation, rural development, infrastructure availabilities such as provision of health services, access roads, pipe-borne water etc. Again the governing bodies should be able to realize and learn from the past mistakes and make amends towards future commitments. Moreover, the citizens' roles are also required especially in their working inputs. Self-reliance through subsistent economic development should be encouraged with the aim of commodity price reduction (especially feeding cost) and labor cost.

On the international scene, the global institutions such as IMF and World Bank have the responsibility to guard the developing economies from the failures or crisis of the developed economies. It has been evident that the poorer countries suffer mostly the sins of financial mismanagement of the Western countries. As it was indicated in chapter five of the work, the global financial crisis have always much negative implications on the economic growth of the developing countries. On the other hand, the hopes and aspirations of most of the developing and poorer countries have not been materialized by the deregulation policies of the global institutions. But how this could be addressed depends on the restructuring of the global institutions. In a way, one could suggest that giving more seats and voices to the developing countries in those global institutions and not just the monopoly of the European and United States based on economic powers or capital contributions to the institutions could be a step in the right direction. This step could fundamentally address the global inequality especially the issues pertaining to global warming, as well as environmental degradation being caused by Multinational Corporations. Therefore, economic growths and their sustainability provide the arena for local, national and global integrative actions towards innovative changes.

7.1.5   Enhancement of Social Cohesion

With diverse social and cultural backgrounds in Nigeria, one often tends to question the common ideological component that unites the state as a nation. This trend usually causes exclusion of one group or the other from the main scheme of things in the state. And of course in the struggle to maintain hold of influence over the national economy or politics brings along with it the issue of clash of interests and violence. This situation threatens the unity of the state often related to the social cleavages in the form of class conflicts, ethnic/regional crisis, religious rivalry, political instability, among others. For instance, the corporate existence of the country seems to be frequently at risk, and stands most often on the verge of collapse from the endless sectarian/ethno-religious violent crisis rocking the parts of the country especially in the North. The crisis situation continues to pose a great challenge to social cohesion.

Furthermore, the lack of social cohesion has both developmental and inequality implications in both local and global relationships. In fact, Stiglitz argues that "social cohesion is important if an economy is to function."[11] Hence instability and violence are usually hostile to local and foreign investments, and discourages economic growth. However, the current wave of globalization seems to have further narrowed down the space for proper social cohesion in terms of emerging individualism as

---

[11] Stiglitz, Joseph E. (2002): p. 219.

against collectivism of the traditional relationship. In that case, through the modern market legislations and their limitations towards general participation, as well as the diminution of the state sovereignty, globalization has on its own part helped to worsen the socio-economic redistribution impasse, thereby increasing the inequality differentials within and among groups and individuals. The gains of globalization can only be successfully harnessed if its integrative processes and interactive systems continue to promote inclusion rather than exclusion.

Finally, a renewed commitment to national unity and social cohesion by the citizens and the government should be a priority in Nigeria. This could be achieved through avoidance of public statements and actions that could indicate a remainder of superiority or an instigation of one group against the other. In this renewed effort, the Nigerian Youth Service Corp (NYSC) that was introduced by former Head of State General Yakubu Gowon, which was designed to create national cohesion after the Nigeria-Biafra civil war, should also be strictly further encouraged and supported. Therefore, this continuous effort can strengthen regional and cultural interactions, as well as the enhancement of social cohesion towards a situation whereby the North and South, Muslims and Christians can live and associate together as part of the whole.

7.2   The Axes of Future Plan

The rising increase of social inequality in Nigeria has been attributed to the various socio-cultural changes in the society, and as a consequence of globalization influences. In this section, our evaluation of inequality and globalization will dwell on the possible strategies or options towards future development of the Nigerian state. The strategies can promote optimism in the sense that notwithstanding the failures of the past and the crises of the present, there are still many possibilities for the future generations. Although the relationship between the past, the present and the future has always been a complex one both on the socio-political and intellectual scenes, yet some of the scholars are convinced that the legacies of the past can be surmounted by the effective future options towards socio-political development. They often use the examples of the newly industrialized countries to illustrate their ideas. As a gradual process, a holistic and efficient handling of the future options can absolutely aid the already addressed approaches towards maximum fruition. With this in mind, we shall then focus our evaluation on the general commitment towards good governance and on balancing the asymmetries created by globalization.

7.2.1   The Necessity of Good Governance

Good governance is all-embracing and all-encompassing. It covers the whole lots of distributional patterns of the society; that is, the formation of various structures and sectors of the government – ranging from political, social, economic, to administrative composites. It gives weight to proper harmonization of those factors necessary for administrative principles. In such instance, the fundamental requirements for good governance are enumerated as follows: "i) an efficient public service; ii) an independent judicial system and legal framework to enforce contracts; iii) the accountable administration of public funds; iv) an independent public auditor, responsible to a representative legislature; v) respect for the law and human rights at all levels of government; vi) a 'pluralistic institutional structure', and a free press."[12] In fact, these fundamental requirements assist in promoting and expanding the inter-relational activities among the various decision-making institutions, and they help to triumph equitable participation, democratic accountability and transparency in the political system. In that perspective, good governance brings out the legitimacy and effective role of state both in political, social and economic processes, and the lack of any of those fundamental requirements results to bad governance and political instability.

However, ensuring good governance in Nigeria is a monumental challenge but certainly not an impossible task. The prerequisite for good governance in Nigeria should begin with proper understanding of the needs

---

[12] Leftwich, Adrian (1993): p. 610. See: The World Bank (1989): Sub-Saharan Africa: From Crisis to Sustainable Growth. Washington DC, pp. 6, 15, 60-61 and 192. Pluralistic institutional structure implies in this setting as: "a state enjoying both legitimacy and authority, derived from a democratic mandate and built on the traditional liberal notion of a clear separation of legislative, executive and judicial powers. And, whether presidential or parliamentary, federal or unitary, it would normally involve a pluralist polity with some kind of freely elected representative legislature, subject to regular elections, with the capacity at the very least to influence and check executive power and protect human rights" (Leftwich, Adrian (1993): p. 611).

of the people and how that could be translated and achieved through policy legislation. That however demands good leadership qualities on the
part of the political leaders,[13] and an institutional framework that is built
on democratic ideals. Suffice it to say according to Natufe that "democratic practices and good governance flourish in an environment where
political elites possess the required leadership skills anchored on the tenets of democracy. It is essential that they represent a broader constituency
beyond their immediate surroundings in articulating their respective policies, which derive from a sound knowledge of the rudiments of interest
aggregation."[14] In other words, good governance should go beyond the
immediate interests of the political elites through proper legislations and
transparency. For instance, the judicial and the legislative arms of the
government should be strengthened in order to check the excesses of the
executive. That implies that the weak structures of the state that hinder
checks and balances; that give the executives the opportunity in embez-
zling the public funds should be adequately addressed through judicial
and legislative actions as well as by independent monitoring. Although
the establishment of Economic and Financial Crimes Commission
(EFCC) by the Obasanjo administration in 2003 as a law enforcement
agency to check corruption and other related crimes in Nigeria has created some positive impact, yet the legitimacy of the commission is always in question whenever its operations are influenced by the ruling
government or targeted to political opponents. Hence the commission
should be allowed to operate freely as an independent agency without
government interference in order to ensure maximum results.

---

[13] With deep despair following the 1983 election in Nigeria and the lack of imaginative
and selfless leadership, Chinua Achebe wrote in one of his books 'The Trouble with
Nigeria' thus: "The trouble with Nigeria is simply and squarely a failure of leadership.
There is nothing basically wrong with the Nigerian character. There is nothing wrong with
the Nigerian land or climate or water or air or anything else. The Nigerian problem is the
unwillingness or inability of its leaders to rise to the responsibility, to the challenges of
personal example which are the hallmarks of true leadership." (Achebe, Chinua (1984):
The Trouble with Nigeria. London: Heinemann African Writers Series, p. 1). This conception of leadership problem in Nigeria by Achebe illustrates for the challenge of good
governance, which is the bedrock of underdevelopment not only in Nigeria but also in the
Sub-Saharan Africa. Although the problem of bad leadership only constitute part of governance setback, yet the inaptitude behaviors of the political leaders can cause serious
upheaval to the stability of the state and become a direct route to crisis development.
[14] Natufe, Igho (2006): p. 7.

Nevertheless, for a democratic development that will ensure good governance, there is also the absolute need for political reforms, which will overhaul constitutional, legislative and operational mechanisms at all levels of government. Here Jega suggests that leadership and good governance in Nigeria "must meet the challenge of simultaneously pursuing political and economic reforms. Without effective political reforms, which would ensure free and fair elections, entrench the Rule of Law, protect basic freedoms and rights, guarantee equitable distribution of state resources and access to state funded services, and decisively penalize corruption and executive lawlessness, economic reforms would not succeed. Nigeria needs a leadership that recognizes that it is in the enlightened self-interest of elite to strengthen institutions of governance, reduce the over-heating of the political atmosphere, put in place effective and reliable machinery for the conduct of credible elections and curtail the excesses of some reckless, 'do-or-die' politicians."[15] It follows that the reform agenda lies not only on the three arms of the government but also on the citizens' commitment to its implementation through strict adherence to the rule of law and then exercising their civic responsibilities. In this perspective, the citizens should also understand their civic rights and their political duties in voting into powers only those leaders who are ready and capable of protecting their rights and aspiration towards good governance without selling their votes, and then thereafter their own rights. This action could therefore enable the political leaders to be visionary and more efficient in the performance of their social and political functions. Thus in realizing the immediate needs of the masses and the demand for social justice, the political leaders should then ensure equitable distribution of power and resources through redistribution. Redistribution can always proffer effective participation in the socio-economic and political systems. For a more detailed examination of this theme, two essential factors that can inspire good governance in Nigeria will further be addressed as follows.

---

[15] Jega, Attahiru M. (2009): 'Nigerian Economy and the Global Economic Crisis'. In: Daily Trust Newspaper Online, 2 & 3. Feb, 2009.

7.2.1.1 Entrenching Political and Economic Decentralization

Decentralization is an important prerequisite for good governance. The issue of political and economic centralization has been one of the bottle-necks to good governance in Nigeria. It means that the political space does not properly allow equitable distribution of power and resources, which continue to remain in the hands of few political elites and big-business men. In that perspective, it has been aptly noted that "the over-centralization favours parasitic groups and individuals who manipulate all governments and thus prevent the prosecution of a programme of mod-ernization and development. The exploitation and plunder of resources of parts of the country are consequences of this inequitable arrangement."[16] In fact, it has been effectively observed that over-centralization has per-sisted, perhaps, because of the pluralistic nature of the Nigerian society on the one hand, and on the other hand, because of the emergence of crude oil as the main source of accumulation. This development has pro-moted the neo-patrimonial system in the socio-political and economic spheres of the country. Without making over-generalization, it appears that the paradigm 'political instrumentalization of disorder' is the bul-wark of Nigerian political atmosphere in this perspective. For instance, the patterns of political and economic competitions especially among and within the ethnic regions have made governance a matter of regional and class interests. In that sense, any political party in power would always ensure that its interests are protected as well as that of its regional con-cern; and would neither have intention of giving up power nor their re-spective leaders withdrawing their hands from the country's resources. The situation of this sort has continued to amount to a constitutional crisis that usually heats up the polity and hurts the poor population.

Thus the language of power struggle and political competition has been that of dominance combined with the 'complex procedural accumulation' of the state resources. It is no doubt that the long period of the military regime in Nigeria has contributed to over-centralization of political and

---

[16] The Nigerian Guardian Newspaper: 6. December, 1999. Cited in: Mustapha, Raufu A. (2004): 'Ethnicity and the Politics of Democratization in Nigeria'. In: Berman, Bruce/Eyoh, Dickson/Kymlicka, Will (eds.): Ethnicity and Democracy in Africa. Oxford: James Currey, p. 267.

economic powers. This of course has encouraged corruption, intense competition for economic access and the widespread pursuant of power personalization.[17] In this effect, the political powers have continued to remain in the hands of few political elites and their clients, unable to relinquish authority and positions to other members of the society. Against this backdrop, General Murtala Mohammed in his opening address to the Constitution Drafting Committee on 18th October, 1975 noted that we should seek to "eliminate over-centralization of power in a few hands, and a matter of principle, decentralize power wherever possible, as a means of diffusing tension. The powers and duties of the leading functionaries of government should be carefully defined."[18] But this is easier said than done. The socio-political environment has entrenched the attitude of the pursuit of personal interests to the detriment of the common good. Each government in Nigeria has in one way or the other proposed various mechanisms and avenues towards decentralization but with little or no positive results. The failure has been as a result of lack of political will, sacrifices and commitments on the part of the political elites to pursue vividly the developmental agendas.

Moreover, the issue of decentralization of the government agencies and structures has continued to be a political rhetoric without a matching policy and administrative capacity to its fulfillment. Unfortunately, the administrative lapses and poor regulations have continued to affect the decentralization efforts and government's policies towards service delivery, accountability and improved government performance. As such, the institutional arrangement of the state is burdened with instability and corruption especially in the public sectors, making the coordinating mechanisms of the state structures even more difficult to function. Thus the efforts

---

[17] Forrest observes that "a consequence of the centrality of state power and resources has been intense political competition for access to the state and over the distribution of state resources. Individuals in positions of power within the public sector are subject to great pressures over the distribution of state patronage. Access to the state is secured through clientilist patterns of politics with support often mobilised on an ethnic basis. Personal ties are essential to the development of horizontal networks, and to vertical ones, which link village and region to the centre through a hierarchy of communities" (Forrest, Tom (1986): p. 5).

[18] Traub, Rudolf (1986): Nigeria Weltmarktintegration und sozial-strukturelle Entwicklung. Hamburg: Institut für Afrika-Kunde, p. 450.

towards decentralization in the past were also highly abridged with the long-term period of the military rule. Even in the civilian regimes, the relationship between the central and local governments has been that of 'the lord and the master', which has not given much space for autonomy at the local levels. Thus the recognition of effective institution with proper administrative balance through fiscal federalism can give way for decentralization and developmental chances.

In order to entrench decentralization process, the concerted effort in reforming the state structures that have long given the political elites advantages over the control of state apparatuses is very necessary. There is also the need to initiate focused policy programmes for the management of the ethnic pluralism and rural development. In this reform strategy, the World Bank report suggests as follows: "amending the constitution to redefine the role of the state, introduce new governance arrangements, change the machinery of the government or alter the balance of power among the executives and the parliament."[19] But in order to achieve the aforementioned ideals from the World Bank, a strong institution built on 'democratic principles'[20] and devoid of corruption is required. This will promote national unity amidst ethnic differences, shared ideology amidst individual differences and equal distribution amidst class differences. These aspects of decentralization can yield a desired result only if a proper institutionalization of the political system is put in place. On the other hand, sustainable measures should be taken in order to foster the democratization process that would establish a clear separation between political powers and administrative powers. By that it implies that the administrative standard should not be politicized in order to achieve per-

---

[19] World Bank (2000): Reforming Public Institutions and Strengthening Governance, p. 77.

[20] Ibeanu notes that "democratization is a phased process of decentralizing state power and promoting appropriate values and attitudes that enable justice and equity to be institutionalized in political relations. There are various aspects of the decentralization of state power. One involves the transfer of certain powers from the authoritarian state to an emerging civil society. Another involves the decentralization of power within civil society. And yet another involves the decentralization of power within the state system itself" (Ibeanu, Okechukwu (2000): pp. 52-53. See also: Nnoli, Okwudiba (1995): 'Ethnic Conflicts and Democratization in Africa'. Paper presented at the 8th General Assembly of CODESRIA, Dakar).

sonal ends, but should follow the bureaucratic norms. Though this separation may appear totally unfeasible at the moment, it requires time and effort both on the part of the citizens and the leaders in understanding the democratic processes.

Furthermore, in separating administrative power from political power through proper institutionalization of state apparatuses, democratic process should be based on the recognition of the individual capabilities and the appropriate redistribution of powers. The exercise of this nature can facilitate mutuality of purpose and inclusiveness especially in treating all citizens as equal before the law, equally free and equally important. It also calls for equal participation of all community or society members in the public affairs, as well as ensuring and granting financial autonomies to the three levels or arms of the government. And as a means of socio-economic and political development, it enables the citizens to understand the real import of democratization. In that case, it is the duty of the government and its agencies to define clearly the economic and power distribution in a democratic setting in order to ensure equal participation, and proper planning and implementation of developmental policies.

In his analysis, Aka sees decentralization of power and the economy in two different perspectives. On the one hand, he suggests that "as a means of socio-cultural development, it provides an important component of the social infrastructure and local organizational capacity which nurtures the creation, demand, and supply of local services and amenities. Finally, as a means of politico-administrative development, it fosters the creation of a local bureaucratic constituency which improves the participation rate and the initiative necessary for integrated regional development."[21] Although, Aka's position may to some extent sound hypothetical in the context of Nigerian situation, yet it is the sure route in laying adequate foundation for unbridled realization and consolidation of developmental strategies and redistribution mechanisms.

On the other hand, the Nigerian economy is not yet well diversified, relying on oil as one main commodity both for foreign exchange, and for the recurring and capital projects, as well as the major integrating force to-

---

[21] Aka, Ebenezer (1995): p. 76.

wards global capitalism. This formation has affected the development of the other sectors of the economy. Thus the privatization of some of the government agencies that started at the onset of civilian regime in 1999 came as a way of tackling decentralization of the economy towards efficiency and competition. Privatization made some positive impacts in some subsectors of the economy such as communication industry, transportation, solid minerals and banking industry. However, it also gave rise to some difficulties (especially in the communication industries) in ensuring the availability of their services in the low-income areas as well as their high operation charges. Moreover, due to inherent system of corruption, some of the privatization exercises were carried out without detailed guidelines. And on the other hand, it became another means through which the political leaders and business elites enriched themselves. And this is one of the basic reasons why the effective regulation of the privatization exercises has become a major challenge to economic growth.

Lastly, the government intervention failures in harnessing other sectors of the economy especially the agricultural and manufacturing sectors have indeed placed the rural communities and the growing poor population in disadvantaged positions. Likewise, the pattern of infrastructural distributions has been also city-centered, with much concentration on the urban areas and neglect of the rural sectors. Consequently, the increasing rate of social inequality between the rural household and the urban settlers could be justified by the rising rate of economic accumulation especially by the political elites in the urban regions without its corresponding redistribution to reach the rural areas, as well as the concentration of most industries in the urban regions. Here Hayami and Godo suggest that "the most effective way to prevent inequality in income distribution from increasing under strong population pressure is to expand demand for labour at a speed faster than growth in population and the labour force. In this regard, modernization of agriculture and the development of labour-intensive, small- and medium-scale manufacturers, especially in rural areas, are critically important."[22] That means that the expansion of labor force through agricultural development can fundamentally create more economic opportunities, improve the local and rural participations in the

---

[22] Hayami, Yujiro/Godo, Yoshihisa (2005): Development Economics: From the Poverty to the Wealth of Nations, Third Edition. New York: Oxford University Press, p. 223.

economic development and then limit the influx of rural population from rural to urban areas in search of better living conditions. Therefore, it is the task of the political elites to champion the course for economic and political decentralization and that of the citizens to respond to the challenges. These efforts as a matter of fact can create more avenues for investments, productions and poverty reduction.

7.2.1.2 Increased Local Participation in National Matters

As a means of redistribution of economic and political powers of government from the centre, integral strategies for expanded participation should be a fundamental principle in policy decisions and should as well be objectively formulated towards practicability. In such a way, the basic issues that border on local development would be directly addressed to the benefit of all, especially the disadvantaged and the poor masses. This strategy has two-fold intentions: firstly, the empowerment of the poor population and secondly, the development of the local communities. And these intentions are some of the basic tenets of good governance and democratic principles. As such, the government policies should gear not only towards the creation of better opportunities for the citizens, but also for socio-political and economic participations of the local communities. The implementation of the policies can be achieved not without institutional restructuring of the state that can guarantee equality of purpose but can also gears towards social development. In that case, meeting up with the national reform agendas and their consolidation in the society development are always a great challenge to policy makers. The reforms require among other things the availability of fundamental and necessary platforms such as good governance, bureaucratic norms, strong public institutions, political stability etc. But the weakness of these platforms in Nigeria has been the constraint in achieving the desired developmental reforms. This weakness could be attributed to some hindrances like the personalization of state by the political elites, outrageous corruption, ethnic consciousness and religious bigotry, class conflicts etc. that affect the bureaucratic norms. But also some external pressures such as global capitalism and political liberalization that tend to constitute a delimiting factor to the power of the state sovereignty.

Promoting greater participation of the local communities in the national issues demands strong political will, accountability and stability in politics. In that sense, the leadership potentialities and the involvement of the masses become quite significant. As a gradual process towards participatory democracy, the involvement of masses in the policy decisions could aid growth by way of evaluation of the past policies and their failures towards achieving future outcomes. In line with this principle, it may serve as a preventive, integrative and inter-personal mechanism against the backdrop of leadership lapses. But it can also demand both behavioral and organizational changes. And the changes can as well demand a situation whereby the citizens can develop their potentials and capabilities in leading productive and resourceful achievements in accordance with their needs and interests.

Finally, greater participation of the local community require also a set-programme on the part of central government in committing enough resources on the third-tier of the government, which can gear towards supporting local community development. That action could assist in fostering the union and integration of individuals into the community life as well as limiting the influx of rural-urban migration. In that way, it takes cognizance of the changing nature of the society towards an open-sphere and level-ground for all parties in the socio-political system. Therefore, greater participation of the local communities can be a bridge builder that could break the jinx of inequality differences and then also guarantee non-formidable developments.

7.2.1.3 Renewed Civil Society Engagement

In relation to decentralization of economic and political powers as a means of good governance is also the idea of renewed effort towards civil society engagement. In order to restructure the state and create new platforms for inclusion of the marginalized and disadvantaged, as well as equal participation in the societal affairs, the civil society development remains a critical factor and actor, according to various contemporary scholars. Thus, the development of the civil society in Nigeria should base on the anticipated role it plays in the stability of socio-political and economic processes. Although one cannot wholly deny the existence and roles of civil society in Nigeria, yet the contending question remains: how far does civil society come to terms with the ideological synthesis that defines its relevance towards effective implementation of development strategies, and in building a social-compact based on corroborative partnership with a broader consensus? Answering this question forms the beginning of proper crystallization of civil society in Nigeria.

Civil society as a form of social force in regulating the state operations plays an important role in the society by positioning of new ideas and innovations. It cannot be an alternative to the state authority but can be a response to its motives through interactions, especially in mobilizing for open and participatory governance.[23] In that sense, civil society according to Nwosu "does not compete with the state. Rather, it opposes excesses of the state – a veritable platform for demanding accountability. This, of course, means that a state's undemocratic tendencies can be questioned by a civil society whose constituents are also subjects of the state. It follows that civil society can confer a mandate on managers of the state and guard that mandate."[24] In this mandate, Kabeer further notes that "the membership and goal are usually 'chosen', and members determine how resources and responsibilities will be distributed on the basis of some agreed set of principles."[25] It follows that the efforts in renewing the civil society spirit in Nigeria becomes a necessity for the radical transformation of the state structures and protection of the citizens from the oppressive and authoritarian powers of the state. Thus this renewed civil society resonance, of course points to the ability to recognize the contradictions of the state structures, as well as to create enabling spaces that can foster the independent nature of the civil society. In other words, the renewed civil society resonance may sometimes appear as a response to changes required in reworking the existing structures in the state institutions and a force towards democratic development.

In encountering the domineering nature of the state, Nwosu further emphasizes that "the contradiction is that the state suppresses civil society and prevents the consolidation of democracy in Nigeria. Elections remain a farce, while protecting the electoral mandate is regarded with levity

---

[23] The character of interaction between the state and civil society defines the nature of the society. A state that overwhelms civil society is likely to be absolutist and repressive, whereas a civil society that overwhelms the state may tend toward creating anarchy. Striking a balance between the two categories becomes necessary (Nwosu, B. U. (2006): p. 20).

[24] Nwosu, B. U. (2006): p. 22.

[25] Kabeer, Naila (2003): p. 48.

[…]. Civil society's limited and weak engagement with the state in Nigeria could gradually be overcome by strengthening 'institutional civil society' into a social force. The intelligentsia can commence proactive actions on matters of governance, including elections. This can open the space for other professional, community-based, and religious associations to turn proactive in protecting the electoral mandate, demanding accountability in governance, and, ultimately, transforming the nation into a true democratic society."[26] Though Nwosu's conception of 'institutional civil society' may in some point suggest that civil society is to be built or governed by the bureaucratic norms. On the contrary, it is a regulative formation that is in response to the organized body structure, which seeks for the pursuit of common good. In that way, the civil society engagement can always promote the rule of law, encourage more participation and distribution of resources.

Through demonstrations and strikes, some civil groups in Nigeria have sometimes succeeded in pressurizing the government and challenging some of its decisions towards future developmental plans. The groups may comprise of religious groups, professional associations, women empowerment groups, NGOs etc. But there may also arise some difficulties in recognizing which group among them could actually be termed as a civil society organization. This is because; some of those groups are based on ethnic and religious affiliations and could endanger the state formation, rather than creating harmony. Although the role of the religious groups has been embraced by many, yet there may be also the fear that it can exacerbate political tension considering the regional dichotomy and ethnic bias of the religious composition in Nigeria. On that basis, the restriction in the formation of NGOs and other groups is not uncommon due to the fact that political oppositions may use them to generate crisis and instability in the government. That notwithstanding, the existence of civil society is a sine qua non and should be a catalyst and strong element in administrative efficiency, accountability in the politics and democratic processes. It is here that the government is challenged towards recognizing the integrated role of the state and its regulatory functions in promoting civil society organizations as a partnership in governance and an in-

---

[26] Nwosu, B. U. (2006): pp. 25-26.

dependent entity of the state. This role function, of course should be protected by the constitution and guarded by the court of law for an efficient and dynamic coexistence.

Therefore, the state should be able to accommodate and give a free hand in the functioning of the civil society groups based on democratic ideals. And that should especially be achieved independent of the political party influences for the interest of public good. The action should be projected through a renewed civic responsibility and common interest in engaging the state in its roles and obligations, especially in terms of promotion of good governance. With the spread of economic and political liberalization, civil society should at this point attempt to promote the interaction of the state with the wider world, accompanied by the expansion of institutional changes that can sustain the autonomy of the state. In a collaborative resonance towards political transformation, state-civil society relations should therefore be constructed in order to legitimize the governing processes and then assist in policy implementations.

7.2.2   Balancing the Asymmetries of Globalization

In this present discussion, I will try to examine the challenges posed by global integration as well as the relationship between the foreign market trends and the local economy. The rising scope of inequality differences and the changing structure of the social formation are said to be promoted and sustained by the asymmetric nature of globalization. This, of course involves the rapid changes: i) in the market forces and fiscal mechanisms through capitalism; ii) in the international legislations supported by political liberalization. These changes seem to have weakened the state autonomy and still continue to widen the gap between nations and states. It follows that the changes are more intense in the developing countries because of their constitutive weak institutional frameworks unable to counter the growing forces and impositions by the international agencies such as IMF and World Bank. In other words, the unfair economic policies of the industrialized countries through transnational corporations, which influence the pattern of investment and thereby prevent effective competitions, have continued to increase the inequality and imbalance in the global relationships.[27] In fact, the United Nations' Report on Inequality Predicament notes that, "the imbalance between the pace of globalization and the prevailing regulatory framework has produced many asymmetries requiring correction. At the political and institutional levels, emphasis should be placed on the equitable distribution of the benefits in an increasingly open world economy, with actions that promote democratic participation by all countries and peoples in the decision-making processes that govern international relations."[28] It follows that the benefits of globalization on the other note could be harnessed through fair treatment of the global participants especially in the context of growing imbalances in global formation. In fact, equal access to market opportunities and new technological developments, as well as advancement of global economic and political participations, ought to be the operative norm and prerogative of globalization processes and systems. On the contrary, globalization has rather helped to deepen the divide in the world system, creating remote opportunities and stunted economic growth for most of the developing countries.

With the trade barrier policies supported by the IMF and its associates, the export commodities of the developing countries – mainly raw materials – are stringently monitored. This, on the other hand is rarely applicable to the reverse imports of the finished products from industrialized countries. The global inequality is much more evident when the industrialized world determines the modes and prices of the raw materials from the developing countries only to have those materials as finished com-

---

[27] Summarizing the hypocrisy of the advanced industrial countries in the globalization exercise that gave rise to protest in Seattle, Stiglitz observes that "while these countries had preached – and forced – the opening of the markets in the developing countries to their industrial products, they had continued to keep their markets closed to the products of the developing countries, such as textiles and agriculture. While they preached that developing countries should not subsidize their industries, they continue to provide billions in subsidies to their own farmers, making it impossible for the developing countries to compete. While they preached the virtues of competitive markets, the United States was quick to push for global cartels in steel and aluminum when its domestic industries seemed threatened by imports. The United States pushed for liberalization of financial services, but resisted liberalization of the service sectors in which the developing countries have strength, construction and maritime services" (Stiglitz, Joseph E. (2002): pp. 244-245).

[28] United Nations (2005): The Inequality Predicament, p. 132.

modities returned back at exorbitant prices. These market asymmetries promote majorly the interests of the developed countries. On the other hand, the increase of the lending rate by the World Bank and IMF for developmental loans to developing countries also makes it difficult for the developing countries to repay their debts. In 2006, the Nigerian government managed to repay some of its bilateral external debts owed to the Paris Club of the lending nations, which was accrued for many years. Notwithstanding, the external debts of the country has started again to rise as a result of much deflection in the foreign reserves caused by budget deficits.

Hence, there is the absolute need for the central government in Nigeria to be conscious of the fact that globalization has come to stay. This awareness becomes necessary in fashioning the best ways to embrace globalization changes and its operational order. Even though as Yotopoulos rightly pointed out that "the operational formulation of the institutional setting of globalization rests on the universal adoption of a common set of 'rules of the game' for economic interactions."[29] Yet the market forces and the global interests do not allow for the universal adoption in order to promote equity in the economic interaction. The compelling prerogative of this universal adoption should rather be the urgent need in providing an enabling environment for political competition, state autonomy and local economic development that can replace the dictatorship of capital market conditionalities. In that case, the prevailing reform agendas of the global institutions and local economies should be able to pursue an equitable global relationship that goes beyond the mere trade interests, which only favour some and disfavour many. This agenda tends towards securing the advantages of globalization that can reflect a greater participation of the developing countries.

Finally, with the challenges imposed by the capitalist global systems, the key problem also rests on the accumulation attitudes of the political elites and the rich business moguls in Nigeria that benefit mostly from the capitalist system. In this perspective, if a country does not change its domi-

---

[29] Yotopoulos, Pan (2007): 'Asymmetric Globalization: Impact on the Third World'. In: Yotopoulos, Pan/Romano, Donato (eds.): The Asymmetries of Globalization. New York: Routledge, p. 7.

nant economic strategies towards more flexible formation, the overall development of the state may not be stimulated and the poor majority will continue to be subjugated. What is indeed needed in Nigeria is a set of strategic policy decisions concerning an efficient investment in development of market interactions especially in the areas of import-export subsectors, attraction of foreign investors through infrastructural development, and the establishment and maintenance of the trade relations with the major market partners of equal liberalization promise. In the neoliberal policy changes, the state must be a flexible operational actor with de centralized formation to enable it drives its society towards global interdependence in the dynamic environment of global market forces. This can therefore assist in fostering a change in current global asymmetries. As a way of furthering this topic of enquiry, 'globalization from below' and organized information networks can also offer the needed paradigm for global balancing.

7.2.2.1 Fostering Globalization from Below

'Globalization from below' is described as the grassroots involvement in liberating the society from the negative forces of globalization systems and processes. This movement is a critical response to the institutional structures of globalization, which favours mainly the political and business elites, and the industrialized countries. Through cooperative involvement, the institutional framework of globalization could however be restructured to accommodate and expand the participative scope of the disadvantaged, minorities and the developing countries. But the restructuring of the global order may not be simply achieved through indifference to the current wave of globalization or its outright resistance; on the contrary, it should be through a focussed project agenda, revolutionary awareness and understanding, as well as the balanced view of various roles involved in the global interaction and integration. In that sense, Chase Dunn has already observed that from the "earlier efforts to confront and transform capitalism [...], local resistance cannot, by itself, overcome the strong forces of modern capitalism. What is needed is globalization from below [...]."[30] So, with the nature and occurrence of

---

[30] Chase-Dunn notes that "globalization from below means the transnationalization of antisystemic movements and the active participation of popular movements in global

globalization forces, it becomes difficult to be outright from their influence or formation processes. This is because globalization has today constituted part of the changing structure of the society. The most pertinent need is to ensure that the institutional structures of globalization begin to emanate from below, that is, at the local, regional to the national levels.[31] Yet, it does not end at the local or national levels but also goes beyond the immediate environment or territorial boundaries to embrace a more interconnected worldwide reach. This expansion implies devising the means in carrying every class group along, both in the regional and global processes and also in the system developments.

Thereafter, the regional and global formation can have a corporate responsibility in eliminating any form of socio-political or economic dislocation and inequality. This formation, as against the idea of the so-called 'globalization from above' can become the route of comparative advantages between the regional and global societies. This, of course involves new method of cooperation that can recognize the autonomy of various states, but at the same time guarantee the effective coexistence and complementation in the global networks. Within the integration outlook, globalization from below establishes an overreaching collective framework, which both accommodates diversity as well as autonomy in the institutional structure of globalization. It follows that each region should be able to determine its pace of integration in the global setting and as such open to adopt better paths to development. For instance, the major fault of Structural Adjustment Programme in Nigeria was its imposition without proper state institution to harness its gains. In fact, what is required in Nigeria is a more legitimate stabilization and adjustment policies than had occurred previously in early 80s. Thus structural adjustment policy could be a prerequisite for economic growth, only if its basic priority could be for job-creation, instead of restraining the opportunities peo-

---

politics and global citizenship." (Chase-Dunn, Christopher (2005): Social Evolution and the Future of World Society, p. 183)

[31] That is because the "integral human development, sustainable human development depends more on harmonious human relationships at the local level than on the organization and operation of unaccountable national or international political structures or an unfettered free market" (Ike, Obiora (2004): 'The Impact of Globalization on Africa: A Call to Solidarity and Concern'. In: Ike, Obiora (ed.) Globalization and African Self-Determination: What is Our Future? Enugu-Nigeria: CIDJAP Publishing House, p. 19).

ple have in earning their living, all in the name of foreign reserve, deregulation and global integration. But in order for the policy adaptation to gain popularity in the local settings, there ought to be an understanding between the governing bodies and the governed in formulating agendas that gear towards visible growth. In that case, the real import and goal of economic policies should be understood, and with the promise that they can bring about positive changes and sustainable development.

Furthermore, another basic idea of globalization from below is to build an inclusive government that can achieve an increase of cooperation and participation in the global decision-making processes.[32] According to Brecher et al, "globalization from below embrace diversity as one of its central values, and asserts that cooperation need not presuppose uniformity. Its structure tends to be a network of networks, facilitating cooperation without demanding organizational centralization."[33] It follows that the demand for organizational decentralization negates the idea of sociocultural specificity in order to complement different groups. This demand can assist in facilitating collective rationality and innovation in the global cooperation. On the other hand, the facilitation of cooperation through diversity should not presuppose a further avenue for subordination of the weaker group, but a way of confronting the global inequality within the various local capacity levels in order to ensure equitable global society. With the closer economic and political cooperation both at the local and regional levels, it can strengthen the potentialities of interconnections that may revolutionize global economic development and interaction. In fact, the cooperation could embrace the empowerment of the ordinary citizens and the developing world by creating new possibilities of integrations and interactions. Indeed, that may not only slide-down the alliance of the

---

[32] It is on this perspective that Held defined cosmopolitan democracy as "not merely the formal construction of new democratic institutions, but also the construction, in principle, of broad avenues of civic participation in a deliberation over decision-making at regional and global levels" (Held, David (2006): Models of Democracy 3rd Edition. Cambridge: Polity Press, p. 305). Here Chase-Dunn states that "the human species needs both more democratic global governance and more local autonomy, and that the globalization-from-below movements should work together with the local-autonomy movements, or at least with those who are progressive and willing" (Chase-Dunn, Christopher (2005): p. 184).

[33] Brecher, Jeremy/Costello, Tim/Smith, Brendan (2000): Globalization from Below: The Power of Solidarity. Cambridge: South End Press, p. 16.

world powers merely in view of the hegemonial control of the developing countries in the global politics, but can as well help to modify the logic of capitalist economy that aid the concentration of wealth in the hands of few entrepreneurs.

Finally, understanding the repertoire of global inequality could help to transform both the political and economic liberalization processes in a more definite outlook that takes into account the needs of the moment through global supports especially in laying the foundation for national stability and development. In so doing, the local communities can therefore have paramount position in inspiring the continuation of integration as against the eventual hegemonial influences that are reproducing themselves into other forms of domination. And on this point, globalization from below could be a proximal pathway to global involvement.

7.2.2.2 Organized Information Networks

Widening the awareness spaces and engaging the less advantaged segment of the society could assume the fundamental guide to organized information networks. The intergenerational and digital divides between those who are connected and those who are disconnected, as consequence of an unequal access to new information technology, form the compelling interest in this section. Thus the fast growing modern communication and interactive networks separate the global North from the global South, the rural and urban regions, thereby creating the wide margin of differences in communication. The modern communication systems have made it easier to communicate, to gain information from every part of the globe and to enrich the citizens on the current social outlooks around them. It becomes a major challenge when any group or individual is cut-off from the modern informational network.

Castells however comments that "the sense of disorientation is compounded by radical changes in the realm of communications, derived from the revolution of communication technologies. The shift from traditional mass media to a system of horizontal communication networks organized around the Internet and wireless communication has introduced a multiplicity of communication patterns at the source of a fundamental cultural transformation, as virtuality becomes an essential dimension of our reality."[34] It is then evident that the influence of modern network constellation cannot be denied, judging from spatial changes and socio-cultural transformation that is currently in vogue as a consequence of revolutions in the global information infrastructure (GII). This transformation process has really created more open spaces for an enriched cooperation among groups and individuals, as well as an avenue for fast-tracking the increased participation in the global institutions. But the question remains, what is the fate of those who have remained cut off from the promise of information links in this globalization age?

The above question assumes more problematic dimension as new patterns of information networks continue to unfold, promoting important forms of development opportunities, knowledge generation mechanisms and new qualitative changes in the society. [35] The society that is in tune with the new formation reality has the potentials for growth and the one that is yet to embrace the network changes is blocked from the future possibilities. Here Castells however distinguished between information society and informational society. He posits that information society entails the role of information in the society, which as an old process, has been a critical factor in all societies. On the other hand, he identifies the informational society as a specific form of social organization consequent of the new technological conditions in this period of history.[36] Hence the informational society is attributed with the current wave of organized networks. Castells then argues that "as an historical trend, dominant functions and processes in the Information Age are increasingly organized around networks. Networks constitute the new social morphology of our societies, and the diffusion of networking logic

---

[34] Castells, Manuel (2010): The Rise of the Network Society. The Information Age: Economy, Society and Culture Vol. 1, 2nd Edition. Oxford: Wiley-Blackwell, p. xviii.

[35] According to Borgman, "the premise is that this constellation of networks will promote information society that benefits all: peace, friendship, and cooperation through improved interpersonal communications; empowerment through access to information for education, business, and social goods; more productive labor through technology-enriched environment; and stronger economies through open competition in global markets" (Borgman, Christine L. (2000): From Gutenberg to the Global Information Infrastructure: Access to Information in the Networked World. USA: Mit Press, p. 1).

[36] Castells, Manuel (2010): The Rise of the Network Society, p. 21.

substantially modifies the operation and outcomes in processes of production, experience, power, and culture. While the networking form of social organization has existed in other times and spaces, the new information technology paradigm provides the material basis for its pervasive expansion throughout the entire social structure."[37] In other words, as an inter-connecting node and social force, the new information networks become quite essential in the social formation. This is because, they structure as well as transform the pattern of social and power relationships that could enable individuals and societies to participate in the network of global competition. They are also the route through which the asymmetries of globalization could be balanced by creating more spaces for interaction and integration in the local environments.

Dissemination of information usually assists in building relational capacity especially in establishing informed-community that can link individuals and groups in the social networks. On this angle, Rajaee notes that "access to information is a basic right for every citizen. The information infrastructure will be vitally important for social and economic interaction and integration. The benefits of the information society should not be limited to business but should be available to society as a whole. Social cohesion both in a national context as well as on a world scale requires that all citizens, wherever they live, can benefit from essential information services at an affordable price."[38] It then follows that the distributional flexibility of the new information communication networks makes it possible for innovations with its dynamic capacity to regulate as well as diffuse relevant and essential information. For example, the use of mobile telephone as the commonest network in Nigeria was an essential tool that helped to checkmate the politicians against rigging in the 2011 general elections. It significantly assisted in giving out immediate information to the security agents as well as the public media.

Furthermore, the need to expand information networks can also assist in other areas of interests especially in economic transactions, transparency and security. But unfortunately, the Internet accessibility and other sophisticated communication networks that could help in those areas still

---

[37] Castells, Manuel (2010): The Rise of the Network Society, p. 500.
[38] Rajaee, Farhang (2000): p. 121.

remain limited on the hands of the very few, due to their underdevelopment and the lack of maintenance of the already cable-telephone lines, as well as inadequate infrastructural facilities such as electricity. Even the predominant mobile telephone communication has not fared well in providing adequate services to the subscribers and also the high tariff of the network constitute a setback. The challenge of the country therefore is on how to reorganize and devise other alternative means such as information centers in the local communities. This alternative means may be demanding but could provide adequate information networks in which the ordinary men and women in the remote rural areas could boast of their linkages to the external world.

In summary, reducing exclusion and achieving more inclusive developmental goals require an objective and a collaborative rationality towards: i) empowering the marginalized in the society; ii) building stronger social institutions with basic infrastructural development; iii) creating more spaces for informational society and; iv) the maintenance of existing structures of the social formation. Hence both the individuals, groups and more especially the federal government must participate in this important venture. Suffice it to say that the government and its agencies, directly or indirectly are mostly implicated in the crisis of development that has exposed its masses to inequality predicaments due to negligence and system failures. The government on that note should therefore rise up to these challenges of globalization by ensuring proper economic policies, social development and political inclusive environment for peaceful coexistence, which can contribute significantly to the emergence of stable and strong nation-state and civil society.

GENERAL CONCLUSION

In any pluralistic and multicultural society, building a common socio-political ideology that is capable of integrating various interest groups and individuals is always an uphill task. This could also be said to be the experience in the Nigerian context, whereby different ethnic nationalities, with language barriers and diverse cultures are united as one country. In such a situation, the unity in diversity seems to have not enhanced social cohesion and the onward developmental transformation of the state, but rather appears to have deepened the chances of socio-cultural differentiation. The differentiation has hitherto resulted to the increase in social inequalities, political instability, corruption, ethnic rivalry and low economic productivity. Thus findings have revealed that unequal political and economic distributions as a result of various competing interests have led to the increase of insecurity and violence. As one section of the society benefits more than the other from the gains of globalization, the tendency becomes the deterring of progressive investment and production, as well as social cohesion. In other words, the threat of peace both in the local and national levels has been the outcome of inequality and poverty dynamics that exist both among and within groups and individuals. This condition affects greatly the economic growth, in the sense that most investors both local and foreign are often scared at the rate of violent crime in Nigeria.

Besides, very good numbers of the citizens still remain separated from the life chances such as incomes, education, health services and other social amenities, and their basic rights both socially, economically and politically are frequently denied. The distribution of resources and power as it was indicated in the study thus far revealed absolute inequalities according to class, gender, place of residence and regional differentials. From the historico-political standpoint, the research indicated that the changes in structural differentials in Nigeria were majorly characterized within three basic phenomena: the colonial development, the nature of socio-political structure of Nigerian society that gave undue advantage to some groups, and then of recent as a consequent reaction to changes brought about by liberalization processes. As I have argued in this work, most of the problems associated with globalization especially its consequential effect on social inequality in Nigeria should not only be attributed to the global forces but also to the internal and local elements that help to drive the modes of integration into global system. It is on this note that this work identified globalization both as a system of interaction and a process of integration, coupled with the different influences it has on the global relationships.

In this conclusion, I will make effort to evaluate as well as to draw out some conclusions from the important findings and the major issues already raised in the work, by concentrating on the relationship between social inequality and globalization, the resultant effects of global interaction and integration, social structural changes and the main reasons behind unrealizable developmental goals. However, at the beginning of this work, I raised five study questions as the major research priorities. And at this point around, it is pertinent to ask again to what extent has the work addressed or done justice to those questions.

In the first place, question was raised on whether the globalization drive through its uneven processes has any influence on the society and if so, how could that be attributed to the nature of state formation in Nigeria. From the evidence so far, there is no doubt whether globalization has any influence on the society because, it is a force of change either positively or negatively. As was analysed in chapter three and vividly addressed in chapter four, globalization has some success stories in political evolution especially the enthronement of democracy and empowerment of the citizens, as well as in the transformation of national economy from agrarian to modern economies. But the negative impacts of globalization tend to diminish these progressive changes. It is on this note that two major questions were posited namely: In the current instance of neoliberal influence through democratization, how has Nigeria been affected and what are the responses to the many challenges of modern democracy? And, have cosmopolitan ideas and discourse about global capitalism with particular reference to free trade enhanced equality, economic growth and social cohesion? These questions were of course the main burden of this study. Through historical and empirical surveys thus far it could be deduced that in as much as globalization could be a force for positive changes, its consequences on the local population as a result of its unbalanced asymmetries undermined most of its benefits. In that case, the globalization influence on the developing economy through surplus transfers stands the function of protecting the developed economies from market decline.

Moreover, on the question: Have the social changes emanating from the global integration any influence on the endogamous pattern of social network, so also the pattern of income distribution and ethnic associations? In particular, how do those changes affect the individuals and groups both within and without? These questions, as addressed in part three of the study, indicate that the major social changes in Nigeria have been a reaction to the influence of globalization. The manifestation of such changes in the social structure as the study has affirmed is more evident in the political and economic liberalization, income distribution, educational attainment, gender differentiation, and regional and urban development. In addition, the traditional network of sustainability, which initially characterized the society structure, seemed to have been substituted with the neo-patrimonial system of relationship as consequence of modernization. This structural change consequently created more divides than corroboration, more accumulation than distribution, thereby deterring national economic growth and sustainable development.

However, the work further identified some major areas that require immediate attention towards progressive development. From the findings, it was revealed that the foremost set-back in economic growth and the increase of inequality ranges from much dependency on the oil economy, to the lack of autonomy in policy formulation consequent of the conditionality of the global economic institutions, represented by the World Bank and International Monetary Fund. The organizational structure of the institutions has not properly allowed for a dynamic and sustainable economic breakthrough in most of the developing countries. For instance, the imposition of the structural adjustment programme in early 80s on the weak structure of the local economy could not achieve much development gains. On the other hand, the structure of the global economy through trade liberalization may have also hindered the indigenous developmental efforts through economic extraction and value transfer. This condition has made it feasible that the Transnational Corporations in the developing economies control the major foreign market transactions, recalling the stands of the dependency theorists on asymmetrical domination. It is obvious here that the process of value transfer if not well regulated so as to put the market producers in the labor advantage, the economic exploitation will continue to aid the capitalist accumulation processes.

Moreover, it is not enough to have economic potentials and natural resources; what matters most is how to harness those potentials for local sustainable development. And this instance is one of the main challenges of development in Nigeria as was examined in part four. Drawing from the evidence in the study, it indicates that the stagnation of the other sector of the economy especially the agricultural sector has been the outcome of crude oil discovery. In other words, most of the valuable raw materials mainly from agricultural produce and liquid minerals are explored by foreign firms and exported to their respective countries, only to have their finished products from those materials imported in return by the Nigerians. In such a situation, the raw materials are exported in cheaper bargains only to be imported as finished products in exorbitant prices. In that case, labor is also exported; in that, refining and manufacturing those materials in Nigeria would have been a better and sure way of creating jobs and fighting inequality differences. Nevertheless, the attempts already made by the federal government in the middle 70s to promote import-substitutes through the establishment of manufacturing industries could not achieve much result due to: i) import liberalization policies by the IMF, ii) the world market forces that continue to give much advantage to the foreign companies and, iii) lack of proper maintenance culture and indigenous technical operators to manage the industrial machines. As such, most of those industries have folded and some others, their capacity outputs still remain very little to sustain the glowing population.

Although one may also question the rationale behind attributing much of the economic decline and policy failures to the globalization influence on the local economy. But in as much as one would accept the fact that the global integration has no direct impact on all the facets of the economy, yet one would argue that the indirect influence through media penetrations and cultural diffusions have contributed much to the rate of consumerism of the foreign products. As a result, the increasing aversion for locally produced goods has limited the rate of local investments, which has only exploitatively increased the foreign investments on primary goods or raw materials without having much attributes to local economic gains. Hence the prospect of investment on labor-intensive and high-technological sectors becomes a major challenge to the growing economy, and as such would increase opportunities in generating employment and promoting participatory market traditions.

However, adopting only the modern economic culture and financial institution's policies based on savings and productive investments as the modernization theorists would suggest may not be the end view to economic development, but rather recognizing also the input of endogenous elements and the local contents that could aid economic growth. This idea implies that the conscious effort of the government in recognizing the pertinent needs – through the promotion of locally manufactured goods, as was the case in China and other fast growing East Asian countries, and also a diversified economy – will bring about positive changes and the possibility of accelerating the rate of economic growth. Though this may not be easily achieved because of the dictatorship of neo-liberal economic policies and the uncompetitive strength of the local manufacturers in the international investment, but however, it requires time in advocating policies that can withstand and open up more spaces for foreign direct investments. In this conception, most economic analysts would believe that there is also the need to pay much attention to the inner deficiency of the Nigerian economic structure by defining the roles of the state, foreign investors, class compositions, and the business and political elites. From the study carried out, it was discovered that the undefined role differences are some of the barriers that characterize the political economy of Nigeria and then contribute to policy failures.

Furthermore, the increase interference on the local politics as a result of the conditionality of the global institutions has not only been a diminution to the autonomy of the state but has also empowered the local political elites in consonance with their Western backers in infringing hardship on the local population. This situation as it was seen in chapter four was more prominent during the colonial and military regimes. In the colonial periods, the system of indirect rule gave the local authorities power over the community in order to protect the interests of the colonial administrators. In such formation, the colonial or Western powers were allowed to use the state apparatuses to achieve their economic and political ends. A similar formation also manifested during the military governments in Nigeria. For instance, at the time of General Babangida military regime from 1985 to 1993, it seemed to be a bargain between the government and the western powers in imposing the structural adjustment policy on the one hand and the recognition of the military junta on the other hand. This pay-back model between the global powers and the national government has constituted the pattern of political development in Nigeria since early 80s. It gave much room for corruption and transferring the resources to western countries without much concentration on nation-building. Studies have also revealed that the state dominated the society during the long term of the military regime in Nigeria, which helped to entrench and deepen the privatization of the state by the political elites.

Nevertheless, the state is the primary source of accumulation of wealth, and the control of the state through governance in the Nigerian context implies automatic access to the state resources. One could also say that since the state is the decisive means of wealth distribution instead of the market, it becomes difficult in separating politics from state resources. Hence in view of the fact that politics is the accumulation criterion of the state resources and powers, I would propose that political competition is likewise an economic competition. In other words, control of the state is the control of its resources, which gives rise to personalization of state. This condition entails that whoever gets access to the state resources through political means uses them to build up his/her clientele network and political machinery in order to safeguard his/her position. In such circumstance, neutralizing the influence of political elites on the state economy, for instance through civil society involvement or from opposition parties, becomes an uphill task. This is because all the state's apparatuses are under their control, in which case, they use every available means to surmount any opposition. This formation also implies that what underlies political formation in Nigeria is not actually the method of distribution of power and wealth but depends on personal interests that command the mode of distribution.

From the above perspective, the separation of state resources from the private interests will be a proper step in sustaining the required space for desirable economic and political construction as against the capitalist over-accumulation procedures. In other words, if the demarcation between the state and private interests are not well tackled through a strong constitutional clause, the accumulation chances of the political elites in the state resources will still continue to create opportunities for patronages and personalization of state, thereby affecting the distribution of state wealth. Most analysts infer that even the past attempts in restructuring the political system were not actually aimed at the separation of state resources from private interests, but were meant to intervene in the political conflicts that existed among political parties. Thus the separation of state and personal interests will conversely involve the reconfiguration of domestic politics against the dominant forces of neo-patrimonialism as Chabal and Daloz suggested. This formation will open more room for participation as well as assist in an evolution of healthy political opposition parties that are beyond tribal sentiments and without intent usurpation of the state economic. This conclusion also means that attention should properly be given to the mode of evolution of political parties, which should not be grounded on regional or ethnic affinities but could embrace different groups as well as creating common ideology as a unifying instance. This formation process will go a long way in establishing transparency in the political system and smooth transfer of power from one political party to the other in a free and fair election.

Nonetheless, the key problem of political instability as the study suggested was based on the pluralistic nature of the country comprising different ethnic groups with divergent interests. This composition through an amalgamation of the southern and northern proletariats in 1914 by the colonial administration has been widely criticized. In the current composition, there seem to be a reciprocal relationship between the homogenous ethnic groups and the bureaucratic structure of the state, making ethnicity an instrument of politics and a struggle for class supremacy. Each ethnic group continues to struggle for relevance and interest, thereby abandoning the national interest to the interest of ethnic nationalities. The distrust that exists among the ethnic groups has also endangered the country as a nation without common interest and value. The agenda of the nation boils down to the agenda of ethnic nationalities that fight only in favor of their own ethnic groups. This is more evident in the distribution of incomes and political offices. Nevertheless, the minority ethnic groups usually suffer marginalization from the dominant ethnic groups that possess the power and the resources. There are always attempts by each ethnic group to mobilize their members in order to overlay the other (ethnic groups) in the political and economic scheme of the state. Due to this ethnic consciousness, the struggle for the control of the state and its apparatuses could results to regional fragmentation and institutional instability. By such understanding, ethnic consciousness means the unending effort by different ethnic groups to take control of the decision-making organs of the state in order to have exclusive access to state resources.

Nevertheless, it is never impossible in forming a stable and strong state in a multicultural society such as Nigeria. But that entails the recognition of multiple identities and different affiliations, and then developing out new realities from the diversities, which will unite the different interests. In developing new realities, maintaining the legacy of the pluralistic interaction as a unifying entity could aptly be considered as a necessary ingredient to integration and general participation. But facing its challenges will demand a relevant ideological construct that could integrate the ethnic groups into nationhood, navigate individual interests towards general interests. This ideological construct could as well be a force that could champion a practical strategy for society transformation in the era of globalization.

The study also discovered that the pattern of regional development, based on economic and political interest of the colonial powers has been the major source of regional differentiation. This entails: the development of urban settings only in the regions with economic potentialities, as well as the regions of transnational contact for easy exportation of raw materials. This pattern of development has been a constraint on the part of the government in establishing definite developmental plans and policies that could account for equal distribution of resources among different regions. Part of the problem is that most of the regions have limited potentials for revenue generation and thus depend heavily on the central government for developmental allocations. On the other hand, the survey in chapter six revealed that the developmental model in Nigeria was mostly urban-based leaving most of the rural areas underdeveloped. Most of the cities that were developed during the colonial periods due to economic proximity were further sustained by postcolonial governments, causing the utmost neglect of the peasant farmers and exclusion of the rural population in the provision of basic infrastructure.

Furthermore, the discriminatory distribution of resources has resulted to rapid inflow of the population from rural to urban regions, causing high rate of urban population. Also the natural growth of the urban population contributes to this high increase, causing over-crowding in most of the major cities in the country. This is consequential because of the fact that the rate of urban growth does not match with the available amenities in those cities, as well as the decay in physical infrastructure as a result of poor maintenance. It is in most of these cities such as in Lagos that the rate of inequality within groups is most evident due to high house rents and cost of living. The majority of the residents are however renter and they suffer many hardships in the hands of the house-owners because of inadequate regulatory rent system. The concerted effort by the government in establishing secondary and satellite cities has not either yielded significant results due to poor planning and lack of infrastructural development. What is clear from the study thus far is that, it would be difficult to anticipate immediate reduction in migration rate from rural to urban regions. Therefore, consideration must be given to allocation of resources, employment generation, and then proper regulative units must be put in place in order to promote efficiency and distributive balance.

Among others, the above consideration will involve most importantly a strong and emancipated society from the state domination. As such, the institutional components of the state play an important role in determining the modus operandi of the society. In fact, many contemporary scholars are of the opinion that the state has a central role and remains a critical factor in the formation of emancipated society. In this way, the state can effectively intervene in policy renewal by constructing new strategies, and conditioning them for efficient institutional development. But on the other hand, the state must however be properly equipped and should remain sovereign to be able to construct the required platform that is desirable for this institutional development. In this perspective, Chabal and Daloz likewise point out that the key conditions for this institutional development requires among other things i) "the gradual emancipation of established political structures from the society," and ii) "the emergence of a notion of citizenship binding individuals directly to the state – above and beyond the more proximate ties of kinship, community or faction."[1] Thus Chabal and Daloz may be right in their thought towards proper separation of state from kinship networks and other personal interests. But one has to know that other network of relationships could as well play a major and perhaps predominant role in the Nigerian socio-political development. In that case, consideration could be given to the significant roles of kinship and community relationships in Nigerian context as important tools for social cohesion in the traditional cultural setting, as well as the role of traditional institutions and religions, but they should on the other hand, not be allowed to assume the dominant role in the institutional formation of the state.

Hence building a state that is characterized with strong institutional formation, transparency and accountability to the citizens requires an interactive point of convergence that gears towards the common good of the masses. This ideal is at the heart of democratic ideological principles of good governance and sustainable development that could join forces together in creating unity in diverse socio-cultural autonomies. Thus in building and reforming the foundations of democratic governance that existed and still exist in the traditional local settings may contribute substantially in guaranteeing the proper consensus negotiation that can strengthen the formation of institutionalized state. More pertinently, it can assist in promoting and ensuring equal participation. In this sense, the pursuit for a proper ideological construction could help to offer "individuals a more or less coherent picture of the world not only as it is but also as it ought to be."[2] This ideological formation should of course be a consistent and rational effort in establishing a link between spatial realities and the traditional norms. In that understanding, Agbakoba notes that "ideology basically provides people with an internal control mechanism which places barriers on certain types of behaviour while encouraging or simply allowing other types [...]. It is important to appreciate the strength of an ideology, that is, the capacity of an ideology to determine and guide behaviour in the face of the changing circumstances due to cultural influ-

---

[1] Chabal, Patrick/Daloz, Jean-Pascal (1999): Africa Works, pp. 5&6.
[2] Steger, Manfred B. (2003): p. 93.

339

ences from within and without."[3] In articulating these two opposing-sides mechanism of ideological influences and appreciating their differences, suitable ideological construction may assist in advocating for integrative procedural changes in the society development. The integrative procedural changes could on this note be a rational force in addressing unequal socio-economic and political distributions that constitute the multiplicity of advantages for few and wallowing penury for the majority of the population in the capitalist system.

The integral procedural changes will first of all involve change of mindset and an in-depth understanding and consideration of a more focused developmental agenda with collective/collaborative initiative. On this note, one is required to ask: why does certain agenda or developmental plan work for one nation but does not work for another? In such scenario, there are always significant differentials in developmental outcomes, in the sense that what works in one country may not work in the other, perhaps due to unfavorable economic and political settings, as well as some historical constraints to resource distribution. However, the above question may involve the reexamination of the cohesiveness of societies as well as the efficiency of public institutions in gearing towards society transformation. On the other hand, findings in this study have shown that the key factor to proper policy development and implementation is the strength of the economy. With rich natural and human resources endowment, Nigeria is capable of this transformation agenda and has the potential of being a major player in the global system. But this calls for the ultimate effort in understanding the necessary means of utilizing the available resources and opportunities for onward transformation of society and how that could foster a greater sense of belonging and inclusive-agenda in environments where there are different identities and interests.

In fostering society transformation, the decision-making bodies must also be convinced that any institutional building and procedural changes that should be made are both implementable and desirable for the benefit of the masses. And the masses on the other hand should be ready to comply

---

[3] Agbakoba, J.C.A. (1998): 'Towards a Philosophy of Technology and Development in Africa'. In: Oguejiofor, J. Obi (ed.): Africa: Philosophy and Public Affairs. Enugu: Delta Publication, p. 230.

with those changes. An exercise of such transformation agenda could begin to proffer future policy options in the various sectors as well as assist in the establishment of an emancipated society. This transformation agenda thus represents a movement from old ways of thinking, complex methods of dealing with societal problems, to more simple and 'reflexive' ways of production and relation that will probably embrace the socio-cultural heritage that is authentic and compatible in ensuring minimal external interventions. In that case, the leadership commitments and the people's positive contributions to the ideals of national interest will gradually reawaken the general consciousness towards procedural changes ably articulated to withstand and absolve much of the external pressures.

Most pertinently, the transformation agenda requires the development of knowledge-based society through qualitative education and training. It demands creating an information-society whereby the population has the possibility of interaction with the external world, as well as steady attention to socio-economic strategies with minimal interventions in promoting socio-cultural interaction. In fact, remaining in a world of change demands both internal and external transformations in order to tackle the changing situations. If people are not operating on the same wave length, how could they compete in the same environment? For instance, if one has the opportunity to study in a better institution of learning with every educational facility in one's disposal, and the other studies in a school where it is even very difficult to have qualified teachers, not to mention of study facilities: Are the two expected to compete in the same labor environment? So the difference is obvious in characterizing their abilities and capabilities. Hence empowerment of the citizens through qualitative education becomes a necessity. Unfortunately, with the expansion of the educational institutions since 1970s, much of the emphasis has been on the theoretical expansion to the detriment of vocational and practical formation. One of the reasons is because of inadequate facilities to guarantee technical trainings in most of the educational institutions. Again, it could also be said that the available educational infrastructure does not match with the increasing population of students and that also deters the corresponding qualitative formation of students. The concerted effort of the government in realizing the need to prepare the future entrepreneurs with quality education will be a right direction to transformative options of the society.

Finally, in dealing with globalization and social inequality in Nigeria as a structural niche, the work has thus far outlined some contextual problems and some alternatives based on the perspective of this analysis. Even though no country can afford to remain isolated from the global configuration or to abandon globalization completely, this work therefore advocates a more accommodation of differences in global participation that seeks to reduce inequality and improve the social well-being of every member of the society. In so doing, the benefits and opportunities offered by globalization could be a sure route to sustainable development.

BIBLIOGRAPHY

Abbink, John (2004): 'Violence and State (Re)formation in African Context: Global and Local Aspects of Crisis and Change'. In: Westerfield, Robert E. (ed.): Current Issues in Globalization. New York: Nova Science Publishers Inc.

Abrahamsen, Rita/Williams, Michael (2011): Security beyond the State: Private Security in International Politics. Cambridge: Cambridge University Press.

Achebe, Chinua (1984): The Trouble with Nigeria. London: Heinemann African Writers Series.

Agbakoba, J.C.A. (1998): 'Towards a Philosophy of Technology and Development in Africa'. In: Oguejiofor, J. Obi (ed.): Africa: Philosophy and Public Affairs. Enugu: Delta Publication.

Agbali, Anthony A. (2005): 'A Reflection on Afigbo's Writings on Nigeria'. In: Afigbo, Adiele Eberechukwu/Falola, Toyin (eds.) Nigerian History, Politics and Affairs: The Collected Essays of Adiele Afigbo. Trenton: Africa World Press Inc.

Agbese, Pita O./Udogu, Ike E. (2005): 'Taming of the Shrew: Civil-Military Politics in the Fourth Republic'. In: Udogu, E. Ike (ed.): Nigeria in the Twenty-first Century: Strategies for Political Stability and Peaceful Coexistence. Trenton: Africa World Press.

Agbese, Pita O. (2004): 'Soldiers as Rulers: Military Performance'. In: Kieh, George K./Agbese, Pita O. (eds.): The Military and Politics in Africa: From Engagement to Democratic and Constitutional Control (Contemporary Perspectives on Developing Societies). England: Ashgate.

Agbola, Tunde/Alabi, Moruf (2003): 'Political Economic of Petroleum Resources Development, Environmental Injustice and Selective Victimization: A Case Study of the Niger Delta Region of Nigeria'. In: Agyeman, Julian/Bullard, Robert Doyle/Evans, Bob (eds.): Just Sustainabilities: Development in an Unequal World. London: Mit Press.

344

Ake, Claude (1989): 'How Politics Underdevelops Africa'. In: Ihonvbere, O. Julius (ed.): The Political Economy of Crisis and Underdevelopment in Africa: Selected Works of Claude Ake. Lagos: JAD Publishers.

Alexander, Jeffrey (1982): Theoretical Logic in Sociology, Vol. 1. London and Heney: Routledge and Kegan Paul.

Anderson, Benedict (1983): Imagined Communities: Reflection on the Origin and Spread of Nationalism. London: Verso Editions.

Anikpo, Mark (1985): 'Nigeria's Evolving Class Structure'. In: Ake, Claude (ed.): Political Economy of Nigeria, New York: Longman Inc.

Anthony, Robert Michael (2009): Primacy and Polity: The Role of Urban Population in Political Change. Dissertation: The Ohio State University.

Arrighi, Giovanni (1994): The Long Twentieth Century: Money, Power, and the Origins of Our Times. London/New York: Verso.

Barlösius, Eva (2004): Kämpfe um soziale Ungleichheit: Machttheoretische Perspektiven. Wiesbaden: VS Verlag für Sozialwissenschaften.

Barth, Fredrik (1969): Ethnic Groups and Boundaries: The Social Organization of Cultural Difference. Boston: Little, Brown and Company.

Bayart, Jean-Francois (2009): The State in Africa: The Politics of the Belly, Second Edition. Cambridge: Polity Press.

Bayart, Jean-Francois/Ellis, Stephen/Hibou, Beatrice (1999): The Criminalization of the State in Africa. Indiana: Indiana University Press.

Beck, Ulrich (1992): Risk Society: Towards a New Modernity (First Published in 1986 in German). London: SAGE Publications.

345

Beck, Ulrich (2009): World at Risk (First Published in German in 2007). Cambridge: Polity Press.

Beck, Ulrich/Bonss, Wolfgang/Lau, Christoph (2003): The Theory of Reflexive Modernization: Problematic, Hypotheses and Research Programme. In: Theory, Culture & Society Vol. 20, No. 2. London: SAGE Publications.

Berman, Bruce/Eyoh, Dickson/Kymlicka, Will (2004): 'Conclusion: African Ethnic Politics & the Paradox of Democratic Development'. In: Berman, Bruce/Eyoh, Dickson/Kymlicka, Will (eds.): Ethnicity and Democracy in Africa. Oxford: James Currey.

Berman, Bruce/Lonsdale, John (1992): Unhappy Valley: Conflict in Kenya & Africa, Book Two: Violence & Ethnicity. Oxford: James Currey.

Bienen, Henry (1985): Political Conflict and Economic Change in Nigeria. London: Frank Cass & Co.

Borgman, Christine L. (2000): From Gutenberg to the Global Information Infrastructure: Access to Information in the Networked World. USA: Mit Press.

Bratton, Michael/Van de Walle, Nicolas (1997): Democratic Experiments in Africa: Regime Transitions in Comparative Perspective. Cambridge: Cambridge University Press.

Brecher, Jeremy/Costello, Tim/Smith, Brendan (2000): Globalization from Below: The Power of Solidarity. Cambridge: South End Press.

Burton, John (1979): Deviance, Terrorism and War: The Process of Solving Unsolved Social and Political Problems. New York: St. Martin's Press.

Burton, John (1990): Conflict Resolution and Prevention. New York: St. Martin's Press.

346

Burton, John (1997): 'Violence Experienced: The Source of Conflict Violence and Crime and Their Prevention'. New York: Manchester University Press.

Callaghy, Thomas (2000): 'Africa and the World Political Economy: More Caught Between a Rock and a Hard Place'. In: Harbeson, John W. /Rothchild, Donald (eds.): Africa in the World Politics: The African State System in Flux, 3rd Edition. US: Westview Press.

Carroll, David J. /Rosati, Jerel A. /Coate, Roger A. (1988): 'Human Needs Realism: A Critical Assessment of the Power of Human Needs in World Society'. In: Coate, Roger A. /Rosati, Jerel A. (eds.): The Power of Human Needs in World Society. Boulder, CO: Lynne Rienner Publishers.

Castells, Manuel (2010): End of Millennium: The Information Age: Economy, Society, and Culture Vol. III, 2nd Edition. Oxford: Wiley-Blackwell.

Castells, Manuel (2010): The Rise of the Network Society. The Information Age: Economy, Society and Culture Vol. 1, 2nd Edition. Oxford: Wiley Blackwell.

Chabal, Patrick/Daloz, Jean-Pascal (1999): Africa Works: Disorder as Political Instrument. US & Canada: Indiana University Press.

Chase-Dunn, Christopher (2000): 'Globalization: A World-Systems Perspective'. In: Ciprut, Jose V. (ed.): Of Fears and Foes: Security and Insecurity in an Evolving Global Political Economy. USA: Greenwood Publishing Group Inc.

Chiegboka, C. A. (1997): Women Status and Dignity in the Society and the Church: A perspective from Gal. 3, 36-39. Enugu: Pearl Functions.

Coate, Roger A./Rosati, Jerel A. (1988): 'Human Needs in World Society'. In: Coate, Roger A. / Rosati, Jerel A. (eds.): The Power of Human Needs in World Society. Boulder CO: Lynne Rienner Publishers.

Cohen, Robin (1974): Labor and Politics in Nigeria 1945-71. London: Heinemann.

Cohen, Ronald/Goldman, Abe (1992): 'The Society and its Environment'. In: Metz, Helen Chapin (ed.): Nigeria: A Country Study 5th Edition. Washington: GPO for the Library of Congress.

Cooper, Frederick (2002): Africa Since 1940: The Past of the Present. Cambridge: Cambridge University Press.

Croucher, Sheila L. (1997): Imagining Miami: Ethnic Politics in a Postmodern World. USA, Virginia: University Press.

Croucher, Sheila L. (2004): Globalization and Belonging: The Politics of Identity in a Changing World. Oxford: Rowman & Littlefield Publishers.

Davidson, Basil (1971): Which Way Africa? The Search for a New Society 3rd Edition. Middlesex, England: Penguin Books.

Davidson, Basil (1992): The Black Man's Burden: Africa and the Curse of the Nation-State. London: James Currey.

Diamond Larry (1999): Developing Democracy: Toward Consolidation. Maryland: The Johns Hopkins University Press.

Diamond, Larry (1988): Class, Ethnicity and Democracy in Nigeria: The Failure of the First Republic. New York: Syracuse University Press.

Duffield, Mark (2000): Globalization, Transborder Trade, and War Economies. In: Berdal, Mats/Malone, David (eds.): Greed and Grievance: Economic Agendas in Civil Wars. Colorado: Lynne Rienner Publishers Inc.

Durkheim, Emile (1992): Über soziale Arbeitsteilung: Studie über die Organisation höherer Gesellschaften. Frankfurt am Main: Suhrkamp.

Eichelpasch, Rolf/Rademacher, Claudia (2004): Identität. Bielefeld: Transcript Verlag.

Eisenstadt, Shmuel N. /Abitbol, Michel /Chazan, Naomi (1988): 'State Formation in Africa, Conclusions'. In: Eisenstadt, S. N. / Abitbol, M. / Chazan, N. (eds.): The Early State in African Perspective. The Netherlands: E. J. Brill, Leiden.

Eme, Ekekwe (1986): Class and State in Nigeria. London: Longman.

Falola, Toyin/Heaton, Matthew (2008): A History of Nigeria. Cambridge: Cambridge University Press.

Forrest, Tom (1986): 'The Political Economy of Civil Rule and the Economic Crisis in Nigeria (1979-84)'. In: The Review of African Political Economy Vol. 13, No. 35. London: Routledge.

Forsyth, Frederick (1977): The Making of an African Legend: The Biafra Story. New York: Penguin Books.

Fortes, Meyer/Evans-Pritchard, Edward (1940): African Political Systems. New York: Oxford University Press.

Foucault, Michel (1991): Die Ordnung des Diskurses. Frankfurt am Main: Fischer-Taschenbuch-Verlag.

Foucault, Michel (2004): The Order of Things: An Archaeology of the Human Sciences (First Published in 1966 in French). New York: Routledge.

Friedmann, John (1973): Urbanization, Planning and National Development. Newbury Park California: SAGE Publications.

Giddens, Anthony (1990): The Consequences of Modernity. Cambridge: Polity Press.

Giddens, Anthony (2002): Runaway World: How Globalisation is reshaping our Lives. London: Profile Books.

Giddens, Anthony (2006): Sociology, 5th Edition. Cambridge: Polity Press.

349

Goetze, Dieter (2002): Entwicklungssoziologie: Eine Einführung. Weinheim/München: Juventa.

Grusky, David B. (2001): The Past, Present, and Future of Social Inequality. In: Grusky, David B. (ed.): Social Stratification: Class, Race, and Gender in Sociological Perspective 2nd Edition. Westview Press.

Gyekye, Kwame (1998): 'Person and Community in African Traditional Thought.' In: Coetzee, P. H./Roux A. P. J. (eds.): The African Philosophy Reader. London/New York: Routledge.

Hall, Stuart (1997): 'Cultural Identity and Diaspora'. In: Woodward, Kathryn (ed.) Identity and Difference. London: SAGE Publications.

Hall, Stuart (2007): 'Ethnicity: Identity and Difference'. In: Ching, Erik Kristofer/Buckley, Christina/Lozano-Alonso Angélica (eds.): Reframing Latin America: a Cultural Theory Reading of the Nineteenth and Twentieth Centuries. USA: University of Texas Press.

Hauck, Gerhard (2001): Gesellschaft und Staat in Afrika. Frankfurt am Main: Brandes & Apsel.

Hayami, Yujiro/Godo, Yoshihisa (2005): Development Economics: From the Poverty to the Wealth of Nations, Third Edition. New York: Oxford University Press.

Held, David (1995): Democracy and the Global Order: From the Modern State to Cosmopolitan Governance. London: Polity Press.

Held, David (2006): Models of Democracy 3rd Edition. Cambridge: Polity Press.

Held, David/McGrew, Anthony/Goldblatt, David/Perraton, Jonathan (1999): Global Transformations: Politics, Economics and Culture. California: Stanford University Press.

Henriot, Peter S.J (2003): 'Globalization: Implications for Africa'. In: Drischoll, William/Clark, Julie (eds.): Globalization and the

Poor: Exploitation of Equalizer? New York: International Debate Education Association.

Huntington, Samuel P. (1996): The Clash of Civilizations and the Re-making of World Order. New York: Simon & Schuster.

Ihonvbere, Julius O. (1994): Nigeria: the Politics of Adjustment & De-mocracy. New Brunswick, New Jersey: Transaction Publishers.

Ike, Obiora (2004): 'The Impact of Globalization on Africa: A Call to Solidarity and Concern'. In: Ike, Obiora (ed.) Globalization and African Self-Determination: What is Our Future? Enugu-Nigeria: CIDJAP Publishing House.

Iroegbu, Pantaleon (1996): Communalism: Toward Justice in Africa. Owerri: International Universities Press.

Jäger, Siegfried (1999): Kritische Diskursanalyse: Eine Einführung. Duisburg: DISS-Studien 23.

Jarmon, Charles (1988): Nigeria: Reorganization and Development since the Mid-Twentieth Century (Monographs and Theoretical Studies in Sociology and Anthropology in Honour of Nels Anderson) The Netherlands: E. J. Brill Leiden, Publication 23.

Jega, Attahiru (2000): 'The State and Identity Transformation under Structural Adjustment in Nigeria'. In: Jega, Attahiru (ed.): Iden-tity Transformation and Identity Politics under Structural Ad-justment in Nigeria. Stockholm, Sweden: Elanders Gotab.

Jessop, Bob (1990): State Theory: Putting the Capitalist State in its Place. USA: Pennsylvania State University Press.

Johnston, Barry V. ed. (1998): Pitirim A Sorokin 1889-1968: On the Practice of Sociology – The Heritage of Sociology. Chicago: University of Chicago Press.

Josephson, Jyl (2005): 'The Intersectionality of Domestic Violence'. In: Sokoloff, Natalie J./Pratt, Christina (eds.): Domestic Violence at the Margins: Readings on Race, Class, Gender and Culture. USA: Rutger University Press.

Kabeer, Naila (2003): Gender Mainstreaming in Poverty Eradication and the Millennium Development Goals: A Handbook for Policy-Makers and Other Stakeholders. Commonwealth Secretariat, London: Ashford Colour Press.

Kaplinsky, Raphael (2005): Globalization, Poverty and Inequality: Between a Rock and a Hard Place. Cambridge: Polity Press.

Karl, Terry Lynn (2004): 'Oil-Led Development: Social, Political, and Economic Consequences'. In: Encyclopedia of Energy Vol. 4. Elsevier Inc.

Kayongo Male, Diane/Onyango, Philista (1984): The Sociology of the African Family. London/New York: Longmans.

Kieh, George K. (2004): 'Military Engagement in Politics in Africa'. In: Kieh, George K./Agbese, Pita O. (eds.): The Military and Politics in Africa: From Engagement to Democratic and Constitutional Control (Contemporary Perspectives on Developing Societies). England: Ashgate.

Kößler, Reinhart (1994): Postkoloniale Staaten: Elemente eines Bezugsrahmens. Hamburg: Deutsches Übersee-Institut.

Kößler, Reinhart/Wienold, Hanns (2001): Gesellschaft bei Marx. Münster: Westfälisches Dampfboot.

Kreckel, Reinhard (1992): Politische Soziologie der sozialen Ungleichheit. Frankfurt am Main: Campus.

Leftwich, Adrian (2000): States of Development: On the Primacy of Politics in Development. Cambridge: Polity Press.

Lewellen, Ted C. (2002): The Anthropology of Globalization: Cultural Anthropology enters the 21st Century. USA: Greenwood Publishing Group.

352

Lewis, Peter M. (2007): Growing Apart; Oil, Politics, and Economic Change in Indonesia and Nigeria. Ann Arbor: University of Michigan Press.

Loimeier, Roman (1997): Islamic Reform and Political Change in Northern Nigeria. Evanston, Illinois: Northwestern University Press.

Lopez, Jose (2003): Society and its Metaphors: Language, Social Theory and Social Structure. London & New York: Continuum.

Lopez, Jose/Scott, John (2000): Social Structure. Glasgow: Harper Collins.

Luhmann, Niklas (1999): Funktionen und Folgen formaler Organisation (5. Auflage). Berlin: Duncker &. Humblot.

Mahalingam, Ramaswami (2007): 'Essentialism and Cultural Narratives: A Social-Marginality Perspective'. In: Fuligni, Andrew J. (ed.): Contesting Stereotypes and Creating Identities: Social Categories, Social Identities and Educational Participation. New York: Russell Sage Foundation.

Mamdani, Mahmood (1996): Citizen and Subject: Contemporary Africa and the Legacy of Late Colonialism. Princeton, New Jersey: Princeton University Press.

Mandel, Ernest (1981): Marx's Theory of Surplus Value. In: International Viewpoint: Fourth International.

Mbiti, S. John (1989): African Religions and Philosophy 2nd Edition. Oxford: Heinemann Educational Publishers.

McGrew, Anthony G. (1992): 'Conceptualizing Global Politics'. In: McGrew, Anthony G. /Lewis, Paul G. (eds.): Global Politics: Globalization and the Nation-states. Cambridge: Polity Press.

Meredith, Martin (2006): The State of Africa: A History of Fifty Years of Independence. Reading: Cox & Wyman.

Mentan, Tatah (2010): The State in Africa: An Analysis of Impacts of Historical Trajectories of Global Capitalist Expansion and Domination in the Continent. Cameroon: Langaa RPCIG.

Meyer, Birgit/Geschiere, Peter eds. (1999): Globalization and Identity: Dialectics of Flow and Closure. Oxford: Blackwell.

Miller, David (1999): ,Justice and Global Inequality'. In: Hurrell, Andrew/Woods, Ngaire (eds.): Inequality, Globalization, and World Politics. New York: Oxford University Press.

Moore, Wilbert E. (1968): 'Social Change'. In: Sills, David (ed.): International Encyclopedia of the Social Sciences, Vol. 14. New York: The Free Press.

Mossmann, Jannis (2007): Modern World System Theory: Essay. Norderstedt: GRIN Verlag.

Mustapha, Raufu A. (2004): 'Ethnicity and the Politics of Democratization in Nigeria'. In: Berman, Bruce/Eyoh, Dickson/Kymlicka, Will (eds.): Ethnicity and Democracy in Africa. Oxford: James Currey.

Nafziger, Wayne E. (1992): 'The Economy'. In: Metz, Helen Chapin (ed.): Nigeria: A Country Study 5th Edition. Washington: GPO for the Library of Congress.

Naples, Nancy A. (2003): Feminism and Method: Ethnography, Discourse Analysis, and Activist Research. New York/London: Routledge.

Nnoli, Okwudiba (1978): Ethnic Politics in Nigeria. Enugu: Fourth Dimensions Publishers.

Nnoli, Okwudiba (1995): Ethnicity and Development in Nigeria. Aldershot: Avebury.

Northrup, Terrell A (1989): 'The Dynamic of Identity in Personal and Social Conflict'. In: Kriesberg, Louis/Northrup, Terrell A.

/Thorson, Stuart J. (eds.): Intractable Conflicts and their Transformation. New York: Syracuse University Press.

Ntibagirirwa, Symphorien (2001): 'A Wrong Way: From Being to Having in the African Value System'. In. Giddy, Patrick (ed.): Protest and Engagement: Philosophy after Apartheid at an Historically Black South African University, Cultural Heritage and Contemporary Change Series II, Africa, Volume 7. Washington, D.C.: The Council for Research in Values and Philosophy.

Nugent, Paul (2004): Africa since Independence: A Comparative History. UK: Palgrave Macmillan.

Obodoechina, Uchechukwu (2006): The Imperative of Self-Reliance for the Churches in Africa: A Study in Christian Social Ethics. Frankfurt am Main: Peter Lang GmbH.

Oborji, Francis A. (2005): Trends in African Theology since Vatican II: A Missiological Orientation. Rome: Leberit SRL Press.

Okere, Theophilus (2005): Philosophy, Culture and Society in Africa: Essays. Nsukka-Nigeria: Afro-Orbis Publications.

Oman, Charles (1999): 'Globalization, Regionalization, and Inequality'. In: Hurrell, Andrew/Woods, Ngaire (eds.): Inequality, Globalization, and World Politics. New York: Oxford University Press.

Onyeonoru, Ifeanyi P. (2003): 'Globalisation and Industrial Performance in Nigeria'. In: Journal of Africa Development Vol. 28, No. 3 and 4. Dakar: Council for the Development of Social Science Research in Africa (CODESRIA).

Osberg, Lars (1991): 'Introduction'. In: Osberg, Lars (ed.): Economic Inequality and Poverty: International Perspectives. New York: M.E. Sharpe, Inc.

Paris, Peter J. (1995): The Spirituality of African Peoples: The Search for a Common Moral Discourse. Minneapolis: Fortress Press.

Parsons, Talcott (2003): Das System moderner Gesellschaften (6. Auflage). Weinheim/München: Juventa Verlag.

Pelczynski, Z. A. (1984): 'Introduction: The Significance of Hegel's Separation of the State and Civil Society'. In: Pelczynski, Z. A. (ed.): The State and Civil Society: Studies in Hegel's Political Philosophy. Cambridge: Cambridge University Press.

Pereira, Charmaine (2000): 'National Council of Women's Societies and the State, 1985-1993: The Use of Discourses of Womanhood by the NCWS'. In: Jega, Attahiru (ed.): Identity Transformation and Identity Politics under Structural Adjustment in Nigeria. Stockholm, Sweden: Elanders Gotab.

Polanyi, Karl (1944): The Great Transformation. Boston, MA, USA: Beacon Press.

Prakash, A. /Hart, Jeffrey A. (1999): Globalization and Governance. London/New York: Routledge.

Rajaee, Farhang (2000): Globalization on Trail: The Human Condition and the Information Civilization. West Hartford, USA: Kumarian Press Inc.

Reno, William (1999): Warlord Politics and African States Boulder: Lynne Rienner Publishers.

Richardson, David J. (2001): 'Exports Matter ... And So Does Trade Finance'. In: Hufbauer, C. Gary/Rodríguez, M. Rita (eds.): Ex-Im Bank in the 21st Century: A New Approach? Washington, DC: Institute for International Economics.

Robertson, Roland (1992): Globalization: Social Theory and Global Culture. London: SAGE Publications.

Rodney, Walter (2012): How Europe Underdeveloped Africa. Cape Town/Dakar/Nairobi & Oxford: Pambazuka Press.

Rostow, Walt Whitman (1990): The Stages of Economic Growth: A Non-Communist Manifesto, Third Edition. Cambridge: Cambridge University Press.

Rothman, Jay (1997): Resolving Identity-Based Conflict in Nations, Organizations, and Communities. San Francisco, CA: Jossey-Bass Publishers.

Schützeichel, Rainer (2007): ‚Soziale Repräsentationen'. In Schützeichel, Rainer (Hrsg.): Handbuch Wissenssoziologie und Wissensforschung. Konstanz: UVK.

Scott, John/Marshall, Gordon (2005): Oxford Dictionary of Sociology 3rd Edition. New York: Oxford University Press.

Sen, Amartya (1995): Inequality Reexamined. New York: Harvard University Press.

Sen, Amartya (2001): Development as Freedom. Oxford: Oxford University Press.

Sen, Amartya (2008): 'Many Faces of Gender Inequality'. In: Webber, Michelle/Bezanson, Kate (eds.): Rethinking Society in the 21st Century: Critical Readings in Sociology 2nd Edition. Toronto: Canadian Scholars' Press Inc.

Sen, Amartya/Foster, James (1997): On Economic Inequality, Expanded Edition with a Substantial Annexe. New York: Oxford University Press.

Shaka, Femi O. (2004): Modernity and African Cinema: A Study in Colonialist Discourse, Postcoloniality, and Modern African Identities. Trenton, New Jersey: Africa World Press Inc.

Sharma, Rajendra K. (2007): Fundamentals of Sociology. New Delhi: Atlantic Publishers.

Shorter, Aylward (1998): African Culture: An Overview. Nairobi: Paulines Publications.

Sklar, Richard L. (2003): 'The Premise of Mixed Government in African Political Studies'. In: Vaughan, Olufemi (ed.): Indigenous Political Structures and Governance in Africa. Ibadan, Nigeria: Sefer Books Ltd.

Smith, Dorothy E. (2006): 'Introduction'. In: Smith, Dorothy E. (ed.): Institutional Ethnography as Practice. Oxford: Rowman and Littlefield Publishers, Inc.

Solomos, John/Schuster, Lisa (2000): 'Citizenship, Multiculturalism and the politics of Identity Politics: Contemporary Dilemmas and Policy Agendas'. Koopmans, Ruud/Statham, Paul (eds.): Challenging Immigration and Ethnic Relations Politics: Comparative European Perspectives. Oxford: Oxford University Press.

Steger, Manfred B. (2003): Globalization: A Very Short Introduction. Oxford: Oxford University Press.

Steger, Manfred B. (2010): Globalization: A Brief Insight. New York: Sterling Publishing Co. Inc.

Stein, Howard (2006): 'Rethinking African Development'. In: Chang, Ha-Joon (ed.): Rethinking Development Economics. London and New York: Anthem Press.

Stewart, Frances/Berry, Albert (1999): 'Globalization, Liberalization and Inequality: Expectations and Experience'. In: Hurrell, Andrew/Woods, Ngaire (eds.): Inequality, Globalization, and World Politics. New York: Oxford University Press.

Stiglitz, Joseph E. (2002): Globalization and its Discontents. London: Penguin Books.

Stiglitz, Joseph E. (2007): Making Globalization Work. New York: W. W. Norton & Company, Inc.

Suberu, Rotimi T. (2001): Federalism and Ethnic Conflict in Nigeria. Washington, DC: United States Institute of Peace.

Traub, Rudolf (1986): Nigeria Weltmarktintegration und sozial-strukturelle Entwicklung. Hamburg: Institut für Afrika-Kunde.

Ujomu, Philip Ogo (2008): 'The Bounds of Security Theorising: Envisioning Discursive Inputs for the Rectification of a Post-Colonial Situation'. In: Adelugba, Dapo/Ujomu, Philip Ogo (eds.): Rethinking Security in Nigeria: Conceptual Issue in the Quest for Social Order and National Integration. Senegal: CODESRIA.

Ujomu, Philip Ogo/Adelugba, Dapo (2008): 'An Aesthetic Theorising of the Challenge of National Security in the Post-Colonial Context'. In: Adelugba, Dapo/Ujomu, Philip Ogo (eds.): Rethinking Security in Nigeria: Conceptual Issue in the Quest for Social Order and National Integration. Senegal: CODESRIA.

Vaughan, Olufemi (2000): Nigerian Chiefs: Traditional Power in Modern Politics, 1890s-1990s. Rochester, New York: University of Rochester Press.

Walby, Sylvia (2009): Globalization & Inequalities: Complexities and Contested Modernities. London: SAGE Publication.

Wallerstein, Immanuel (1974): The Modern World-System: Capitalist Agriculture and the Origins of the European World Economy in the Sixteenth Century. New York: Academic Press.

Wallerstein, Immanuel (1976): 'The Three Stages of African Involvement in the World Economy'. In: Gutkind, Peter/Wallerstein, Immanuel (eds.): The Political Economy of Africa. Los Angeles: Univ. of California Press.

Wallerstein, Immanuel (2004): 'The Rise and Future Demise of the World-Capitalist System'. In: Lechner, Frank J./Boli, John (eds.): The Globalization Reader 2nd Edition. Oxford: Blackwell Publishing Ltd.

Weedon, Chris (2000): Feminism, Theory, and the Politics of Difference. Oxford: Blackwell Publishers.

Weiss, Thomas G./Thakur, Ramesh C. (2010): Global Governance and the UN: An Unfinished Journey (The United Nations Intellectual History Project Series). Indiana: Indiana University Press.

Williams, Lizzie (2008): Nigeria: The Bradt Travel Guides 2nd Edition. USA: The Globe Pequot Press Inc.

Winters, Alan (2002): 'Trade Policies for Poverty Alleviation' In: Hoekman, Bernard/Mattoo, Aaditya/English, Philip (eds): Development, Trade and the WTO: A Handbook, World Bank, Washington DC.

Wood, Ellen M. (2002): 'Global Capital, National States'. In: Rupert, Mark/Smith, Hazel (eds.): Historical Materialism and Globalization. New York: Routledge.

Wood, Allen W. (2004): Karl Marx 2nd Edition. New York and London: Routledge.

Woodward, Kathryn ed. (1997): Identity and Difference. London: SAGE Publication.

Yotopoulos, Pan (2007): 'Asymmetric Globalization: Impact on the Third World'. In: Yotopoulos, Pan/Romano, Donato (eds.): The Asymmetries of Globalization. New York: Routledge.

Young, Crawford (2000): 'The Heritage of Colonialism'. In: Harbeson, John W. /Rothchild, Donald (eds.): Africa in the World Politics: The African State System in Flux, 3rd Edition. US: Westview Press.

Zündorf, Lutz (2008): Das Weltsystem des Erdöls: Entstehungszusammenhang, Funktionsweise, Wandlungstendenzen. Wiesbaden: VS Verlag für Sozialwissenschaften.

Journal Articles/Internet Sources/Unpublished Papers

Ajayi, Dickson D. (2007): 'Recent Trends and Patterns in Nigeria's Industrial Development'. In: Journal of Africa Development Vol.

32, No. 2. Dakar: Council for the Development of Social Science Research in Africa (CODESRIA).

Ajibola, M. A. (2008): Innovations and Curriculum Development for Basic Education in Nigeria: Policy Priorities and Challenges of Practice and Implementation. In: Research Journal of International Studies, Issue 8. http://www.eurojournals.com/rjis_8_05.pdf [accessed: 23.02.2010]

Aka, Ebenezer (1995): 'Regional Inequalities in the Process of Nigeria's Development: Socio-Political and Administrative Perspective'. In: Journal of Social Development in Africa Vol. 10, No. 2. http://archive.lib.msu.edu/DMC/African Journals.pdf [accessed: 25.03.2010]

Akinade, Akintunde E. (2002): The Precarious Agenda: Christian-Muslim Relations in Contemporary Nigeria. Duncan Black Macdonald Center for the Study of Islam and Christian-Muslim Relations: Hartford. http://macdonald.hartsem.edu/articles_akinade. htm [accessed: 21.06.2010]

Akindele, S. T./Gidado, T. O./Olaopo, O. R. (2002): 'Globalisation: Its Implications and Consequences for Africa'. In: In: Globalization Vol. 1, No. 2. Pueblo, USA: Colorado State University (Published Online by the International Consortium for the Advancement of Academic Publication (ICAAP)). http://globalization. icaap.org/content/v2.1/01_akindele_etal.html [accessed: 28.06. 2010]

Akintoye, Ishola R. (2008): 'Reducing Unemployment through the Informal Sector: A Case Study of Nigeria'. In: European Journal of Economics, Finance and Administrative Sciences, Issue 11. EuroJournals, Inc. http://www.eurojournals.com/ejefas_11_10. pdf [accessed: 12.08.2010]

Alalade, F. O. (2004): 'Trade Unions and Democratic Option in Nigeria'. In: Journal of Social Sciences Vol. 9, No. 3, Kamla-Raj.

Alexander, Malcolm L. (2007): Visualizing Social Structure: Bridging the Gap between Contemporary Social Theory and Social Network Analysis. In: Curtis, B./Matthewman, S./McIntosh T. (eds.): Public Sociologies: Lessons and Trans-Tasman Comparisons, TASA & SAANZ Joint Conference 2007 http://www.tasa.org. au/conferences/conferencepapers07/papers/199.pdf [accessed: 22. 03.2010].

Anugwom, Edlyne E (2007): 'Globalisation and Labour Utilisation in Nigeria: Evidence from the Construction Industry'. In: Journal of Africa Development Vol. 32, No. 2. Dakar: Council for the Development of Social Science Research in Africa (CODESRIA).

Araar, Abdelkrim/Taiwo, Awoyemi (2006): Poverty and Inequality Nexus. Illustrations with Nigeria Data. http://www.cirpee.org/fileadmin/documents/Cahiers_2006/CIRPEE06-38.pdf [Accessed: 12.04.2012]

Banjo, Lanre (2010): Zoning of Elective Offices is Destructive and fosters Disunity! In: Sahara Reporters online, 16 March.

Barrow, Clyde W. (2005): 'The Return of the State: Globalization, State Theory, and the New Imperialism'. In: New Political Science: A Journal of Politics and Culture Vol. 27, No. 2. London: Routledge.

Bartels, Larry M. (2005): Economic Inequality and Political Representation, Princeton University. http://www.princeton.edu/~bartels/economic.pdf [accessed: 24.05.2010]

Blair, Tony (2001): The Power of Community can Change the World. Address at the Labour Party Conference. http://www.american rhetoric.com/speeches/tblair10-02-01.htm [accessed: 30.08.2009]

Bollen, Kenneth/Jackman, Robert (1985): 'Economic and Noneconomic Determinants of Political Democracy in the 1960's'. In: Research in Political Sociology, Vol. 1. JAI Press Inc.

Bollen, Kenneth/Jackman, Robert (1989): 'Democracy, Stability, and Dichotomies'. In: American Sociological Review, Vol. 54.

Bratton, Michael/Van de Walle, Nicolas (1994): 'Neopatrimonial Regimes and Political Transitions in Africa'. In: Journal of World Politics Vol. 46, No. 4, John Hopkins University Press.

Caldwell, John/Caldwell, Pat/Quiggin, Pat (1989): 'Disaster in an Alternative Civilization: The Social Context of AIDS in Sub-Saharan Africa'. In: Population and Development Review Vol. 15, No. 2.

Chase-Dunn, Christopher (1981): 'Interstate System and Capitalist World-Economy: One Logic or Two?' In: International Studies Quarterly, Vol. 25, No. 1, JSTOR.

Chase-Dunn, Christopher (2005): 'Social Evolution and the Future of World Society'. In: Herkenrath, Mark/König, Claudia/Scholtz, Hanno/Volken, Thomas (eds.): Globalizations from 'Above' and 'Below' – The Future of World Society, Journal of World-Systems Research Vol. XI, No. 2. http://jwsr.ucr.edu [accessed: 23.07.2009]

Cheru, Fantu (2005): Globalization and Uneven Urbanization in Africa: The Limits to Effective Urban Governance in the Provision of Basic Services. Los Angeles: African Studies Center. http://www. international.ucla.edu/media/files/57.pdf [accessed: 12.03.2010]

Coate, Bromeyn/Handmer, John/Choong, Wei (2006): Taking Care of People and Communities: Rebuilding Livelihoods through NGOs and the Informal Economy in Southern Thailand. In: Shaw, Rajib (ed.): Disaster Prevention and Management: An International Journal Vol. 15, No. 1. Emerald Group Publishing Ltd.

Cole, Elizabeth R. (2009): Intersectionality and Research in Psychology. In: American Psychologist: 2009 American Psychological Association Vol. 64, No. 3. http://aurora.wells.edu/~vim/Intersectionality_Psy.pdf [accessed: 11.09.2009]

Conzen, Kathleen et al (1992): 'The Invention of Ethnicity: A Perspective from the USA'. In: Journal of American Ethnic History Vol. 12, No. 1. USA, Illinois: University Press.

Delaney, Joan (1971): Pareto's Theory of Elites and Education. Studium: No. III. http://sunzi.lib.hku.hk/hkjo/view/32/3200052.pdf [accessed: 23.05.2010]

Durotoye, Adeolu A. (2008): Weathering the Storm/Reaping the Harvest? Democratic Dividends in Africa. In: All Academic Research. All Academic, Inc. http://www.allacademic.com/ [accessed: 28.09. 2009]

Dutceac, Anamaria (2004): Globalization and Ethnic Conflict: Beyond the Liberal – Nationalist Distinction. In: The Global Review of Ethnopolitics Vol. 3, no. 2.

Falana, Femi (2010): Civil Society and the Challenge of Anti-corruption Struggle in Nigeria. In: SaharaReporter Online, Sunday, 16 May.

Falana, Femi (2010): Religion and Political Reforms in Nigeria. A public lecture delivered at the 51st birthday anniversary of Rt. Rev Alfred Adewale Martins, Catholic Bishop of Abeokuta, Ogun State on Saturday June 5, 2010. In: SaharaReporter Online.

Gaughran, Audrey (2009): 'Petroleum, Pollution and Poverty in the Niger Delta'. In: The Guardian Newspaper Online, June 30.

Goldthorpe, John H. (2009): 'Analysing Social Inequality: A Critique of Two Recent Contributions from Economics and Epidemiology'. In: European Sociological Review. Oxford: Oxford University Press

Hund, Wulf D. (2003): 'Inclusion and Exclusion: Dimensions of Racism'. In: Wiener Zeitschrift zur Geschichte der Neuzeit, 3. Jg. Heft 1/6 – 19. http://www.wiso.uni-hamburg.de/fileadmin.pdf [accessed: 25.09.2009]

Hungwe, Kedmon/Hungwe, Chipo (2000): 'Essay Review on Africa Works: Disorder as Political Instrument'. In: Zambezia Vol. 27, No. 2, University College of Rhodesia.

Ibeanu, Okechukwu (2000): 'Ethnicity and Transition to Democracy in Nigeria: Explaining the Passing of Authoritarian Rule in a Multi-ethnic Society'. In: African Journal of Political Science Vol. 5, No. 2.

Idowu, William (1999): 'Citizenship Status, Statehood Problems and Political Conflict: The Case of Nigeria'. In: Nordic Journal of African Studies Vol. 8, No. 2, Nordic Association of African Studies.

Ifidon, Ehimika A. (1998): 'The Appropriated State: Political Structure and Cycles of Conflict in Nigeria, 1900 — 1993'. In: African Journal of Political Science Vol. 3, No. 2.

Ifidon, Ehimika A. (1999): 'Social Rationality and Class Analysis of National Conflict in Nigeria: A Historiographical Critique'. In: Journal of Africa Development Vol. 24, Nos. 1 & 2.

Jega, Attahiru M. (2009): 'Nigerian Economy and the Global Economic Crisis'. In: Daily Trust Newspaper Online, 2 & 3. Feb, 2009.

Joseph, Richard A. (1978): Affluence and Underdevelopment: The Nigerian Experience. In: The Journal of Modern African Studies Vol. 16, No. 2. Cambridge: University Press.

Kariuki, Angela (2010): Violence begets Violence: Nigeria's Deathly Religious History. In: Consultancy Africa Intelligence. http://www.consultancyafrica.com/ [accessed: 24.10.2010]

Knudsen, Susanne V. (2004): Intersectionality - A Theoretical Inspiration in the Analysis of Minority Cultures and Identities in Textbooks. In: Caught in the Web or Lost in the Textbook, Paris. http://www. caen.iufm.fr/colloque_iartem/pdf/knudsen.pdf [accessed: 12.08. 2009]

Kolawole, Dipo (2005): 'Colonial and Military Rule in Nigeria: A Symmetrical Relationship'. In: Pakistan Journal of Social Sciences Vol. 3, No. 6, Grace Publications.

Leftwich, Adrian (1993): Governance, Democracy and Development in the Third World. In: Third World Quarterly Vol. 14, No 3. Available at http://www.jstor.org/ [accessed: 12.04.2009]

Mbembe, Achille (1992): 'The Banality of Power and the Aesthetics of Vulgarity in the Postcolony', translated by Janet Roitman. In: Public Culture Journal Vol. 4, No. 2. Duke University Press.

Mitchell, Timothy (1991): 'The Limits of the State: Beyond Statist Approaches and Their Critics'. In: American Political Science Review Vol. 85, No. 1.

Natufe, Igho (2006): Governance and Politics in Nigeria. A Lecture Delivered on November 21, 2006 at The Staff and Graduate Seminar Department of Political Science & Public Administration University of Benin. http://www.okpenation.org/doc/governance_and_politics_in_nigeria.pdf [accessed: 28.09.2009]

Njoku, Uzochukwu J. (2006): 'Corruption and Social Change in Nigeria's Public Service: The Agency Structure Debate'. In: Adibe, Jideofor (ed.): Is It in Our Stars? Culture and the Current Crises of Governance in Africa. The Journal of African Renaissance Vol. 3, No.6. http://www.hollerafrica.com/pdf/nov-dec-06.pdf [accessed: 28.06.2009]

Nwosu, B. U. (2006): 'Civil Society and Electoral Mandate Protection in Southeastern Nigeria'. In: Bates, Stephen (ed.): The International Journal of Not-for-Profit Law Volume 9, Issue 1. Washington D.C.: The International Center for Not-for-Profit Law. http://www.icnl.org/knowledge/ijnl/vol9iss1/ijnl_vol9iss1.pdf [accessed: 23.02.2010]

Olayode, Kehinde (2005): 'Reinventing the African State: Issues and Challenges for Building a Developmental State'. In: African Journal of International Affairs, Vol. 8, Nos. 1&2. Dakar: Council for the Development of Social Science Research in Africa (CODESRIA). http://www.codesria.org/IMG/pdf/2-Olayode.pdf [accessed: 15.10.2010]

Olesin, Ayo (2011): Nigeria's Jobless Growth. In: National Mirror, 19. September, 2011. http://nationalmirroronline.net/index.php/ business/business-and-finance/matrix-with-ayo-olesin/20978.html [Accessed: 14.03.2012]

Oshikoya, Temitope W (2008): 'Nigeria in the Global Economy: Nigeria's Integration into the Global Economy is below its Potential'. In: Business Economics Vol. 43, Issue 1. UK: Palgrave Macmillan.

Paul, Axel T. (2008): 'Reciprocity and Statehood in Africa: from Clientelism to Cleptocracy'. In: International Review of Economics Vol. 55, Nos. 1-2. Springer-Verlag.

Petithomme, Mathieu (2007): Political Power and the Development of Under-development in Sub-Saharan Africa, 4th ECPR General Conference. http://www.essex.ac.uk/pisa.pdf [accessed: 14.02.2010].

Reno, William (2003): Patrick Chabal and Jean-Pascal Daloz. 1999. Africa Works: the Political Instrumentalization of Disorder (Book Review). In: Journal of Asian and African Studies Vol. 38, No. 1. http://jas.sagepub.com [accessed: 16.11.2009]

Van den Boom, Rob (2001): 'Africa's Crisis: A Crisis of Modernity'. In: Newsletter: Association for Law and Administration in Developing and Transition Countries (ALADIN), Vol. 2, No. 3. http://www.aladinweb.org [accessed: 13.04.2010]

Weber, Cameron M. (2008): "Adam Smith and Globalization". Brooklyn, NY. http://cameroneconomics.com/smith.pdf [accessed: 12.04.2010]

Wood, Ellen M. (1999): 'Unhappy Families: Global Capitalism in a World of Nation-States.' In: Monthly Review Vol. 51, No. 3.

Country Reports:

A report from the Committee of African Finance Ministers and Central Bank Governors established to monitor the crisis (March 17, 2009) Impact of the Crisis on African Economies – Sustaining Growth and Poverty Reduction: African Perspectives and Recommendations to the G20, London Summit. http://www.londonsummit.gov.uk/resources/en/PDF/africa-recommendations [accessed: 12.04.2010]

367

Abrahamsen, Rita/Williams, Michael (2005): The Globalization of Private Security. Country Report: Nigeria. http://users.aber.ac.uk/ rbh/privatesecurity/countryreport-nigeria.pdf [accessed: 26.09. 2009]

Ajakaiya, Olu/Fakiyesi, 'Tayo (2009): 'Global Financial Crisis Discussion Series Paper 8: Nigeria'. In: Overseas Development Institute (ODI). London. http://www.odi.org.uk/resources/download/3310. pdf [accessed: 22.03.2010]

Ajomale, Olayinka (2007): 'Country Report: Ageing in Nigeria – Current State, Social and Economic Implications'. In: Hoff, Andreas (ed.): Summer Newsletter 2007 of the Research Committee (RC11) on the Sociology of Aging of the International Sociological Association (ISA). Oxford: Oxford Institute of Ageing. http://www.rc11-sociology-of-aging.org/system/files/2007News-letter.pdf [accessed: 12.04.2010]

Asume, Osuoka/Roderick, Peter (2005): Gas Flaring in Nigeria: a Human Rights, Environmental and Economic Monstrosity (A report by the Climate Justice Programme and Environmental Rights Action/Friends of the Earth Nigeria). Amsterdam: The Climate Justice Programme. http://www.foe.co.uk/resource/reports/gas_ flaring_nigeria.pdf [accessed: 26.05.2009]

Blench, Roger/Longtau, Selbut/Hassan, Umar/Walsh, Martin (2006): The Role of Traditional Rulers in Conflict Prevention and Mediation in Nigeria. A Final Report prepared for Department for International Development (DFID) Nigeria. http://rogerblench.info/ Development/Nigeria 2006.pdf [accessed: 11.10.2010]

British Council (2012): Gender in Nigeria Report 2012: Improving the Lives of Girls and Women in Nigeria. Issues, Policies, Action 2nd Edition: British Council Nigeria.

Federal Republic of Nigeria (1987): Report of the Political Bureau. Lagos: Federal Government Printer.

Human Rights Watch (2003): The Warri Crisis: Fueling Violence. Human Rights Watch Vol. 15, No. 18 (A).

International Labor Office (1972): Employment, Incomes and Equality: A strategy for Increasing Productive Employment in Kenya. ILO Geneva.

Kirwin, Matthew/Cho, Wonbin (2009): Weak States and Political Violence in Sub-Saharan Africa: A Comparative Series of National Public Attitude Surveys on Democracy, Market and Civil Society in Africa. In: AFROBAROMETER Working Paper No. 111. http://www.afrobarometer.org/papers/AfropaperNo111_2.pdf [accessed: 11.05.2010]

Library of Congress (2008): Federal Research Division. Country Profile: Nigeria. http://lcweb2.loc.gov/frd/cs/profiles/Nigeria.pdf [accessed: 23.02.2009]

Mustapha, Raufu A. (2006): 'Ethnic Structure, Inequality and Governance of the Public Sector in Nigeria'. In: United Nations Research Institute for Social Development: Democracy, Governance and Human Rights Programme. Paper Number 24, Geneva. http://www.unrisd.org/Mustapha.pdf [accessed: 24.03.2009]

National Bureau of Statistics (2007): The Middle Class in Nigeria Analysis of Profile, Determinants and Characteristics (1980-2007): [Produced under the Auspices of the Economic Reform & Governance Project, ERGP] Federal Republic of Nigeria. http://www.nigerianstat.gov.ng/ [accessed: 03.04.2009]

National Bureau of Statistics (2011): 2011 Annual Socio-Economic Report, Abuja.

National Planning Commission (2004): Nigeria: National Economic Empowerment Development Strategy (NEEDS). Abuja: The NEEDS Secretariat/Federal Secretariat. http://www.cenbank.org/out/ publications/guidelines/rd/2004/needs.pdf [accessed: 16.09.2009]

Nigeria Union of Petroleum and Natural Gas Workers (NUPENG): History of Trade Union in Nigeria. Lagos-Nigeria: NUPENG House. http://nupeng.org/id17.html [accessed: 21.09.2010]

United Nations (2005): The Inequality Predicament: Report on the World Social Situation 2005. Department of Economic and Social Affairs, New York: Academic Foundation.

United Nations Development Programme (2006): Niger Delta Human Development Report. Garki-Abuja: UNDP Nigeria. http://web. ng.undp.org/reports/nigeria_hdr_report.pdf [accessed: 08.02. 2009]

United Nations Development Programme (2011): Human Development Report Nigeria 2008 – 2009: Achieving Growth with Equity. UNDP, Abuja. http://www.ng.undp.org/documents/NHDR2009/ NHDR_MAIN-REPORT_2008-2009.pdf [Accessed: 24.02.2012]

US Department of State (2010): Bureau of African Affairs November 1, 2010. Background Note: Nigeria. http://www.state.gov/r/pa/ei/ bgn/2836.htm [accessed: 6.11.2010]

World Bank (2000): Reforming Public Institutions and Strengthening Governance: A World Bank Strategy November 2000. Washington D.C.: The International Bank for Reconstruction and Development/the World Bank.

World Bank (2003): School Education in Nigeria: Preparing for Universal Basic Education. Human Development III: Africa Region. http://siteresources.worldbank.org/AFRICAEXT/Resources/no_5 3.pdf [accessed: 12.08.2010]

World Bank (2008): Project Appraisal Document on a Proposed Credit In The Amount of SDR 100.7 Million (US$150million Equivalent) to the Federal Republic of Nigeria for Commercial Agriculture Development Project. Report No: 46830-NG. http://cadpnigeria.org/documentation/Project%20Appraisal%20Document.pdf [accessed: 16.02.2010]

Soziologie

Tanja Carstensen; Wibke Derboven;
Gabriele Winker
Soziale Praxen Erwerbsloser
Gesellschaftliche Teilhabe – Internetnutzung – Zeithandeln. Unter Mitarbeit von Kathrin Englert, Doris Gerbig und Betje Schwarz
Erwerbslosigkeit ist eng mit Einschränkungen gesellschaftlicher Teilhabe und Herausforderungen an das alltägliche Zeithandeln verbunden. Gleichzeitig sind mit dem Internet neue Möglichkeiten der Information und Kommunikation und damit auch Hoffnungen auf neue Formen von gesellschaftlicher Teilhabe entstanden. Das Buch geht den Fragen nach, in welchen Bereichen der Gesellschaft Erwerbslose Teilhabe verwirklichen, inwieweit die Nutzung des Internets dabei Teilhabe erweitert und wie Erwerbslose ihre Zeit jenseits von Erwerbsarbeit strukturieren.
Bd. 75, 2012, 112 S., 19,90 €, br.,
ISBN 978-3-643-11824-0

Kristin Mundt
Vom Delegierten der sozialistischen Moderne zum gläubigen Zuwanderer?
Religiöser Wandel vietnamesischer Migranten in der DDR und Ostdeutschland
Vietnamesische Zuwanderer in Ostdeutschland interessieren sich zunehmend für Religion. Wirklich verstehen lässt sich dieses Phänomen jedoch nur im Zusammenspiel von Makro- und Mikroprozessen, die mit dem Systemwandel und der Reform des Doi Moi einhergingen. Anhand der Biographien von bereits in die DDR migrierten Vertragsarbeitern und Studenten zeigt die Autorin, in welcher Weise das veränderte Verhältnis von Religion und Politik in Vietnam mit den postsozialistischen Rahmenbedingungen des Migrationsarrangements und der spezifischen biographischen Verarbeitung dieser Veränderungen verwoben ist.
Bd. 76, 2012, 296 S., 34,90 €, br.,
ISBN 978-3-643-11855-4

LIT Verlag Berlin – Münster – Wien – Zürich – London
Auslieferung Deutschland / Österreich / Schweiz: siehe Impressumsseite